THE TEACHINGS OF THE CHURCH FATHERS

THE TEACHINGS
OF THE
CHURCH FATHERS

EDITED BY JOHN R. WILLIS, S.J.

HERDER AND HERDER

1966
HERDER AND HERDER NEW YORK
232 Madison Avenue, New York 10016

Library of Congress Catalog Card Number: 66-13067
©1966 by Herder and Herder, Inc.
Manufactured in the United States

Reginae Societatis Jesu

Introduction

The aim of this book is to present a brief outline of Catholic doctrine as it appears in some of the more typical writings of the Church Fathers. It is based on the *Enchiridion Patristicum* of Rouët de Journel, but it departs from that work in two ways. It seeks to present the Church Fathers under topical headings rather than following a strict chronology, although a chronology is adhered to under the separate topical headings themselves. It also attempts to give the best English translation possible for the Greek and Latin texts taken by M. Rouët de Journel from the Migne *Patrologia*.

The idea for this book came from *The Church Teaches*,* a collection of *Documents of the Church in English Translation* based on Denzinger's *Enchiridion Symbolorum*.

There has been no attempt to present an exhaustive selection of writings from all of the early Church Fathers on all the possible topics in Catholic doctrine. Rather, the intention is to present typical selections from the better-known sources and to include as many representative selections as time and space will allow. With a few exceptions, each selection appears only once in full, and then it is referred to later only by number if it should have a bearing on some succeeding doctrinal point. The numbers in parentheses refer to M. Rouët de Journel's *Enchiridion Patristicum,* twenty-first edition, and a table of coördinating numbers will be found in the Reference Table at the end of this work.

Our intention is to let the Fathers speak for themselves, and so, apart

---

* *The Church Teaches*, published by B. Herder Book Company of St. Louis in 1955, was prepared for publication under the guidance of Gerald Van Ackeren, S.J., and his able collaborators: John F. Clarkson, S.J., John H. Edwards, S.J., William J. Kelly, S.J., and John J. Welch, S.J., of St. Mary's College, St. Marys, Kansas.

from short introductions to each of the chapters, commentary has been excluded as well as any interpretation. Yet we have been very careful that each quotation shall be faithful to the context in which it is found.

With the permission of the publishers, to whom grateful acknowledgment is here made, the translations used in *The Teachings of the Church Fathers* have been based on the following series:

Ancient Christian Writers. The Works of the Fathers in Translation. Edited by J. Quasten, S.T.D., and Walter J. Burghardt, S.J., S.T.D., and the late J. C. Plumpe, Ph.D. Westminster, The Newman Press, 1946–. Abbreviation: *ACW*.

The Ante-Nicene Christian Library. Translations of the Writings of the Fathers down to A.D. *325.* The Rev. Alexander Roberts, D.D., and James Donaldson, LL.D., editors. Edinburgh, T. & T. Clark, 1873. Abbreviation: *ANCL*.

The Ante-Nicene Fathers. Translations of the Writings of the Fathers down to A.D. *325.* The Rev. Alexander Roberts, D.D., and James Donaldson, LL.D., editors (American reprint of the Edinburgh edition). Revised and Chronologically Arranged, with Brief Prefaces and Occasional Notes, by A. Cleveland Coxe, D.D. New York, Charles Scribner's Sons, 1899. Abbreviation: *ANF*.

The Church Teaches. Documents of the Church in English Translation. The Rev. John F. Clarkson, S.J., *et al.,* editors. St. Louis, B. Herder Book Company, 1955. Abbreviation: *TCT*.

Didascalia et Constitutiones Apostolorum. 2 vols. Paderborn, 1905. Abbreviation: *F*.

S. Ephraemi Syri Carmino Nisibena. G. S. Bickell, editor. Lipsiae, 1866. Abbreviation: *BK*.

S. Ephraemi Syri Humni et Sermones. 4 vols. T. J. Lamy, editor. Mechelen, 1882–1902. Abbreviation: *L*.

The Fathers of the Church. A New Translation. Founded by Ludwig Schopp. Editorial Director: Roy J. Deferrari, Ph.D. Washington, D.C., The Catholic University of America Press, 1948–. Abbreviation: *FC*. *A New Eusebius. Documents Illustrative of the History of the Church to* A.D. *337.* James Stevenson, editor. Based on the collection edited by B. J. Kidd. London, S.P.C.K., 1957 (*The Muratorian Fragment*). Abbreviation: *S*.

Nicene and Post-Nicene Fathers of the Christian Church. Translated into English with Prologomena and Explanatory Notes under the Editorial Supervision of Philip Schaff, D.D., LL.D., and Henry Wace, D.D. New York, Charles Scribner's Sons, 1904. Abbreviation: *NPNF.*

Patres Apostolici. ed. 2, 2 vols. F. X. Funk, editor. Tübingen, 1901. Abbreviation: *F.*

Patrologia Graeca. J. P. Migne, editor. Paris, 1857 *sqq.* Abbreviation: *MG.*

Patrologia Latina. J. P. Migne, editor. Paris, 1844 *sqq.* Abbreviation: *ML.*

Patrologia Syriaca. R. Graffin, editor. Paris, 1894 *sqq.* Abbreviation: *PS.*

Finally, it should be stressed that this work has no polemical intention. There is no attempt to prove or disprove any doctrinal point from the writings of the Fathers. The aim has simply been to correlate interesting and more or less pertinent writings under various selected doctrinal topics. These topics have been carefully chosen and kept to a minimum. Nor should the importance or relevance of a particular topic be judged by the number of citations which have been placed under it. Moreover, items upon which the Fathers may have written rather copiously, but which are of doubtful interest to the average reader, have simply been omitted. Practical considerations of size and utility have been the norms for determining what could be conveniently included in a volume of this sort.

The author wishes to thank the numerous priests and scholastics of Weston College, Weston, Massachusetts, who made valuable suggestions, comments, and criticisms. His special thanks go to Miss Madeleine Stotz of Cambridge, Massachusetts, who laboriously typed the entire manuscript. Any inadequacies, shortcomings, and faults of the book the author naturally accepts as his own.

Table of Contents

11

IV.

ONE GOD

V.

THE TRIUNE GOD

IX.

HABITUAL GRACE

XI.

MARY, MOTHER OF GOD AND VIRGIN

XII.

THE SACRAMENTS

I.

Revealed Religion

Man is by nature religious. The new revelation of God which burst upon the ancient world in the person of Jesus Christ was meant to be a culmination of all the divine aspirations which man had had since the ages began. Perhaps Tertullian expressed this idea most succinctly and memorably when he exclaimed that the soul of man is Christian by its very nature. Writing at about the same time in the late second century, Minucius Felix appealed to the common consent of the human race to establish the existence of God. Some years later, in the early part of the fourth century, Lactantius in his *The Divine Institutes* devoted some attention to the phenomenon of religion itself, and his ideas were further enlarged by the great St. Augustine himself in his *On the Profit of Believing.*

At the same time, it was necessary to show that the new revelation of God in Jesus Christ did not do violence to human reason, but merited its assent. Theophilus of Antioch addressed himself to this task in the latter part of the second century in his defense of Christianity in three books to Autolycus. Origen and St. Cyprian also touched on the subject in the first half of the third century, but it remained for St. John Chrysostom in his homilies on the Gospel of St. Matthew to defend with eloquence (along with Augustine) the great profit of believing. Indeed, the famed Bishop of Hippo declared that revelation was morally necessary for man in his present condition, and in this he had been anticipated by Tertullian at about the turn of the second century, and Origen writing a short time later.

The appeal to miracles to substantiate the divine truth of Christianity was largely the work of Augustine, although Origen in his work against Celsus declared that miracles offered an external criterion of revelation but were not sufficient of themselves to confirm the truth of any particular doctrine. The Fathers seem to prefer prophecy as a more certain external criterion of revelation, and we find St. Ignatius of Antioch as early as the first quarter of the second century holding this position. St. Theophilus of Antioch in the late second century, as well as Origen in the third and Lactantius in the early fourth, are also of this opinion. Later writers such as St. Basil in the fourth century and likewise St. Ambrose seem to prefer the affections of the soul as internal criteria of revelation, and it hardly needs to be added that St. Augustine expressed himself on all of these viewpoints.

The challenge of Marcion forced the Church to consider seriously the position of the Old Testament vis-à-vis the New Dispensation, and as early as the second century St. Ignatius of Antioch showed that the Law and the prophets pointed clearly to the Gospel. Not only was the old Law designed to prepare and prefigure the coming of Christ, but St. Irenaeus specifically declared that God was the Author of the Old as well as the New Testament. This position is echoed again and again up to the time of St. Leo the Great in the middle of the fifth century. But St. Ignatius of Antioch had also been careful to show that the old Law had been abrogated by the revelation of the new, and his position is mirrored in the *Epistle to Diognetus,* written by an unknown author, probably late in the second century. These positions are explicitated by St. Augustine in his celebrated *Reply to Faustus the Manichaean.*

That the four Gospels are genuine seems to be the unanimous agreement of the ancient writers. St. Justin Martyr (mid-second century) has a good deal to say about it, and so also does St. Irenaeus writing in the latter part of the second century. All of them have Marcion in mind as the chief opponent, and Irenaeus's work *Against Heresies* is directed chiefly against him and the Gnostics. The *Muratorian Fragment,* about the year 200, is a valuable piece of evidence. The *Against Marcion* of Tertullian continues the assault, and we find the defense of the Gospels again in St. Clement of Alexandria as quoted by the Church historian Eusebius. St. Augustine deals with the more sophisticated problem of apparent contradiction in Scripture, and defends its inerrancy by saying that either the manuscript is faulty, or the translation is wrong, or it has been misunderstood (*Reply to Faustus the Manichaean,* Bk. 11, Ch. 5). The testimony of both Papias and Polycarp in the early second century is considered weighty proof that the witnesses who assert the genuinity of the Gospels are worthy of belief.

The central message of Christianity is that Jesus Christ truly came into the world as a divine legate and that his miracles and prophecies prove his divine mission, attested principally by the central fact of His resurrection. All of the major writers concur in this; one finds it as early as St. Clement of Rome at the end of the first century, and there is no major writer and hardly a minor one that does not allude to it in some way. Much of the writing is directed against the Docetists and the Gnostics, many of whom denied that Jesus had actually lived and suffered truly in the flesh.

To prove the divine origin of Christianity, St. Justin Martyr cites its wonderful propagation and perpetuity as early as the middle of the second century, and Tertullian in some famous passages dwells on this at considerable length a half-century later. So do Origen and Arnobius writing in the third, and St. Augustine mentions it in the *City of God.* The beautiful *Letter to Diognetus,* written probably in the late second century, contrasts the virtues of the Christians with the pagan vices, and Minucius Felix and Tertullian emphasize this point at about the same time. Thus the change of morals induced by Christianity argues for the divinity of its doctrine, as St. Justin contends. We can expect Tertullian to dwell on martyrdom as a testimony of the truth of the Christian religion, but St. Clement of Rome mentions it as early as the closing years of the first century, and so do St. Ignatius of Antioch, St. Justin Martyr, and St. Irenaeus in the second, Origen and Lactantius in the third, and of course St. Augustine in the fourth.

1. The notion of religion.

LACTANTIUS

1
(631)

By these things it is evident how closely connected are wisdom and religion. Wisdom relates to sons, and this relation requires love; religion to servants, and this relation requires fear. For as the former are bound to love and honor their father, so are the latter bound to respect and venerate their lord. But with respect to God, who is one only, inasmuch as He sustains the twofold character both of Father and Lord, we are bound both to love Him, inasmuch as we are sons, and to fear Him, inasmuch as we are servants. Religion, therefore, cannot be divided from wisdom, nor can wisdom be separated from religion; because it is the same God, who ought to be understood, which is the part of wisdom, and to be honored, which is the part of religion. But wisdom precedes, religion follows; for the knowledge of God comes first, His worship is the result of knowledge.

THE DIVINE INSTITUTES, Bk. 4, Ch. 4
ML 6, 456
ANF VII, 103

2
(635)

For we are created on this condition, that we pay just and due obedience to God who created us, that we should know and follow Him alone. We are bound and tied to God by this chain of piety; from which religion itself received its name, not, as Cicero explained it, from carefully gathering.

THE DIVINE INSTITUTES, Bk. 4, Ch. 28
ML 6, 535
ANF VII, 131

ST. AUGUSTINE

3
(1603)

It is true that Christians pay religious honor to the memory of the martyrs, both to excite us to imitate them, and to obtain a share in their merits, and the assistance of their prayers. But we build altars not to any martyr, but to the God of martyrs, although it is to the memory of the martyrs. No one officiating at the altar in the saints' burying-place ever says, 'We bring an offering to you, O Peter! or O Paul! or O Cyprian!' The offering is made to God who gave the crown of martyrdom. . . . What is properly divine worship, which the Greeks call *latria,* and for which there is no word in Latin, both in doctrine and in practice we give only to God.

REPLY TO FAUSTUS THE MANICHAEAN, Bk. 20, Ch. 21
ML 42, 384
NPNF IV, 262

[God] is the source of our happiness and the very end of all our aspirations. We elect Him, whom, by neglect, we lost. We offer Him our allegiance—for 'allegiance' and 'religion' are, at root, the same. We pursue Him with our love so that when we reach Him we may rest in perfect happiness in Him who is our goal.

4
(1743)

THE CITY OF GOD, Bk. 10, Ch. 3
ML 41, 298
FC XIV, 121

ST. FULGENTIUS

True religion consists in the service of the one true God. That God is one, is truth itself. And just as without that one truth there is no other truth, so also without the one true God there is no other true God. For that one truth is one divinity. And so we cannot say truly that there are two true gods, just as truth itself cannot naturally be divided.

5
(2236)

EIGHTH LETTER
ML 65, 365

ST. JOHN OF DAMASCUS

We should certainly fall into error if we should make an image of the invisible God; since that which is not corporeal, nor visible, nor circumscribed, nor imagined, cannot be depicted at all. Again, we should act impiously if we thought images made by men were gods, and bestowed honors upon them as if they were. But we do not admit to doing any of these things.

6
(2377)

AGAINST THOSE WHO DESTROY SACRED IMAGES, Or. 2, 5
MG 94, 1288

We adore only the Creator and Maker of things, God, to whom we offer *latria* since God is to be adored according to His nature. We also adore the holy mother of God, not as God, but as mother of God according to the flesh. We also adore the saints, the chosen friends of God, by whom we have easy access to Him.

7
(2378)

AGAINST THOSE WHO DESTROY SACRED IMAGES, Or. 3, 41
MG 94, 1357

2. *Natural religion exists in man.*

MINUCIUS FELIX

8
(270)

By His Word God calls into existence all things that are, disposes them according to His wisdom, and perfects them by His goodness. God is invisible, because too bright for our sight; intangible, because too fine for our sense of touch; immeasurable, because He is beyond the grasp of our senses; infinite, limitless, His real magnitude being known to Himself alone. Our intelligence is too limited to comprehend Him, therefore we can only measure Him fittingly when we call Him immeasurable. Here is my candid opinion: a man who thinks to know God's magnitude diminishes it; he who does not wish to diminish it knows it not. And do not search for a name for God: 'God' is His name. There is a need for names when, among a crowd, individuals have to be distinguished by giving them their specific appellations. To God, who is the only One, the name 'God' belongs in an exclusive and total manner. If I should call Him 'Father,' you would think Him made of flesh; if 'King' you would infer that He is of this world; if 'Lord' you surely would understand Him to be a mortal. Away with these added names, and you will behold Him in His splendor. Besides, do not all men share my opinion about this point? Hearken to the common people: when they stretch forth their hands to heaven, they say nothing else but 'God' or 'God is great' or 'God is true' or 'If God grant it.' Is that the natural language of the common crowd or is it the prayerful profession of faith made by a Christian?

LETTER TO OCTAVIUS, 18
ML 3, 290
FC X, 353–354

TERTULLIAN

9
(275)

What we worship is the one God, Who, out of nothing, simply for the glory of His majesty, fashioned this enormous universe with its whole supply of elements, bodies, and spirits, and did so simply by the Word wherewith He commanded it, the Reason whereby He ordered it, the Power wherewith He was powerful. Hence it is that even the Greeks apply the appropriate word 'cosmos' to the universe. . . . And this is the gravest part of the sin of those who are unwilling to recognize Him, of Whom they cannot remain in ignorance.

Do you wish us to prove His existence from His numerous, mighty works by which we are supported, sustained, delighted, and even startled? Do you wish us to prove Him from the testimony of the soul itself? The soul, though it be repressed by the prison house of the body, though it be circumscribed by base institutions, weakened by lust and concupiscence, and enslaved to false gods, yet, when it revives, as from intoxication or sleep or some sickness and enjoys health again, names 'God' with this name alone because, properly speaking, He alone is true. 'Good God!' 'God Almighty!' and 'God grant it!' are expressions used by all mankind. That He is a Judge, also, is testified by the phrases: 'God sees,' and 'I commend it to God,' and 'God will reward me.' O testimony of the soul, which is by natural instinct Christian! In fine, then, the soul, as it utters these phrases, looks not to the Capitol but to heaven. It knows the abode of the living God; from Him and from there it has come.

APOLOGY, 17
ML 1, 375
FC X, 52–53

ST. AUGUSTINE

For this name of God, by which He is called, could not but be known in some way to the whole creation, and so to every nation, before they believed in Christ. For such is the energy of true Godhead, that it cannot be altogether and utterly hidden from any rational creature, so long as it makes use of its reason. For, with the exception of a few in whom nature has become outrageously depraved, the whole race of man acknowledges God as the maker of this world. In respect, therefore, of His being the maker of this world that is visible in heaven and earth around us, God was known unto all nations even before they were indoctrinated into the faith of Christ.

10
(1841)

ON THE GOSPEL OF JOHN, Tract 106:4
ML 35, 1910
NPNF VII, 400

3. *Revelation merits the assent of human reason.*

ST. THEOPHILUS OF ANTIOCH

When you have put off mortality, and put on immortality, then will you see God worthily. For God will raise your flesh immortal with your soul; and then, having become immortal, you will see the Immortal, if now you believe on Him; and then you shall know that you have spoken unjustly against Him. But you do not believe that the dead are

11
(173)

29

raised. When the event takes place, then you will believe, whether you like it or not; and your faith shall be reckoned for unbelief, unless you believe now. And why do you not believe? Do you not know that faith is the leading principle in all matters? For what farmer can reap, unless he first trust his seed to the earth? Or who can cross the sea, unless he first entrust himself to the boat and the pilot? And what sick person can be healed, unless first he trust himself to the care of the physician? And what art or knowledge can any one learn, unless he first apply and entrust himself to the teacher? If, then, the farmer trusts the earth, and the sailor the boat, and the sick the physician, will you not place confidence in God, even when you hold so many and such great pledges from His hand?

TO AUTOLYCUS, Bk. 1, Ch. 7
MG 6, 1036
ANF II, 91

ORIGEN

12
(514)

And why should it not be more reasonable, seeing all human things are dependent upon faith, to believe God rather than them? For who enters upon a voyage, or takes a wife, or becomes the father of children, or casts seed into the ground, without believing that better things will result from so doing, although the contrary might and sometimes does happen?

AGAINST CELSUS, Bk. 1, Ch. 11
MG 11, 676
ANF IV, 401

ST. CYPRIAN

13
(562)

If an influential and reputable man were to promise you something, you would have confidence in his promise and you would not believe that you would be deceived or cheated by the man who you knew stood by his words and actions. God is speaking to you, and do you waver faithless in your unbelieving mind? God promises immortality and eternity to you leaving this world, and do you doubt? This is not to know God at all. This is to offend Christ, the Teacher of believing, by the sin of disbelief. This is, though one is in the Church, not to have faith in the House of Faith.

ON MORTALITY
ML 4, 586
FC XXXVI, 203

ST. JOHN CHRYSOSTOM

Let us then in everything believe God, and contradict Him in nothing, though what is said seem to be contrary to our thoughts and senses, but let His word be of higher authority than both our reasoning and sight. Thus let us do in the mysteries also, not looking at the things set before us, but keeping in mind His sayings. For His word cannot deceive, but our senses are easily beguiled. His word has never failed, but our senses in most things go wrong. Since then the Word says, 'This is my Body' (Mt. 26:26) let us both be persuaded and believe, and look at It with the eyes of the mind. For Christ has given us nothing sentient, but though things are sensible, yet all are to be perceived spiritually. So also in baptism, the gift is bestowed by a sensible thing, that is, by water; but that which is done is perceived by the mind: —the birth and the renewal. For if you had been incorporeal, He would have delivered to you the incorporeal gifts bare; but because the soul has been locked up in a body, He delivers you the things that the mind perceives, in things sensible. How many now say, I would wish to see His form, His figure, His clothes, His shoes. You *do* see Him, you *do* touch Him, you *do* eat Him, And you indeed desire to see His clothes, but He gives Himself to you not only to see, but also to touch and eat and receive within you.

14
(1179)

THE GOSPEL OF ST. MATTHEW, Homily 82
MG 58, 743
NPNF X, 495

ST. AMBROSE

It is good for faith to precede reason, lest we seem to require reason not only from man but from God our Lord as well. For how unworthy it would be that we should believe human testimonies of another, and yet not believe the utterances of God!

15
(1321)

ON ABRAHAM, Bk. 1, Ch. 3
ML 14, 428

4. Revelation is morally necessary for us in the present order.

TERTULLIAN

We maintain that God must first be known from nature, and afterwards authenticated by instruction: from nature, by His works; by instruction through His revealed announcements. Now, in a case where nature is excluded, no natural means [of knowledge] are furnished. He ought,

16
(334)

31

therefore, to have carefully supplied a revelation of himself, even by announcements, especially as he had to be revealed in opposition to One, who, after so many and so great works, both of creation and revealed announcement, had with difficulty succeeded in satisfying men's faith.

AGAINST MARCION, Bk. 1, Ch. 18
ML 2, 266
ANF III, 284

ORIGEN

17
(513)

And [Celsus] asserts that certain [Christians] who do not wish either to give or receive a reason for their belief, keep repeating, 'Do not examine, but believe!' and, 'Your faith will save you!' And he alleges that such also say, 'The wisdom of this life is bad, but that foolishness is a good thing!' To which we have to answer, that if it were possible for all to leave the business of life, and devote themselves to philosophy, no other method ought to be adopted by any one, but this alone. For in the Christian system also it will be found that there is, not to speak at all arrogantly, at least as much of investigation into articles of belief, and of explanation of dark sayings, occurring in the prophetical writings, and of the parables in the Gospels, and of countless other things, which either were narrated or enacted with a symbolic signification (as is the case with other systems). But since the course alluded to is impossible, partly on account of the necessities of life, partly on account of the weakness of men, as only a very few individuals devote themselves earnestly to study, what better method could be devised with a view of assisting the multitude, than that which was delivered by Jesus to the heathen? And let us inquire, with respect to the great multitude of believers, who have washed away the mire of wickedness in which they formerly wallowed, whether it were better for them to believe without a reason, and [so] to have become reformed and improved in their habits, through the belief that men are chastised for sins, and honored for good works; or not to have allowed themselves to be converted on the strength of mere faith, but [to have waited] until reasons. For it is manifest that, [on such a plan], all men, with very few exceptions, would not obtain this [amelioration of conduct] which they have obtained through a simple faith, but would continue to remain in the practice of a wicked life.

AGAINST CELSUS, Bk. 1, Ch. 9
MG 11, 672
ANF IV, 400

LACTANTIUS

[The philosophers] frequently approach the truth. But those precepts have no weight, because they are human, and are without a greater, that is, that divine authority. No one therefore believes them, because the hearer imagines himself to be a man, just as he is, who enjoins them.

THE DIVINE INSTITUTES, Bk. 3, Ch. 27
ML 6, 433
ANF VII, 96

18
(629)

But if there had been any one to collect together the truth which was dispersed among individual [philosophers] and scattered among sects, and to reduce it to a body, he assuredly would not disagree with us. But no one is able to do this, unless he has experience or knowledge of the truth. And to know the true, belongs only to him who has been taught by God.

THE DIVINE INSTITUTES, Bk. 7, Ch. 7
ML 6, 759
ANF VII, 204

19
(644)

ST. AUGUSTINE

For, if the Providence of God preside not over human affairs, we have no need to busy ourselves about religion. But if both the outward form of all things, which we must believe assuredly flows from some fountain of truest beauty, and some, I know not what, inward conscience exhorts, as it were, in public and in private, all the better order of minds to seek God, and to serve God; we must not give up all hope that the same God Himself has appointed some authority, on which, resting as on a sure step, we may be lifted up to God.

ON THE PROFIT OF BELIEVING, Ch. 16, n. 34
ML 42, 89
NPNF III, 363

20
(1557)

But since the mind itself, though naturally capable of reason and intelligence, is disabled by befuddling and inveterate vices not merely from delighting and abiding in, but even from tolerating His unchangeable light, until it has been gradually healed, and renewed, and made capable of such felicity, it had, in the first place, to be impregnated with faith, and so purified. And that in this faith it might advance the more confidently towards the truth, the truth itself, God, God's Son, assuming humanity without destroying His divinity, established and founded

21
(1746)

33

this faith, that there might be a way for man to man's God through a God-man. For this is the Mediator between God and men, the man Christ Jesus. (1 Tim. 2:5) For it is as man that He is the Mediator and the Way. . . . Now the only way that is infallibly secured against all mistakes, is when the very same person is at once God and man, God our end, man our way.

THE CITY OF GOD, Bk. 11, Ch. 2
ML 41, 318
NPNF II, 206

THE NEW LAW: THE GOSPEL

5. The Gospel—senses of the word: one and four.

THE DIDACHE

22
(5)

And do not pray as the hypocrites, but as the Lord directed in His Gospel, 'Thus shall you pray: "Our Father in heaven, hallowed be Thy name," ' etc. (Mt. 6:9ff.)

Ch. 8
F 1, 18
FC I, 178

ST. IGNATIUS OF ANTIOCH

23
(60)

There are some whom I heard to say, 'Unless I find it in the documents, I do not believe in what is preached.' When I said, 'It is the written word,' they replied, 'That is what is in question.' For me, Jesus Christ is the written word; His cross and death and resurrection and faith through Him make up the untampered documents. Through these, with the help of your prayers, I desire to be justified.

LETTER TO THE PHILADELPHIANS, Ch. 8
MG 5, 704
FC I, 178

ST. JUSTIN MARTYR

24
(128)

There is then brought to the president of the brethren bread and a cup of wine mixed with water; and he taking them gives praise and glory to the Father of the universe, through the name of the Son and of the

Holy Ghost, and offers thanks at considerable length for our being counted worthy to receive these things at His hands. And when he has concluded the prayers and thanksgivings, all the people present express their assent by saying Amen. This word *Amen* answers in the Hebrew language to "so be it." And when the president has given thanks, and all the people have expressed their assent, those who are called by us deacons give to each of those present to partake of the bread and wine mixed with water over which the thanksgiving was pronounced, and to those who are absent they carry away a portion.

And this food is called among us the Eucharist, of which no one is allowed to partake but the man who believes that the things which we teach are true, and who has been washed with the washing that is for the remission of sins, and unto regeneration, and who is so living as Christ has enjoined. For not as common bread and common drink do we receive these; but in like manner as Jesus Christ our Saviour, having been made flesh by the Word of God, had both flesh and blood for our salvation, so likewise have we been taught that the food which is blessed by the prayer of His word, and from which our blood and flesh by transmutation are nourished, is the flesh and blood of that Jesus who was made flesh. For the apostles, in the memoirs composed by them, which are called Gospels, have thus delivered unto us what was enjoined upon them; that Jesus took bread and when He had given thanks, said, 'This do in remembrance of Me, this is My body'; (Lk. 22:19) and that after the same manner, having taken the cup and given thanks, He said, 'This is My blood'; (Mt. 26:28) and gave it to them alone. Which the wicked devils have imitated in the mysteries of Mithras, commanding the same thing to be done. For, that bread and a cup of water are placed with certain incantations in the mystic rites of one who is being initiated, you either know or can learn.

FIRST APOLOGY, Ch. 65, 66

MG 6, 428

ANF I, 185

ST. IRENAEUS

We have learned from none others the plan of our salvation, than from those through whom the Gospel has come down to us, which they did at one time proclaim in public, and, at a later period, by the will of God, handed down to us in the Scriptures, to be the ground and pillar of our faith. . . . [The apostles] went to the ends of the earth . . . proclaiming the peace of heaven to men, who indeed do all equally and individually possess the Gospel of God.

25

(208)

35

Matthew also issued a written Gospel among the Hebrews in their own dialect, while Peter and Paul were preaching at Rome, and laying the foundations of the Church. After their departure, Mark, the disciple and interpreter of Peter, did also hand down to us in writing what had been preached by Peter. Luke, also, the companion of Paul, recorded in a book the Gospel preached by him. Afterwards, John, the disciple of the Lord, who also had leaned upon His breast, did himself publish a Gospel during his residence at Ephesus in Asia.

AGAINST HERESIES, Bk. 3, Ch. 1
MG 7, 844
ANF I, 414

26
(215)

It is not possible that the Gospels can be either more or fewer in number than they are. For, since there are four zones of the world in which we live, and four principal winds, while the Church is scattered throughout all the world, and the 'pillar and ground' of the Church is the Gospel and the spirit of life; it is fitting that she should have four pillars, breathing out immortality on every side, and vivifying men afresh. From which fact, it is evident that the Word, and the Artificer of all, He that sits upon the cherubim, and contains all things, He who was manifested to men, has given us the Gospel under four aspects, but bound together by one Spirit.

AGAINST HERESIES, Bk. 3, Ch. 11
MG 7, 885
ANF I, 428

TATIAN

27
(659)

Tatian composed a kind of combination and collection of the gospels, I know not how, to which he gave the name Diatessaron, and this is in circulation even today among some.

Eusebius of Caesarea, ECCLESIASTICAL HISTORY, Bk. 4, Ch. 29
MG 20, 401
FC XIX, 268

ST. AUGUSTINE

28
(1825)

In the four Gospels, or rather in the four books of the one Gospel, Saint John the apostle, not undeservedly in respect of his spiritual understanding compared to the eagle, has elevated his preaching higher and far more sublimely than the other three; and in this elevating of it he would have our hearts likewise lifted up. For the other three evangelists walked with the Lord on earth as with a man; concerning His divinity they have said but little; but this evangelist, as if he disdained to walk on earth, just as in the very opening of his discourse he thundered on us and soared ... to reach Him through Whom all things are made, saying: "In the beginning was the Word," etc. (Jn. 1:1ff.)

ON THE GOSPEL OF ST. JOHN, Tr. 36:1
ML 35, 1662
NPNF VII, 208

ST. GREGORY THE GREAT

I confess that I receive and revere, as the four books of the Gospel so also the four Councils: the Nicene, in which the perverse doctrine of Arius is overthrown; the Constantinopolitan also, in which the error of Eunomius and Macedonius is refuted; further, the first Ephesine, in which the impiety of Nestorius is condemned; and the Chalcedonian, in which the depravity of Eutyches and Dioscorus is reprobated. These with full devotion I embrace, and adhere to with most entire approval; since on them, as on a foursquare stone, rises the structure of the holy faith; and whosoever, of whatever life and behaviour he may be, holds not fast to their solidity, even though he is seen to be a stone, yet he lies outside the building.... But all persons whom the aforesaid venerable Councils repudiate I repudiate; those whom they venerate I embrace; since, they having been constituted by universal consent, he overthrows not them but himself, whosoever presumes either to loose those whom they bind, or to bind those whom they loose. Whosoever, therefore, thinks otherwise, let him be anathema.

29
(2291)

LETTER TO JOHN, BISHOP OF CONSTANTINOPLE, AND THE OTHER
PATRIARCHS, Bk. 1, No. 25
ML 77, 478
NPNF XII, 81

6. *The genuineness of the four Gospels was acknowledged by Christian antiquity.*

ST. JUSTIN MARTYR

And on the day called Sunday, all who live in cities or in the country gather together to one place, and the memoirs of the apostles or the writings of the prophets are read, as long as time permits ...

30
(129)

FIRST APOLOGY, Ch. 67
MG 6, 429
ANF I, 186

31
(139)

For when John remained by the Jordan, and preached the baptism of repentance, wearing only a leathern girdle and a vesture made of camels' hair, eating nothing but locusts and wild honey, men supposed him to be Christ; but he cried to them: 'I am not the Christ, but the voice of one crying; for He that is stronger than I shall come, whose shoes I am not worthy to bear.'

DIALOGUE WITH TRYPHO, Ch. 88
MG 6, 688
ANF I, 244

32
(141)

And since we find it recorded in the memoirs of His apostles that [Christ] is the Son of God, and since we call Him the Son, we have understood that He proceeded before all creatures from the Father by His power and will (for He is addressed in the writings of the prophets in one way or another as Wisdom, and the Day, and the East, and a Sword, and a Stone, and a Rod, and Jacob, and Israel); and that He became man by the Virgin, in order that the disobedience which proceeded from the serpent might receive its destruction in the same manner in which it derived its origin. For Eve, who was a virgin and undefiled, having conceived the word of the serpent, brought forth disobedience and death. But the Virgin Mary received faith and joy, when the angel Gabriel announced the good tidings to her that the Spirit of the Lord would come upon her, and the power of the Highest would overshadow her: wherefore also the Holy Thing begotten of her is the Son of God; and she replied, 'Be it done unto me according to your word.'

DIALOGUE WITH TRYPHO, Ch. 100
MG 6, 709
ANF I, 249

33
(143)

For in the memoirs which I say were drawn up by His apostles and those who followed them, [it is recorded] that His sweat fell down like drops of blood while He was praying, (Lk. 22:44) and saying, 'If it be possible, let this cup pass. . . .' (Mt. 26:39)

DIALOGUE WITH TRYPHO, Ch. 103
MG 6, 717
ANF I, 251

ST. IRENAEUS
See No. 25.

34
(214)

So firm is the ground upon which these Gospels rest, that the very heretics themselves bear witness to them, and starting from these [documents], each one of them endeavors to establish his own peculiar doctrine. For the Ebionites, who use Matthew's Gospel only, are confuted out of this very same, making false suppositions with regard to the Lord. But Marcion, mutilating that according to Luke, is proved to be a blasphemer of the only existing God, from those [passages] which he still retains. Those, again, who separate Jesus from Christ, alleging that Christ remained impassible, but that it was Jesus who suffered, preferring the Gospel by Mark, if they read it with a love of truth, may have their errors rectified. Those, moreover, who follow Valentinus, making copious use of that according to John, to illustrate their conjunctions, shall be proved to be totally in error by means of this very Gospel.

AGAINST HERESIES, Bk. 3, Ch. 11

MG 7, 884

ANF I, 428

These things being so, all who destroy the form of the Gospel are vain, unlearned, and also audacious; those, [I mean] who represent the aspects of the Gospel as being either more in number than as aforesaid, or, on the other hand fewer. The former class [do so] that they may seem to have discovered more than is of the truth; the latter, that they may set the dispensations of God aside.

AGAINST HERESIES, Bk. 3, Ch. 11

MG 7, 890

ANF I, 429

35
(216)

THE MURATORIAN FRAGMENT

. . . but at some he was present, and so he set them down. The third book of the Gospel, that according to Luke, was compiled in his own name on Paul's authority by Luke the physician, when after Christ's ascension Paul had taken him to be with him like a legal expert. Yet neither did *he* see the Lord in the flesh; and he too, as he was able to ascertain events, begins his story from the birth of John.

The fourth of the Gospels was written by John, one of the disciples. When exhorted by his fellow-disciples and bishops, he said, 'Fast with me this day for three days; and what may be revealed to any of us, let us relate it to one another.' The same night it was revealed to Andrew, one of the apostles, that John was to write all things in his own name, and they were all to certify.

And therefore, though various ideas are taught in the several books

36
(268)

39

of the Gospels, yet it makes no difference to the faith of believers, since by one sovereign Spirit all things are declared in all of them concerning the Nativity, the Passion, the Resurrection, the conversation with his disciples and his two comings, the first in lowliness and contempt, which has come to pass, the second glorious with royal power, which is to come.

What marvel therefore if John so firmly sets forth each statement in his Epistles too, saying of himself, "What we have seen with our eyes and heard with our ears and our hands have handled, these things we have written to you"? For so he declares himself not an eye-witness and a hearer only, but a writer of all the marvels of the Lord in order. The Acts, however, of all the Apostles are written in one book. Luke, 'to the most excellent Theophilus,' includes events because they were done in his own presence, as he also plainly shows by leaving out the passion of Peter, and also the departure of Paul from the City on his journey to Spain.

The Epistles, however, of Paul themselves make plain to those who wish to understand it, what epistles were sent by him, and from what place or for what cause. He wrote at some length first of all to the Corinthians, forbidding the schisms of heresy; next to the Galatians, forbidding circumcision; then he wrote to the Romans at greater length, impressing on them the rule of the Scriptures, and also that Christ is the first principle of them, concerning which severally it is not necessary for us to discuss. For the blessed Apostle Paul himself, following the rule of his predecessor John, writes only by name to seven churches in the following order—to the Corinthians a first, to the Ephesians a second, to the Philippians a third, to the Colossians a fourth, to the Galatians a fifth, to the Thessalonians a sixth, to the Romans a seventh; although for the sake of admonition there is a second to the Corinthians and to the Thessalonians, yet *one* Church is recognized as being spread over the entire world. For John too in the Apocalypse, though he writes to seven churches, yet speaks to all. Howbeit to Philemon one, to Titus one, and to Timothy two were put in writing from personal inclination and attachment, to be in honor however with the Catholic Church for the ordering of ecclesiastical discipline. There is in circulation also one to the Laodicenes, another to the Alexandrians, both forged in Paul's name to suit the heresy of Marcion, and several others, which cannot be received into the Catholic Church; for it is not fitting that gall be mixed with honey.

The Epistle of Jude no doubt, and the couple bearing the name of John, are accepted in the Catholic Church; and the Wisdom written by the friends of Solomon in his honor. The Apocalypse also of John, and of Peter only we receive, which some of our friends will not have read in the Church. But the Shepherd was written quite lately in our times in the city of Rome by Hermas, while his brother Pius, the bishop, was sitting in the chair of the church of the city of Rome; and therefore it ought indeed to be read, but it cannot to the end of time be publicly read in the Church to the people, either among the prophets, who are complete in number, or among the Apostles.

But of Arsinous, called also Valentinus, or of Miltiades we receive nothing at all; those who have also composed a new book of Psalms for Marcion, together with Basileides and the Asian founder of the Cataphrygians are rejected.

S, pp. 144–146

TERTULLIAN

I pass on to give a proof of the Gospel—not, to be sure, of Jewry, but of Pontus—having become meanwhile [occasionally] adulterated; and this shall indicate the order by which we proceed. We lay it down as our first position, that the evangelical Testament has apostles for its authors, to whom was assigned by the Lord Himself this office of publishing the gospel. . . . Of the apostles, therefore, John and Matthew first instill faith into us; while of apostolic men, Luke and Mark afterwards renew it.

37
(339)

AGAINST MARCION, Bk. 4, Ch. 2
ML 2, 363
ANF III, 347

On the whole, then, if that is evidently more true which is earlier, if that is earlier which is from the very beginning, if that is from the beginning which has the apostles for its authors, then it will certainly be quite as evident, that that comes down from the apostles, which has been kept as a sacred deposit in the churches of the apostles. Let us see what milk the Corinthians drank from Paul; to what rule [of faith] the Galatians were brought for correction; what the Philippians, the Thessalonians, the Ephesians read [out of it]; what utterance also the Romans give, so very near [to the apostles], to whom Peter and Paul conjointly bequeathed the gospel, even sealed with their own blood. We have also [St.] John's foster churches. For although Marcion rejects his Apocalypse, the order of the bishops [thereof], when traced up to their origin, will yet rest on John as their author. In the same manner

38
(341)

is recognized the excellent source of the other churches. I say, therefore, that in them (and not simply such of them as were founded by apostles, but in all those which are united with them in the fellowship of the mystery [of the gospel of Christ]) that Gospel of Luke which we are defending with all our might has stood its ground from its very publication; whereas Marcion's Gospel is not known to most people, and to none whatever is it known without being at the same time condemned. It too, of course, has its churches, but specially its own—as late as they are spurious; and should you want to know their origin, you will more easily discover apostasy in it than apostolicity, with Marcion as their founder, or some one of Marcion's swarm. Even wasps make combs; so also these Marcionites make churches. The same authority of the apostolic churches will afford evidence to the other Gospels also, which we possess equally through their means, and according to their usage—I mean the Gospels of John and Matthew—while that which Mark published may be affirmed to be Peter's, whose interpreter Mark was. For even Luke's form of the Gospel men usually ascribe to Paul.

AGAINST MARCION, Bk. 4, Ch. 5
ML 2, 366
ANF III, 349–350

ST. CLEMENT OF ALEXANDRIA

39
(439)

Again, in the same books Clement has set down a tradition which he had received from the elders before him, in regard to the order of the Gospels, to the following effect. He says that the Gospels containing the genealogies were written first, and that the Gospel according to Mark was composed in the following circumstances:—Peter having preached the word publicly at Rome, and by the Spirit proclaimed the Gospel, those who were present, who were numerous, entreated Mark, inasmuch as he had attended him from an early period, and remembered what had been said, to write down what had been spoken. On his composing the Gospel, he handed it to those who had made the request to him; which coming to Peter's knowledge, he neither hindered nor encouraged. But John, the last of all, seeing that what was corporeal was set forth in the Gospels, on the entreaty of his intimate friends, and inspired by the Spirit, composed a spiritual Gospel.

Eusebius of Caesarea, ECCLESIASTICAL HISTORY, Bk. 6, Ch. 14
MG 9, 749 20, 551
FC XXIX, 27

ORIGEN

Among the four Gospels, which are the only indisputable ones in the
Church of God under heaven, I have learned by tradition that the first
was written by Matthew, who was once a publican, but afterwards an
apostle of Jesus Christ, and it was prepared for the converts from
Judaism, and published in the Hebrew language. The second is by
Mark, who composed it according to the instructions of Peter . . . . the
third by Luke, the Gospel commended by Paul, and composed for
Gentile converts. Last of all that by John.

40
(503)

> Eusebius of Caesarea, ECCLESIASTICAL HISTORY, Bk. 6, Ch. 25
> *MG* 13, 829 20, 581
> *FC* XXIX, 48

TATIAN
See No. 27.

ST. AUGUSTINE

If we are perplexed by an apparent contradiction in Scripture, it is not
allowable to say, "The author of this book is mistaken"; but either the
manuscript is faulty, or the translation is wrong, or you have not
understood. . . . But in consequence of the distinctive peculiarity of the
sacred writings, we are bound to receive as true whatever the canon
shows to have been said by even one prophet, or apostle, or evangelist.
Otherwise, not a single page will be left for the guidance of human
fallibility, if contempt for the wholesome authority of the canonical
books either puts an end to that authority altogether, or involves it in
hopeless confusion.

41
(1597)

> REPLY TO FAUSTUS THE MANICHAEAN, Bk. 11, Ch. 5
> *ML* 42, 249
> *NPNF* IV, 180

7. *The witnesses who assert the genuineness of the Gospels are worthy of belief.*

ST. PAPIAS

Whenever anyone came my way, who had been a follower of my
seniors, I would ask for the accounts of our seniors: What did Andrew
or Peter say? Or Philip or Thomas or James or John or Matthew, or
any of the Lord's disciples? I also asked: What did Aristion and John

42
(94)

the Presbyter, disciples of the Lord say. For, as I see it, it is not so much from books as from the living and permanent voice that I must draw profit.

Eusebius of Caesarea, ECCLESIASTICAL HISTORY, Bk. 3, Ch. 39
MG 20, 297
FC, I, 374

ST. IRENAEUS

43
(212)

But Polycarp also was not only instructed by apostles, and conversed with many who had seen Christ, but was also, by apostles in Asia, appointed bishop of the Church in Smyrna, whom I also saw in my early youth, for he tarried [on earth] a very long time, and, when a very old man, gloriously and most nobly suffered martyrdom, departed this life, having always taught the things which he had learned from the apostles, and which the Church has handed down, and which alone are true. To these things all the Asiatic Churches testify, as do also those men who have succeeded Polycarp down to the present time.

AGAINST HERESIES, Bk. 3, Ch. 3 *
MG 7, 851
ANF I, 416

44
(264)

These opinions, Florinus, these presbyters who preceded us, and who were conversant with the apostles, did not hand down to you. For, while I was yet a boy, I saw you in Lower Asia with Polycarp, distinguishing yourself in the royal court, and endeavoring to gain his approbation. For I have a more vivid recollection of what occurred at that time than of recent events (inasmuch as the experiences of childhood, keeping pace with the growth of the soul, become incorporated with it); so that I can even describe the place where the blessed Polycarp used to sit and discourse—his going out, too, and his coming in—his general mode of life and personal appearance, together with the discourses which he delivered to the people; also how he would speak of his familiar intercourse with John, and with the rest of those who had seen the Lord; and how he would call their words to remembrance. Whatsoever things he had heard from them respecting the Lord, both with regard to His miracles and His teaching, Polycarp having thus received [information] from the eye-witnesses of the Word of life, would recount them all in harmony with the Scriptures. These things, through God's mercy which was upon me, I then listened to attentively,

* See also Bk. 2, Ch. 22.

and treasured them up not on paper, but in my heart; and I am continually, by God's grace, revolving these things accurately in my mind. And I can bear witness before God, that if that blessed and apostolical presbyter had heard any such thing, he would have cried out, and stopped his ears, exclaiming as he was wont to do: "O good God, for what times have You reserved me, that I should endure these things?" And he would have fled from the very spot where, sitting or standing, he had heard such words.

Letter to Florinus in Eusebius of Caesarea, ECCLESIASTICAL HISTORY,
Bk. 5, Ch. 20
MG 7, 1225 20, 485
ANF I, 568

EUSEBIUS OF CAESAREA

[Papias] presents other accounts as having come to him from unwritten tradition, and some strange parables of the Saviour and teachings of His and other more mythical accounts. Among these he says that there will be a period of about a thousand years after the resurrection of the dead, when the kingdom of Christ will be established on this earth in material form. I suppose that he got these ideas through a perverse reading of the accounts of the Apostles, not realizing that these were expressed by them mystically in figures. For he appears to be a man of very little intelligence, to speak judging from his books, but he was responsible for the great number of Church writers after him holding the same opinion as himself, who proposed in their support the antiquity of the man, as, for instance, Irenaeus and whoever else appeared to hold similar views.

45
(658)

ECCLESIASTICAL HISTORY, Bk. 3, Ch. 39
MG 20, 300
NPNF I, 116

8. *The four Gospels contain true history.*

ST. IGNATIUS OF ANTIOCH
See No. 23.

ST. IRENAEUS

[Marcion] mutilates the Gospel which is according to Luke, removing all that is written respecting the generation of the Lord, and setting aside a great deal of the teaching of the Lord, in which the Lord is recorded as most clearly confessing that the Maker of this universe is

46
(195)

His Father. He likewise persuaded his disciples that he himself was more worthy of credit than are those apostles who have handed down the Gospel to us, furnishing them not with the Gospel, but merely a fragment of it.

AGAINST HERESIES, Bk. 1, Ch. 27
MG 7, 688
ANF I, 352

See Nos. 36 and 44.

ORIGEN

47
(519)

Now if they had not been sincere, but, as Celsus supposes, had written lies, they would not have represented Peter as denying, nor His disciples as being offended. For although these events actually happened, who could have proved that they turned out in that manner? And yet, according to all probability, these were matters which ought to have been passed over in silence by men who wished to teach the readers of the Gospels to despise death for the sake of confessing Christianity.

AGAINST CELSUS, Bk. 2, Ch. 15
MG 11, 825
ANF IV, 437

ARNOBIUS

48
(619)

But [the Gospels] were written by unlearned and ignorant men, and occurrence, and who saw them done before their eyes—the very best witnesses and the most trustworthy authorities—both believed them themselves, and transmitted them to us who follow them, to be believed with no scanty measure of confidence. Who are these? you perhaps ask. Tribes, peoples, nations, and that incredulous human race; but if the matter were not plain, and, as the saying is, clearer than day itself, they would never grant their assent with so ready belief to events of such a kind. But shall we say that the men of that time were untrustworthy, false, stupid, and brutish to such a degree that they pretended to have seen what they never had seen, and that they put forth under false evidence, or alleged with childish asseveration things which never took place, and that when they were able to live in harmony and to maintain friendly relations with you, they wantonly incurred hatred, and were held in execration?

AGAINST THE HEATHEN, Bk. 1, Ch. 54
ML 5, 792
ANF VI, 428

But [the Gospels] were written by unlearned and ignorant men, and should not therefore be readily believed. See that this be not rather a stronger reason for believing that they have not been adulterated by any false statements, but were put forth by men of simple mind, who knew not how to trick out their tales with meretricious ornaments. But the language is mean and vulgar. For truth never seeks deceitful polish, nor in that which is well ascertained and certain does it allow itself to be led away into excessive prolixity.

49
(620)

AGAINST THE HEATHEN, Bk. 1, Ch. 58
ML 5, 796
ANF VI, 429

ST. JOHN CHRYSOSTOM

In many places [the evangelists] are convicted of disagreement. Nay, this very thing is a very great evidence of their truth. For if they had agreed in all things exactly even to time, place, and to the very words, none of our enemies would have believed but that they had met together, and had written what they wrote by some human compact; because such entire agreement as this does not come of simplicity. But now even that discordance which seems to exist in little matters delivers them from all suspicion, and speaks clearly in behalf of the character of the writers.

50
(1170)

HOMILIES ON MATTHEW, No. 1:6
MG 57, 16
NPNF X, 3

CHRIST, THE DIVINE LEGATE

9. *Jesus Christ truly came into the world as a divine legate.*

ST. IGNATIUS OF ANTIOCH

I say these things to forewarn you against falling into the snares of an empty doctrine. I hope, rather, that you may be fully convinced of the birth and passion and the resurrection that took place during the period of the governorship of Pontius Pilate. These things were really and

51
(47)

truly done by Jesus Christ, our hope; and from this hope may God forbid that any of you should be turned aside.

LETTER TO THE MAGNESIANS, Ch. 11
MG 5, 672
FC I, 99–100

52
(51)

And so be deaf when anyone speaks to you apart from Jesus Christ, who was of the race of David, the son of Mary, who was truly born and ate and drank, who was truly persecuted under Pontius Pilate and was really crucified and died in the sight of those 'in heaven and on earth and under the earth.' Moreover, He was truly raised from the dead by the power of His Father.

LETTER TO THE TRALLIANS, Ch. 9
MG 5, 681
FC I, 104

TERTULLIAN

53
(290)

Now the rule of faith—that we may at this point confess what it is that we maintain—is that whereby it is believed that there is in any wise but one God, and no other than the Creator of the world, Who, by His own Word first of all sent forth, brought all things out of nothing: that this Word is called His Son, Who, with the Name of God, was in divers manners seen by the Patriarchs, ever heard in the Prophets, brought down at last by the Spirit and the Power of God the Father into the Virgin Mary, made flesh in her womb, and, being born of her, appeared under the character of Jesus Christ: that thenceforth He preached a new law, and a new promise of the Kingdom of Heaven; worked miracles; was nailed to the cross; rose again the third day; was taken up to Heaven, and sat down at the right hand of the Father; sent in His stead the power of the Holy Spirit, to work upon believers; and that He shall come with glory to take the saints to the enjoyment of eternal life and of the heavenly promises, and to condemn the ungodly to everlasting fire, having caused the resurrection of both classes to take place, with the restoration of their bodies.

THE PRESCRIPTION OF HERETICS, Ch. 13
ML 2, 26
ANF III, 249

ST. CLEMENT OF ALEXANDRIA

54
(405)

For with a celerity unsurpassable, and a benevolence to which we have ready access, the divine power, casting its radiance on the earth, has filled the universe with the seed of salvation. For it was not without divine care that so great a work was accomplished in so brief a space by the Lord, who, though despised as to appearance, was in reality adored, the expiator of sin, the Saviour, the clement, the Divine Word, He that is truly most manifest Deity, He that is made equal to the Lord of the universe; because He was His Son, and the Word was in God, (Jn. 1:1) not disbelieved in by all when He was first preached, nor altogether unknown when, assuming the character of man, and fashioning Himself in flesh, He enacted the drama of human salvation: for He was a true champion and a fellow-champion with the creature. And being communicated most speedily to men, having dawned from His Father's counsel quicker than the sun, with the most perfect ease He made God shine on us. Whence He was and what He was, He showed by what He taught and exhibited, manifesting Himself as the Herald of the Covenant, the Reconciler, our Saviour, the Word, the Fount of Life, the Giver of peace, diffused over the whole face of the earth; by whom, so to speak, the universe has already become an ocean of blessing.

EXHORTATION TO THE HEATHEN, Ch. 10: 110
MG 8, 225
ANF II, 202

ORIGEN

But we do not view His sufferings as having been merely in appearance, in order that His resurrection also may not be a false, but a real event. For he who really died, actually arose, if he did arise; whereas he who appeared only to have died, did not in reality arise.

55
(520)

AGAINST CELSUS, Bk. 2, Ch. 16
MG 11, 828
ANF IV, 438

If it had been recorded that several individuals had appeared in human life as sons of God in the manner in which Jesus did, and if each of them had drawn a party of adherents to his side, so that, on account of the similarity of the profession (in the case of each individual) that he was the Son of God, he to whom his followers bore testimony to that effect was an object of dispute, there would have been ground for his saying, 'If these bring forward this person, and others a different individual, while the common and ready cry of all parties is, "Believe, if you will be saved, or else begone," ' and so on; whereas it

56
(531)

49

has been proclaimed to the entire world that Jesus Christ is the only Son of God who visited the human race.

AGAINST CELSUS, Bk. 6, Ch. 11
MG 11, 1305
ANF IV, 578

ST. AUGUSTINE

57
(1506)

[Christ] did these [miracles], yet was He despised by the many, who considered not so much what great things He did, as how small He was; as though they said within themselves, 'These are divine things, but He is a man.' Two things then you see, divine works, and a man. If divine works cannot be wrought but by God, take heed lest in This Man God lie concealed. Attend, I say, to what you see, believe what you see not. He has not abandoned you, who has called you to believe; though He enjoin you to believe that which you cannot see: yet has He not given you up to see nothing whereby you may be able to believe what you do not see. Is the creation itself a small sign, a small indication of the Creator? He also came, He did miracles. You could not see God, a man you could; so God was made Man, that in One you might have both what to see, and what to believe.

SERMONS, No. 126
ML 38, 700

See No. 21.

NPNF VI, 482

ST. CYRIL OF ALEXANDRIA

58
(2077)

Therefore, as God, He abrogated the first precept, and on His Own authority enjoined the second. For this is what 'But I say to you' seems to mean. How therefore is God made or created since He sanctions laws naturally?

TREASURY OF THE HOLY AND CONSUBSTANTIAL TRINITY, 33
MG 75, 516

10. The prophecies prove this divine mission to be fulfilled in Christ.

ST. JUSTIN MARTYR

59
(122)

But lest any one should meet us with the question, What should prevent that He whom we call Christ, being a man born of men, performed what we call His mighty works by magical art, and by this appeared to be the Son of God? we will now offer proof, not trusting mere assertions, but being of necessity persuaded by those who prophesied [of Him] before these things came to pass, for with our own eyes we behold things that have happened and are happening just as they were predicted; and this will, we think, appear even to you the strongest and truest evidence.

FIRST APOLOGY, Ch. 30
MG 6, 373
ANF I, 172

For with what reason should we believe of a crucified man that He is the first-born of the unbegotten God, and Himself will pass judgment on the whole human race, unless we had found testimonies concerning Him published before He came and was born as man, and unless we saw that things had happened accordingly?

FIRST APOLOGY, Ch. 53
MG 6, 405
ANF I, 180

60
(125)

But so much is written, [the testimonies of the prophets] for the sake of proving that Jesus the Christ is the Son of God and His Apostle, being of old the Word, and appearing sometimes in the form of fire, and sometimes in the likeness of angels; but now, by the will of God, having become man for the human race, He endured all the sufferings which the devils instigated the senseless Jews to inflict upon Him.... 'No one knows the Father, but the Son; nor the Son but the Father, and those to whom the Son will reveal Him.' (Mt. 11:27) The Jews, accordingly, being throughout of opinion that it was the Father of the universe who spoke to Moses, though He who spoke to him was indeed the Son of God, who is called both Angel and Apostle, are justly charged, both by the Spirit of prophecy and by Christ Himself, with knowing neither the Father nor the Son. For they who affirm that the Son is the Father, are proved neither to have become acquainted with the Father, nor to know that the Father of the universe has a Son; who also, being the first-begotten Word of God is even God. And of old He appeared in the shape of fire and the likeness of an angel to Moses and to the other prophets; but now in the times of your reign, having, as we before said, become Man by a virgin, according to the counsel of the Father, for the salvation of those who believe

61
(127)

51

on Him, He endured both to be set at nought and to suffer, that by dying and rising again He might conquer death.

FIRST APOLOGY, Ch. 63

MG 6, 424

ANF I, 184

ST. IRENAEUS

62
(222)

But being ignorant of Him who from the Virgin is Emmanuel, they are deprived of His gift which is eternal life; and not receiving the incorruptible Word, they remain in mortal flesh, and are debtors to death, not obtaining the antidote of life. . . . But that He is Himself in His own right, beyond all men who ever lived, God, and Lord, and King Eternal, and the Incarnate Word, proclaimed by all the prophets, the apostles, and by the Spirit Himself, may be seen by all who have attained to even a small portion of the truth. Now, the Scriptures would not have testified these things of Him, if, like others, He had been a mere man. But that He had, beyond all others, in Himself that pre-eminent birth which is from the Most High Father, and also experienced that pre-eminent generation which is from the Virgin, the divine Scriptures do in both respects testify of Him.

AGAINST HERESIES, Bk. 3, Ch. 19

MG 7, 938

ANF I, 448

LACTANTIUS

63
(638)

Learn, therefore, if you have any sense, that [Christ] was not believed by us to be God on this account, because He did wonderful things, but because we saw that all things were done in His case which were announced to us by the prediction of the prophets. He performed wonderful deeds; we might have supposed Him to be a magician, as you now suppose Him to be, and the Jews then supposed Him, if all the prophets did not with one accord proclaim that Christ would do those very things. Therefore we believe Him to be God, not more from His wonderful deeds and works, than from that very cross which you as dogs lick, since that also was predicted at the same time. It was not therefore on His own testimony (for who can be believed when he speaks concerning himself?), but on the testimony of the prophets who long before foretold all things which He did and suffered, that He gained a belief in His divinity, which could have happened neither to

Apollonius, nor to Apuleius, nor to any of the magicians; nor can it happen at any time.

THE DIVINE INSTITUTES, Bk. 5, Ch. 3
ML 6, 560
ANF VII, 139

ST. AUGUSTINE

For whenever we wish to show Christ prophesied about, we produce for the heathen these writings. And lest by chance men hard of belief should say that we Christians have composed these books, so that together with the Gospel which we have preached we have forged the Prophet, through whom there might seem to be foretold that which we preach: by this we convince them, namely, that all the very writings wherein Christ has been prophesied are with the Jews, all these very writings the Jews have. We produce documents from enemies, to confound other enemies. In what sort of reproach therefore are the Jews? A document the Jew carries, from which a Christian may believe. Our librarians they have become, just as slaves are wont behind their masters to carry documents, in such sort that these faint in carrying, those profit by reading.

64
(1470)

EXPOSITIONS ON THE PSALMS, Ps. 56
ML 36, 666
NPNF VIII, 227

11. Christ's miracles prove His divine mission.

ST. QUADRATUS

But the works of our Saviour were always at hand, for they were true, those who were cured, those who rose from the dead, who were seen not only when being cured and when rising, but also, being always at hand, not only when the Saviour was on earth, but even after He had departed, survived for a considerable time, so that some of them have even come down to our own time.

65
(109)

Eusebius of Caesarea, ECCLESIASTICAL HISTORY, Bk. 4, Ch. 3
MG 20, 308
FC XIX, 210

ST. JUSTIN MARTYR
See No. 59.

ORIGEN

66
(522)
The works of Christ and His disciples had for their fruit, not deceit, but the salvation of human souls. And who would rationally maintain that an improved moral life, which daily lessened the number of a man's offences, could proceed from a system of deceit?

AGAINST CELSUS, Bk. 2, Ch. 50
MG 11, 876
ANF IV, 451

67
(524)
Place yourself, then, as a neutral party, between what is related of Aristeas and what is recorded of Jesus, and see whether, from the result, and from the benefits which have accrued to the reformation of morals, and to the worship of the God who is over all things, it is not allowable to conclude that we must believe the events recorded of Jesus not to have happened without the divine intervention, but that this was not the case with the story of Aristeas the Proconnesian.

AGAINST CELSUS, Bk. 3, Ch. 27
MG 11, 953
ANF IV, 475

ARNOBIUS

68
(618)
Can you specify and point out to me any one of all those magicians who have ever existed in past ages, that did anything similar, in the thousandth degree, to Christ?

AGAINST THE HEATHEN, Bk. 1, Ch. 43
ML 5, 773

See No. 48.

ANF VI, 425

ST. GREGORY OF NYSSA

69
(1031)
Should you, however, ask in what way Deity is mingled with humanity, you will have occasion for a preliminary inquiry as to what the coalescence is of soul with flesh. But supposing you are ignorant of the way in which the soul is in union with the body, do not suppose that that other question is bound to come within your comprehension; rather, as in this case of the union of soul and body, while we have reason to believe that the soul is something other than the body, because the flesh when isolated from the soul becomes dead and inactive, we have yet no exact knowledge of the method of the union,

so in that other inquiry of the union of Deity with manhood, while we are quite aware that there is a distinction as regards degree of majesty between the Divine and the mortal perishable nature, we are not capable of detecting how the Divine and human elements are mixed together. We do not doubt, however, that God was born in the nature of a man, because of those miracles narrated.

THE GREAT CATECHISM, No. 11
MG 45, 44
NPNF V, 486

When we take a wide survey of the universe, and consider the dispensations throughout the world, and the Divine benevolences that operate in our life, we grasp the conception of a power overlying all, that is creative of all things that come into being, and is conservative of them as they exist. On the same principle, as regards the manifestation of God in the flesh, we have established a satisfactory proof of that apparition of Deity, in those wonders of His operations; for in all his work as actually recorded we recognize the characteristics of the Divine nature.

70
(1032)

THE GREAT CATECHISM, No. 12
MG 45, 44
NPNF V, 486

ST. AUGUSTINE
See No. 57.

12. Christ's prophecies prove His divine mission.

ST. JUSTIN MARTYR

That all these things should come to pass [the persecutions against Christians], I say, our Teacher foretold, He who is both Son and Apostle of God the Father of all and the Ruler, Jesus Christ; from whom also we have the name of Christians. Whence we become more assured of all the things He taught us, since whatever He beforehand foretold should come to pass, is seen in fact coming to pass; and this is the work of God, to tell of a thing before it happens, and as it was foretold so to show it happening.

71
(116)

FIRST APOLOGY, Ch. 12
MG 6, 344
ANF I, 166

EUSEBIUS OF CAESAREA

72
(654)
If one should compare the words of our Saviour with the other narratives of the historian [Josephus on the Jewish War], how could he help but marvel and confess the truly divine and supernaturally wonderful foreknowledge and prophecy of our Saviour?

ECCLESIASTICAL HISTORY, Bk. 3, Ch. 7
MG 20, 233
FC XIX, 154

13. The resurrection of Christ rests on arguments that are certain.

ST. CLEMENT OF ROME

73
(13)
Let us consider, beloved, how the Lord is continually revealing to us the resurrection that is to be. Of this He has constituted the Lord Jesus Christ the first-fruits, by raising Him from the dead. Let us look, beloved, at the resurrection in regard to the seasons. Day and night demonstrate a resurrection; the night sleeps and the day arises; the day departs and night returns.

LETTER TO THE CORINTHIANS, Ch. 24
MG 1, 260
FC I, 29

ST. IGNATIUS OF ANTIOCH
See Nos. 51 and 52.

ORIGEN

74
(523)
But Celsus . . . will have it that some dreamed a waking dream, and, under the influence of a perverted imagination, formed to themselves such an image as they desired. Now it is not irrational to believe that a dream may take place while one is asleep; but to suppose a waking vision in the case of those who are not altogether out of their senses, and under the influence of delirium or hypochondria, is incredible.

AGAINST CELSUS, Bk. 2, Ch. 60
MG 11, 892
ANF IV, 455

ST. AUGUSTINE

At the earth quaking, the Lord rose again: such miracles were done
about the sepulchre, that even the very soldiers that had come for
guards were made witnesses, if they chose to tell the truth: but the
same covetousness which had led captive a disciple, the companion of
Christ, led captive also the soldier that was guard of the sepulchre.
We give you, they say, money; and say, while yourselves were sleeping
there came His disciples, and took Him away (Mt. 28:13). . . . Sleeping
witnesses, you adduce: truly you yourself have fallen asleep, that in
searching such devices have failed. If they were sleeping, what could
they see? If they saw nothing, how are they witnesses?

75
(1471)

> EXPOSITIONS ON THE PSALMS, Ps. 63
> *ML* 36, 767
> *NPNF* VIII, 266

14. *The wonderful propagation and perpetuity of Christianity
prove its divine origin.*

ST. JUSTIN MARTYR

Now it is evident that no one can terrify or subdue us who have
believed in Jesus over all the world. For it is plain, that though
beheaded, and crucified, and thrown to wild beasts, and chains, and
fire, and all other kinds of torture, we do not give up our confession;
but the more such things happen, the more do others and in larger
numbers become faithful, and worshippers of God through the name
of Jesus. For just as if one should cut away the fruit-bearing parts of
a vine, it grows up again, and yields other branches flourishing and
fruitful; even so the same things happen with us.

76
(144)

> DIALOGUE WITH TRYPHO, Ch. 110
> *MG* 6, 729
> *ANF* I, 254

TERTULLIAN

Truth and hatred came into existence simultaneously. As soon as the
former appeared, the latter began its enmity. It has as many foes as
there are outsiders, particularly among Jews because of their jealousy,
among soldiers because of their blackmailing, and even among the

77
(274)

very members of our own household because of corrupt human nature. Day by day we are besieged; day by day we are betrayed; oftentimes, in the very midst of our meetings and gatherings, we are surprised by an assault. Who has ever come upon a baby wailing, as the accusation has it? Who has ever kept for the judge's inspection the jaws of Cyclopes and Sirens, bloodstained as he had found them? Who has ever found any traces of impurity upon [Christian] wives? Who has discovered such crimes, yet concealed them or been bribed to keep them secret when dragging these men off to court? If we always keep under cover, whence the betrayal of our crimes?

Rather, who could have been the traitors? Certainly not the accused themselves, since the obligation of pledged silence is binding upon all mysteries by their very nature. The mysteries of Samothrace and of Eleusis are shrouded in silence; how much more such rites as these which, if they were made public, would provoke at once the hatred of all mankind—while God's wrath is reserved for the future? If, then, Christians themselves are not the betrayers, it follows that outsiders are. Whence do outsiders get their knowledge since even holy initiation rites always ban the uninitiated and are wary of witnesses? Unless you mean that the wicked are less afraid.

APOLOGY, Ch. 7
ML 1, 307
FC X, 26–27

78
(279)

We are but of yesterday, yet we have filled every place among you—cities, islands, fortresses, towns, marketplaces, camps, tribes, town councils, the palace, the senate, the forum; we have left nothing to you but the temples of your gods. For what war would we not have been fit and ready, even though unequally matched in military strength, we who are so ready to be slain, were it not that, according to our rule of life, it is granted us to be killed rather than to kill?

Even unarmed and without any uprising, merely as malcontents, simply through hatred and withdrawal, we could have fought against you. For, if such a multitude of men as we are had broken loose from you and had gone into some remote corner of the earth, the loss of so many citizens, of whatever kind they might be, would certainly have made your power blush for shame; in fact, it would even have punished you by this very desertion. Without a doubt, you would have been exceedingly frightened at your loneliness, at the silence of your surroundings, and the stupor, as it were, of a dead world. You would have had to look around for people to rule; there would have been more enemies than citizens left to you.

APOLOGY, Ch. 37
ML 1, 462
FC X, 95–96

[They consider] that the Christians are the cause of every public calamity and every misfortune of the people. If the Tiber rises as high as the city walls, if the Nile does not rise to the fields, if the weather will not change, if there is an earthquake, a famine, a plague— straightway the cry is heard: 'Toss the Christians to the lion!'

APOLOGY, Ch. 40
ML 1, 479
FC X, 102

79
(282)

Should she hesitate and investigate and speculate constantly whether a man will be a proper husband to receive her dowry, when God has entrusted him with His own treasures? How shall we ever be able adequately to describe the happiness of that marriage which the Church arranges, the Sacrifice strengthens, upon which the blessing sets a seal, at which angels are present as witnesses, and to which the Father gives His consent?

TO HIS WIFE, Bk. 2, Ch. 9
ML 1, 1302
ACW, 34–35

80
(320)

Though our numbers are so great—constituting all but the majority in every city—we conduct ourselves so quietly and modestly; I might perhaps say, known rather as individuals than as organized communities, and remarkable only for the reformation of our former vices.

TO SCAPULA, Ch. 2
ML 1, 700
ANF III, 106

81
(369)

ORIGEN

But in the case of the Christians, the Roman Senate, and the princes of the time, and the soldiery, and the people, and the relatives of those who had become converts to the faith, made war upon their doctrine, and would have prevented [its progress], overcoming it by a confederacy of so powerful a nature, had it not, by the help of God, es-

82
(511)

caped the danger, and risen above it, so as [finally] to defeat the whole world in its conspiracy against it.

AGAINST CELSUS, Bk. 1, Ch. 3
MG 11, 661
ANF IV, 398

83
(516)
Could it have come to pass without divine assistance, that Jesus, desiring during these years to spread abroad His words and teaching, should have been so successful, that everywhere throughout the world, not a few persons, Greeks as well as Barbarians, learned as well as ignorant, adopted His doctrine, so that they struggled even to death in its defence, rather than deny it, which no one is ever related to have done for any other system? . . . And if any one, on a candid consideration of these things, shall admit that no improvement ever takes place among men without divine help, how much more confidently shall he make the same assertion regarding Jesus, when he compares the former lives of many converts to His doctrine with their after-conduct, and reflects in what acts of licentiousness and injustice and covetousness they formerly indulged, until, as Celsus, and they who think with him, allege, 'they were deceived,' and accepted a doctrine which, as these individuals assert, is destructive of the life of men; but who, from the time that they adopted it, have become in some way meeker, and more religious, and more consistent, so that certain among them, from a desire of exceeding chastity, and a wish to worship God with greater purity, abstain even from the permitted indulgences of [lawful] love.

Any one who examines the subject will see that Jesus attempted and successfully accomplished works beyond the reach of human power. For although, from the very beginning, all things opposed the spread of His doctrine in the world, —both the princes of the times, and their chief captains and generals, and all, to speak generally, who were possessed of the smallest influence, and in addition to these, the rulers of the different cities, and the soldiers, and the people, —yet it proved victorious, as being the Word of God, the nature of which is such that it cannot be hindered.

AGAINST CELSUS, Bk. 1, Ch. 26
MG 11, 709
ANF IV, 407

ARNOBIUS

84
(621)
Do not even these proofs at least give you faith to believe, viz., that already, in so short and brief a time, the oaths of this vast army have

spread abroad over all the earth? that already there is no nation so rude and fierce that it has not, changed by His love, subdued its fierceness, and with tranquillity hitherto unknown, become mild in disposition: that men endowed with so great abilities, orators, critics, rhetoricians, lawyers, and physicians, those, too, who pry into the mysteries of philosophy, seek to learn these things, despising those in which but now they trusted?

AGAINST THE HEATHEN, Bk. 2, Ch. 5

ML 5, 816

ANF VI, 435

ST. AUGUSTINE

'Give heed unto me,' the Church says unto you; give heed unto me, whom you see, although to see you are, unwilling. For the faithful, who were in those times in the land of Judaea, were present at, and learned as present, Christ's wonderful birth of a virgin, and His passion, resurrection, ascension; all His divine words and deeds. These things you have not seen, and therefore you refuse to believe. Therefore behold these things, fix your eyes on these things, these things which you see reflect on, which are not told you as things past, nor foretold you as things future, but are shown you as things present. What does it seem to you a vain or a light thing, and do you think it is none, or a little, divine miracle, that in the name of One Crucified the whole human race runs?

85
(1614)

CONCERNING FAITH OF THINGS NOT SEEN, Ch. 7

ML 40, 176

NPNF III, 340

It is incredible that Jesus Christ should have risen in the flesh and ascended with flesh into heaven; it is incredible that the world should have believed so incredible a thing; it is incredible that a very few men, of mean birth and the lowest rank, and no education, should have been able so effectually to persuade the world, and even its learned men, of so incredible a thing. . . . But if they do not believe that these miracles were wrought by Christ's apostles to gain credence to their preaching of His resurrection and ascension, this one grand miracle suffices for us, that the whole world has believed without any miracles.

86
(1783)

THE CITY OF GOD, Bk. 22, Ch. 5

ML 41, 756

NPNF II, 482

15. *Christian virtues versus pagan vices.*

LETTER TO DIOGNETUS

87
(97)

Christians are not different from the rest of men in nationality, speech, or customs; . . . They live each in his native land—but as though they were not really at home there. They share in all duties like citizens and suffer all hardships like strangers. Every foreign land is for them a fatherland and every fatherland a foreign land. They marry like the rest of men and beget children, but they do not abandon the babies that are born. They share a common board, but not a common bed. In the flesh as they are, they do not live according to the flesh. They dwell on earth, but they are citizens of heaven. They obey the laws that men make, but their lives are better than the laws. They love all men, but are persecuted by all. They are unknown, and yet they are condemned. They are put to death, yet are more alive than ever. They are paupers, but they make many rich. They lack all things, and yet in all things they abound. They are dishonored, yet glory in their dishonor. They are maligned, and yet are vindicated. They are reviled, and yet they bless. They suffer insult, yet they pay respect. They do good, yet are punished with the wicked. When they are punished, they rejoice, as though they were getting more of life. In a word, what the soul is to the body, Christians are to the world.

Ch. 5:1
MG 2, 1173
FC I, 358–360

ARISTIDES

88
(112.)

[Christians] have the commandments of the Lord Jesus Christ himself engraven on their hearts, and these they observe, looking for the resurrection of the dead and the life of the world to come. They commit neither adultery nor fornication; nor do they bear false witness, nor covet other men's goods: they honor father and mother, and love their neighbors: they give right judgment. They do not unto others that which they would not have done unto themselves. They comfort such as wrong them, and make friends of them: they labor to do good to their enemies. . . . They despise not the widow, and grieve not the orphan. He that has distributes liberally to him that does not have. If they see a stranger, they bring him under their roof, and rejoice over him, as it were their own brother: for they call themselves brethren, not after the flesh, but after the spirit.

APOLOGY, Ch. 15
MG 96, 1121
S, p. 56

MINUCIUS FELIX

We, on the other hand, prove our modesty not by external appearance but by character; with a good heart we cling to the bond of one marriage; in our desire for offspring we have only one wife or none at all. The banquets we conduct are distinguished not only by their modesty, but also by their soberness. We do not indulge in sumptuous meals or produce good fellowship by drawn out wine bibbing, but hold in check our cheerful spirits by the sobriety of our manners. Chaste in conversation and even more chaste in body, very many enjoy the perpetual virginity of a body undefiled rather than boast of it. In short, the desire of incest is so far from our thoughts that some blush even at the idea of a chaste union.

LETTER TO OCTAVIUS, Ch. 31
ML 3, 337
FC X, 388

89
(271)

Nor is there set any limit or end to these torments. The fire there below, endowed with ingenuity, consumes and renews, wears away and sustains the limbs. As the fiery flashes of lightning strike the bodies without consuming them, as the fires of Etna, and Vesuvius, and volcanoes all the world over burn without being exhausted, so that avenging fire is not fed by destroying those who are exposed to the flames, but is sustained by the never ending mangling of their bodies. That those who do not know God are tortured for their impiety and injustice according to their deserts, none but an atheist can doubt, since the crime of ignoring the Father and Lord of all is not less than that of offending Him. And, although ignorance of God is sufficient reason for punishment, just as knowledge of Him helps to obtain His pardon, still, if we Christians are compared with you, although some fail to come up to the standard of our teaching, we shall be found far better than you. For, you prohibit adultery, yet practice it, while we are found to be husbands for our wives alone. You punish crimes committed, while with us the mere thought of crime is sin. You are afraid of witnesses, while we even dread our mere conscience which

90
(273)

always accompanies us. Finally, while the jails are crammed with people of your kind, they do not hold a single Christian, unless he be accused on account of his religion, or unless he be an apostate.

LETTER TO OCTAVIUS, Ch. 35
ML 3, 348
FC X, 394–395

TERTULLIAN
See No. 77.

91
(280)

Our tongues, our eyes, our ears have nothing to do with the madness of the circus, the shamelessness of the theater, the brutality of the arena, the vanity of the gymnasium.

APOLOGY, Ch. 38
ML 1, 466
FC X, 97

92
(281)

The practice of such a special love brands us in the eyes of some. 'See,' they say, 'how they love one another'; (for *they* hate one another), 'and how ready they are to die for each other.' (They themselves would be more ready to kill each other.)

APOLOGY, Ch. 39
ML 1, 471
FC X, 99

93
(283)

It is with men from your own midst that the jail is always bulging, with your own that the mines are always humming, with your own that the wild beasts are always fattened, with your own that the producers of gladiatorial shows feed the herds of criminals. No one there is a Christian—unless he is *merely* that; if he is something else, too, then he is not longer a Christian.

APOLOGY, Ch. 44
ML 1, 497
FC X, 109

94
(285)

Crucify us—torture us—condemn us—destroy us! Your iniquity is the proof of our innocence. For this reason God permits us to suffer these things. In fact, by recently condemning a Christian maid to the pander rather than to the panther (ad lenonem quam ad leonem), you confessed that among us a stain on our virtue is considered worse than any punishment or any form of death. Yet, your tortures accomplish nothing, though each is more refined than the last; rather, they are an enticement to our religion. We become more numerous every time we are hewn down by you: the blood of Christians is seed.

APOLOGY, Ch. 50
ML 1, 534
FC X, 125

ORIGEN

Whereas the churches of God which are instructed by Christ, when carefully contrasted with the assemblies of the districts in which they are situated, are as beacons in the world; for who would not admit that even the inferior members of the church, and those in comparison with the better are less worthy, are nevertheless more excellent than many of those who belong to the assemblies in the different districts?

95
(525)

AGAINST CELSUS, Bk. 3, Ch. 29
MG 11, 957
ANF IV, 476

LACTANTIUS

Nor is it difficult to show why the worshippers of the gods cannot be good and just. For how shall they abstain from the shedding of blood who worship bloodthirsty deities, Mars and Bellona? or how shall they spare their parents who worship Jupiter, who drove out his father? or how shall they spare their own infants who worship Saturnus? how shall they uphold chastity who worship a goddess who is naked, and an adulteress, and who prostitutes herself as it were among the gods? how shall they withhold themselves from plunder and frauds who are acquainted with the thefts of Mercurius, who teaches that to deceive is not the part of fraud, but of cleverness? how shall they restrain their lusts who worship Jupiter, Hercules, Liber, Apollo, and the others, whose adulteries and debaucheries with men and women are not only known to the learned, but are even set forth in the theatres, and made the subject of songs, so that they are notorious to all? Among these things is it possible for men to be just, who, although they were naturally good, would be trained to injustice by the very gods themselves? For, that you may propitiate the god whom you worship, there is need of those things with which you know that he is pleased and delighted. Thus it comes to pass that the god fashions the life of his

96
(639)

worshippers according to the character of his own will, since the most religious worship is to imitate.

THE DIVINE INSTITUTES, Bk. 5, Ch. 10
ML 6, 583
ANF VII, 146

16. Martyrdom is a testimony of the truth of the Christian religion.

ST. CLEMENT OF ROME

97
(11)
But, to leave the ancient examples, let us come to the heroes nearest ourselves; let us consider the noble examples of our own generation. Through jealousy and envy the greatest and holiest pillars [of the Church] were persecuted, and they endured to the death. Let us put before our eyes the good apostles: Peter, because of unrighteous jealousy, underwent not one or two but many sufferings, and having thus borne testimony went to his well-deserved place of glory. Because of jealousy and dissension Paul pointed out the way to the reward of endurance: Seven times he was put in chains; he was banished, stoned; he became a herald in the East and in the West and received the noble renown of his faith. He taught righteousness to the whole world, and after reaching the confines of the West, and having given testimony before rulers, passed from the world and was taken up to the Holy place, having become the outstanding model of endurance.

Besides these men who lived such holy lives, there was a great multitude of the elect who suffered many outrages because of jealousy and became a shining example among us. It was because of jealousy that women were paraded as Danaids and Dircae and put to death after they had suffered horrible and cruel indignities. They kept up the race of faith to the finish and, despite their physical weakness, won the prize they deserved.

LETTER TO THE CORINTHIANS, Chs. 5 and 6
MG 1, 217
FC I, 13

ST. JUSTIN MARTYR
See No. 76.

ST. IRENAEUS

Wherefore the Church does in every place, because of that love which she cherishes towards God, send forward, throughout all time, a multitude of martyrs to the Father; while all others not only have nothing of this kind to point to among themselves, but even maintain that such witness-bearing is not at all necessary.

98
(243)

> AGAINST HERESIES, Bk. 4, Ch. 33
> *MG* 7, 1078
> *ANF* I, 508

TERTULLIAN

See Nos. 78 and 94.

ORIGEN

See No. 83.

LACTANTIUS

For when the people see that men are lacerated by various kinds of tortures, and that they retain their patience unsubdued while the executioners are wearied, they think, as is really the case, that neither the agreement of so many nor the constancy of the dying is without meaning, and that patience itself could not surmount such great tortures without [the aid of] God. Robbers and men of robust frame are unable to endure lacerations of this kind: they utter exclamations, and send forth groans; for they are overcome by pain, because they are destitute of patience infused into them. But in our case (not to speak of men), boys and delicate women in silence overpower their torturers, and even the fire is unable to extort from them a groan. Let the Romans go and boast in their Mutius or Regulus, . . . Behold, the weak sex and fragile age endure to be lacerated in the whole body, and to be burned: not of necessity, for it is permitted them to escape if they wished to do so; but of their own will, because they put their trust in God.

99
(640)

> THE DIVINE INSTITUTES, Bk. 5, Ch. 13
> *ML* 6, 592
> *ANF* VII, 149

ST. AUGUSTINE

'Attend to My judgment; even to My cause, My God, and My Lord' (Ps. 34:23). Not to My punishment, but to My cause. . . . For punish-

100
(1465)

ment is equal to good and bad. Therefore the cause, not the punishment, makes Martyrs, for if punishment made Martyrs, all the mines would be full of martyrs, every chain would drag martyrs, all that are executed with the sword would be crowned.

EXPOSITIONS ON THE PSALMS (Ps. 34)
ML 36, 340
NPNF VIII, 85

17. *The internal nature of Christian doctrine proves its divinity.*

ST. IRENAEUS

101
(192)

The Church, having received this preaching and this faith, although scattered throughout the whole world, yet as if occupying but one house, carefully preserves it. She also believes these points [of doctrine] just as if she had but one soul, and one and the same heart, and she proclaims them, and teaches them, and hands them down, with perfect harmony, as if she possessed only one mouth. For, although the languages of the world are dissimilar, yet the import of the tradition is one and the same. For the Churches which have been planted in Germany do not believe or hand down anything different, nor do those in Spain, nor those in Gaul, nor those in the East, nor those in Egypt, nor those in Libya, nor those which have been established in the central regions of the world. But as the sun, that creature of God, is one and the same throughout the whole world, so also the preaching of the truth shines everywhere, and enlightens all men that are willing to come to a knowledge of the truth. Nor will any one of the rulers in the Churches, however highly gifted he may be in point of eloquence, teach doctrines different from these (for no one is greater than the Master); nor, on the other hand will he who is deficient in power of expression inflict injury on the tradition. For the faith being ever one and the same, neither does one who is able at great length to discourse regarding it, make any addition to it, nor does one, who can say but little, diminish it.

AGAINST HERESIES, Bk. 1, Ch. 10
MG 7, 552
ANF I, 331

ST. CLEMENT OF ALEXANDRIA
See No. 54.

ORIGEN

If any one were to come from the study of Greek opinions and usages
to the gospel, he would not only decide that its doctrines were true, but
would by practice establish their truth, and supply whatever seemed
wanting, from a Grecian point of view, to their demonstration, and thus
confirm the truth of Christianity.

102
(510)

AGAINST CELSUS, Bk. 1, Ch. 2
MG 11, 656
ANF IV, 397

II.

The Church

Jesus Christ preached a kingdom which was indeed eschatological and spiritual, but which existed already on earth and was visible as well as invisible, external as well as internal. This hierarchical society He called the Church, and He entrusted her to the apostles with the power of ruling, teaching, and sanctifying. As early as the end of the first century, the writings of St. Clement of Rome already indicate that the Church is conscious of herself and the apostolic succession of her bishops from the apostles. That the Church is hierarchically constituted is likewise clearly shown by the *Didache* which may be as late as the third century, but could be contemporary with the Pauline epistles. What is certain is that St. Ignatius of Antioch, at the beginning of the second century exhorts his readers to obedience to the bishops, priests, and deacons. This idea is echoed in St. Polycarp's *Letter to the Philippians* about the middle of the second century.

Shortly before this time the Shepherd of Hermas declared that in a sense the Church could be said to have existed from the beginning of the world, and the *Letter to Diognetus* implies that Christians are spread throughout the entire world. St. Irenaeus, at the end of the second century, declares that the Church is to continue Christ's own life on earth, and also testifies to the universality of the Church. Moreover, he declares that the Church is necessary for all men to obtain their salvation. This ties in with his notion that apostolicity belongs only to the true church of Christ, and he makes clear his belief that Peter founded his chair at Rome and instituted a Roman bishop as his successor in the primacy. This would indicate that the supreme power of the Roman pontiff as the successor of Peter was recognized in the entire Church.

The vigorous and salty style of Tertullian sharpens the polemic. Heretics and schismatics are not members of the Church at all; unity of faith and government belongs only to the true Church of Christ which alone can make the claim of apostolicity. Peter received from Christ the primacy of jurisdiction, he went to Rome and died there, and the supreme power of the Roman pontiff as the successor of Peter was recognized in the entire Church. Tertullian even deplored the relaxation of Church discipline on both adultery and fornication (near the beginning of the third century), although in *The Prescription of Heretics* there is a defense of the Church's infallibility when teaching *ex cathedra.*

A more subdued tone is taken by St. Clement of Alexandria, who emphasizes the ancient character of the Church and its unity, which is now vigorously defended by St. Cyprian in the middle of the third century during the persecution of Decius. Although he finds himself at odds with Pope Cornelius with regard to the treatment of the lapsed, he nonetheless has a highly developed ecclesiology, as indicated by his *On the Unity of the Catholic Church.* His letters show that the Church is a monarchical society which is necessary for salvation and alone can boast a unity of faith and government. Catholicity and apostolicity are also hers because she is in union with Peter's successor. He testifies to the preëminence of Rome and its authority in the preaching of the faith.

In the fourth century the Church was involved in the homoousion controversy with the Arians and the Semi-Arians. St. Athanasius is the key figure here, but he does not add anything which has not already been said before about the Church. St. Cyril of Jerusalem writing in the fourth century emphasizes the notion of sanctity as belonging only to the true Church of Christ and St. Gregory Nazianzen declares that she has a body and soul, a visible and invisible element. For this reason, the Church on earth has good and evil mixed together, St. Augustine will add. The notion of the Church as a monarchical society outside of which there is no salvation reappears in St. Jerome, and St. Ambrose (in his struggle with the emperor) will insist on the independence of the Church, a concept with which St. John Chrysostom was much less fortunate in his controversy with the Byzantine empress.

All of these ideas receive full treatment at the hands of St. Augustine, especially in his writings against the Donatists. Perhaps he is the first to state that the true Church of Christ can be recognized by certain notes; his contribution is mainly that of synthesis. It is even conceivable that his entire position is stated when he says in the *Epistle of Manichaeus,* "I should not believe the Gospel except as moved by the authority of the Catholic Church."

In the middle of the fifth century St. Leo the Great was asserting the infallibility of the Roman Pontiff when teaching *ex cathedra,* and the idea is echoed a century and a half later by St. Gregory the Great (590–604). By this time the East and West began to embark on separate courses, the East in a Church-state relationship which was to last until the fall of the Byzantine Empire, the West on an independent course which freed her from subservience to the state, and allowed her to mould the new barbarian kingdoms more after her own ideals.

18. *Jesus Christ instituted a society which was to last forever which He called His Church.*

ST. CLEMENT OF ROME

The Apostles received the Gospel for us from the Lord Jesus Christ; Jesus Christ was sent from God. Christ, therefore is from God and the Apostles are from Christ. Both, accordingly, came in proper order by the will of God. Receiving their orders, therefore, and being filled with confidence because of the Resurrection of the Lord Jesus Christ, and confirmed in the word of God, with full assurance of the Holy Spirit, they went forth preaching the Gospel of the Kingdom of God that was about to come. Preaching, accordingly, throughout the country and the cities, they appointed their first-fruits, after testing them by the Spirit, to be bishops and deacons of those who should believe.

103
(20)

LETTER TO THE CORINTHIANS, Ch. 42
MG 1, 292
FC I, XXX

ST. CYPRIAN

104
(555)
The Lord speaks to Peter: 'I say to you,' He says, 'you are Peter, and upon this rock I will build my church, and the gates of hell shall not prevail against it. And I will give you the keys of the kingdom of heaven; and whatever you shall bind on earth shall be bound also in heaven, and whatever you shall loose on earth shall be loosed also in heaven' (Mt. 16:16–18). Upon him, being one, He built His Church, and although after His resurrection He bestows equal power upon all the Apostles, and says: 'As the Father has sent me, I also send you. Receive the Holy Spirit: if you forgive the sins of anyone, they will be forgiven him; if you retain the sins of anyone, they will be retained' (Jn. 20:21ff.), that He might display unity, He established by His authority the origin of the same unity as beginning from one. Surely the rest of the Apostles also were that which Peter was, endowed with an equal partnership of office and of power, but the beginning proceeds from unity, that the Church of Christ may be shown to be one.

ON THE UNITY OF THE CATHOLIC CHURCH, Ch. 4

ML 4, 498

FC XXXVI, 98

105
(571)
Our Lord, whose precepts and admonitions we ought to observe, describing the honor of a bishop and the order of His Church, speaks in the Gospel, and says to Peter: 'I say unto you, that you are Peter, and upon this rock will I build my Church; and the gates of hell shall not prevail against it. And I will give unto you the keys of the kingdom of heaven: and whatsoever you shall bind on earth shall be bound in heaven; and whatsoever you shall loose on earth shall be loosed in heaven' (Mt. 16:16–18). Thence, through the changes of times and successions, the ordering of bishops and the plan of the Church flow onwards; so that the Church is founded upon the bishops, and every act of the Church is controlled by these same rulers. Since this, then, is founded on the divine law, I marvel that some, with daring temerity, have chosen to write to me as if they wrote in the name of the Church; when the Church is established in the bishop and the clergy, and all who stand fast in the faith.

LETTER No. 33

ML 4, 298

ANF V, 305

ST. AUGUSTINE

106
(1535)
This same is the holy Church, the one Church, the true Church, the catholic Church, fighting against all heresies: fight, it can; be fought

down, it cannot. As for heresies, they all went out of it, like unprofitable branches pruned from the vine: but itself abides in its root, in its Vine, in its charity.

ON THE CREED: A SERMON TO THE CATECHUMENS, 1:6
ML 40, 635
NPNF III, 374

19. The Church was to continue Christ's own life on earth.

ST. IGNATIUS OF ANTIOCH

I give glory to Jesus Christ, the God who has imbued you with such wisdom. I am well aware that you have been made perfect in unwavering faith, like men nailed, in body and spirit, to the Cross of our Lord, Jesus Christ, and confirmed in love by the blood of Christ. In regard to our Lord, you are thoroughly convinced that He was of the race of David according to the flesh, and the Son of God by His will and power; that He was truly born of the Virgin and baptized by John in order that all due observance might be fulfilled by Him (Mt. 3:15); that in His body He was truly nailed to the Cross for our sake under Pontius Pilate and Herod, the tetrarch—of His most blessed Passion we are the fruit—so that, through His resurrection, He might raise, for all ages, in the one body of His Church a standard for the saints and the faithful, whether among Jews or Gentiles.

107
(62)

LETTER TO THE SMYRNAEANS, Ch. 1
MG 5, 708
FC I, 118

ST. IRENAEUS

And thus one God the Father is declared, who is above all, and through all, and in all. The Father is indeed above all, and He is the Head of Christ; but the Word is through all things, and is Himself the Head of the Church; while the Spirit is in us all, and He is the living water, which the Lord grants to those who rightly believe in Him, and love Him, and who know that 'there is one Father, who is above all, and through all, and in us all' (Eph. 4:6).

108
(256)

AGAINST HERESIES, Bk. 5, Ch. 18
MG 7, 1173
ANF I, 546

20. The Church is hierarchically constituted.

THE DIDACHE

109
(9)

Elect therefore for yourselves bishops and deacons worthy of the Lord, humble men and not covetous, and faithful and well tested; for they also serve you in the ministry of the prophets and teachers. Do not, therefore, despise them, for they are the honored men among you along with the prophets and teachers.

Ch. 15
F 1, 32
FC I, 183

ST. CLEMENT OF ROME

110
(19)

Since all these things are clear to us, and we have looked into the depths of divine knowledge, we ought in proper order to do all things which the Lord has commanded us to perform at appointed times. He has commanded the offerings and ministrations to be carried out, and not carelessly or disorderly, but at fixed times and seasons. . . . For the high priest has been allotted his proper ministrations, and to the priests their proper place has been assigned, and on the Levites their own duties are laid. The lay man is bound by the lay ordinances.

LETTER TO THE CORINTHIANS, Ch. 40
MG 1, 288

See No. 103.

FC I, 41

111
(21)

Our Apostles also knew, through our Lord Jesus Christ, that there would be contention over the bishop's office. So, for this cause, having received complete foreknowledge, they appointed the above-mentioned men, and afterwards gave them a permanent character, so that, as they died, other approved men should succeed to their ministry. Those, therefore, who were appointed by the Apostles or afterwards by other eminent men, with the consent of the whole Church, and who ministered blamelessly to the flock of Christ in humility, peaceably and nobly, being commended for many years by all—these men we consider are not justly deposed from their ministry.

LETTER TO THE CORINTHIANS, Ch. 44
MG 1, 296
FC I, 43

It is disgraceful, beloved, very disgraceful, and unworthy of your training in Christ, to hear that the stable and ancient Church of the Corinthians, on account of one or two persons, should revolt against its presbyters. And this report has come not only to us, but also to those who dissent from us. The result is that blasphemies are brought upon the name of the Lord through your folly, and danger accrues for yourselves.

112
(25)

LETTER TO THE CORINTHIANS, Ch. 47
MG 1, 308
FC I, 46

ST. IGNATIUS OF ANTIOCH

I exhort you to be careful to do all things in the harmony of God, the bishop having the primacy after the model of God and the priests after the model of the council of the Apostles, and the deacons (who are so dear to me) having entrusted to them the ministry of Jesus Christ— who from eternity was with the Father and at last appeared to us.

113
(44)

LETTER TO THE MAGNESIANS, Ch. 6
MG 5, 668
FC I, 97

In the same way all should respect the deacons as they would Jesus Christ, just as they respect the bishop as representing the Father and the priests as the council of God and the college of the Apostles. Apart from these there is nothing that can be called a Church.

114
(49)

LETTER TO THE TRALLIANS, Ch. 2
MG 5, 677
FC I, 102

Anyone who is within the sanctuary is pure and anyone who is outside is impure, that is to say, no one who acts apart from the bishop and the priests and the deacons has a clear conscience.

115
(50)

LETTER TO THE TRALLIANS, Ch. 7
MG 5, 680
FC I, 104

For, all who belong to God and Jesus Christ are with the bishop. And those, too, will belong to God who have returned, repentant, to the unity of the Church so as to live in accordance with Jesus Christ. Make no mistake, brethren. No one who follows another into schism inherits

116
(56)

the kingdom of God (1 Cor. 6:9). No one who follows heretical doctrine is on the side of the passion.

LETTER TO THE PHILADELPHIANS, Ch. 3

MG 5, 700

FC I, 114

117
(65)

[Shun schisms, as the source of troubles.] Let all follow the bishop as Jesus Christ did the Father, and the priests, as you would the Apostles. Reverence the deacons as you would the command of God. Apart from the bishop, let no one perform any of the functions that pertain to the Church. Let that Eucharist be held valid which is offered by the bishop or by one to whom the bishop has committed this charge. Wherever the bishop appears, there let the people be; as wherever Jesus Christ is, there is the Catholic Church. It is not lawful to baptize or give communion without the consent of the bishop. On the other hand, whatever has his approval is pleasing to God. Thus, whatever is done will be safe and valid.

LETTER TO THE SMYRNAENS, Ch. 8

MG 5, 713

FC I, 121

ST. HEGESIPPUS

118
(188)

Now Hegesippus, in the five Memoirs which have come down to us, has left behind a very complete record of his personal views. And in his Memoirs he tells us that on a journey as far as Rome he associated with very many bishops, and that he had received the same teaching from all. In fact, we may listen to what he says, when, after some remarks on the epistle of Clement to the Corinthians, he adds as follows:

And the church of the Corinthians continued in the true doctrine until Primus was bishop at Corinth. . . . With them I associated on my voyage to Rome, and I abode with the Corinthians many days; during which we were refreshed together in the true doctrine. But when I came to Rome, I made for myself a succession-list as far as Anicetus; whose deacon was Eleutherus. And from Anicetus Soter received the succession and in every city that which the Law and the Prophets and the Lord preach is faithfully followed.

Eusebius of Caesarea, ECCLESIASTICAL HISTORY, Bk. 4, Ch. 22

MG 20, 377

FC XIX, 253–254

ST. CLEMENT OF ALEXANDRIA

Innumerable counsels relating to particular individuals have been
written in these holy books, some to priests, some to bishops and
deacons, others to widows (about whom there would be occasion to
speak in another place).

119
(413)

> CHRIST THE EDUCATOR, Bk. 3, Ch. 12
> *MG* 8, 676
> *FC* XXIII, 273

Since, according to my opinion, the grades here in the Church, of
bishops, presbyters, deacons, are imitations of the angelic glory, and of
that economy which, the Scriptures say, awaits those who, following the
footsteps of the apostles, have lived in perfection of righteousness
according to the Gospel.

120
(427)

> STROMATA, Bk. 6, Ch. 13
> *MG* 9, 328
> *ANF* II, 505

For when, on the tyrant's death, [John] returned to Ephesus from
the isle of Patmos, he went away, being invited, to the contiguous
territories of the nations, here to appoint bishops, there to set in order
whole Churches, there to ordain such as were marked out by the
Spirit.

121
(438)

> WHO IS THE RICH MAN THAT SHALL BE SAVED?, Ch. 42
> *MG* 9, 648
> *ANF* II, 603

ST. CORNELIUS I

Nor are we unaware that there is one God, and one Lord Christ whom
we confess, one Holy Spirit, and that there ought to be one bishop in
the Catholic [Church? city of Rome?]

122
(546)

> LETTER TO ST. CYPRIAN, #49
> *ML* 3, 222
> *ANF* V, 323

ST. CYPRIAN
See No. 105.

ST. JOHN CHRYSOSTOM

123
(1205)

'To the fellow-Bishops and Deacons' (Phil. 7:1). What is this? were there several Bishops of one city? Certainly not; but he called the Presbyters so. For then they still interchanged the titles, and the Bishop was called a Deacon. For this cause in writing to Timothy, he said, 'Fulfill your ministry' (2 Tim. 4:5), when he was a Bishop. For that he was a Bishop appears by his saying to him, 'Lay hands hastily on no man' (1 Tim. 5:22). And again, 'Which was given you with the laying on of the hands of the Presbytery' (1 Tim. 4:14). Yet Presbyters would not have laid hands on a Bishop.

HOMILIES ON PHILIPPIANS, 1:1
MG 62, 183
NPNF XIII, 184

ST. JEROME

124
(1357)

I am told that some one has been mad enough to put deacons before presbyters, that is, before bishops. For when the apostle clearly teaches that presbyters are the same as bishops, must not a mere server of tables and of widows be insane to set himself up arrogantly over men through whose prayers the body and blood of Christ are produced? Do you ask for proof of what I say? . . . In the Acts of the Apostles Paul thus speaks to the priests of a single church: 'Take heed unto yourselves and to all the flock, in the which the Holy Ghost has made you bishops, to feed the church of God which He purchased with His own blood' (Acts 20:28). And lest any should in a spirit of contention argue that there must then have been more bishops than one in a single church, there is the following passage which clearly proves a bishop and a presbyter to be the same. Writing to Titus the apostle says: 'For this cause left I you in Crete, that you should set in order the things that are wanting, and ordain presbyters in every city, as I had appointed you; if any be blameless, the husband of one wife, having faithful children not accused of riot or unruly. For a bishop must be blameless as the steward of God' (Tit. 1:5–7). . . . When subsequently one presbyter was chosen to preside over the rest, this was done to remedy schism and to prevent each individual from rending the Church of Christ by drawing it to himself. For even at Alexandria from the time of Mark the Evangelist until the episcopates of Heraclas and Dionysius the presbyters always named as bishop one of their own number chosen by themselves and set in a more exalted position, just as an army elects a general, or as deacons appoint one of themselves

80

whom they know to be diligent and call him archdeacon. For what function, excepting ordination, belongs to a bishop that does not also belong to a presbyter?

LETTERS, No. 146
ML 22, 1192
NPNF VI, 288

21. *Heretics and schismatics are not members of the Church.*

TERTULLIAN

If these things be so, so that the truth be adjudged to belong to us as many as walk according to this rule, which the Churches have handed down from the Apostles, the Apostles from Christ, Christ from God, the reasonableness of our proposition is manifest, which determines that heretics are not to be allowed to enter upon an appeal to the Scriptures, whom we prove, without the Scriptures, to have no concern with the Scriptures. For if they be heretics, they cannot be Christians, in that they have not from Christ that, which following according to their own choosing, they admit the name of heretics. Therefore, not being Christians, they can have no right to Christian writings. To such it may be justly said, who are you? when and from where do you come? not being mine, what do you in that which is mine? In brief, by what right do you, Marcion, cut down my wood? By what license do you, Valentine, turn the course of my waters? by what power do you, Apelles, remove my landmarks? This is my possession. Why do the rest of you sow and feed here at your own pleasure? It is my possession; I have held it of old; I held it first: I have a sure title down from the first owners themselves, whose the estate was. I am the heir of the Apostles. As they provided by their own testament, as they committed it in trust, as they have adjured, so I hold it. You, assuredly, they have ever disinherited and renounced, as aliens, as enemies.

125
(298)

THE PRESCRIPTION OF HERETICS, Ch. 37
ML 2, 50
ANF III, 261

There is to us one, and but one baptism; as well, according to the Lord's Gospel as according to the apostle's letters, inasmuch as [he says] 'One God, and one baptism, and one church in the heavens.' But it must be admitted that the question, 'What rules are to be observed with regard to heretics?' is worthy of being treated. For it is to us that

126
(308)

that assertion refers. Heretics, however, have no fellowship in our discipline, whom the mere fact of their excommunication testifies to be outsiders. I am not bound to recognise in them a thing which is enjoined on me, because they and we have not the same God, nor one—that is, the same—Christ: and therefore their baptism is not one [with ours] either, because it is not the same; [a baptism] which, since they have it not duly, doubtless they not [at all]; nor is that capable of being counted which is not had: thus they cannot receive it either, because they have it not. But this point has already received a fuller discussion from us in Greek. We enter, then, the font once: once are sins washed away, because they ought never to be repeated.

ON BAPTISM, Ch. 15
ML 1, 1216
ANF III, 676

ST. AUGUSTINE

127
(1478)

Let us love our Lord God, let us love His Church: Him as a Father, Her as a Mother: Him as a Lord, Her as His Handmaid, as we are ourselves the Handmaid's sons. But this marriage is held together by a bond of great love: no man offends the one, and wins favor of the other. Let no man say, 'I go indeed to the idols, I consult possessed ones and fortunetellers: yet I abandon not God's Church; I am a Catholic.' While you hold to your Mother, you have offended your Father. Another says, Far be it from me; I consult no sorcerer, I seek out no possessed one, I never ask advice by sacrilegious divination, I go not to worship idols, I bow not before stones; though I am in the party of Donatus. What does it profit you not to have offended your Father, if he avenges your offended Mother. . . . Hold then, most beloved, hold all with one mind to God the Father, and the Church our Mother.

EXPOSITIONS ON THE PSALMS, No. 88
ML 37, 1140
NPNF VIII, 440

128
(1562)

We believe also in The Holy Church, [intending thereby] assuredly the Catholic. For both heretics and schismatics style their congregations churches. But heretics, in holding false opinions regarding God, do injury to the faith itself; while schismatics, on the other hand, in wicked separations break off from brotherly charity, although they may believe just what we believe. Wherefore neither do the heretics belong to the

Church catholic, which loves God; nor do the schismatics form a part of the same, inasmuch as it loves the neighbor.

ON FAITH AND THE CREED, Ch. 10
ML 40, 193
NPNF IV, 331

22. *The Church is necessary for all men to attain their salvation.*

ST. IGNATIUS OF ANTIOCH
See No. 116.

ST. IRENAEUS

But [it has on the other hand been shown] that the preaching of the Church is everywhere consistent, and continues in an even course, and receives testimony from the prophets, the apostles, and all the disciples. . . . and that well-grounded system which tends to man's salvation, namely, our faith; which, having been received from the Church, we do preserve, and which always, by the Spirit of God, renewing its youth, as if it were some precious deposit in an excellent vessel, causes the vessel itself, containing it to renew its youth also. . . . 'For in the Church, God has set apostles, prophets, teachers' (1 Cor. 12:28), and all the other means through which the Spirit works; of which all those are not partakers who do not join themselves to the Church, but defraud themselves of life through their perverse opinions and infamous behaviour. For where the Church is, there is the Spirit of God; and where the Spirit of God, there is the Church, and every kind of grace; but the Spirit is truth.

129
(226)

AGAINST HERESIES, Bk. 3, Ch. 24
MG 7, 966
ANF I, 458

ST. CYPRIAN

The spouse of Christ cannot be defiled; she is uncorrupted and chaste. She knows one home, with chaste modesty she guards the sanctity of one couch. She keeps us for God; she assigns the children whom she has created to the kingdom. Whoever is separated from the Church and is joined with an adulteress is separated from the promises of the Church, nor will he who has abandoned the Church arrive at the rewards of Christ. He is a stranger; he is profane; he is an enemy. He

130
(557)

cannot have God as a father who does not have the Church as a mother. If whoever was outside the ark of Noe was able to escape, he too who is outside the Church escapes. The Lord warns, saying: 'He who is not with me is against me, and who does not gather with me, scatters.' He who breaks the peace and concord of Christ acts against Christ; he who gathers somewhere outside the Church scatters the Church of Christ. The Lord says: 'I and the Father are one' (Jn. 10:30). And again of the Father and Son and the Holy Spirit it is written: 'And these three are one' (Jn. 5:7). Does anyone believe that this unity which comes from divine strength, which is closely connected with the divine sacraments, can be broken asunder in the Church and be separated by the divisions of colliding wills? He who does not hold this unity, does not hold the law of God, does not hold the faith of the Father and the Son, does not hold life and salvation.

ON THE UNITY OF THE CATHOLIC CHURCH, Ch. 6
ML 4, 502
FC XXXVI, 100–101

LACTANTIUS

131
(637)

Therefore it is the Catholic Church alone which retains true worship. This is the fountain of truth, this is the abode of faith, this is the temple of God; into which if any one shall not enter, or from which if any shall go out, he is estranged from the hope of life and eternal salvation. No one ought to flatter himself with persevering strife. For the contest is respecting life and salvation, which, unless it is carefully and diligently kept in view, will be lost and extinguished. But, however, because all the separate assemblies of heretics call themselves Christians in preference to others, and think that theirs is the Catholic Church, it must be known that the true Catholic Church is that in which there is confession and repentance, which treats in a wholesome manner the sins and wounds to which the weakness of the flesh is liable.

THE DIVINE INSTITUTES, Bk. 4, Ch. 30
ML 6, 542
ANF VII, 133

ST. JEROME

132
(1346)

[To Damasus, a. 374–379] As I follow no leader save Christ, so I communicate with none but your blessedness, that is with the chair of Peter. For this, I know, is the rock on which the Church is built! This is the house where alone the paschal lamb can be rightly eaten. This is the ark of Noah, and he who is not found in it shall perish when the flood prevails.

LETTERS, No. 15
ML 22, 355
NPNF VI, 16

ST. AUGUSTINE

One cannot have [salvation] except in the Catholic Church. Outside of the Catholic Church one can have everything except salvation. One can have honor, one can have the sacraments, one can sing the alleluia, one can answer Amen, one can have the Gospel, one can have faith in the name of the Father and of the Son and of the Holy Spirit and preach, but never can one find salvation except in the Catholic Church.

SERMON TO THE PEOPLE OF THE CHURCH OF CAESAREA, Ch. 6
ML 43, 695

133
(1858)

ST. FULGENTIUS

From that time when the Saviour said to us: 'If any man is not born again from water and the Holy Spirit, he cannot enter into the Kingdom of God' (Jn. 3:5), without the sacrament of baptism—apart from those who without baptism in the Catholic Church shed their blood for Christ—no one can receive the Kingdom of God or eternal life. Either in the Catholic [Church] or any old heresy or schism one can receive the sacrament of baptism in the name of the Father and of the Son and of the Holy Spirit, and he receives the entire sacrament. But he will not have salvation, which is the strength of the sacrament, if he has that sacrament outside the Catholic Church. So therefore he must return to the Church, not to receive the sacrament of baptism again, for no one should repeat it for a baptized person, but in order that he may receive life eternal in a Catholic society, which no one can attain, who with the sacrament of baptism remains a stranger to the Catholic Church.

ON FAITH, TO PETER, Ch. 3
ML 65, 692

134
(2269)

Firmly hold and never doubt that every baptized person outside of the Catholic Church cannot share in eternal life, if before the end of his life he does not return and is incorporated into the Church.

ON FAITH, TO PETER, Ch. 37
ML 65, 703

135
(2274)

85

136
(2275)

Most firmly hold and never doubt that not only all pagans but also all Jews, all heretics and schismatics who finish this life outside of the Catholic Church, will go into eternal fire, prepared for the devil and his angels (Mt. 25:41).

ON FAITH, TO PETER, Ch. 38
ML 65, 704

23. The true Church of Christ can be recognized by certain notes.

ST. AUGUSTINE
See No. 106.

137
(1580)

For in the Catholic Church, not to speak of the purest wisdom, to the knowledge of which a few spiritual men attain in this life, so as to know it, in the scantiest measure, indeed, because they are but men, still without any uncertainty (since the rest of the multitude derive their entire security not from acuteness of intellect, but from simplicity of faith—not to speak of this wisdom, which you do not believe to be in the Catholic Church, there are many other things which most justly keep me in her bosom. The consent of peoples and nations keeps me in the Church; so does her authority, inaugurated by miracles, nourished by hope, enlarged by love, established by age. The succession of priests keeps me, beginning from the very seat of the Apostle Peter, to whom the Lord, after His resurrection, gave it in charge to feed His sheep, down to the present episcopate. And so, lastly, does the name itself of Catholic, which, not without reason, amid so many heresies, the Church has thus retained; so that, though all heretics wish to be called Catholics, yet when a stranger asks where the Catholic Church meets, no heretic will venture to point to his own chapel or house.

AGAINST THE EPISTLE OF MANICHAEUS CALLED FUNDAMENTAL,
Ch. 4
ML 42, 175
NPNF IV, 130

24. Sanctity of principles and members belongs only to the true Church of Christ.

ST. IRENAEUS
See No. 129.

ORIGEN
  See No. 83.

TERTULLIAN
  See No. 95.

ST. CYRIL OF JERUSALEM

[The Church] is called Catholic then because it extends over all the 138
world, from one end of the earth to the other; and because it teaches (838)
universally and completely one and all the doctrines which ought to
come to men's knowledge, concerning things both visible and invisible,
heavenly and earthly; and because it brings into subjection to godliness
the whole race of mankind, governors and governed, learned and
unlearned; and because it universally treats and heals the whole class
of sins, which are committed by soul or body, and possesses in itself
every form of virtue which is named, both in deeds and words, and in
every kind of spiritual gifts.

> CATECHESES, No. 18:23
> *MG* 33, 1044
> *NPNF* VII, 139

25. Unity of faith and government belongs only to the true Church of Christ.

ST. IGNATIUS OF ANTIOCH
  See No. 116.

ST. HEGESIPPUS
  See No. 118.

ST. IRENAEUS
  See No. 101.

Since therefore we have such proofs, it is not necessary to seek the truth 139
among others which it is easy to obtain from the Church; since the (213)
apostles, like a rich man [depositing his money] in a bank, lodged in
her hands most copiously all things pertaining to the truth: so that
every man, whosoever will, can draw from her the water of life. For

she is the entrance to life; all others are thieves and robbers. On this account we are bound to avoid *them,* but to make choice of the things pertaining to the Church with the utmost diligence, and to lay hold of the tradition 'of the truth. For how stands the case? Suppose there arise a dispute relative to some important question among us, should we not have recourse to the most ancient Churches with which the apostles held constant intercourse, and learn from them what is certain and clear in regard to the present question? For how should it be if the apostles themselves had not left us writings? Would it not be necessary [in that case] to follow the course of the tradition which they handed down to those to whom they did commit the Churches?

AGAINST HERESIES, Bk. 3, Ch. 4

MG 7, 855

ANF I, 416

140
(241)

[The spiritual disciple] shall also judge those who give rise to schisms, who are destitute of the love of God, and who look to their own special advantage rather than to the unity of the Church; and who for trifling reasons, or any kind of reason which occurs to them, cut in pieces and divide the great and glorious body of Christ.

AGAINST HERESIES, Bk. 4, Ch. 33

MG 7, 1076

ANF I, 508

141
(257)

Now all these [heretics] are of much later date than the bishops to whom the apostles committed the Churches; . . . [These heretics] are forced into various by-paths. . . . But the path of those belonging to the Church circumscribe the whole world, as possessing the sure tradition from the apostles, and gives unto us to see that the faith of all is one and the same.

AGAINST HERESIES, Bk. 5, Ch. 20

MG 7, 1177

ANF I, 547

TERTULLIAN

142
(292)

The apostles . . . went forth into the world, and preached the same doctrine of the same Faith to the nations, and forthwith founded Churches in every city, from whence the other churches thenceforward borrowed the tradition of the Faith and the seeds of doctrine, and are daily borrowing them, that they may become Churches. And for this cause they are themselves also accounted Apostolical, as being the off-spring of Apostolical Churches. The whole kind must needs be classed under their original. Wherefore these churches, so many and so great, are but that one primitive Church from the Apostles, whence they all spring. Thus all are the primitive, and all Apostolical, while all are one. The communication of peace, the title of brotherhood, and the token of hospitality prove this unity, which rights no other principle directs than the unity of the tradition of the same mystery.

THE PRESCRIPTION OF HERETICS, Ch. 20

ML 2, 32

ANF III, 252

But if there be any heresies, which venture to plant themselves in the midst of the age of the Apostles, that they may therefore be thought to have been handed down from the Apostles, because they existed under the Apostles, we may say, let them then make known the origins of their Churches; let them unfold the roll of their Bishops so coming down in succession from the beginning, that their first Bishop had for his ordainer and predecessor some one of the Apostles, or of Apostolic men, so he were one that continued steadfast with the Apostles. For in this manner do the Apostolic Churches reckon their origin: as the Church of Smyrna recounts that Polycarp was placed there by John; as that of Rome does that Clement was in like manner ordained by Peter. Just so can the rest also show those, whom being appointed by the Apostles to the Episcopate, they have as transmitters of the Apostolic seed. Let the heretics invent something of the same sort; for after blasphemy what is withheld from them? But even though they invent it, they will advance never a step: for their doctrine, when compared with that of the Apostles, will of itself declare, by the difference and contrariety between them, that it had neither any Apostle for its author, nor any Apostolic man: because, as the Apostles would not have taught things differing from each other, so neither would Apostolic men have set forth things contrary to the Apostles, unless those who learned from Apostles preached a different doctrine! To this test then they will be challenged by those Churches, which although they can bring forward as their founder no one of the Apostles or of Apostolic men, as being of much later date, and indeed being founded daily, nevertheless, since they agree in the same faith, are by reason of their consanguinity in doctrine counted not the less Apostolical. So let all

143
(296)

89

heresies, when challenged by our Churches to both these tests, prove themselves apostolical in whatever way they think themselves so to be. But in truth they neither are so nor can they prove themselves to be what they are not, nor are they received into union and communion by Churches in any way apostolical, simply because they are in no way apostolical, by reason of the difference of the sacred mystery which they teach.

THE PRESCRIPTION OF HERETICS, Ch. 32
ML 2, 44
ANF III, 258

ST. CYPRIAN
See No. 104.

144
(556)

This unity we ought to hold firmly and defend, especially we bishops who watch over the Church, that we may prove that also the episcopate itself is one and undivided. Let no one deceive the brotherhood by lying; let no one corrupt the faith by a perfidious prevarication of the truth. The episcopate is one, the parts of which are held together by the individual bishops. The Church is one which with increasing fecundity extends far and wide into the multitude, just as the rays of the sun are many but the light is one, and the branches of the tree are many but the strength is one founded in its tenacious root, and, when many streams flow from one source, although a multiplicity of waters seems to have been diffused from the abundance of the overflowing supply nevertheless unity is preserved in their origin. Take away a ray of light from the body of the sun, its unity does not take on any division of its light; break a branch from a tree, the branch thus broken will not be able to bud; cut off a stream from its source, the stream thus cut off dries up. Thus too the Church bathed in the light of the Lord projects its rays over the whole world, yet there is one light which is diffused everywhere, and the unity of the body is not separated. She extends her branches over the whole earth in fruitful abundance; she extends her richly flowing streams far and wide; yet her head is one, and her source is one, and she is the one mother copious in the results of her fruitfulness. By her womb we are born; by her milk we are nourished; by her spirit we are animated.

ON THE UNITY OF THE CATHOLIC CHURCH, Ch. 5
ML 4, 501
FC XXXVI, 99–100

[To Florentius, a. 254] Peter speaks there, on whom the Church was to be built, teaching and showing in the name of the Church, that although a rebellious and arrogant multitude of those who will not hear and obey may depart, yet the Church does not depart from Christ; and they are the Church who are a people united to the priest, and the flock which adheres to its pastor. Whence you ought to know that the bishop is in the Church, and the Church in the bishop; and if any one be not with the bishop, that he is not in the Church, and that those flatter themselves in vain who creep in, not having peace with God's priests, and think that they communicate secretly with some; while the Church which is Catholic and one, is not cut nor divided, but is indeed connected and bound together by the cement of priests who cohere with one another.

145
(587)

LETTERS, No. 66
ML 4, 406
ANF V, 374

ST. HILARY

Since the Church, instituted by the Lord and strengthened by the Apostles, is the one Church of all men, from which the raging error of the different blasphemous teachings has cut itself off, and it cannot be denied that the separation from the faith has come about as the result of a defective and perverted understanding, while that which was read was adapted to one's views rather than one's views being submissive to what was read, still, while the individual groups contradict one another, she is to be understood not only by her own teachings but also by those of her adversaries, so that, while all are directed against her alone, she refutes the most godless error of all of them by the very fact that she is alone and is one. All the heretics, therefore, rise up against the Church, but, while all the heretics mutually conquer themselves, they gain no victories for themselves. Victory in their case is the triumph of the Church over each of them, while one heresy wages war against that teaching in another heresy which the faith of the Church condemns in the other heresy (for there is nothing which the heretics hold in common), and, meanwhile, they confirm our faith while they contradict one another.

146
(865)

ON THE TRINITY, Bk. 7, Ch. 4
ML 10, 202
FC XXV, 227–228

26. *Catholicity belongs only to the true Church of Christ.*

THE MARTYRDOM OF ST. POLYCARP

147
(79)

When finally he concluded his prayer, after remembering all who had at any time come his way—small folk and great folk, distinguished and undistinguished, and the whole Catholic Church throughout the world —the time for departure came. So they placed him on an ass, and brought him into the city on a great Sabbath.

> Ch. 8
> *MG* 5, 1036
> *FC* I, 154–155

ST. CYPRIAN
See No. 144.

ST. CYRIL OF JERUSALEM
See No. 138.

148
(839)

And if ever you are sojourning in cities, inquire not simply where the Lord's House is (for the other sects of the profane also attempt to call their own dens houses of the Lord), nor merely where the Church is, but where is the Catholic Church. For this is the peculiar name of this Holy Church, the mother of us all.

> CATECHESES, No. 17:14
> *MG* 33, 1048
> *NPNF* VII, 140

ST. AUGUSTINE

149
(1422)

[To Vincent, ca. 408] You imagine you are saying something clever when you derive the name Catholic, not from its universal membership in the world, but from the observance of all divine commands and all the sacraments, as if we rely on the meaning of the word to prove that the Church is world-wide, and not rather on the promise of God, and on so many and such clear pronouncements of truth itself. Yet it does happen that the Church is called Catholic, too, because it embraces all truth, and there are even some fragments of this truth to be found in different heresies.

> LETTERS, No. 93
> *ML* 33, 333
> *FC* XVIII, 79

See Nos. 128 and 137.

27. *Apostolicity belongs only to the true Church of Christ.*

ST. IRENAEUS

Since, however, it would be very tedious in such a volume as this, to
reckon up the successions of all the Churches, we do put to confusion
all those who, in whatever manner, whether by an evil self-pleasing, by
vainglory, or by blindness and perverse opinion, assemble in unauthor-
ized meetings; [we do this, I say] by indicating that tradition derived
from the apostles, of the very great, the very ancient, and universally
known Church founded and organized at Rome by the two most
glorious apostles, Peter and Paul; as also [by pointing out] the faith
preached to men, which comes down to our time by means of the
successions of the bishops. For it is a matter of necessity that every
Church should agree with this Church, on account of its pre-eminent
authority, that is, the faithful everywhere, inasmuch as the apostolical
tradition has been preserved continuously by those [faithful men] who
exist everywhere.

150
(210)

AGAINST HERESIES, Bk. 3, Ch. 3
MG 7, 848
ANF I, 415

See No. 139.

Therefore it is necessary to obey the presbyters who are in the
Church, —those who, as I have shown, possess the succession from the
apostles; those who, together with the succession of the episcopate,
have received the certain gift of truth, according to the good pleasure
of the Father. But [it is also necessary] to hold in suspicion others who
depart from the primitive succession, and assemble themselves together
in any place whatsoever.

151
(237)

AGAINST HERESIES, Bk. 4, Ch. 26
MG 7, 1053
ANF I, 497

TERTULLIAN
See No. 142.

On this principle therefore we shape our rule: that, if the Lord Jesus
Christ sent the Apostles to preach, no others ought to be received as
preachers than those whom Christ appointed: for no man knows the
Father save the Son, and to whomsoever the Son has revealed Him
(Mt. 11:27). Neither does the Son seem to have revealed Him to any

152
(293)

93

other than to the Apostles, whom He sent to preach, that which He revealed unto them. Now what they did preach, that is, what Christ did reveal unto them, I will here also rule, must be proved in no other way than by those same Churches which the Apostles themselves founded; themselves, I say, by preaching to them as well 'viva voce' [as men say], as afterwards by Epistles. If these things be so, it becomes quite apparent that all doctrine, which agrees with these Apostolic Churches, the matrices and origins of the faith, must be accounted true, as without doubt containing that which the Churches have received from the Apostles, the Apostles from Christ, Christ from God: and that all other doctrine must be judged at once to be false, which savors things contrary to the truth of the Churches, and of the Apostles, and of Christ, and of God. It remains therefore that we show whether this our doctrine, the rule of which we have above declared, be derived from the tradition of the Apostles, and, from this very fact, whether the other doctrines come of falsehood. We have communion with the Apostolic Churches, because we have no doctrine differing from them. This is evidence of truth.

THE PRESCRIPTION OF HERETICS, Ch. 21
ML 2, 33
See No. 143.   ANF III, 246

153   Go through the Apostolic Churches, in which the very seats of the
(297)   Apostles, at this very day, preside over their own places; in which their
own authentic writings are read, speaking with the voice of each, and making the face of each present to the eye. Is Achaia near you? You have Corinth. If you are not far from Macedonia, you have Philippi, you have the Thessalonians. If you can travel into Asia, you have Ephesus. But if you are near Italy, you have Rome, where we also have an authority close at hand. What a happy Church that is! on which the Apostles poured out all their doctrine, with their blood: where Peter had a like Passion with the Lord; where Paul has for his crown the same death with John; where the Apostle John was plunged into boiling oil, and suffered nothing, and was afterwards banished to an island.

THE PRESCRIPTION OF HERETICS, Ch. 36
ML 2, 49
See No. 125.   ANF III, 260

154   But I have proposed [as models] those churches which were founded
(329)   by apostles or apostolic men; and antecedently, I think, to certain
[founders, so shall be nameless]. Those churches therefore, as well [as

others], have the selfsame authority of custom [to appeal to]; they range in opposing phalanx 'times' and 'teachers,' more than these [later churches do]. What shall we observe? What shall we choose? We cannot contemptuously reject a custom which we cannot condemn, inasmuch as it is not 'strange,' with whom we share the law of peace and the name of brotherhood. They and we have one faith, one God, the same Christ, the same hope, the same baptismal sacraments; let me say it once for all, we are one church.

ON THE VEILING OF VIRGINS, Ch. 2
ML 2, 890
ANF IV, 28

See No. 38.

ST. AUGUSTINE
See No. 137.

THE PRIMACY OF PETER
AND OF THE ROMAN PONTIFF

28. *Among the apostles Peter received the primacy of jurisdiction in the Church from Christ.*

TERTULLIAN

Peter alone do I find—through [the mention of] his 'mother-in-law' —to have been married. Monogamist I am led to presume him by consideration of the church, which, built upon him, was destined to appoint every grade of her Order from monogamists. The rest, while I do not find them married, I must of necessity understand to have been either eunuchs or continent.

155
(381)

ON MONOGAMY, Ch. 8
ML 2, 939
ANF IV, 65

'But,' you say, '*the church* has the power of forgiving sins.' This I acknowledge and adjudge more [than you; I] who have the Paraclete Himself in the persons of the new prophets, saying, 'The church has

156
(387)

the power to forgive sins; but I will not do it, lest they commit others.' 'What if a pseudo-prophetic spirit has made that declaration?' Nay, but it would have been more the part of a subverter on the one hand to commend himself on the score of clemency, and on the other to influence all others to sin. Or if, again, [the pseudo-prophetic spirit] has been eager to affect this [sentiment] in accordance with 'the Spirit of truth,' it follows that 'the Spirit of truth' has indeed the power of indulgently granting pardon to fornicators, but wills not to do it if it involve evil to the majority.

I now inquire into your opinion, [to see] from what source you usurp this right to 'the church.'

If, because the Lord has said to Peter, 'Upon this rock will I build my church,' 'to you have I given the keys of the heavenly kingdom'; or, 'Whatsoever you shall have bound or loosed in earth, shall be bound or loosed in the heavens' (Mt. 16:16–18), you therefore presume that the power of binding and loosing has derived to you, that is, to every church akin to Peter; what sort of man are you, subverting and wholly changing the manifest intention of the Lord, conferring [as that intention did] this [gift] personally upon Peter? 'On you,' He says, 'will I build my church'; and, 'I will give to you the keys,' not to the church; and, 'Whatsoever you shall have loosed or bound,' not what they shall have loosed or bound.

ON MODESTY, Ch. 21
ML 2, 1024
ANF III, 99

ST. CLEMENT OF ALEXANDRIA

157
(436)

Nor does the kingdom of heaven belong to sleepers and sluggards, 'but the violent take it by force' (Mt. 11:12). Therefore on hearing those words, the blessed Peter, the chosen, the pre-eminent, the first of the disciples, for whom alone and Himself the Saviour paid tribute, quickly seized and comprehended the saying. And what does he say? 'Lo, we have left all and followed Thee' (Mt. 19:27; Mk. 10:28).

WHO IS THE RICH MAN THAT SHALL BE SAVED?, Ch. 21
MG 9, 625
ANF II, 597

ST. CYPRIAN
See Nos. 104 and 105.

ST. CYRIL OF JERUSALEM

The Lord is loving unto man, and swift to pardon, but slow to punish. Let no man therefore despair of his own salvation. Peter, the chiefest and foremost of the Apostles, denied the Lord thrice before a little maid: but he repented himself, and wept bitterly. Now weeping shows the repentance of the heart: and therefore he not only received forgiveness for his denial, but also held his Apostolic dignity unforfeited.

158
(810)

CATECHESES, No. 2:19
MG 33, 408
NPNF VII, 13

29. Peter founded his chair at Rome and instituted a Roman bishop as his successor in the primacy.

ST. IGNATIUS OF ANTIOCH

I am writing to all the Churches to tell them all that I am, with all my heart, to die for God—if only you do not prevent it. I beseech you not to indulge your benevolence at the wrong time. Please let me be thrown to the wild beasts; through them I can reach God. I am God's wheat; I am ground by the teeth of the wild beasts that I may end as the pure bread of Christ. If anything, coax the beasts on to become my sepulcher and to leave nothing of my body undevoured so that, when I am dead, I may be no bother to anyone. I shall be really a disciple of Jesus Christ if and when the world can no longer see so much as my body. Make petition, then, to the Lord for me, so that by these means I may be made a sacrifice to God. I do not command you, as Peter and Paul did. They were Apostles; I am a condemned man. They were free men; I am still a slave. Still, if I suffer, I shall be emancipated by Jesus Christ and, in my resurrection, shall be free. But now in chains I am learning to have no wishes of my own.

159
(54)

LETTER TO THE ROMANS, Ch. 4
MG 5, 689
FC I, 109–110

ST. HEGESIPPUS
See No. 118.

ST. IRENAEUS
See Nos. 25 and 150.

The blessed apostles, then, having founded and built up the Church, committed into the hands of Linus the office of the episcopate. Of this

160
(211)

Linus, Paul makes mention in the Epistles to Timothy. To him succeeded Anacletus; and after him, in the third place from the apostles, Clement was allotted the bishopric. This man, as he had seen the blessed apostles, and had been conversant with them, might be said to have the preaching of the apostles still echoing [in his ears], and their traditions before his eyes. Nor was he alone [in this], for there were many still remaining who had received instructions from the apostles. In the time of this Clement, no small dissension having occurred among the brethren at Corinth, the Church in Rome despatched a most powerful letter to the Corinthians, exhorting them to peace, renewing their faith, and declaring the tradition which it had lately received from the apostles.

> AGAINST HERESIES, Bk. 3, Ch. 3
> *MG* 7, 849
> *ANF* I, 416

TERTULLIAN
See No. 143.

ST. CYPRIAN

161
(575)
[To Antonianus, a. 251–252] Moreover, Cornelius was made bishop by the judgment of God and of His Christ, by the testimony of almost all the clergy, by the suffrage of the people who were then present and by the assembly of ancient priests and good men, when no one had been made so before him, when the place of Fabian, that is, when the place of Peter and the degree of the sacerdotal throne was vacant; which being occupied by the will of God, and established by the consent of all of us, whosoever now wishes to become a bishop, must needs be made from without; and he cannot have the ordination of the Church who does not hold the unity of the Church.

> LETTERS, No. 55:8
> *ML* 3, 770
> *ANF* V, 329

ST. AUGUSTINE

162
(1418)
[To Generosus, ca. 400] For, if the order of succession of bishops is to be considered, how much more surely, truly and safely do we number them from Peter, to whom, as representing the whole Church, the Lord said: 'Upon this rock I will build my church and the gates of hell shall

not prevail against it' (Mt. 16:18). For, to Peter succeeded Linus, to Linus Clement, to Clement Anacletus, to Anacletus Evaristus, to Evaristus Sixtus, to Sixtus Telesphorus, to Telesphorus Hyginus, to Hyginus Anicetus, to Anicetus Pius, to Pius Soter, to Soter Alexander, to Alexander Victor, to Victor Zephyrinus, to Zephyrinus Calistus, to Calistus Urban, to Urban Pontian, to Pontian Antherus, to Antherus Fabian, to Fabian Cornelius, to Cornelius Lucius, to Lucius Stephen, to Stephen Sixtus, to Sixtus Dionysius, to Dionysius Felix, to Felix Eutychian, to Eutychian Gaius, to Gaius Marcellus, to Marcellus Eusebius, to Eusebius Melchiades, to Melchiades Sylvester, to Sylvester Marcus, to Marcus Julius, to Julius Liberius, to Liberius Damasus, to Damasus Siricius, to Siricius Anastasius.

> LETTERS, No. 53
> ML 33, 196
> FC 95–96

30. The Roman pontiffs have always attributed the primacy to themselves.

ST. CLEMENT OF ROME
See Nos. 110, 111, and 112.

You, therefore who laid the foundation of rebellion, submit to the presbyters, and accept chastisement for repentance, bending the knees of your heart.

163
(27)

> LETTER TO THE CORINTHIANS, Ch. 57
> MG 1, 324
> FC I, 52–53

For you will afford us joy and gladness if you obey what we have written through the Holy Spirit and get rid of the wicked passion of jealousy, according to the plea for peace and harmony which we have made in this letter. We have sent trustworthy and prudent men, who have lived among us irreproachably from youth to old age; and they will be witnesses between you and us.

164
(29)

> LETTER TO THE CORINTHIANS, Ch. 63
> F 1, 182
> FC I, 57

ST. LEO THE GREAT

165
(2179)

[To the bishops of Mauretania, a. 446] 'Lay hands hastily on no one, and do not share in other men's sins' (1 Tim. 5:22). What is to lay on hands hastily but to confer the priestly dignity on unproved men before the proper age, before there has been time to test them, before they have deserved it by their obedience, before they have been tried by discipline? And what is to share in other men's sins but for the ordainer to become such as is he who ought not to have been ordained by him?

LETTERS, No. 12
ML 54, 647
NPNF XII, 13

166
(2186)

My respect for the Nicene canons is such that I never have allowed nor ever will the institutions of the holy Fathers to be violated by any innovation. For although the desserts of individual prelates are sometimes different, yet the rights of their Sees are Permanent: and although rivalry may perchance cause some disturbance about them, yet it cannot impair their dignity.

LETTERS, No. 119
ML 54, 1043
NPNF XII, 86

BISHOPS

31. Bishops were the legitimate successors of the apostles.

ST. CLEMENT OF ROME
See Nos. 103 and 111.

ST. IGNATIUS OF ANTIOCH
See Nos. 114, 116, and 117.

167
(48)

For it seems to me that, when you are obedient to the bishop as you would be to Jesus Christ, you are living, not in a human way, but according to Jesus Christ, who died for us that by faith in His death you might escape death. You must continue, then, to do nothing apart from the bishop. Be obedient, too, to the priests as to the apostles of Jesus Christ, our hope—in whom we shall be found, if only we live in Him. And, as ministers of the mysteries of Jesus Christ, the deacons should please all in every way they can; for they are not merely ministers of food and drink, but the servants of the Church of God. They must avoid all reproach as they would beware of fire.

LETTER TO THE TRALLIANS, Ch. 2
MG 5, 676
FC I, 102

ST. HEGESIPPUS
See No. 118.

ST. IRENAEUS

It is within the power of all, therefore, in every Church, who may wish to see the truth, to contemplate clearly the tradition of the apostles manifested throughout the whole world; and we are in a position to reckon up those who were by the apostles instituted bishops in the Churches, and [to demonstrate] the succession of these men to our own times; those who neither taught nor knew of anything like what these [heretics] rave about. For if the apostles had known hidden mysteries, which they were in the habit of imparting to 'the perfect' apart and privately from the rest, they would have delivered them especially to those to whom they were also committing the Churches themselves.

168
(209)

AGAINST HERESIES, Bk. 3, Ch. 3
MG 7, 848
See Nos. 43, 98, 141, and 151.   *ANF* I, 415

TERTULLIAN
See Nos. 38 and 143.

ST. CLEMENT OF ALEXANDRIA
See No. 121.

ST. CORNELIUS I
See No. 122.

FIRMILIAN

But what is the greatness of his error, and what the depth of his blindness, who says that remission of sins can be granted in the synagogues

169
(602)

of heretics, and does not abide on the foundation of the one Church which was once based by Christ upon the rock, may be perceived from this, that the power of remitting sins was given to the apostles, and to the churches which they, sent by Christ, established, and to the bishops who succeeded to them by vicarious ordination (cf. Mt. 16:19).

LETTER TO CYPRIAN
ML 3, 1168
ANF V, 394

INFALLIBILITY

32. The Church is infallible in transmitting Christ's doctrine.

ST. IRENAEUS
See No. 139.

TERTULLIAN

170
(295)

Well then: be it that all have erred; that the Apostle also was deceived in the testimony he gave in favor of some; that the Holy Spirit had regard to no one of them so as to guide it into truth, although for this sent by Christ, asked of the Father, that He might be the Teacher of truth; that He, the Steward of God, the Deputy of Christ, neglected His office, suffering the Churches the while to understand differently, to believe differently, that which He Himself preached by the Apostles— is it probable that so many Churches, and so great should have gone astray into the same Faith?

THE PRESCRIPTION OF HERETICS, Ch. 28
ML 2, 40
ANF III, 256

ST. AUGUSTINE

171
(1581)

But should you meet with a person not yet believing the Gospel, how would you reply to him were he to say, I do not believe? For my part, I should not believe the Gospel except as moved by the authority of the Catholic Church.

AGAINST THE EPISTLE OF MANICHAEUS CALLED FUNDAMENTAL,
Ch. 5
ML 42, 176

33. The Roman pontiff is infallible when teaching ex cathedra.

TERTULLIAN

But if Peter was reproved because, after having lived with the Gentiles, he separated himself from their company out of respect for persons, surely this was a fault in his conversation, not in his preaching.

172
(294)

> THE PRESCRIPTION OF HERETICS, Ch. 23
> ML 2, 36
> ANF III, 254

ST. LEO THE GREAT

[The Lord] has suffered us to sustain no harm in the person of our brethren, but has corroborated by the irrevocable assent of the whole brotherhood what He had already laid down through our ministry: to show that, what had been first formulated by the foremost See of Christendom, and then received by the judgment of the whole Christian world, had truly proceeded from Himself: that in this, too, the members may be at one with the Head.

173
(2187)

> LETTERS, No. 120
> ML 54, 1046
> NPNF XII, 87

34. The bishops assembled in ecumenical council have always been recognized as infallible judges of the faith.

ST. ATHANASIUS

Without prefixing Consulate, month, and day, [the Fathers] wrote concerning Easter, 'It seemed good as follows,' for it did then seem good that there should be a general compliance; but about the faith they wrote not, 'It seemed good,' but, 'Thus believes the Catholic Church'; and thereupon they confessed how they believed, in order to show that their own sentiments were not novel, but Apostolic; and what they wrote down was no discovery of theirs, but is the same as was taught by the Apostles.

174
(785)

> LETTER ON THE COUNCILS OF ARIMINUM AND SELEUCIA
> MG 26, 688
> NPNF IV, 453

ST. AMBROSE

175
(1250)

This decree [denial of the divinity of Christ] was made at the Synod of Ariminum and I rightfully despise that council, for I follow the rule of the Council of Nicaea from which neither death nor the sword can separate me.

LETTER TO THE EMPEROR VALENTINIAN, No. 21
ML 16, 1005
NPNF X, 428

ST. AUGUSTINE

176
(1419)

[To Januarius, ca. 400] In the first place, I want you to hold as the basic truth of this discussion that our Lord Jesus Christ, as He Himself said in the Gospel, has subjected us to His yoke and His burden, which are light. Therefore, He has laid on the society of His new people the obligation of sacraments, very few in number, very easy of observance, most sublime in their meaning, as, for example, baptism hallowed by the name of the Trinity, Communion of His Body and His Blood, and whatever else is commended in the canonical writings, with the exception of those burdens found in the five books of Moses, which imposed on the ancient people a servitude in accord with their character and the prophetic times in which they lived. But, regarding those other observances which we keep and all the world keeps, and which do not derive from Scripture but from tradition, we are given to understand that they have been ordained or recommended to be kept by the Apostles themselves, or by plenary councils, whose authority is well founded in the Church.

LETTERS, No. 54
ML 33, 200
FC 252–253

ST. LEO THE GREAT
See No. 166.

ST. GREGORY THE GREAT
See No. 29.

III.

Sacred Scripture and Tradition

To offset the errors of the Reformers, the Council of Trent maintained that the faith of the universal Church was contained in written books and in the unwritten traditions that the apostles received from Christ Himself or that were handed on through the inspiration of the Holy Spirit, via the apostles down to us. The books of the Old and New Testaments are to be accepted as sacred and canonical in their entirety, with all their parts, not on the ground that they were produced by mere human ingenuity and afterwards approved by her authority, but because they were written as a result of the prompting of the Holy Spirit, and have God for their author.

That there are sacred books, written under the inspiration of the Holy Spirit, having God as their author, is clearly attested by St. Clement of Rome as early as the end of the first century. The same position is at least attributed to St. Justin Martyr a half century later, as well as to St. Theophilus of Antioch late in the second century, along with St. Irenaeus. It receives mention in St. Clement of Alexandria, and in such later writers as St. Ambrose and St. Augustine.

It is Athenagoras and most especially St. Theophilus of Antioch writing in the latter part of the second century who develop the notion of inspiration consisting in God's action moving the mind and the will of the hagiographer to the mode of the instrument. St. Augustine elaborates on this idea in the latter part of the fourth century, and adds that the primary object of this inspiration are things pertaining to salvation. This inspiration truly extends to all parts of Scripture, even in some sense to the words themselves, as St. Gregory Nazianzen, writing in the fourth century, and Theodoret assert. But it is not until the time of St. Augustine that we have a sophisticated disentangling of the roles of the writer himself, the divine assistance in writing, and the revelation to be recorded.

That no error can be found in the sacred books is held by St. Clement of Rome as early as the end of the first century, St. Justin Martyr in the second, and, of course, St. Jerome in the latter part of the fourth. He and St. Augustine even corresponded with each other on this matter. They agreed that every assertion of the sacred writers expressed the sense which they themselves wished to express and did express. In this way apparent errors in the sciences and history could be explained, and St. Cyril of Alexandria supports this view early in the fifth century.

The sole criterion of canonicity is Catholic tradition, which has its foundation in apostolic tradition, says Tertullian, and lists of the canonical Scriptures are furnished us by St. Cyril of Jerusalem (fourth century), St. Athanasius, and St. Gregory Nazianzen, as well as Rufinus and St. Augustine. Even as late as the eighth century, St. John of Damascus feels obliged to furnish one. These lists for the Old Testament vary a bit: the Tridentine canon of the New Testament has a surer footing in tradition, although the Apocalypse of St. John is occasionally missing, and some are hesitant about the authorship of Hebrews.

St. Paul in his second letter to the Thessalonians wrote, "So then, brethren, stand firm and hold to the traditions which you were taught by us, either by word of mouth or by letter" (2 Thess. 2:15). Against the Protestant Reformers the Council of Trent declared that tradition as well as sacred Scripture was a source of the Church's teaching magisterium. St. Irenaeus at the end of the second century is most emphatic and eloquent on this point, and so is Tertullian writing some time later. One finds the idea again in the writings of St. Basil in the fourth century, and St. John Chrysostom specifically comments on the text. We might expect to find it in St. Jerome and St. Augustine, but nowhere is it more beautifully expressed than by St. Vincent of Lérins in his *Commonitory*.

This tradition completes Scripture through an authentic interpretation according to St. Irenaeus, for apostolic tradition has always been regarded as a rule of faith. St. Polycarp himself had affirmed this earlier in his Letter to the Philippians, and apostolic tradition is mentioned several times not only by St. Irenaeus but also by Tertullian and Origen. In the fourth century, St. Eusebius of Caesarea, St. Athanasius, St. Epiphanius, and Theodoret all witness to it.

While there was, however, progress in revelation until the death of the apostles (so Irenaeus), from that time the deposit of revelation can neither grow nor decrease. This is the position of the *Didache* and it is explicitated by Tertullian in *The Prescription of Heretics* when he asks, "What has Athens to do with Jerusalem?" St. Basil and St. John Chrysostom echo his words, but the freshest presentation is again in that of St. Vincent of Lérins, in the *Commonitory*. It is he who argues for progress in the understanding of traditional doctrines, and he at once shows himself both an ancient and a modern, for his writing indicates a marked advance over that, say, of Tertullian and Origen. While admitting that the Fathers, speaking as private doctors, were still able to err, he holds that the consent of the Fathers in matters of faith and morals produces certitude, and in these ideas he is at one with the Bishop of Hippo, St. Augustine.

INSPIRATION

35. There are sacred books, written under the inspiration of the Holy Spirit, that have God as their author.

ST. CLEMENT OF ROME

You have studied the Holy Scriptures, which are true and inspired by the Holy Spirit. You know that nothing contrary to justice or truth has been written in them.

177
(22)

LETTER TO THE CORINTHIANS, Ch. 45
MG 1, 300
FC I, 42

ST. JUSTIN MARTYR (?)

178
(149)
Since therefore it is impossible to learn anything true concerning religion from your teachers, who by their mutual disagreement have furnished you with sufficient proof of their own ignorance, I consider it reasonable to recur to our progenitors, who both in point of time have by a great way the precedence of your teachers, and who have taught us nothing from their own private fancy, nor differed with one another, nor attempted to over-turn one another's positions, but without wrangling and contention received from God the knowledge which also they taught to us. For neither by nature nor by human conception is it possible for men to know things so great and divine, but by the gift which then descended from above upon the holy men, who had no need of rhetorical art, nor of uttering anything in a contentious or quarrelsome manner, but to present themselves pure to the energy of the Divine Spirit, in order that the divine plectrum itself, descending from heaven, and using righteous men as an instrument like a harp or lyre, might reveal to us the knowledge of things divine and heavenly.

HORTATORY ADDRESS TO THE GREEKS, Ch. 8
MG 6, 256
ANF I, 276

ST. THEOPHILUS OF ANTIOCH

179
(185)
Confirmatory utterances are found both with the prophets and in the Gospels, because they all spoke inspired by one Spirit of God.

TO AUTOLYCUS, Ch. 3
MG 6, 1137
ANF II, 114

ST. IRENAEUS

180
(203)
If, however, we cannot discover explanations of all those things in Scripture which are made the subject of investigation, yet let us not on that account seek after any other God besides Him who really exists. For this is the very greatest impiety. We should leave things of that nature to God Who created us, being most properly assured that the Scriptures are indeed perfect, since they were spoken by the Word of God and His Spirit.

AGAINST HERESIES, Bk. 2, Ch. 28
MG 7, 804
ANF I, 399

ST. CLEMENT OF ALEXANDRIA

I could adduce ten thousand Scriptures of which not 'one tittle shall pass away' without being fulfilled; for the mouth of the Lord the Holy Spirit has spoken these things.

181
(404)

> EXHORTATION TO THE HEATHEN, Ch. 9:82
> *MG* 8, 192
> *ANF* II, 195

ST. AMBROSE

How, then, does He not possess all that pertains to God, Who is named by priests in baptism with the Father and the Son, and is invoked in the oblations, is proclaimed by the Seraphim in heaven with the Father and the Son, dwells in the Saints with the Father and the Son, is poured upon the just, is given as the source of inspiration to the prophets? And for this reason in the divine Scripture all is called θεόπνευστος because God inspires what the Spirit has spoken.

182
(1286)

> ON THE HOLY SPIRIT, Bk. 3, Ch. 16
> *ML* 16, 803
> *NPNF* X, 151

36. *Inspiration consists in God's action moving the mind and the will of the hagiographer to the mode of the instrument.*

ST. JUSTIN MARTYR (?)

See No. 178.

ATHENAGORAS

But we have for witnesses of the things we apprehend and believe, prophets, men who have pronounced concerning God and the things of God, guided by the Spirit of God. And you too will admit, excelling all others as you do in intelligence and in piety towards the true God (τὸ ὄντως θεῖον) that it would be irrational for us to cease to believe in the Spirit from God, who moved the mouths of the prophets like musical instruments, and to give heed to mere human opinions.

183
(162)

> A PLEA FOR THE CHRISTIANS, Ch. 7
> *MG* 6, 904
> *ANF* II, 132

[The prophets] lifted in ecstasy above the natural operations of their minds by the impulses of the Divine Spirit, uttered the things with

184
(163)

which they were inspired, the Spirit making use of them as a flute-player breathes into a flute.

A PLEA FOR THE CHRISTIANS, Ch. 9
MG 6, 908
ANF II, 133

ST. THEOPHILUS OF ANTIOCH

185
(179)

And first, [the prophets] taught us with one consent that God made all things out of nothing; for nothing was coeval with God: but He being His own place, and wanting nothing, and existing before all ages, willed to make man by whom He might be known; for him, therefore, He prepared the world. For he that is created is also needy; but He that is uncreated stands in need of nothing. God, then, having His own Word internal within His own bowels, begat Him, emitting Him along with His own wisdom before all things. He had this Word as a helper in the things that were created by Him, and by Him He made all things. He is called 'governing principle' (*arché*) because He rules, and is Lord of all things fashioned by Him. He, then, being Spirit of God, and governing principle, and wisdom, and power of the highest, came down upon the prophets, and through them spoke of the creation of the world and of all other things. For the prophets were not when the world came into existence, but the wisdom of God which was in Him, and His holy Word which was always present with Him. . . . And Moses, who lived many years before Solomon, or, rather, the Word of God by him as by an instrument, says, 'In the beginning God created the heavens and the earth' (Gen. 1:1).

TO AUTOLYCUS, Bk. 2
MG 6, 1064
ANF II, 97–98

ST. HIPPOLYTUS

186
(388)

For these fathers were furnished with the Spirit, and largely honored by the Word Himself; and just as it is with instruments of music, so had they the Word always, like the plectrum, in union with them, and when moved by Him the prophets announced what God willed. For they spoke not of their own power (let there be no mistake as to that), neither did they declare what pleased themselves.

ON CHRIST AND ANTICHRIST, Ch. 2
MG 10, 728
ANF V, 204

ST. AUGUSTINE

Therefore, when those disciples [the evangelists] have written matters which He declared and spoke to them, it ought not by any means to be said that He has written nothing Himself; since the truth is, that His members have accomplished only what they became acquainted with by the repeated statements of the Head. For all that He was minded to give for our perusal on the subject of His own doings and sayings, He commanded to be written by those disciples, whom He thus used as if they were His own hands.

187
(1609)

THE HARMONY OF THE GOSPELS, Bk. 1, Ch. 35
ML 34, 1070
NPNF VI, 101

"The Lord will seek Him a man" (1 Sam. 13:14) meaning either David or the Mediator of the New Testament, who was figured in the chrism with which David also and his offspring was annointed. But it is not as if He knew not where he was that God thus seeks Him a man, but, speaking through a man, He speaks as a man, and in this sense seeks us.

188
(1766)

THE CITY OF GOD, Bk. 17, Ch. 6
ML 41, 537
NPNF II, 346

37. *The primary object of this inspiration are things pertaining to salvation.*

ST. AUGUSTINE

The Spirit of God, who spoke through [the divine authors] was unwilling to teach men things of no profit for salvation.

189
(1687)

ON GENESIS, Bk. 2, Ch. 9
ML 34, 270

38. *Inspiration truly extends to all parts of Scripture, even in some sense to the words themselves.*

ST. GREGORY NAZIANZEN

We however, who extend the accuracy of the Spirit to the merest stroke and tittle, will never admit the impious assertion that even the smallest

190
(979)

matters were dealt with haphazardly by those who have recorded them, and have thus been borne in mind down to the present day.

ORATIONS, 2:105
MG 35, 504
NPNF VII, 225

THEODORET

191
(2158)

They said, however, that all of the psalms were not by David, but some were by others. But I say nothing about those; what do I care . . . since all of them were written by the divine inspiration of the Spirit.

ON THE PSALMS, Preface
MG 80, 861

39. *The writer, the revelation, and the divine assistance.*

ST. AUGUSTINE

192
(1612)

For of what consequence is it in what place any of them may give his account; or what difference does it make whether he inserts the matter in its proper order, or brings in at a particular point what was previously omitted, or mentions at an earlier stage what really happened at a later, provided only that he contradicts neither himself nor a second writer in the narrative of the same facts or of others? For as it is not in one's own power, however admirable and trustworthy may be the knowledge he has once obtained of the facts to determine the order in which he will recall them to memory (for the way in which one thing comes into a person's mind before or after another is something which proceeds not as we will, but simply as it is given to us), it is reasonable enough to suppose that each of the evangelists believed it to have been his duty to relate what he had to relate in that order in which it had pleased God to suggest to his recollection the matters he was engaged in recording. At least this might hold good in the case of those incidents with regard to which the question of order, whether it were this or that, detracted nothing from evangelical authority and truth.

THE HARMONY OF THE GOSPELS, Bk. 2, Ch. 21
ML 34, 1102
NPNF VI, 127

193
(1767)

In the very history of the kings of Judah and Israel containing their acts, which we believe to belong to the canonical Scripture, very many things are mentioned which are not explained there, but are said to be found in other books which the prophets wrote, the very names of these prophets being sometimes given, and yet they are not found in the canon which the people of God received (1 Chr. 29:29; 2 Chr. 9:29). Now I confess the reason of this is hidden from me; only I think that even those men, to whom certainly the Holy Spirit revealed those things which ought to be held as of religious authority, might write some things as men by historical diligence, and others as prophets by divine inspiration; and these things were so distinct, that it was judged that the former should be ascribed to themselves, but the latter to God speaking through them; and so the one pertained to the abundance of knowledge, the other to the authority of religion. In that authority the canon is guarded.

THE CITY OF GOD, Bk. 18, Ch. 38
ML 41, 598
NPNF II, 383

40. *No error can be found in the sacred books.*

ST. CLEMENT OF ROME
See No. 177.

ST. JUSTIN MARTYR

But I shall not venture to suppose or to say such a thing [that the Scriptures err]; and if a Scripture which appears to be of such a kind be brought forward, and if there be a pretext [for saying] that it is contrary [to some other] since I am entirely convinced that no Scripture contradicts another, I shall admit rather that I do not understand what is recorded, and shall strive to persuade those who imagine that the Scriptures are contradictory, to be rather of the same opinion as myself.

DIALOGUE WITH TRYPHO, Ch. 65
MG 6, 625
ANF I, 230

194
(138)

ST. IRENAEUS
See No. 180.

ST. JEROME

[To Marcella, 382–385] Let my [detractors] take my answer as follows: I am not so dull-witted nor so coarsely ignorant (qualities which they take for holiness, calling themselves the disciples of fishermen as if

195
(1347)

113

men were made holy by knowing nothing)—I am not, I repeat, so ignorant as to suppose that any one of the Lord's words is either in need of correction or is not divinely inspired; but the Latin manuscripts of the Scriptures are proved to be faulty by the variations which all of them exhibit, and my object has been to restore them to the form of the Greek original, from which my detractors do not deny that they have been translated.

LETTERS, No. 27
MC 22, 431
NPNF VI, 44

ST. AUGUSTINE

196
(1417)

[To Jerome, a. 394–395] I think it is extremely dangerous to admit that anything in the Sacred Books should be a lie. . . . If we once admit in that supreme authority even one polite lie, there will be nothing left of those books, because, whenever anyone finds something difficult to practise or hard to believe, he will follow this most dangerous precedent and explain it as the idea or practice of a lying author.

LETTERS, No. 28
ML 33, 112
FC XII, 95–96

197
(1421)

[To Jerome, shortly after 405] For, I admit to your Charity that it is from those books alone of the Scriptures, which are now called canonical, that I have learned to pay them such honor and respect as to believe most firmly that not one of their authors has erred in writing anything at all. If I do find anything in those books which seems contrary to truth, I decide that either the text is corrupt, or the translator did not follow what was really said, or that I failed to understand it.

LETTERS, No. 82
ML 33, 277
FC XII, 392

See Nos. 41 and 192.

TRADITION

"So then, brethren, stand firm and hold to the traditions which you were taught by us, either by word of mouth or by letter" (2 Th. 2:15). So wrote St. Paul in his second letter to the Thessalonians. Against the

Protestant Reformers the Council of Trent maintained that tradition as well as Sacred Scripture was a source of the Church's teaching magisterium. Since earliest times sacred tradition has always been recognized as a true font of revelation. Indeed, Scripture alone cannot be the sole source of faith because the Canon of Scripture cannot be determined from the writings themselves, nor can their inspiration be so determined. But how is tradition safely transmitted? By means of the creeds, the writings of the fathers, the constant and unanimous consent of Catholic Schools on matters of faith, the ancient ecclesiastical monuments, the common belief of the faithful, but most of all by the solemn judgment of the Church which is always an infallible proof of divine tradition. Whether we regard tradition as the teaching authority of the Church, or the body of teaching itself, or the Church's act of teaching the deposit of faith, all three are involved in the history of the authentic transmission of God's revelation of Himself to man in the person of the God-Man Jesus Christ.

41. Sacred tradition is also a true font of revelation.

ST. IRENAEUS

For even creation reveals Him who formed it, and the very work made suggests Him who made it, and the world manifests Him who ordered it. The Universal Church, moreover, through the whole world, has received this tradition from the Apostles.

198
(198)

AGAINST HERESIES, Bk. 2, Ch. 9
MG 7, 734
ANF I, 369

True knowledge is [that which consists in] the doctrine of the Apostles, and the ancient constitution of the Church throughout all the world, and the distinctive manifestation of the body of Christ according to the successions of the bishops, by which they have handed down that Church which exists in every place, and has come even unto us, being guarded and preserved, without any forging of Scriptures, by a very complete system of doctrine, and neither addition nor [suffering] curtailment [in the truths which she believes]; and [it consists in] reading [the Word of God] without falsification, and a lawful and diligent exposition in harmony with the Scriptures, both without danger and without blasphemy; and [above all, it consists in] the pre-eminent gift

199
(242)

of love, which is more precious than knowledge, more glorious than prophecy, and which excels all the other gifts [of God].

AGAINST HERESIES, Bk. 4, Ch. 33
MG 7, 1077
ANF I, 508

TERTULLIAN

200
(291)

For wherever both the true Christian rule and Faith shall be shown to be, there will be the true Scriptures, and the true expositions, and all the true Christian traditions.

THE PRESCRIPTION OF HERETICS, Ch. 19
ML 2, 31
ANF III, 251–252

201
(371)

We . . . believe that there is only one God, but under the following dispensation, or *oikonomía* as it is called, that this one only God has also a Son, His Word, who proceeded from Himself, by whom all things were made, and without whom nothing was made (Jn. 1:3). Him [we believe] to have been sent by the Father into the Virgin, and to have been born of her—being both Man and God, the Son of Man and the Son of God, and to have been called by the name of Jesus Christ. . . . That this rule of faith has come down to us from the beginning of the gospel, even before any of the older heretics, much more before Praxeas [a pretender] of yesterday, will be apparent both from the lateness of date which marks all heresies, and also from the absolutely novel character of our new-fangled Praxeas. In this principle also we must henceforth find a presumption of equal force against all heresies whatsoever—that whatever is first is true, whereas that is spurious which is later in date. But keeping this prescriptive rule inviolate, still some opportunity must be given for reviewing [the statements of heretics], with a view to the instruction and protection of divers persons; were it only that it may not seem that each perversion [of the truth] is condemned without examination, and simply pre- judged; especially in the case of this heresy, which supposes itself to possess the pure truth, in thinking that one cannot believe in One Only God in any other way than by saying that the Father, the Son, and the Holy Spirit are the very selfsame Person. As if in this way also one were not All, in that All are of One, by unity [that is] of substance; while the mystery of the *oikonomía* [or, dispensation] is still guarded, which distributes the Unity into a Trinity, placing in their order the

three Persons—the Father, the Son, and the Holy Ghost: three, however, not in condition, but in degree; not in substance, but in form;
not in power, but in aspect; yet of one substance, and of one condition,
and of one power, inasmuch as He is one God, from whom these degrees
and forms and aspects are reckoned, under the name of the Father, and
of the Son, and of the Holy Ghost.

AGAINST PRAXEAS, Ch. 2

ML 2, 156

ANF III, 598

ST. BASIL

Nor do we speak of the Holy Spirit as begotten, for by the tradition   202
of the faith we have been taught one Only-begotten: the Spirit of truth   (917)
we have been taught to proceed from the Father, and we confess Him to
be of God without creation. We are also bound to anathematize all who
speak of the Holy Spirit as ministerial, inasmuch as by this term they
degrade Him to the rank of a creature. . . . It is necessary to add yet
this further, that they are to be shunned, as plainly hostile to true
religion, who invert the order left us by the Lord, and put the Son
before the Father, and the Holy Spirit before the Son. For we must
keep unaltered and inviolable that order which we have received from
the very words of the Lord, 'Go therefore and teach all nations,
baptizing them in the name of the Father and of the Son, and of the
Holy Spirit' (Mt. 28:19).

LETTERS, No. 125

MG 32, 549

NPNF VIII, 195–196

Of the beliefs and practices whether generally accepted or publicly   203
enjoined which are preserved in the Church some we possess derived   (954)
from written teaching; others we have received delivered to us 'in a
mystery' by the tradition of the Apostles; and both of these in relation
to true religion have the same force. And these no one will contradict;
—no one, at all events, who is even moderately versed in the institutions
of the Church. For were we to attempt to reject such customs as have
no written authority, on the ground that the importance they possess
is small, we should unintentionally injure the Gospel in these matters
especially, or, rather, should make our public definition a mere phrase
and nothing more. . . . Which of the saints has left us in writing the

words of the invocation at the displaying of the bread of the Eucharist and the cup of blessing? For we are not, as is well known, content with what the apostle or the Gospel has recorded, but both in preface and conclusion we add other words as being of great importance to the validity of the ministry, and these we derive from unwritten teaching. Moreover we bless the water of baptism and the oil of the chrism, and besides this the Catechumen who is being baptized. On what written authority do we do this? Is not our authority silent and mystical tradition? Nay, by what written word is the anointing of oil itself taught? and whence comes the custom of baptizing thrice? And as to the other customs of baptism from what Scripture do we derive the renunciation of Satan and his angels? Does not this come from that unpublished and secret teaching which our fathers guarded in a silence out of the reach of curious meddling and inquisitive investigation? . . . In the same manner the Apostles and Fathers who laid down laws for the Church from the beginning thus guarded the awful dignity of the mysteries in secrecy and silence, for what is bruited abroad at random among the common folk is not mystery at all.

ON THE HOLY SPIRIT, Ch. 27
MG 32, 188
NPNF VIII, 40–41

ST. JOHN CHRYSOSTOM

204
(1213)

'So then, brethren, stand fast, and hold the traditions which you were taught, whether by word, or by Epistle of ours' (2 Th. 2:15). Hence it is manifest, that they did not deliver all things by Epistle, but many things also unwritten, and in like manner both the one and the other are worthy of credit. Therefore let us think the tradition of the Church also worthy of credit. It is a tradition, seek no farther.

HOMILIES ON SECOND THESSALONIANS
MG 62, 488
NPNF XIII, 390

ST. JEROME

205
(1358)

Don't you know that the laying on of hands after baptism and then the invocation of the Holy Spirit is a custom of the Churches? Do you demand Scripture proof? You may find it in the Acts of the Apostles. And even if it did not rest on the authority of Scripture the consensus of the whole world in this respect would have the force of a command.

For many other observances of the Churches, which are due to tradition, have acquired the authority of the written law.

THE DIALOGUE AGAINST THE LUCIFERIANS, Ch. 8
ML 23, 163
NPNF VI, 324

ST. AUGUSTINE
See No. 176.

Holy and blessed priests, famous in their treatment of sacred doctrine, Irenaeus, Cyprian, Reticius, Olympius, Hilary, Ambrose, Gregory, Innocent, John [Chrysostom], Basil, to whom I add, whether you wish it or not, the priest Jerome, omitting those who are still alive, have pronounced against you their opinion about the succession of all men which is bound by original sin, whence no one can rescue them except Him Whom a virgin conceived without the law of sin warring against the law of the mind. . . . What they found in the Church they held; what they learned they taught; what they received from the fathers they handed down to the sons. We were not as yet involved with you before these judges; they tried our case.

206
(1899)

AGAINST JULIAN, Bk. 2, Ch. 10
ML 44, 697
FC XXXV, 97–98

ST. VINCENT OF LÉRINS

I have often then inquired earnestly and attentively of very many men eminent for sanctity and learning, how and by what sure and so to speak universal rule I may be able to distinguish the truth of Catholic faith from the falsehood of heretical pravity; and I have always, and in almost every instance, received an answer to this effect: That whether I or any one else should wish to detect the frauds and avoid the snares of heretics as they rise, and to continue sound and complete in the Catholic faith, we must, the Lord helping, fortify our own belief in two ways: first, by the authority of the Divine Law, and then, by the Tradition of the Catholic Church.

207
(2168)

But here some one perhaps will ask, Since the canon of Scripture is complete, and sufficient of itself for everything, and more than sufficient, what need is there to join with it the authority of the Church's interpretation? For this reason, —because, owing to the depth of Holy Scripture, all do not accept it in one and the same sense, but one understands its words in one way, another in another. . . . Therefore, it is very necessary, on account of so great intricacies of such various error, that the rule for the right understanding of the prophets and apostles should be framed in accordance with the standard of Ecclesiastical and Catholic interpretation.

Moreover, in the Catholic Church itself, all possible care must be taken, that we hold that faith which has been believed everywhere, always, by all. For that is truly and in the strictest sense 'Catholic' which, as the name itself and the reason of the thing declare, comprehends all universally.' This rule we shall observe if we follow universality, antiquity, consent. We shall follow universality if we confess that one faith to be true, which the whole Church throughout the world confesses; antiquity, if we in no wise depart from those interpretations which it is manifest were notoriously held by our holy ancestors and fathers; consent, in like manner, if in antiquity itself we adhere to the consentient definitions and determinations of all, or at the least of almost all priests and doctors.

COMMONITORY, Ch. 2
ML 50, 639
NPNF XI, 132

208
(2172)

He is the true and genuine Catholic who loves the truth of God, who loves the Church, who loves the Body of Christ, who esteems divine religion and the Catholic Faith, above every thing, above the authority, above the regard, above the genius, above the eloquence, above the philosophy, of every man whatsoever; who sets light by all of these, and continuing steadfast and established in the faith, resolves that he will believe that, and that only, which he is sure the Catholic Church has held universally and from ancient time.

COMMONITORY, Ch. 20
ML 50, 665
NPNF XI, 146

42. This tradition completes Scripture through an authentic interpretation.

ST. IRENAEUS
See Nos. 199 and 220.

120

ORIGEN

Seeing there are many who think they hold the opinions of Christ, and yet some of these think differently from their predecessors, yet as the teaching of the Church, transmitted in orderly succession from the Apostles, and remaining in the churches to the present day, is still preserved, that alone is to be accepted as truth which differs in no respect from ecclesiastical and apostolical tradition.

209
(443)

ON FIRST PRINCIPLES, Bk. 1, Preface, 2
MG 11, 116
ANF IV, 239

ST. AUGUSTINE
See No. 171.

ST. VINCENT OF LÉRINS
See No. 207.

43. *Apostolic tradition has always been regarded as a rule of faith.*

ST. POLYCARP

For 'everyone who does not confess that Jesus Christ has come in the flesh is an antichrist' (1 Jn. 4:2, 3); and whoever does not confess the witness of the Cross is of the devil; and whoever perverts the sayings of the Lord to his own evil desires and says there is neither resurrection nor judgment, that one is the first-born of Satan. Therefore, let us abandon the vanities of the crowd and their false teachings; let us return to the word which was delivered to us from the beginning.

210
(74)

LETTER TO THE PHILIPPIANS, No. 7
MG 5, 1012
FC I, 139

ST. PAPIAS
See No. 42.

ST. IRENAEUS

The Church, though dispersed throughout the whole world, even to the ends of the earth has received from the Apostles and their disciples this faith: [She believes] in one God, the Father Almighty, Maker of

211
(191)

heaven, and earth, and the sea, and all things that are in them (Ps. 145:6; Acts 4:24, 14:15), and in one Christ Jesus, the Son of God, who became incarnate for our salvation; and in the Holy Spirit, who proclaimed through the prophets the dispensations of God, and the advent, and the birth from a virgin, and the passion, and the resurrection from the dead, and the ascension into heaven in the flesh of the beloved Christ Jesus, our Lord, and His [future] manifestation from heaven in the glory of the Father 'to gather all things in one,' and to raise up anew all flesh of the whole human race, in order that to Christ Jesus, our Lord, and God, and Saviour, and King, according to the will of the invisible Father, 'every knee should bow, of things in heaven, and things in earth, and things under the earth, and that every tongue should confess' to Him, and that He should execute just judgment towards all; that He may send 'spiritual wickednesses,' and the angels who transgressed and became apostates, together with the ungodly, and unrighteous, and wicked, and profane among men, into everlasting fire; but may, in the exercise of His grace, confer immortality on the righteous, and holy, and those who have kept His commandments, and have persevered in His love, some from the beginning [of their Christian course], and others from [the date of] their repentance, and may surround them with everlasting glory.

AGAINST HERESIES, Ch. 1
MG 7, 549
ANF I, 330–331

See Nos. 101, 168, 150, 160, 43, 139, 141, and 44.

TERTULLIAN
See No. 152, 143, 125, 154, and 38.

ORIGEN
See No. 209.

212
(445)

The particular points clearly delivered in the teaching of the Apostles are as follows: First, That there is one God, Who created and arranged all things, and Who, when nothing existed, called all things into being— . . . and that this God in the last days, as He had announced beforehand by His prophets, sent our Lord Jesus Christ . . . Himself who came [into the world], was born of the Father before all creatures; that, after He had been the servant of the Father in the creation of all things—'For by Him were all things made' (Jn. 1:3)—He in the last times, divesting Himself [of His glory), became a man, and was incarnate although God, and while made a man remained the God which He was; that He assumed a body like to our own, differing in this respect only, that it was born of a virgin and of the Holy Spirit: that this Jesus Christ was truly born, and did truly suffer, and did not endure this death common [to man] in appearance only, but did truly die; that He did truly rise from the dead; and that after His resurrection He conversed with His disciples, and was taken up [into heaven].

Then, thirdly, the Apostles related that the Holy Spirit was associated in honor and dignity with the Father and the Son. But in His case it is not clearly distinguished whether He is to be regarded as born or innate, or also as a Son of God or not.

ON FIRST PRINCIPLES, Bk. 1, Preface, 4

MG 11, 118

ANF IV, 240

EUSEBIUS OF CAESAREA

While [Ignatius of Antioch] was making the journey through Asia   **213** under the strictest military guard, he strengthened the diocese in each   **(657)** city where he stayed by spoken sermons and exhortations, and he especially exhorted them above all to be on their guard against the heresies which then for the first time were prevalent and he urged them to hold fast to the tradition of the Apostles to which he thought it necessary, for security's sake, to give form by written testimony.

ECCLESIASTICAL HISTORY, Bk. 3, Ch. 36

MG 20, 288

FC XIX, 196

ST. ATHANASIUS
See No. 174.

THEODORET

[To Florentius, a patrician] I have ever kept the faith of the Apostles   **214** undefiled. . . . So have I learnt not only from the Apostles and the   **(2142)** prophets but also from the interpreters of their writings, Ignatius, Eustathius, Athanasius, Basil, Gregory, John, and the rest of the lights of the world; and before these from the holy Fathers in council at Nicaea, whose confession of the faith I preserve in its integrity, like an ancestral inheritance [styling corrupt and enemies of the truth all who dare to transgress its decrees].

LETTERS, No. 89

MG 83, 1284

NPNF III, 283

44. *All progress in dogma, however, is not to be rejected.*

ST. IRENAEUS
See No. 129.

TERTULLIAN
See No. 201.

ORIGEN

215
(444)
Now it ought to be known that the holy Apostles, in preaching the faith of Christ, delivered themselves with the utmost clearness on certain points which they believed to be necessary to every one, even to those who seemed somewhat dull in the investigation of divine knowledge; leaving, however, the grounds of their statements to be examined into by those who should deserve the excellent gifts of the Spirit, and who, especially by means of the Holy Spirit Himself, should obtain the gift of language, of wisdom, and of knowledge: while on other subjects they merely stated the fact that things were so, keeping silence as to the manner of origin of their existence; clearly in order that the more zealous of their successors, who should be lovers of wisdom, might have a subject of exercise on which to display the fruit of their talents, —those persons, I mean who should prepare themselves to be fit and worthy receivers of wisdom.

ON FIRST PRINCIPLES, Bk. 1, Preface, 3
MG 11, 116
ANF IV, 239

ST. AUGUSTINE

216
(1765)
For while the hot restlessness of heretics stirs questions about many articles of the Catholic faith, the necessity of defending them forces us both to investigate them more accurately, to understand them more clearly, and to proclaim them more earnestly.

THE CITY OF GOD, Bk. 16, Ch. 2
ML 41, 477
NPNF II, 310

ST. VINCENT OF LÉRINS

217
(2174)
But some one will say perhaps, Shall there, then, be no progress in Christ's Church? Certainly; all possible progress. For what being is

124

there, so envious of men, so full of hatred to God, who would seek to forbid it? Yet on condition that it be real progress, not alteration of the faith. For progress requires that the subject be enlarged in itself; alteration, that it be transformed into something else. The intelligence, then, the knowledge, the wisdom, as well of individuals as of all, as well of one man as of the whole Church, ought, in the course of ages and centuries, to increase and make much and vigorous progress; but yet only in its own kind; that is to say, in the same doctrine, in the same sense, and in the same meaning.

The growth of religion in the soul must be analogous to the growth of the body, which, though in process of years it is developed and attains its full size, yet remains still the same. . . . For example: Our forefathers in the old time sowed wheat in the Church's field. It would be most unmeet and iniquitous if we, their descendants, instead of the genuine truth of corn, should reap the counterfeit error of tares. This should rather be the result, —there should be no discrepancy between the first and the last. From doctrine which was sown as wheat, we should reap, in the increase, doctrine of the same kind—wheat also; so that when in process of time any of the original seed is developed, and now flourishes under cultivation, no change may ensue in the character of the plant. There may supervene shape, form, variation in outward appearance, but the nature of each kind must remain the same.

COMMONITORY, Ch. 23
ML 50, 667
NPNF XI, 147–148

IV.

One God

We can know God in many different ways—from the order we see around us in nature, from the governing of Providence, and even from the dictates of our own conscience. While revelation is necessary in order that man may reach his supernatural end, nevertheless God's existence, His attributes, and His providential care are truths that can easily be known by all men because they are by their nature accessible to human reason.

There is hardly a Church Father who does not express and comment on these ideas in one way or another. St. Irenaeus (ca. 130–200), St. Clement of Alexandria (early third century), Origen at about the same time, Lactantius in the early fourth century, as well as St. Basil and St. Gregory Nazianzen all tell us that the existence of God can certainly be known through the natural light of reason. Tatian (mid-second century), St. Theophilus of Antioch (late second century), St. Athanasius (third century), St. John Chrysostom (late fourth century), St. Augustine (early fifth century), St. Cyril of Alexandria (fifth century), and St. John of Damascus (eighth century) join them in telling us that man can draw knowledge of God from the order of the visible world. As early as about 140, Aristides, the author of the *Apology,* asserted the knowledge of God from the governing of providence, and other writers add the argument from man's conscience. An early writer, St. Justin Martyr, declares that this knowledge is somehow inborn in all men, and a dozen other writers agree.

The essence of God is His very existence, and He is completely independent of the world He has created; all other beings, however, are not their own essence: they possess a derived existence and they are said to participate in being. Since God is pure Substance, pure Act, He is utterly simple and admits of no composition whatever. His attributes of infinity, immensity, ubiquity, eternity, immutability, and omnipotence are actually one with His divine essence.

The equation of essence with existence fascinates St. Gregory Nazianzen writing in the fourth century. St. Athanasius emphasizes that God is *per se* independent existence. St. Augustine shortly afterwards reminds us that the divine attributes are really the same as the divine substance, and all are intrigued with the idea of God as utter simplicity, admitting of no composition whatever. Athenagoras, writing about 180, describes beautifully the spiritual nature of God and summarizes all of His attributes, and other writers dwell now on one quality, now on another, St. Irenaeus and St. Clement of Alexandria on his infinite perfection, Hermas and Novatian on His immensity and ubiquity, St. Cyril of Jerusalem on His immutability, Athenagoras on His eternity, Tertullian and Lactantius on His oneness and unicity, St. Theophilus of Antioch and Tertullian on His omnipotence.

No creature can naturally see God, but creatures can be elevated to the vision of God, and this is done for the angels and the blessed in heaven. The Greek writers are particularly articulate on this point, especially St. Basil and St. Gregory Nazianzen, as well as St. John Chrysostom.

We learn about God's attributes only by studying His creatures in a threefold manner: the way of negation, by which we determine what God is not; the way of causality, by which we argue from effect to cause; and the way of eminence, by which all deficiency is removed from God. God's knowledge embraces everything at a glance —what actually is now, what will be, what could be, or what would be under given circumstances that might exist. The usual chorus of voices is heard, but a new one, that of St. Ephraem, the poet-musician of the Syriac Church celebrates the divine attributes in his famous *Nisibene Hymns.*

God's knowledge is also His will; He sees all men in the divine idea, and He wills the salvation of each one of them. But salvation is achieved only by the elect, because God has already predestined them for salvation and mercifully dispenses to them the grace necessary to achieve their final end. Hence those who fail to do so have only themselves to blame, and unwittingly show that while God is merciful, He is also just. So we are to work out our own salvation with fear and trembling, as St. Paul says, because God is at work in us, both to will and to work for His good pleasure (see Phil. 2:12).

God's foreknowledge is not explicitated at any great length until the fourth century by St. Ambrose, St. Jerome, and St. Augustine. The question of salvific will, predestination, and reprobation likewise does not much occur before their time. Hippolytus touched upon it, but it is the great St. Augustine who tackled the problem and wrote volumes on it. *On the Predestination of the Saints* and *On the Gift of Perseverance* both try to reconcile the doctrine of predestination with God's desire for the salvation of all men as stated in 1 Timothy 2:4. Predestination for faith and justification is completely gratuitous, and ultimately Augustine must agree that the whole matter is an occult work of God. There are other writers, but they are few, and Augustine towers over all of them in significance. We must finally say that those who are damned are damned through their own fault (it is not a double-barreled predestination as in Calvin), and while leaving predestination as a hidden counsel of God (so Fulgentius), insist that it never destroys free will. Those who are damned perish through their own neglect according to St. Prosper of Aquitaine, and St. John Chrysostom asserts that God reprobates only those who He knows will freely be sinners.

THE EXISTENCE OF GOD

45. The existence of God can certainly be known through the natural light of reason.

ST. IRENAEUS

For since [God's] invisible essence is mighty, it confers on all a profound mental intuition and perception of His most powerful, yes, omnipotent greatness. Wherefore, although 'no one knows the Father,

218
(197)

except the Son, nor the Son except the Father, and those to whom the Son will reveal Him' (Mt. 11:27; Lk. 10:22), yet all beings do know this one fact at least, because reason, implanted in their minds, moves them, and reveals to them [the truth] that there is one God, the Lord of all.

AGAINST HERESIES, Bk. 2, Ch. 6
MG 7, 724
ANF I, 365

219
(228)
For by means of the creation itself, the Word reveals God the Creator; and by means of the world [does He declare] the Lord the Maker of the world; and by means of the formation [of man] the Artificer who formed him; and by the Son that Father who begat the Son; and these things do indeed address all men in the same manner, but all do not in the same way believe them.

AGAINST HERESIES, Bk. 4, Ch. 6
MG 7, 989
ANF I, 469

MINUCIUS FELIX
See No. 8.

TERTULLIAN
See Nos. 9 and 16.

220
(287)
Now nobody denies what nobody is ignorant of—for Nature herself is teacher of it—that God is the Maker of the universe, and that it is good, and that it is man's by free gift of its Maker.

ON THE SPECTACLES, Ch. 2
ML 1, 631
ANF III, 80

ST. CLEMENT OF ALEXANDRIA

221
(416)
'And what is hidden or manifest I know; for Wisdom, the artificer of all things, taught me' (Wis. 7:21). You have, in brief, the professed aim of our philosophy; and learning of these branches, when pursued with right course of conduct, leads through Wisdom, the artificer of all things, to the Ruler of all, —a Being difficult to grasp and apprehend, ever receding and withdrawing from him who pursues.

STROMATA, Bk. 2, Ch. 2
MG 8, 936
ANF II, 348

Who, then, is so impious as to disbelieve God, and to demand 222
proofs from God as from men? Again, some questions demand the (422)
evidence of the senses, as if one were to ask whether the fire be warm,
or the snow white; and some admonition and rebuke, as the question
if you ought to honor your parents. And there are those that deserve
punishment, as to ask proofs of the existence of Providence. There being
then a Providence, it would be impious to think that the whole of
prophecy and the economy of reference to a Saviour did not take place
in accordance with Providence. And perhaps one should not even
attempt to demonstrate such points, the divine Providence being
evident from the sight of all its skillful and wise works which are
seen, some of which take place in order, and some appear in order.

STROMATA, Bk. 5, Ch. 1
MG 9, 16
ANF II, 445

ORIGEN

For no one who has learnt that God is invisible, and that certain of 223
His works are invisible, that is to say, apprehended by the reason, can (534)
say, as if to justify his faith in a resurrection, 'How can they know God,
except by the perception of the senses?' or, 'How otherwise than
through the senses can they gain any knowledge?' For it is not in any
secret writings, perused only by a few wise men, but in such as are
most widely diffused and most commonly known among the people,
that these words are written: 'The invisible things of God from the
creation of the world are clearly seen, being understood by the things
that are made' (Rom. 1:20). From whence it is to be inferred, that
though men who live upon the earth have to begin with the use of the
senses upon sensible objects, in order to go on from them to a knowledge of the nature of things intellectual, yet their knowledge must
not stop short with the objects of sense.

AGAINST CELSUS, Bk. 7, Ch. 37
MG 11, 1473
ANF IV, 625

For 'the invisible things of God,' that is, the objects of the reason, 224
'from the creation of the world are clearly seen' by the reason, 'being (535)
understood by the things that are made' (Rom. 1:20). And when
they have risen from the created things of this world to the invisible

131

things of God, they do not stay there; but after they have sufficiently exercised their minds upon these, and have understood their nature, they ascend to 'the eternal power of God,' in a word, to His divinity. For they know that God, in His love to men, has 'manifested' His truth, and 'that which is known of Him,' not only to those who devote themselves to His service, but also to some who are far removed from the purity of worship and service which He requires; and that some of those who by the providence of God had attained a knowledge of these truths, were yet doing things unworthy of that knowledge, and 'holding the truth in unrighteousness,' and who are unable to find any excuse before God after the knowledge of such great truths which He has given them.

AGAINST CELSUS, Bk. 7, Ch. 46
MG 11, 1489
ANF IV, 630

LACTANTIUS

225
(645)

God is not to be perceived by us through the sight or other frail sense; but He is to be beheld by the eyes of the mind, since we see His illustrious and wonderful works. For as to those who have altogether denied the existence of God, I should not only refuse to call them philosophers, but even deny them the name of men, who, with a close resemblance to dumb animals, consisted of body only, discerning nothing with their mind, and referring all things to the bodily senses, who thought that nothing existed but that which they beheld with their eyes.

THE DIVINE INSTITUTES, Bk. 7, Ch. 9
ML 6, 764
ANF VII, 205

ST. BASIL

226
(924)

Which is first in order, knowledge or faith? I reply that generally, in the case of disciples, faith precedes knowledge. But, in our teaching, if any one asserts knowledge to come before faith, I make no objection; understanding knowledge so far as is within the bounds of human comprehension. In our lessons we must first believe that the letter *A* is said to us; then we learn the characters and their pronunciation, and last of all we get the distinct idea of the force of the letter. But in our belief about God, first comes the idea that God is. This we gather from

His works. For, as we perceive His wisdom, His goodness, and all His invisible things from the creation of the world (Rom. 1:20), so we know Him. So, too, we accept Him as our Lord. For since God is the Creator of the whole world, and we are a part of the world, God is our Creator. This knowledge is followed by faith, and this faith by worship.

LETTERS, No. 235
MG 32, 872
NPNF VIII, 274–275

ST. GREGORY NAZIANZEN

'I will consider the heavens, the work of Your fingers, the moon and the stars' (Ps. 8:4), and the settled order therein; not as if he were considering them now, but as destined to do so hereafter. But far before them is that Nature Which is above them, and out of which they spring, the Incomprehensible and Illimitable—not, I mean, as to the fact of His being, but as to Its nature. . . . Now our very eyes and the Law of Nature teach us that God exists and that He is the Efficient and Maintaining Cause of all things; our eyes, because they fall on visible objects, and see them in beautiful stability and progress, immovably moving and revolving if I may so say; natural Law, because through these visible things and their order, it reasons back to their Author.

227
(984)

ORATIONS, 28:2
MG 36, 32
NPNF VII, 289

ST. AUGUSTINE

[To Evodius, a. 415] You also have some help in the book on religion, if you would review it and look into it, you would never think that reason can prove the necessity of God's existence, or that by reasoning it can ever be established that God must necessarily exist [see *On the True Religion*, 31:58]. In the science of numbers which we certainly make use of in everyday life, if we say seven plus three ought to be ten—they *are* ten. [Evodius had written this in "Letter 160":] ('Reason itself demonstrates that God exists, or must necessarily exist, and that it must be that He cannot be other than God.')

228
(1437)

LETTERS, No. 162
ML 33, 655
FC XX, 375

133

46. *Man can draw knowledge of God from the order of the visible world.*

TATIAN

229
(152)

Our God did not begin to be in time: He alone is without beginning, He Himself is the beginning of all things. God is a Spirit, not pervading matter, but the Maker of material spirits, and of the forms that are in matter; He is invisible, impalpable, being Himself the Father of both sensible and invisible things. Him we know from His creation, and apprehend His invisible power by His works.

ORATION AGAINST THE GREEKS, Ch. 4
MG 6, 813
ANF II, 66

ST. THEOPHILUS OF ANTIOCH

230
(172)

Consider, O man, His works, —the timely rotation of the seasons, and the changes of temperature; the regular march of the stars; the well-ordered course of days and nights, and years; . . . and the providence with which God provides nourishment for all flesh, or the subjection in which He has ordained that all things subserve mankind. He alone is God Who made light out of darkness, and brought forth light from his treasures, and formed the treasure-houses of the deep, and the bounds of the seas. . . .

TO AUTOLYCUS, Bk. 1, Ch. 6
MG 6, 1033
ANF II, 90

ST. IRENAEUS
See No. 198.

TERTULLIAN

231
(332)

For indeed, as the Creator of all things, God was from the beginning discovered equally with them, they having been themselves manifested that He might become known as God. . . . From the beginning the knowledge of God is the dowry of the soul, one and the same amongst the Egyptians, and the Syrians, and the tribes of Pontus.

AGAINST MARCION, Bk. 1, Ch. 10
ML 2, 257
ANF III, 278

ORIGEN

How much more manifest (and how much better than all these inventions!) is it that, convinced by what we see, in the admirable order of the world, we should worship the Maker of it as the one Author of one effect, and which, as being wholly in harmony with itself, cannot on that account have been the work of many makers.

AGAINST CELSUS, Bk. 1, Ch. 23

MG 11, 701

ANF IV, 405

232

(515)

ST. METHODIUS

I began to praise the Creator, as I saw the earth fast fixed, and living creatures in such variety, and the blossoms of plants with their many hues. But my mind did not rest upon these things alone; but thereupon I began to inquire whence they have their origin—whether from some source eternally co-existent with God, or from Himself alone, none co-existing with Him; for that He has made nothing out of that which has no existence appeared to me the right view to take, unless my reason were altogether untrustworthy. For it is the nature of things which come into being to derive their origin from what is already existing. And it seemed to me that it might be said with equal truth, that nothing is eternally co-existent with God distinct from Himself, but that whatever exists has its origin from Him, and I was persuaded of this also by the undeniable disposition of the elements, and by the orderly arrangement of nature about them.

ON FREE WILL, Ch. 2

MG 18, 244

ANF VI, 357

233

(614)

LACTANTIUS

But there is no one so uncivilized, and of such an uncultivated disposition, who, when he raises his eyes to heaven, although he knows not by the providence of what God all this visible universe is governed, does not understand from the very magnitude of the objects, from their motion, arrangement, constancy, usefulness, beauty, and temperament, that there is some providence, and that that which exists with wonderful method must have been prepared by some greater intelligence.

THE DIVINE INSTITUTES, Bk. 1, Ch. 2

MG 6, 121

ANF VII, 11

234

(624)

ST. ATHANASIUS

235
(746)

For the soul is made after the image and likeness of God, as divine Scripture also shows, when it says in the person of God: 'Let us make man after our Image and likeness' (Gen. 1:26). Whence also when it gets rid of all the filth of sin which covers it and retains only the likeness of the Image in its purity, then surely this latter being thoroughly brightened, the soul beholds as in a mirror the Image of the Father, even the Word, and by His means reaches the idea of the Father, Whose Image the Saviour is. Or, if the soul's own teaching is insufficient, by reason of the external things which cloud its intelligence, and prevent its seeing what is higher, yet it is further possible to attain to the knowledge of God from the things which are seen, since Creation, as though in written characters, declares in a loud voice, by its order and harmony, its own Lord and Creator.

AGAINST THE HEATHEN*, Ch. 34
MG 25, 68
NPNF IV, 22

236
(747)

For God, being good and loving to mankind, and caring for the souls made by Him, —since He is by nature invisible and incomprehensible, having His being beyond all created existence, for which reason the race of mankind was likely to miss the way to the knowledge of Him, since they are made out of nothing while He is unmade, —for this cause God by His own Word gave the Universe the Order it has, in order that since He is by nature invisible, men might be enabled to know Him at any rate by His works.

AGAINST THE HEATHEN*, Ch. 35
MG 25, 69
NPNF IV, 22

ST. BASIL
See No. 226.

ST. GREGORY NAZIANZEN
See No. 227.

237
(987)

For suppose that its existence is accidental, to what will you let us ascribe its order? And if you like we will grant you this: to what then will you ascribe its preservation and protection in accordance with the

* ca. A.D. 318.

terms of the first creation? Do these belong to the accidental or something else? Surely not to the Accidental. And what can this Something Else be but God? Thus reason that proceeds from God, that is implanted in all from the beginning and is the first law in us, and is bound up in all leads us up to God through visible things. Let us begin again and reason this out.

ORATIONS, No. 28
MG 36, 48
NPNF VII, 294

ST. JOHN CHRYSOSTOM

For [creation] is not wicked, but is both beautiful and a token of the wisdom and power and lovingkindness of God. . . . Hear, too, Paul saying, 'For the invisible things of Him, since the creation of the world, are clearly seen, being perceived through the things that are made' (Rom. 1:20). For each of these by which he spoke declared that the creation leads us to the knowledge of God, because it causes us to know the Master fully.

238
(1117)

RESISTING THE TEMPTATIONS OF THE DEVIL, Hom. 2:3
MG 49, 260
NPNF IX, 188

The knowledge of Himself God placed in men from the beginning. But this knowledge they invested stocks and stones with, and so dealt unrighteously to the truth, as far at least as they might. For it abides unchanged, having its own glory immutable. 'And whence is it plain that He placed in them this knowledge, O Paul?' 'Because,' says he, 'that which may be known of Him is manifest in them' (Rom. 1:19). This, however, is an assertion, not a proof. But do you make it good, and show me that the knowledge of God was plain to them, and that they willingly turned aside. Whence was it plain then? did He send them a voice from above? By no means. But what was able to draw them to Him more than a voice, that He did, by putting before them the Creation, so that both wise, and unlearned, and Scythian, and barbarian, having through sight learned the beauty of the things which were seen, might mount up to God.

239
(1182)

HOMILIES ON THE LETTER TO THE ROMANS, No. III
MG 60, 412
NPNF XI, 352

ST. AUGUSTINE

240
(1508)
'Whence do these ungodly men detain the truth?' (Rom. 1:18). Has God spoken to any one of them? Have they received the Law as the people of the Israelites by Moses? Whence then do they detain the truth, though it be even in this unrighteousness?' Hear what follows, and he shows. 'Because that which can be known of God,' he says, 'is manifest in them; for God has manifested it to them' (Rom. 1:19). Manifested it to them to whom He has not given the Law? Hear how He has manifested it. 'For the invisible things of Him are clearly seen, being understood by the things that are made' (Rom. 1:20). Ask the world, the beauty of the heaven, the brilliancy and ordering of the stars . . . ask all things, and see if they do not as if it were by a language [sensu] of their own make answer to you, 'God made us.' These things have illustrious philosophers sought out, and by the art have come to know the Artificer.

SERMONS, No. 141
See No. 10.　　　　　　　　　　　　　　　　　　ML 38, 776
NPNF VI, 531

ST. CYRIL OF ALEXANDRIA

241
(2137)
We emphatically declare that the knowledge of God is embedded in human nature and that the Creator has implanted in it native knowledge of all things necessary and useful for salvation. It was fitting for him, for whom such great things had been prepared, to show how great His wisdom and power are, by the origin and order and beauty of the world and its perseverance, a straight path to the Creator Who called it into existence, Who surpasses all knowledge.

AGAINST THE EMPEROR JULIAN, Bk. 3
MG 76, 653

ST. JOHN OF DAMASCUS

242
(2338)
'No one has seen God at any time; the Only-begotten Son, Who is in the bosom of the Father, He has declared Him' (Jn. 1:18). The Deity, therefore, is ineffable and incomprehensible. 'For no one knows the Father, save the Son, nor the Son, save the Father' (Mt. 11:27). . . . God, however, did not leave us in absolute ignorance. For the knowledge of God's existence has been implanted by Him in all by

138

nature. This creation, too, and its maintenance, and its government, proclaim the majesty of the Divine nature.

EXPOSITION OF THE ORTHODOX· FAITH, Bk. 1, Ch. 1
MG 94, 789
NPNF IX, 1

47. Man can draw knowledge of God from the governing of providence.

ARISTIDES

Seeing that the world and all that is in it is moved by necessity, I learned that it was God Who moves and conserves it. For whatever moves is stronger that what is moved, and that which conserves is stronger than that which is conserved. Therefore I say it is God Himself Who creates and conserves all things, Who is without beginning, eternal, immortal, and needing nothing, above all changes and defects, wrath, forgetfulness, ignorance, and all other such things.

243
(110)

APOLOGY, 1
MG 96, 1108

ST. THEOPHILUS OF ANTIOCH
See No. 230.

MINUCIUS FELIX

If, upon entering some house, you found there everything kept in neatness, perfect order, and in accordance with good taste, you would no doubt assume that some master was in charge of it, one far superior to those fine possessions of his: so, in this house of the world, when you see providence, order, and law prevailing in heaven and on earth, you may rest assured that there is a Master and Author of the universe, one more beautiful than the stars themselves and the single parts of the world.

244
(269)

LETTER TO OCTAVIUS, Ch. 18
ML 3, 288
FC 352

ST. CLEMENT OF ALEXANDRIA
See No. 222.

ST. GREGORY NAZIANZEN
See No. 237.

ST. GREGORY OF NYSSA

See No. 70.

ST. AUGUSTINE

See No. 20.

48. Man can draw knowledge of God from the dictates of conscience.

ST. CLEMENT OF ALEXANDRIA

245
(411)

To know oneself has always been, so it seems, the greatest of all lessons. For, if anyone knows himself, he will know God.

CHRIST THE EDUCATOR, Bk. 3, Ch. 1
MG 8, 556
FC XXIII, 199

ORIGEN

246
(512)

In reply to which we have to say, that unless all men had naturally impressed upon their minds sound ideas of morality, the doctrine of the punishment of sinners would have been excluded by those who bring upon themselves the righteous judgments of God. It is not therefore a matter of surprise that the same God should have sown in the hearts of all men those truths which He taught by the prophets and the Saviour, in order that at the divine judgment every man may be without excuse, having the 'requirements of the law written upon his heart' (Rom. 2:15).

AGAINST CELSUS, Bk. 1, Ch. 4
MG 11, 661
ANF IV, 398

ST. AUGUSTINE

See No. 20.

49. This knowledge is somehow inborn in all men.

ST. JUSTIN MARTYR

247
(130)

But to the Father of all, who is unbegotten, there is no name given. For by whatever name He be called, He has as His elder the person who gives Him the name. But these words, Father, and God, and Creator, and Lord and Master are not names, but appellations derived from His good deeds and functions. And His Son, who alone is properly called Son, the Word, who also was with Him and was begotten before the works, when at first He created and arranged all things by Him, is called Christ, in reference to His being anointed and God's ordering all things through Him; this name itself also containing an unknown significance; as also the appellation 'God' is not a name, but an opinion implanted in the nature of men of a thing that can hardly be explained. But 'Jesus,' His name as man and Saviour, has also significance. For He was made man also, as we before said, having been conceived according to the will of God the Father, for the sake of believing men, and for the destruction of the demons.

THE SECOND APOLOGY, Ch. 6
MG 6, 453
ANF I, 190

MINUCIUS FELIX
See No. 8.

TERTULLIAN
See No. 231.

ST. CLEMENT OF ALEXANDRIA

For into all men whatever, especially those who are occupied with intellectual pursuits, a certain divine effluence has been instilled; wherefore, though reluctantly, they confess that God is one, indestructible, unbegotten, and that somewhere above in the tracts of heaven, in His own peculiar·appropriate eminence, whence He surveys all things, He has an existence true and eternal.

248
(403)

EXHORTATION TO THE HEATHEN, Ch. 6:68
MG 8, 173
ANF II, 173

For now that is clearly shown 'which was not made known to other ages, which is now revealed to the sons of men' (Eph. 3:5). For there was always a natural manifestation of the one Almighty God, among all right-thinking men; and the most, who had not quite divested themselves of shame with respect to the truth, apprehended the eternal beneficence in divine providence.

249
(425)

STROMATA, Bk. 5, Ch. 13
MG 9, 128
ANF II, 465

ORIGEN
See No. 246.

ST. GREGORY NAZIANZEN
See No. 237.

ST. JOHN CHRYSOSTOM
See No. 239.

ST. AUGUSTINE
See No. 10.

ST. CYRIL OF ALEXANDRIA

250
(2093)
Although among the worshippers of idols the reason for discerning who the Maker of all things is, is corrupt nor seems to be correct, nevertheless a necessary and innate law moves, and spontaneous knowledge excites us to believe that there is something more excellent and incomparably better for us: that is God.

See No. 241.

ON GENESIS, Bk. 1
MG 69, 36

ST. JOHN OF DAMASCUS
See No. 242.

GOD'S ESSENCE AND ATTRIBUTES

50. The essence of God is His very existence. His name is Yah-weh.

ST. HILARY

251
(857)
"I am Who am" (Ex. 3:14). I was filled with admiration at such a clear definition of God, which spoke of the incomprehensible nature in language most suitable to our human understanding. It is known that there is nothing more characteristic of God than to be, because that

142

itself which is does not belong to those things which will one day end or to those which had a beginning. But, that which combines eternity with the power of unending happiness could never not have been, nor is it possible that one day it will not be, because what is divine is not liable to destruction nor does it have a beginning. And since the eternity of God will not be untrue to itself in anything, He has revealed to us in a fitting manner this fact alone, that He is, in order to render testimony to His everlasting eternity.

ON THE TRINITY, Bk. 1, Ch. 5
ML 10, 28
FC XXV, 5

ST. GREGORY NAZIANZEN

As far then as we can reach, He Who Is, and God, are the special names of His Essence; and of these especially He Who Is, not only because when He spoke to Moses in the mount, and Moses asked what His Name was, this was what He called Himself, bidding him say to the people, "I Am has sent me" (Ex. 3:14), but also because we find that this Name is the more strictly appropriate. But we are enquiring into a Nature Whose Being is absolute and not into Being bound up with something else. But Being is in its proper sense peculiar to God, and belongs to Him entirely, and is not limited or cut short by any Before or After, for indeed in Him there is no past or future.

252
(993)

ORATIONS, No. 30
MG 36, 125
NPNF VII, 316

God always was and always is, and always will be; or rather, God always Is, for Was and Will Be are fragments of our time and of changeable nature. But He is Eternal Being; and this is the Name He gives Himself when giving the Oracles to Moses in the Mount. For in Himself He sums up and contains all Being, having neither beginning in the past nor end in the future . . . like some great Sea of Being, limitless and unbounded, transcending all conception of time and nature, only adumbrated by the mind, and that very dimly and scantily . . . not by His Essentials but by His Environment, one image being got from one source and another from another, and combined into some sort of presentation of the truth, which escapes us before we have caught, and which takes to flight before we have conceived it. . . . God, then, is boundless and hard to understand, and all that we can

253
(1015)

comprehend of Him is His boundlessness; even though one may conceive that because He is of a simple Nature He is therefore either wholly incomprehensible or perfectly comprehensible.

ORATIONS, No. 45
MG 36, 625
NPNF VII, 423

ST. AUGUSTINE

254
(1489)

And [God] said, 'Say this to the people of Israel, "I AM has sent me to you"' (Ex. 3:14). For He is such, that in comparison to Him, those things which are made have no existence. Not compared to Him, they do exist, because they are from Him; but compared to Him, they do not exist, because it is true that His Being cannot be given away, because He alone exists.

EXPOSITIONS ON THE PSALMS, 134:4
ML 37, 1741
NPNF VIII, 625

255
(1649)

But the same Scripture rarely employs those things which are spoken properly of God, and are not found in any creature; as, for instance, that which was said to Moses, 'I am Who AM'; and, 'I AM has sent me to you' (Ex. 3:14). For since both body and soul also are said in some sense to *be,* Holy Scripture certainly would not so express itself unless it meant to be understood in some special sense of the term.

ON THE TRINITY, Bk. 1, Ch. 1
ML 42, 821
NPNF III, 18

256
(1669)

Therefore neither changeable nor simple things are properly called substances. . . . But it is an impiety to say that God subsists, and is a subject in relation to His own goodness, and that this goodness is not a substance or rather essence, and that God Himself is not His own goodness, but that it is in Him as in a subject. And hence it is clear that God is improperly called substance, in order that He may be understood to be, by the more usual name essence, which He is truly and properly called; so that perhaps it is right that God alone should be called essence. For His is truly alone, because He is unchangeable; and declared this to be His own name to His servant Moses, when He says,

144

'I am Who am'; and, 'Thus shall you say unto the children of Israel: "He Who is has sent me to you"' (Ex. 3:14).

ON THE TRINITY, Bk. 7, Ch. 5
ML 42, 942
NPNF III, 111

ST. JOHN OF DAMASCUS

It appears then that the most proper of all the names given to God is 'He that is,' as He Himself said in answer to Moses on the mountain, 'Say to the sons of Israel, He that is has sent me' (Ex. 3:14). For He keeps all being in His own embrace, like a sea of essence infinite and unseen.

257
(2345)

THE ORTHODOX FAITH, Bk. 1, Ch. 9
MG 94, 836
NPNF IX, 12

51. God is per se independent existence.

ST. ATHANASIUS

For God creates, and to create is also ascribed to men; and God has being, and men are said to be, having received from God this gift also. Yet does God create as men do? or is His being as man's being? Perish the thought; we understand the terms in one sense of God, and in another of men. For God creates, in that He calls what is not into being, needing nothing thereunto; but men work some existing material, first praying, and so gaining the wit to make, from that God who has framed all things by His proper Word. And again men, being incapable of self-existence, are enclosed in place, ɪ   sist in the Word of God; but God is self-existent, enclosing aɪ   ɪgs, and enclosed by none; within all according to His own goodness ɪd power, yet outside all in His proper nature. As then men create not as God creates, as their being is not such as God's being, so men's generation is in one way, and the Son is from the Father in another. For the offspring of men are portions of their fathers, since the very nature of bodies is not uncompounded but in a state of flux, and composed of parts; . . . but God, being without parts, is Father of the Son without partition or passion; for there is neither effluence of the Immaterial, nor influx from without, as among men; and being uncompounded in nature, He is Father of One Only Son. This is why He is Only-begotten, and alone

258
(754)

145

in the Father's bosom, and alone is acknowledged by the Father to be from Him, saying, This is My beloved Son, in whom I am well pleased (Mt. 3:17). And He too is the Father's Word, from which may be understood the impassible and impartitive nature of the Father, in that not even a human word is begotten with passion or partition, much less the Word of God.

DEFENSE OF THE NICENE DEFINITION, Ch. 11
MG 25, 441
NPNF IV, 157

ST. HILARY

259
(860)

It is the Father from whom everything that exists has been formed. He is in Christ and through Christ the source of all things. Moreover, His being is in Himself and He does not derive what He is from anywhere else, but possesses what He is from Himself and in Himself. He is infinite because He Himself is not in anything and all things are within Him; He is always outside of space because He is not restricted; He is always before time because time comes from Him. . . . But, God is also present everywhere and is present in His entirety wherever He is. Thus, He transcends the realm of understanding, outside of whom nothing exists and of whom eternal being is always characteristic. This is the true nature of the mystery of God; this is the name of the impenetrable nature in the Father.

ON THE TRINITY, Bk. 2, Ch. 6
ML 10, 54
FC XXV, 39–40

260
(861)

God is invisible, ineffable, infinite. In speaking of Him, even speech is silent; the mind becomes weary in trying to fathom Him; the understanding is limited in comprehending Him. He possesses, indeed, as we have said, the name of His nature in the Father, but He is only the Father. He does not receive His Fatherhood in a human way from anywhere else. He Himself is unborn, eternal, and always possesses in Himself what He is.

I would rather think of these things about the Father than speak of them, for I am not unaware that all language is powerless to express what must be said. Moreover, in regard to what He is in Himself, that He is invisible, incomprehensible, and immortal, in these words there is admittedly an encomium of His majesty, an intimation of our thoughts, and a sort of definition of our meaning, but speech will

146

surrender to the nature and words do not portray the subject as it is. . . .
Consequently, a confession in name is defective. No matter what kind
of language is used, it will be unable to speak of God as He is and
what He is. The perfection of learning is to know God in such a
manner that, although you realize He is not unknown, you perceive
that He cannot be described. We must believe in Him, understand
Him, adore Him, and by such actions we shall make Him known.

ON THE TRINITY, Bk. 2, Ch. 6, 7

ML 10, 56

FC XXV, 41

ST. GREGORY NAZIANZEN

What among all things that exist is unoriginate? The Godhead. For no   261
one can tell the origin of God, that otherwise would be older than   (991)
God. But what is the cause of the Manhood, which for our sake God
assumed? It was surely our salvation. What else could it be?

ORATIONS, No. 30

MG 36, 105

See No. 252.   NPNF VII, 310

ST. AUGUSTINE
See No. 254.

52. The divine attributes are really the same as the divine substance.

ST. AUGUSTINE

God's substance is eternity itself, which has nothing changeable. There   262
nothing is past as if it were no longer: nothing is future, as if it existed   (1481)
not as yet. There is nothing there but, Is.

EXPOSITIONS ON THE PSALMS, 101:2:10

ML 37, 1311

NPNF VIII, 502

Since, in the human mind, to be is not the same as to be strong, or   263
prudent, or just, or temperate; for a mind can exist, and yet have   (1664)
none of these virtues. But in God to be is the same as to be strong, or

147

to be just, or to be wise, or whatever is said of that simple multiplicity, or multifold simplicity, whereby to signify His substance.

ON THE TRINITY, Bk. 6, Ch. 4
ML 42, 927
NPNF III, 100

264
(1666)
But God is truly called in manifold ways, great, good, wise, blessed, true, and whatsoever other thing seems to be said of Him not unworthily: but His greatness is the same as His wisdom; for He is not great by bulk, but by power; and His goodness is the same as His wisdom and greatness, and His truth the same as all those things; and in Him it is not one thing to be blessed, and another to be great, or wise, or true, or good, or in a word to be Himself.

ON THE TRINITY, Bk. 6, Ch. 7
ML 42, 929

See No. 256.   *NPNF* III, 101

265
(1676)
And the knowledge of God is itself also His wisdom, and His wisdom is itself His essence or substance. Because in the marvellous simplicity of that nature, it is not one thing to be wise and another to be, but to be wise is to be.

ON THE TRINITY, Bk. 15, Ch. 13
ML 42, 1076
NPNF III, 101

266
(1748)
And this Trinity is one God; and none the less simple because a Trinity. . . . it is simple, because it is what it has, with the exception of the relation of the persons to one another. For, in regard to this relation, it is true that the Father has a Son, and yet is not Himself the Son; and the Son has a Father, and is not Himself the Father.

THE CITY OF GOD, Bk. 11, Ch. 10
ML 41, 325
NPNF II, 210

53. God is utter simplicity, and admits of no composition whatever.

TERTULLIAN

267
(321)
We affirm, then, that the name of God always existed with Himself and in Himself—but not eternally so the Lord. Because the condition of the one is not the same as that of the other. God is the designation

of the substance itself, that is, of the Divinity; but Lord is [the name] not of substance, but of power. I [maintain] that the substance existed always with its own name, which is God; [the title]Lord was afterwards added, as the indication indeed of something accruing.

AGAINST HERMOGENES, Ch. 3
ML 2, 199
ANF III, 478

ST. CLEMENT OF ALEXANDRIA

Nor are any parts to be predicated of Him. For the One is indivisible; wherefore also it is infinite, not considered with reference to inscrutability, but with reference to its being without dimensions, and not having a limit. And therefore it is without form and name. And if we name it, we do not do so properly, terming it either the One, or the Good, or Mind, or Absolute Being, or Father, or God, or Creator, or Lord. We speak not as supplying His name, but for want, we use good names, in order that the mind may have these as points of support, so as not to err in other respects. For each one by itself does not express God; but all together are indicative of the power of the Omnipotent. For predicates are expressed either from what belongs to things themselves, or from their mutual relation. But none of these are admissible in reference to God. Nor any more is He apprehended by the science of demonstration. For it depends on primary and better known principles. But there is nothing antecedent to the Unbegotten.

268
(424)

STROMATA, Bk. 5, Ch. 12
MG 9, 121
ANF II, 464

ORIGEN

As, therefore, our understanding is unable of itself to behold God Himself as He is, it knows the Father of the world from the beauty of His works and the comeliness of His creatures. God, therefore, is not to be thought of as being either a body so as existing in a body, but as an uncompounded intellectual nature, admitting within Himself, no addition of any kind; so that He cannot be believed to have within Him a greater and a less, but is such that He is in all parts [μονας], and, so to speak [ἐνάς], is the mind and source from which all intellectual nature or minds takes its beginning.

269
(451)

ON FIRST PRINCIPLES, Bk. 1, Ch. 1
MG 11, 124
ANF IV, 243

ST. ATHANASIUS
See No. 258.

270
(756)

If then any man conceives God to be compound, as accident is in essence, or to have any external envelopment and to be encompassed, or as if there is anything about Him which completes the essence, so that when we say 'God,' or name 'Father,' we do not signify the invisible and incomprehensible essence, but something about it, then let them complain of the Council's stating that the Son was from the essence of God; but let them reflect, that in thus considering they utter two blasphemies; for they make God corporeal, and they falsely say that the Lord is not Son of the very Father, but of what is about Him. . . . If then the Word is not in such sense from God, as a son, genuine and natural, from a father, but only as creatures because they are framed, and as 'all things are from God,' then neither is He from the essence of the Father, nor is the Son again Son according to essence, but in consequence of virtue, as we who are called sons by grace. But if He only is from God, as a genuine Son, as He is, then the Son may reasonably be called from the essence of God. Again, the illustration of the Light and Radiance has this meaning. For the Saints have not said that the Word was related to God as fire kindled from the heat of the sun, which is commonly put out again, for this is an external work and a creature of its author, but they all preach of Him as Radiance, thereby to signify His being from the essence, proper and indivisible, and His oneness with the Father.

DEFENSE OF THE NICENE DEFINITION, Ch. 22, 23
MG 25, 453
NPNF IV, 164–165

271
(786)

But if, when we hear it said, 'I am who am' (Ex. 3:14), and, 'In the beginning God created the heaven and the earth' (Gen. 1:1), and, 'Hear, O Israel, the Lord our God is one Lord' (Deut. 6:4; Mk. 12:29), and, 'Thus says the Lord Almighty' we understand nothing else than the very simple, and blessed, and incomprehensible essence itself of Him that is (for though we be unable to master what He is, yet hearing 'Father,' and 'God,' and 'Almighty,' we understand nothing else to be meant than the very essence of Him that is).

LETTER ON THE COUNCILS OF ARIMINUM AND SELEUCIA, Ch. 35
MG 26, 753
NPNF IV, 469

ST. BASIL

[To the Caesareans, a. 360] They ought to confess that the Father is
God, the Son God, and the Holy Spirit God, as they have been taught
by the divine words, and by those who have understood them in their
highest sense. Against those who cast it in our teeth that we are
Tritheists, let it be answered that we confess one God not in number
but in nature. For everything which is called one in number is not one
absolutely, nor yet simple in nature; but God is universally confessed
to be simple and not composite.

272
(911)

LETTERS, No. 8
MG 32, 248
NPNF VIII, 116

The operations [of God] are various, and the essence simple, but
we say that we know our God from His operations, but do not undertake to approach near to His essence. His operations come down to us,
but His essence remains beyond our reach. . . . Recognize that the voice
is the voice of mockers, when they say, if you are ignorant of the
essence of God, you worship what you do not know. I do know that
He exists; what His essence is, I look at as beyond intelligence. How
then am I saved? Through faith. It is faith sufficient to know that God
exists, without knowing what He is: and 'He is a rewarder of them
that seek Him' (See Heb. 11:6). So knowledge of the divine essence
involves perception of His incomprehensibility, and the object of our
worship is not that of which we comprehend the essence, but of which
we comprehend that the essence exists.

273
(923)

LETTERS, No. 234
MG 32, 869
NPNF VIII, 274

ST. AMBROSE

God is of an uncompounded nature; nothing can be added to Him,
and that alone which is Divine has He in His nature; filling all things,
yet nowhere Himself confounded with anything; penetrating all things,
yet Himself nowhere to be penetrated; present in all His fullness at
one and the same moment, in heaven, in earth, in the deepest depth
of the sea, to sight invisible, by speech not to be declared, by feeling
not to be measured; to be followed by faith, to be adored with devotion;
so that whatsoever title excels in depth of spiritual import, in setting

274
(1266)

151

forth glory and honour, in exalting power, this you may know to belong of right to God.

TO GRATIAN ON THE CHRISTIAN FAITH, Bk. 1, Ch. 16
ML 16, 552
NPNF X, 218

ST. AUGUSTINE

275
(1660)

For in created and changeable things, that which is not said according to substance, must, by necessary alternative, be said according to accident. . . . But in God nothing is said to be according to accident, because in Him nothing is changeable; and yet everything that is said, is not said according to substance. For it is said in relation to something, as the Father in relation to the Son and the Son in relation to the Father, which is not accident; because both the one is always Father, and the other is always Son; yet not 'always,' meaning from the time when the Son was born [natus], so that the Father ceases not to be the Father because the Son never ceases to be the Son, but because the Son was *always* born, and never began to be the Son. . . . Wherefore, although to be the Father and to be the Son is different, yet their substance is not different; because they are so called, not according to substance, but according to relation, which relation, however, is not accident, because it is not changeable.

ON THE TRINITY, Bk. 5, Ch. 5
ML 42, 914

See No. 256.

NPNF III, 20

ST. CYRIL OF ALEXANDRIA

276
(2081)

We are made to [God's] image and likeness. But . . . we are at an infinite distance. For we are not simple by nature, whereas the divinity, which is perfectly simple and not composite, possesses in itself every perfection, and nothing is lacking to it.

DIALOGUES ON THE HOLY AND CONSUBSTANTIAL TRINITY, No. 1
MG 75, 673

54. *God is omnipotent.*

ST. THEOPHILUS OF ANTIOCH

277
(171)

And [God] is without beginning, because He is unbegotten; and He is unchangeable, because He is immortal. And he is called God [θεός] on account of His having placed [διὰ τὸ τεθεικέναι] all things in security afforded by Himself; and on account of [διὰ τὸ θέειν] for the same means running, and moving, and being active, and nourishing, and foreseeing, and governing, and making all things alive. But he is Lord, because He rules over the universe; Father, because he is before all things; Fashioner and Maker, because He is creator and maker of the universe; the Highest, because of His being above all; and Almighty, because He Himself rules and embraces all . . . and all things God has made out of things that were not into things that are, in order that through His works His greatness may be known and understood.

TO AUTOLYCUS, Bk. 1:4

MG 6, 1029

ANF II, 90

ST. IRENAEUS

The rule of truth which we hold, is, that there is one God Almighty   278
who made all things by His Word, and fashioned and formed, out of   (194)
that which had no existence, all things which exist. Thus says the
Scripture, to that effect: 'By the Word of the Lord were the heavens
established, and all the might of them, by the spirit of His mouth'
(Ps. 32:6). And again, 'All things were made by Him, and without
Him was nothing made' (Jn. 1:3). There is no exception or deduction
stated; but the Father made all things by him, whether visible or invisible, objects of sense or of intelligence, temporal, on account of a
certain character given them, or eternal; and these eternal things He
did not make by angels, or by any power separated from His Ennoea.
For God needs none of all these things, but is He who, by His Word
and Spirit, makes and disposes, and governs all things, and commands
all things into existence. . . . Holding, therefore, this rule, we shall
easily show, notwithstanding the great variety and multitude of their
opinions, that these men have deviated from the truth. [There follow
comments on Saturninus, Basilides, Cerinthus, the Ebionites and Nicola-
itans, Cerdo, and others.]

AGAINST HERESIES, Bk. 1, Ch. 22

MG 7, 669

ANF I, 347

TERTULLIAN

And so, [Hermogenes] even prefers Matter to God, and rather subjects   279
God to it, when he will have it that God made all things out of Matter.   (323)

153

For if He drew His resources from it for the creation of the world, Matter is already found to be the superior, inasmuch as it furnished Him with the means of effecting His works; and God is thereby clearly subjected to Matter, of which the substance was indispensable to Him. For there is no one but requires that which he makes use of; no one but is subject to the thing which he requires, for the very purpose of being able to make use of it. So, again, there is no one who, from using what belongs to another, is not inferior to him of whose property he makes use; and there is no one who imparts of his own for another's use, who is not in this respect superior to him to whose use he lends his property. On this principle, Matter itself, no doubt, was not in want of God, but rather lent itself to God, who was in want of it— rich and abundant and liberal as it was—to one who was, I suppose, too small and too weak, and too unskilful, to form what He willed out of nothing. A grand service, indeed, did it confer on God in giving Him means at the present time whereby He might be known to be God, and be called Almighty—only that He is no longer Almighty, since He is not powerful enough for this, to produce all things out of nothing.

AGAINST HERMOGENES, Ch. 8
ML 2, 204
ANF III, 481

280
(325)

This rule is required by the nature of the One-only God, who is One-only in no other way than as the sole God; and in no other way sole, than as having nothing else [co-existent] with Him. So also He will be first, because all things are after Him; and all things are after Him, because all things are by Him; and all things are by Him, because they are of nothing: so that reason coincides with the Scripture.

AGAINST HERMOGENES, Ch. 17
ML 2, 212
ANF III, 486

ST. CLEMENT OF ALEXANDRIA

281
(402)

Human art, moreover, produces houses, and ships, and cities, and pictures. And how shall I tell what God makes? Behold the whole universe; it is His work: and the heaven, and the sun, and angels, and men, are the works of His fingers. How great is the power of God! His bare volition was the creation of the universe. For God alone made it, because He alone is truly God. By the bare exercise of volition

He creates; His mere willing was followed by the springing into being of what He willed.

EXHORTATION TO THE HEATHEN, Ch. 4, No. 63

MG 8, 164

ANF II, 189–190

ST. AUGUSTINE

But assuredly [God] is rightly called omnipotent, though He can neither die nor fall into error. For He is called omnipotent on account of His doing what He wills, not on account of His suffering what He wills not; for if that should befall Him, He would by no means be omnipotent. Wherefore, He cannot do some things for the very reason that He is omnipotent.

282
(1741)

THE CITY OF GOD, Bk. 5, Ch. 10

ML 41, 152

NPNF II, 92

55. *Creatures can be elevated to the vision of God, and this is done for the angels and the blessed.*

ST. CYRIL OF JERUSALEM

What then, some man will say, is it not written, The little one's Angels do always behold the face of My Father which is in heaven? (Mt. 18:10). Yes, but the Angels see God not as He is, but as far as they themselves are capable. For it is Jesus Himself who says, Not that any man has seen the Father, save He which is of God, He has seen the Father (Jn. 6:46). The Angels therefore behold as much as they can bear, and Archangels as much as they are able; and Thrones and Dominions more than the former, but yet less than His worthiness: for with the Son the Holy Spirit alone can rightly behold Him.

283
(822)

CATECHESES, No. 6:6

MG 33, 545

NPNF VII, 34

ST. GREGORY NAZIANZEN

What God is in nature and essence, no man ever yet has discovered or can discover. Whether it will ever be discovered is a question which he who will may examine and decide. In my opinion it will be dis- covered when that within us which is godlike and divine, I mean our

284
(988)

155

mind and reason, shall have mingled with its Like, and the image shall have ascended to the Archetype, of which it has now the desire. And this I think is the solution of that vexed problem as to 'We shall know even as we are known' (See 1 Cor. 13:12). But in our present life all that comes to us is but a little effluence, and as it were a small effulgence from a great Light.

ORATIONS, No. 28:17
MG 36, 48
NPNF VII, 294

285
(989)

[The Angel] then is called spirit and fire; Spirit, as being a creature of the intellectual sphere; Fire, as being of a purifying nature; for I know that the same names belong to the First Nature. But, relatively to us at least, we must reckon the Angelic Nature incorporeal, or at any rate as nearly so as possible. Do you see how we get dizzy over this subject, and cannot advance to any point, unless it be as far as this, that we know there are Angels and Archangels, Thrones, Dominions, Princedoms, Powers, Splendours, Ascents, Intelligent Powers or Intelligences, pure natures and unalloyed, immovable to evil, or scarcely movable; ever circling in chorus round the First Cause, . . . singing the praises of the divine majesty, eternally contemplating the Eternal Glory, not that God may thereby gain an increase of glory, for nothing can be added to that which is full—to Him, who supplies good to all outside Himself—but that there may never be a cessation of blessings to these first natures after God.

ORATIONS, No. 28:31
MG 36, 72
NPNF VII, 300

ST. JOHN CHRYSOSTOM

286
(1114)

Hear what the blessed Peter says: 'it is good for us to be here' (Mt. 17:4). But if he, when he beheld some dim image of the things to come, immediately cast away all other things out of his soul, on account of the pleasure produced in it by that vision; what would any one say when the actual reality of the things is presented, when the palace is thrown open and it is permitted to gaze upon the King Himself, no longer darkly, or by means of a mirror, but face to face; no longer by means of faith, but by sight?

LETTER TO THE FALLEN THEODORE, Bk. 1, Ch. 11
MG 47, 292
NPNF IX, 100

ST. AUGUSTINE

Those holy angels come to the knowledge of God not by audible words, but by the presence to their souls of immutable truth, i.e., of the only-begotten Word of God; and they know this Word Himself, and the Father, and their Holy Spirit, and that this Trinity is indivisible, and that the three persons of it are one substance, and that there are not three Gods but one God; and this they so know, that it is better understood by them than we are by ourselves. 287 (1752)

THE CITY OF GOD, Bk. 11, Ch. 29
ML 41, 343
NPNF II, 222

GOD'S KNOWLEDGE AND PROVIDENCE

*56. God knows all things in a single gaze, not only those things
which are, but those things which will be.*

ATHENAGORAS

For if we believed that we should live only the present life, then we might be suspected of sinning, through being enslaved to flesh and blood, or overmastered by gain or carnal desire; but since we know that God is witness to what we think and what we say both by night and by day, and that He, being Himself light, sees all things in our heart, we are persuaded that when we are removed from the present life we shall live another life, better than the present one, and heavenly, not earthly (since we shall abide near God, and with God, free from all change or suffering in the soul, not as flesh, even though we shall have flesh, but as heavenly spirit), or falling with the rest, a worse one and in fire; for God has not made us as sheep or beasts of burden, a mere by-work, and that we should perish and be annihilated. On these grounds it is not likely that we should wish to do evil, or deliver ourselves over to the great Judge to be punished. 288 (166)

A PLEA FOR THE CHRISTIANS, Ch. 31
MG 6, 961
ANF II, 146

ST. IRENAEUS

289
(202)
But if any one should ask us whether every number of all the things which have been made, and which are made, is known to God, and whether every one of these [numbers] has, according to His Providence, received that special amount which it contains; and on our agreeing that such is the case, and acknowledging that not one of the things which have been, or are, or shall be made, escapes the knowledge of God, but that through His Providence every one of them has obtained its nature, and rank, and number, and special quantity . . . if, [I say] any one, on obtaining our adherence and consent to this, should proceed to reckon up the sand and pebbles of the earth, yea also the waves of the sea and the stars of heaven, and should endeavor to think out the causes of the number which he imagines himself to have discovered would not his labor be in vain, and would not such a man be justly declared mad, and destitute of reason, by all possessed of common sense?

AGAINST HERESIES, Bk. 2, Ch. 26
MG 7, 801
ANF I, 397–398

ST. CLEMENT OF ALEXANDRIA

290
(429)
For God knows all things—not those which exist, but those also which shall be—and how each thing shall be. And foreseeing the particular movements, 'He surveys all things, and hears all things,' seeing the soul naked within, and possesses from eternity the idea of each thing individually. And what applies to theatres, and to the parts of each object, in looking at, looking around, and taking in the whole in one view, applies also to God. For in one glance He views all things together, and each thing by itself; but not all things, by way of primary intent. Now, then, many things in life take their rise in some exercise of human reason, having received the kindling spark from God.

STROMATA, Bk. 6, Ch. 17
MG 9, 388
ANF II, 517

57. God foreknows everything which is future in the free will of man.

ST. JUSTIN MARTYR
See No. 71.

ST. AMBROSE

Then, speaking of the Father, He added: 'For whom it has been pre-   291
pared' (Mt. 20:23), to show that the Father also is not wont to give   (1272)
heed merely to requests, but to merits; for God is not a respecter of
persons (Acts 10:34). Wherefore also the Apostle says: 'Whom He
did foreknow, He also did predestinate' (Rom. 8:29). He did not
predestinate them before He knew them, but He did predestinate the
reward of those whose merits He foreknew.

> TO GRATIAN, ON THE CHRISTIAN FAITH, Bk. 5, Ch. 6
> *ML* 16, 665
> *NPNF* X, 294

ST. JEROME

This is what Marcion asks, and the whole pack of heretics who mutilate   292
the Old Testament, and have mostly spun an argument something   (1405)
like this: Either God knew that man, placed in Paradise, would
transgress His command, or He did not know. If He knew, man is
not to blame, who could not avoid God's foreknowledge, but He Who
created him such that he could not escape the knowledge of God. If He
did not know, in stripping Him of foreknowledge you also take away
His divinity. Upon the same showing God will be deserving of blame
for choosing Saul, who was to prove one of the worst of kings. And
the Saviour must be convicted either of ignorance, or of unrighteousness, inasmuch as He said in the Gospel, 'Did I not choose you the
twelve, and one of you is a devil?' (Jn. 6:71). Ask Him why He
chose Judas, a traitor? Why He entrusted to him the bag when He
knew that he was a thief? Shall I tell you the reason? God judges the
present, not the future. He does not make use of His foreknowledge
to condemn a man though He knows that he will hereafter displease
Him; but such is His goodness and unspeakable mercy that He chooses
a man who, He perceives, will meanwhile be good, and who, He knows,
will turn out badly, thus giving him the opportunity of being converted and repenting. . . . For Adam did not sin because God knew
that he would do so; but God, inasmuch as He is God, foreknew what
Adam would do of his own free choice.

> DIALOGUE AGAINST THE PELAGIANS, Bk. 3, Ch. 6
> *ML* 23, 575
> *NPNF* VI, 474

ST. AUGUSTINE

293
(1740)

For one who is not prescient of all future things is not God. Wherefore our wills also have just so much power as God willed and foreknew that they should have; and therefore whatever power they have, they have it within most certain limits; and whatever they are to do, they are most assuredly to do, for He whose foreknowledge is infallible foreknew that they would have the power to do it, and would do it.

THE CITY OF GOD, Bk. 5, Ch. 9

ML 41, 152

NPNF II, 74

294
(1742)

It is not the case, therefore, that because God foreknew what would be in the power of our wills, there is for that reason nothing in the power of our wills. For he who foreknew this did not foreknow nothing. Moreover, if He who foreknew what would be in the power of our wills did not foreknow nothing, but something, assuredly, even though He did foreknow, there is something in the power of our wills. Therefore we are by no means compelled, either, retaining the prescience of God, to take away the freedom of the will, to deny that He is prescient of future things, which is impious. But we embrace both. We faithfully and sincerely confess both. . . . For a man does not therefore sin because God foreknew that he would sin. Nay, it cannot be doubted but that it is the man himself who sins when he does sin, because He, whose foreknowledge is infallible, foreknew not that fate, or fortune, or something else would sin, but that the man himself would sin, who, if he wills not, sins not.

THE CITY OF GOD, Bk. 5, Ch. 10

ML 41, 153

NPNF II, 93

295
(1928)

Wherefore, God would have been willing to preserve even the first man in that state of salvation in which he was created, and after he had begotten sons to remove him at a fit time, without the intervention of death, to a better place, where he should have been not only free from sin, but free even from the desire of sinning, if He had foreseen that man would have the steadfast will to persist in the state of innocence in which he was created. But as He foresaw that man would make a bad use of his free-will, that is, would sin, God arranged His own designs rather with a view to do good to man even in his sinful-

160

ness, that thus the good will of the Omnipotent might not be made void by the evil of man, but might be fulfilled in spite of it.

ON FAITH, HOPE, AND LOVE (ENCHIRIDION), Ch. 104
ML 40, 281
NPNF III, 271

ST. JOHN OF DAMASCUS

We ought to understand that while God knows all things beforehand, yet He does not predetermine all things. For He knows beforehand those things that are in our power, but He does not predetermine them. For it is not His will that there should be wickedness nor does He choose to compel virtue. So that predetermination is the work of the divine command based on foreknowledge. But on the other hand God predetermines those things which are not within our power in accordance with His prescience. For already God in His prescience has prejudged all things in accordance with His goodness and justice.

Bear in mind, too, that virtue is a gift from God implanted in our nature, and that He Himself is the source and cause of all good, and without His co-operation and help we cannot will or do any good thing. But we have it in our power either to abide in virtue and follow God, Who calls us into ways of virtue, or to stray from the paths of virtue.

EXPOSITION OF THE ORTHODOX FAITH, Bk. 2, Ch. 30
MG 94, 969
NPNF IX, 240

296
(2359)

58. *God has providence for all of His creatures.*

ST. IRENAEUS
See No. 289.

ST. CLEMENT OF ALEXANDRIA
See No. 222.

ST. GREGORY NAZIANZEN

Believe that all that is in the world, both all that is seen and all that is unseen, was made out of nothing by God, and is governed by the Providence of its Creator, and will receive a change to a better state. . . . Believe that the Son of God, the Eternal Word, Who was begotten

297
(1014)

of the Father before all time and without body, was in these latter days for your sake made also Son of Man, born of the Virgin Mary ineffably and stainlessly (for nothing can be stained where God is, and by which salvation comes), in His own Person at once entire Man and perfect God, for the sake of the entire sufferer, that He may bestow salvation on your whole being, having destroyed the whole condemnation of your sins: impassible in His Godhead, passible in that which He assumed; as much Man for your sake as you are made God for His. Believe that for us sinners He was led to death; was crucified and buried, so far as to taste of death; and that He rose again the third day, and ascended into heaven, that He might take you with Him who were lying low; and that He will come again with His glorious Presence to judge the quick and the dead; no longer flesh, nor yet without a body, according to the laws which He alone knows of a more godlike body, that He may be seen by those who pierced Him, and on the other hand may remain as God without carnality.

ORATIONS, No. 40:45
MG 36, 424
NPNF VII, 377

SALVIFIC WILL, PREDESTINATION, REPROBATION

59. *God wants all men to be saved.*

ST. HIPPOLYTUS

298
(389)

For He casts away none of His servants as unworthy of the divine mysteries. . . . But He seeks all, and desires to save all, wishing to make all the children of God, and calling all the saints unto one perfect man. For there is also one Son (or Servant) of God, by whom we too, receiving the regeneration through the Holy Spirit, desire to come all unto one perfect and heavenly man. For whereas the Word of God was without flesh, He took upon Himself the holy flesh by the holy Virgin, and prepared a robe which He wove for Himself, like a bridegroom, in the sufferings of the cross, in order that by uniting His own power with our mortal body, and by mixing the incorruptible with the corruptible, and the strong with the weak, He might save perishing man. . . and the workers are the patriarchs and prophets who weave the fair, long, perfect tunic for Christ; and the Word passing through these, like the combs (or rods), completes through them that which His Father wills.

ON CHRIST AND ANTICHRIST, Ch. 3

MG 10, 732

ANF V, 205

ST. JOHN CHRYSOSTOM

'According to the good pleasure of His will' (Eph. 1:5). That is to say, because He earnestly willed it. This is, as one might say, His earnest desire. For the word 'good pleasure' everywhere means the precedent will, for there is also another will. As for example, the first will is that sinners should not perish; the second will is, that, if men become wicked, they shall perish. For surely it is not by necessity that He punishes them, but because He wills it. You may see something of the sort even in the words of Paul, where he says, 'I would that all men were even as I myself' (1 Cor. 7:7). And again, 'I desire that the younger widows marry, bear children' (1 Tim. 5:14). By 'good pleasure' then he means the first will, the earnest will, the will accompanied with earnest desire . . . what Paul means to say then is this, God earnestly aims at, earnestly desires, our salvation.

299
(1202)

LETTER TO THE EPHESIANS, Ch. 1:2

MG 62, 13

NPNF XIII, 52

ST. AMBROSE

For it was clear that the laborers could not be saved without a remedy, and so he distributed medicine to the sick, he brought to all the strength of health, so that, whoever should perish should ascribe to himself the causes of his death since he was unwilling to be cured, since he had the remedy by which he could avoid death. However the clear mercy of Christ is preached in all things, from the fact that those who perish do so from their own neglect. Those on the other hand who are saved are liberated through Christ's purpose, Who will have all men to be saved and come to a knowledge of the truth (1 Tim. 2:4).

300
(1279)

ON CAIN AND ABEL, Bk. 2, Ch. 3

ML 14, 346

FC XLII, 412

163

ST. JOHN OF DAMASCUS

301
(2358)

Also one must bear in mind that God's original wish was that all should be saved and come to His Kingdom (1 Tim. 2:4). For it was not for punishment that He formed us but to share in His goodness, inasmuch as He is a good God. But inasmuch as He is a just God, His will is that sinners should suffer punishment.

The first then is called God's antecedent will and pleasure, and springs from Himself, while the second is called God's consequent will and permission, and has its origin in us. . . . But of actions that are in our hands the good ones depend on His antecedent good-will and pleasure, while the wicked ones depend neither on His antecedent nor on His consequent will, but are a concession to free-will.

EXPOSITION OF THE ORTHODOX FAITH, Bk. 2, Ch. 29
MG 94, 968
NPNF IX, 42

60. God "predestined some to eternal life, most merciful Dispenser of grace."

ST. AUGUSTINE

302
(1882)

I simply hold what I see the apostle has most plainly taught us: That owing to one man all pass into condemnation who are born of Adam (Rom. 5:18) unless they are born again in Christ, even as He has appointed them to be regenerated, before they die in the body, whom He predestinated to everlasting life, as the most merciful bestower of grace; while to those whom He has predestinated to eternal death, He is also the most righteous awarder of punishment, not only on account of the sins which they add in the indulgence of their own will, but also because of their original sin, even if, as in the case of infants, they add nothing thereto. Now this is my definite view on that question, so that the hidden things of God may keep their secret, without impairing my own faith.

ON THE SOUL AND ITS ORIGIN, Bk. 4, Ch. 11
ML 44, 533
NPNF V, 361

303
(1951)

But because [Adam] forsook God of his free will, he experienced the just judgment of God, that with his whole race, which being as yet all placed in him had sinned with him, he should be condemned. For

as many of this race as are delivered by God's grace are certainly
delivered from the condemnation in which they are already held bound.
Whence, even if none should be delivered, no one could justly blame
the judgment of God. That, therefore, in comparison of those that
perish *few,* but in their absolute number *many,* are delivered, is effected
by grace, is effected freely: thanks must be given, because it is effected,
so that no one may be lifted up as of his own deservings, but that
every mouth may be stopped, and he that glories may glory in the
Lord (1 Cor. 1:31).

ON REBUKE AND GRACE, Ch. 10:28
ML 44, 933
NPNF V, 482

For what is more true than that Christ foreknew who should believe on Him, and at what times and places they should believe? But
whether by the preaching of Christ to themselves by themselves they
were to have faith, or whether they would receive it by God's gift,
—that is, whether God only foreknew them, or also predestinated them,
I did not at that time think it necessary to inquire or to discuss. Therefore what I said, 'that Christ willed to appear to men at that time, and
that His doctrine should be preached among them when He knew, and
where He knew, that there were those who would believe on Him'
("Letter 102"; see No. 307), may also thus be said, 'That Christ
willed to appear to men at that time, and that His gospel should be
preached among those, whom He knew, and where He knew, that
there were those who had been elected in Himself before the foundation of the world' (Eph. 1:4).

ON THE PREDESTINATION OF THE SAINTS, Ch. 9:18
ML 44, 974
NPNF V, 507

304
(1985)

Therefore they were elected before the foundation of the world with
that predestination in which God foreknew what He Himself would do;
but they were elected out of the world with that calling whereby God
fulfilled that which He predestinated. For whom He predestinated,
them He also called, with that calling which is according to the purpose. Not others, therefore, but those whom He predestinated, them He
also called; nor others, but those whom He so called, them ·He also
justified; nor others, but those whom He predestinated, called, and
justified, them He also glorified (Rom. 8:30). . . . By choosing them,
therefore, He makes them rich in faith, as He makes them heirs of the

305
(1988)

kingdom; because He is rightly said to choose that in them, in order to make in them what He chose them for.*

ON THE PREDESTINATION OF THE SAINTS, Ch. 17:34

ML 44, 986

NPNF V, 515

306
(2002)

See now how foreign it is from the truth to deny that perseverance even to the end of this life is the gift of God; since He Himself puts an end to this life when He wills, and if He puts an end before a fall that is threatening, He makes the man to persevere even unto the end. But more marvellous and more manifest to believers is the largess of God's goodness, that this grace is given even to infants, although there is no obedience at that age to which it may be given.

ON THE GIFT OF PERSEVERANCE, Ch. 17:41

ML 45, 1018

NPNF V, 542

61. Predestination for faith and justification is completely gratuitous.

ST. AUGUSTINE

307
(1427)

What answer could the [pagans] make if, leaving out of view that depth of the wisdom and knowledge of God within which it may be that some other divine purpose lies much more deeply hidden, and without prejudging the other reasons possibly existing, which are fit subjects for patient study by the wise, we confine ourselves, for the sake of brevity in this discussion, to the statement of this one position, that it pleased Christ to appoint the time in which He would appear and the persons among whom His doctrine was to be proclaimed, according to His knowledge of the times and places in which men would believe on Him?

LETTERS, No. 102:14

ML 33, 375

FC XVIII, 157

308
(1428)

The saving grace of this religion, the only true one, through which alone true salvation is truly promised, has never been refused to anyone who was worthy of it, and whoever lacked it was unworthy of it.

* *"Recte quippe in iis hoc eligere dicitur, quod ut in iis faciat, eos eligit."*

From the beginning of human history to the end, this is made known
for the reward of some and the punishment of others.

LETTERS, No. 102:15
ML 33, 376
FC XVIII, 159

With a brevity as concise as his authority is compelling, the blessed   309
Apostle explains the reason for the creation of those also of whom the   (1447)
Creator knows that they are to belong to damnation, not to grace. . . .
But it would seem unjust that vessels of wrath should be made unto
destruction (see Rom. 9:22) if the whole lump of clay had not been
condemned in Adam. The fact that men become vessels of wrath at
birth is due to the penalty deserved, but that they become vessels of
mercy at their second birth is due to an undeserved grace.

LETTERS, No. 190:3
ML 33, 859
FC XXX, 276

For had He chosen us on the ground that He foreknew that we   310
should be good, then would He also have foreknown that we would   (1837)
not be the first to make choice of Him. For in no other way could we
possibly be good: unless, indeed, one could be called good who has
never made good his choice. What was it then that He chose in those
who were not good? For they were not chosen because of their goodness, inasmuch as they could not be good without being chosen. Otherwise grace is no more grace, if we maintain the priority of merit (Rom.
11:6).

ON THE GOSPEL OF ST. JOHN, Tr. 86
ML 35, 1851
NPNF VII, 353

And, consequently, both those who have not heard the gospel, and   311
those who, having heard it and been changed by it for the better, have   (1946)
not received perseverance, and those who, having heard the gospel,
have refused to come to Christ, that is, to believe on Him, since He
Himself says, 'No man comes to me, except it were given him, of my
Father' (Jn. 6:66), and those who by their tender age were unable to
believe, but might be absolved from original sin by the sole laver of
regeneration, and yet have not received this laver, and have perished in

death: are not made to differ from the lump which it is plain is condemned, as all go from one into condemnation.

ON REBUKE AND GRACE, Ch. 7:12
ML 44, 923
See No. 304.   NPNF VII, 476

312
(1986)

Moreover, that which I said, 'That the salvation of this religion has never been lacking to him who was worthy of it, and that he to whom it was lacking was not worthy,'—if it be discussed and it be asked whence any man can be worthy, there are not wanting those who say— by human will. But we say, by divine grace or predestination. Further, between grace and predestination there is only this difference, that predestination is the preparation for grace, while grace is the donation itself.

ON THE PREDESTINATION OF THE SAINTS, Ch. 10:19
ML 44, 974
NPNF V, 507

313
(1989)

'Therefore,' says the Pelagian, 'He foreknew who would be holy and immaculate by the choice of free will, and on that account elected them before the foundation of the world in that same foreknowledge of His in which He foreknew that they would be such. Therefore He elected them,' says he, 'before they existed, predestinating them to be children whom He foreknew to be holy and immaculate. Certainly He did not make them so; nor did He foresee that He would make them so, but that they would be so.' Let us, then, look into the words of the apostle . . . 'Even as He has chosen us in Himself before the foundation of the world, that we should be holy and unspotted' (Eph. 1:4). Not, then, because we were to be so, but that we might be so. Assuredly it is certain, —assuredly it is manifest. Certainly we were to be such for the reason that He has chosen us, predestinating us to be such by His grace . . . 'that He might show to us the mystery of His will, according to His good pleasure' (ib. 9). In this mystery of His will, He placed the riches of His grace, according to His good pleasure, not according to ours, which could not possibly be good unless He Himself according to His own good pleasure, should aid it to become so.

ON THE PREDESTINATION OF THE SAINTS, Ch. 18:36
ML 44, 987
NPNF V, 515

For He chose us, not because we believed, but that we might believe,
lest we should be said first to have chosen Him, and so His word be
false (which be it far from us to think possible), 'You have not
chosen me, but I have chosen you' (Jn. 15:16). Neither are we called
because we believed, but that we may believe; and by that calling which
is without repentance it is effected and carried through that we should
believe.

314
(1990)

> ON THE PREDESTINATION OF THE SAINTS, Ch. 19:38
> *ML* 44, 988
> *NPNF* V, 517

It is therefore false that the dead are judged in respect also of those
things which they would have done if the gospel had reached them
when they were alive. And if this is false, there is no ground for saying,
concerning infants who perish because they die without baptism, that
this happens in their case deservedly, because God foreknew that if
they should live and the gospel should be preached to them, they
would hear it with unbelief. It remains, therefore, that they are kept
bound by original sin alone, and for this alone they go into condemnation; and we see that in others in the same case this is not remitted,
except by the gratuitous grace of God in regeneration.

315
(1997)

> ON THE GIFT OF PERSEVERANCE, Ch. 9:23
> *ML* 45, 1006
> *NPNF* V, 533–534

So that what we see in those whose deliverance is preceded by no
good deservings of theirs, and in those whose condemnation is only
preceded by original sin, common alike to both, —this we by no means
shrink from as occurring in the case of grown-up people, that is,
because we do not think either that grace is given to any one according
to his own merits, or that any one is punished except for his own
merits.

316
(1998)

> ON THE GIFT OF PERSEVERANCE, Ch. 11:25
> *ML* 45, 1008
> *NPNF* V, 535

There are some, moreover, who either do not pray at all, or pray
coldly, because, from the Lord's words, they have learnt that God knows
what is necessary for us before we ask it of Him. Must the truth of
this declaration be given up, or shall we think that it should be erased
from the gospel because of such people? Nay, since it is manifest that

317
(2001)

God has prepared some things to be given even to those who do not pray for them, such as the beginning of faith, and other things not to be given except to those who pray for them, such as perseverance even unto the end, certainly he who thinks that he has this latter from himself does not pray to have it. Therefore, we must take care lest, while we are afraid of exhortation growing lukewarm, prayer should be stifled and arrogance stimulated.

ON THE GIFT OF PERSEVERANCE, Ch. 16:39
ML 45, 1017
NPNF V, 541

V.

The Triune God

Although man can attain to a knowledge of the one true God by reason alone, nevertheless the ineffable mystery of the most Holy Trinity can only be known through revelation. There are three distinct divine Persons in God, who are also one divine substance. Nor can these three Persons be reduced to merely one Person, as the modalists, monarchians, Sabellians, and Patripassians attempted to do.

As early as the end of the first century the triune nature of God had been stated by St. Clement of Rome, and this was affirmed by St. Ignatius of Antioch in the first part of the second century, followed by St. Justin Martyr shortly afterwards, and Athenagoras and St. Theophilus of Antioch in the late second century. By this time St. Irenaeus was busily engaged in his *Against Heresies* to offset the unacceptable opinions of Marcion and the Gnostics. He designates by name in the first book of this celebrated work, all those whose teaching he intends to refute, and what is at stake here is the divinity of Christ against the notion that he was a mere man, —the basic position of the dynamic or adoptionist monarchians.

The Patripassians or modal monarchians admitted the divinity of Christ, but allowed for a single Person in God, saying that the Father had become man in Jesus Christ and hence had truly suffered. St. Hippolytus (c. 160–235) attacked this position in his *Against the Heresy of Noetus,* and Tertullian wrote copiously and vehemently against Praxeas for the same reason.

As contrasted to the tritheists who held for three gods, the Sabellians held that God was one hypostasis with three *prosopa* or masks

171

which He had used in his three modes of revelation, —as Father in creation, as Son in redemption, and as Holy Spirit in sanctification. Both Pope Callistus (217–222) and Pope Dionysius (259–268) condemned Sabellianism.

By the time of the fourth century, the denial of Catholic Trinitarian doctrine had become more subtle. The Arians denied that the Logos had existed from all eternity, but asserted that there had been a time when He was not. Therefore, while there are indeed three Persons in the Trinity, the second and third Persons are not consubstantial with the first. It was the life work of St. Athenasius to combat this heretical point of view, and he is the most articulate writer on the Trinity in the Nicene period. Almost equally famous is St. Hilary of Poitiers who wrote a long book on the Trinity in the middle of the fourth century. For such a vigorous defense he suffered banishment.

The Semi-Arians compromised between the strict doctrine of Arius and that of the Nicene definition by saying that the Son and the Holy Spirit were *like* the Father; they are sometimes called Homoeans. The Council of Nicea (325) condemned Arianism, and the Council of Rome (382) condemned the errors of the Macedonians who maintained that the Holy Spirit was a creature like the angels. In later times the Church equated more precisely the three divine Persons with the one divine nature against the abbot Joachim, and upheld against the Greeks the famous *filioque* clause which asserts that the Holy Spirit proceeds from both the Father and the Son.

Writers like St. John Chrysostom (later fourth century) and Origen feel that the Old Testament contains hints of the Trinitarian doctrine, and as early a writer as the Shepherd of Hermas declares that the Father, Son, and Holy Spirit are distinct, and yet one. This is repeatedly affirmed by St. Athanasius in the fourth century, as well as by St. Basil, St. Ambrose, and St. Augustine. Tertullian clearly holds for three persons in the unity of the one nature, but it is St. Basil who carefully works out a formula by which there is both an acknowledgment of the hypostases and the true dogma of the monarchy is not lost. This position is amply fortified by St. Gregory Nazianzen and receives some treatment from St. Gregory of Nyssa. St. Irenaeus and especially Lactantius at the beginning of the fourth century and a host of others remind us that after all, the Trinity is a mystery.

Various fathers tell us that the Father alone does not proceed. All insist that the Son was not made but was truly born of the Father, and that his generation is voluntary and natural. They affirm that He is both co-eternal and consubstantial with the Father, and give to him such names as Wisdom, Splendor, Image of the Father, etc.

The doctrines of the Holy Spirit do not come into true focus until the Nicene and post-Nicene period. Here the Cappadocian Fathers are prominent in their attempt to help clarify the terminology of hypostasis and ousía. The Holy Spirit is denominated the Image of the Son, and Tertullian is the first to declare that He proceeds from the Father through the Son. Procession is distinguished from generation by the time of the fourth century, and the various operations of the three Persons are distinctly elaborated.

All of these various strands come together and are integrated in a complete and meaningful whole by St. Augustine whose monumental work *On the Trinity* is a summary statement of Trinitarian doctrine. A similar synthesis is presented by St. John of Damascus in the East, but not until the eighth century. By the end of the classical period the lines are fairly well drawn and guideposts for future speculation firmly established.

THE EXISTENCE AND NATURE OF THE TRINITY

62. *From the first three centuries it is clear from tradition that God is triune.*

ST. CLEMENT OF ROME
See No. 103.

Do we not have one God and one Christ, and one Spirit of Grace poured out upon us? And is there not one calling in Christ?

318
(23)

LETTER TO THE CORINTHIANS, Ch. 46
MG 1, 304
FC I, 45

319
(28)

For, as God lives and the Lord Jesus Christ lives and the Holy Spirit, the faith and hope of the elect, so shall he who with humility of mind, and ready gentleness, and without turning back, has performed the decrees and commandments given by God be enrolled and chosen among the number of those who are saved through Jesus Christ, through whom is the glory to Him forever and ever. Amen.

LETTER TO THE CORINTHIANS, Ch. 58
F 1, 172
FC I, 54

ST. IGNATIUS OF ANTIOCH

320
(40)

I have learned that some strangers holding bad doctrine have passed your way, but that you have not allowed them to sow their seed among you and have stopped your ears lest you should receive what they sowed. Like the stones of a temple, cut for a building of God the Father, you have been lifted up to the top by the crane of Jesus Christ, which is the Cross, and the rope of the Holy Spirit. For your faith has drawn you up and charity has been the road leading to God. You are all fellow pilgrims, carrying with you God and His temple; you are bearers of Christ and of holy offerings, decked out in the commandments of Jesus Christ.

LETTER TO THE EPHESIANS, Ch. 9
MG 5, 652
FC I, 90–91

THE MARTYRDOM OF ST. POLYCARP

321
(80)

For this and for all benefits I praise You, I bless You, I glorify You, through the eternal and heavenly High Priest, Jesus Christ, Your beloved Son, through whom be to you with Him and the Holy Spirit glory, now and for all the ages to come. Amen.   14:3

MG 5, 1040
FC I, 158

ARISTIDES
See No. 87.

ST. JUSTIN MARTYR

322
(113)

Hence are we called atheists. And we confess that we are atheists, so far as gods of this sort are concerned, but not with respect to the most true God, the Father of righteousness and temperance and the other virtues, who is free from all impurity. But both Him, and the Son

174

(who came forth from Him and taught us these things, and the host of the other good angels who follow and are made like to Him), and the prophetic Spirit, we worship and adore, knowing them in reason and truth, and declaring without grudging to every one who wishes to learn, as we ourselves have been taught.

FIRST APOLOGY, Ch. 6
MG 6, 336
ANF I, 164

What sober-minded man, then, will not acknowledge that we are not atheists, worshipping as we do the Maker of this universe? . . . Our teacher of these things is Jesus Christ, who also was born for this purpose, and was crucified under Pontius Pilate, procurator of Judea, in the times of Tiberius Caesar; and that we reasonably worship Him, having learned that He is the Son of the true God Himself, holding Him in the second place, and the prophetic Spirit in the third, we will prove. For they proclaim our madness to consist in this, that we give to a crucified man a place second to the unchangeable and eternal God, the Creator of all; for they do not discern the mystery that is herein, to which, as we make it plain to you, we pray you to give heed.

323
(117)

FIRST APOLOGY, Ch. 13
MG 6, 345
ANF I, 166

As many as are persuaded and believe that what we teach and say is true, and undertake to be able to live accordingly, are instructed to pray and to entreat God with fasting, for the remission of their sins that are past, we praying and fasting with them. They then are brought by us where there is water, and are regenerated in the same manner in which we were ourselves regenerated. For, in the name of God, the Father and Lord of the universe, and of our Saviour Jesus Christ, and of the Holy Spirit, they then receive the washing with water. . . . The reason for this we have received from the Apostles.

324
(126)

FIRST APOLOGY, Ch. 61
MG 6, 420
ANF I, 183

ATHENAGORAS

For, as we acknowledge a God, and a Son his Logos, and a Holy Spirit, united in essence, —the Father, the Son, the Spirit, because the Son is the Intelligence, Reason, Wisdom, of the Father, and the Spirit

325
(165)

175

an effluence, as light from fire; so also do we apprehend the existence of other powers, which exercise dominion about matter, and by means of it.

A PLEA FOR THE CHRISTIANS, Ch. 24
MG 6, 945
ANF II, 141

ST. THEOPHILUS OF ANTIOCH

326
(180)

The three days which were before the luminaries, are types of the Trinity, of God, and His Word, and His wisdom.*

TO AUTOLYCUS, Ch. 2:18
MG 6, 1077
ANF II, 101

ST. IRENAEUS
See No. 211.

327
(235)

It was not angels, therefore, who made us, nor who formed us, neither had angels power to make an image of God, nor any one else, except the Word of the Lord, nor any Power remotely distant from the Father of all things. For God did not stand in need of these [beings], in order to accomplish what He had Himself determined beforehand with Himself should be done, as if He did not possess His own hands. For with Him were always present the Word and Wisdom, the Son and the Spirit, by whom and in whom, freely and spontaneously, He made all things, to whom also He speaks, saying, 'Let Us make man after Our image and likeness' (Gen. 1:26).

AGAINST HERESIES, Bk. 4, Ch. 20
MG 7, 1032
ANF I, 487

328
(256)

And thus one God the Father is declared, who is above all, and through all, and in all. The Father is indeed above all, and He is the Head of Christ; but the Word is through all things, and is Himself the Head of the Church; while the Spirit is in us all, and He is the living water, which the Lord grants to those who rightly believe in Him, and love Him, and who know that 'there is one Father, who is above all, and through all, and in us all' (Eph. 4:6).

AGAINST HERESIES, Bk. 5, Ch. 18
MG 7, 1173
ANF I, 546

* This seems to be the earliest use of the word *Trinity*.

TERTULLIAN

For the law of baptizing has been imposed, and the formula prescribed: 'Go,' says Christ, 'teach the nations, baptizing them in the name of the Father, and of the Son, and of the Holy Spirit' (Mt. 28:19).

329
(307)

ON BAPTISM, Ch. 13
ML 1, 1215

See No. 201.

ANF III, 676

Bear always in mind that this is the rule of faith which I profess; by it I testify that the Father, and the Son, and the Spirit are inseparable from each other, and so will you know in what sense this is said. Now, observe, my assertion is that the Father is one, and the Son one, and the Spirit one, and that They are distinct from Each Other. This statement is taken in a wrong sense by every uneducated as well as every perversely disposed person, as if it predicated a diversity, in such a sense as to imply a separation among the Father, and the Son, and the Spirit. I am moreover, obliged to say this, when (extolling the Monarchy at the expense of the Economy) they contend for the identity of the Father and Son and Spirit, that it is not by way of diversity that the Son differs from the Father, but by distribution: it is not by division that He is different, but by distinction; because the Father is not the same as the Son, since they differ one from the other in the mode of their being. For the Father is the entire substance, but the Son is a derivation and portion of the whole, as He himself acknowledges: 'My Father is greater than I' (Jn. 14:28). In the Psalm His inferiority is described as being 'a little lower than the angels.' Thus the Father is distinct from the Son, being greater than the Son, inasmuch as He who begets is one, and He who is begotten is another; He, too, who sends is one, and He who is sent is another; and He, again, who makes is one, and He through whom the thing is made is another. Happily the Lord Himself employs this expression of the person of the Paraclete, so as to signify not a division or severance, but a disposition (of mutual relations in the Godhead); for He says, 'I will pray the Father, and He shall send you another Comforter. . . . even the Spirit of truth' (Jn. 14:16),—thus making the Paraclete distinct from Himself, even as we say that the Son is also distinct from the Father; so that He showed a third degree in the Paraclete, as we believe

330
(376)

the second degree is in the Son, by reason of the order observed in the *Economy.*

AGAINST PRAXEAS, Ch. 9

ML 2, 164

ANF III, 6

331
(377)

We do indeed definitively declare that Two Beings are God, the Father and the Son, and, with the addition of the Holy Spirit, even Three, according to the principle of the [divine] economy, which introduces number, in order that the Father may not, as you perversely infer, be Himself believed to have been born and to have suffered, which it is not lawful to believe, forasmuch as it has not been so handed down. That there are, however, two Gods or two Lords, is a statement which at no time proceeds out of our mouth: not as if it were untrue that the Father is God, and the Son is God, and the Holy Spirit is God, and each is God; but because in earlier times Two were actually spoken of as God, and two as Lord, that when Christ should come He might be both acknowledged as God and designated as Lord, being the Son of Him who is both God and Lord.

AGAINST PRAXEAS, Ch. 13

ML 2, 169

ANF III, 608

ST. CLEMENT OF ALEXANDRIA

332
(414)

The Word does all these things, and teaches all things, and uses all things to educate us. . . . So great is the Word, this Educator, the Creator of the world and of man, become the Educator of the world, also, in His own person. By His command both of us are united together, awaiting His judgment. . . . O Educator, be gracious to your children, O Educator, Father, Guide of Israel, Son and Father, both one, Lord. . . . Grant . . . we may sing eternal thanksgiving to the one only Father and Son, Son and Father, Educator and Teacher with the Holy Spirit. All things are for the One, in whom are all things, through whom, being the One are all things, through whom eternity is, of whom all men are members, to whom is glory and all the ages.

CHRIST THE EDUCATOR, Bk. 3, Ch. 12

MG 8, 677

FC XXIII, 274

ORIGEN
See No. 212.

We however believe that there are three persons, Father, Son and Holy   333
Spirit, and at the same time we believe nothing to be uncreated but the   (479)
Father. We therefore as the more pious and the truer course, admit that
all things were made by the Logos, and that the Holy Spirit is the
most excellent and the first in order of all that was made by the
Father through the Word.

COMMENTARY ON JOHN, Bk. 2, Ch. 10
MG 14, 128

ST. CORNELIUS I
See No. 122.

ST. CYPRIAN

[To Jubianus, a. 256] For if any one could be baptized among heretics,   334
certainly he could also obtain remission of sins. If he attained remission   (596)
of sins, he was also sanctified. If he was sanctified, he also was made the
temple of God. I ask, of what God? If of the Creator; he could not be,
because he has not believed in Him. If of Christ; he could not become
His temple, since he denies that Christ is God. If of the Holy Spirit;
since the three are one, how can the Holy Spirit be at peace with him
who is the enemy either of the Son or of the Father?

LETTERS, No. 73
ML 3, 1117
ANF V, 382

ST. GREGORY THAUMATURGUS

There is one God, the Father of the living Word, who is His subsistent   335
Wisdom and Power and Eternal Image: perfect Begetter of the perfect   (611)
Begotten, Father of the only-begotten Son. There is one Lord, Only
of the Only, God of God, Image and Likeness of Deity, Efficient Word,
Wisdom comprehensive of the constitution of all things, and Power
formative of the whole creation, true Son of true Father, Invisible of
Invisible, and Incorruptible of Incorruptible, and Immortal of Immortal, and Eternal of Eternal. And there is One Holy Spirit, having
His subsistence from God, and being made manifest by the Son to
men: Image of the Son, Perfect Image of the Perfect; Life, the Cause
of the living; Holy Fount; Sanctity, the Supplier, or Leader, of Sanctification; in whom is manifested God the Father, who is above all and in

all, and God the Son, who is through all. There is a perfect Trinity, in glory and eternity and sovereignty, neither divided nor estranged. Wherefore there is nothing either created or in servitude in the Trinity; nor anything superinduced, as if at some former period it was non-existent, and at some later period it was introduced. And thus neither was the Son ever wanting to the Father, nor the Spirit to the Son; but without variation and without change, the Same Trinity abides forever.

DECLARATION OF FAITH
MG 10, 984
ANF VI, 7

APHRAATES

336
(681)

This is faith: when a man believes in God the Lord of all Who made the heavens and the earth and the seas and all that is in them; and He made Adam in His image; and He gave the Law to Moses; He sent of His Spirit upon the prophets; He sent moreover His Christ into the world. Furthermore that a man should believe in the resurrection of the dead; and should furthermore also believe in the sacrament of baptism. This is the faith of the Church of God.

DEMONSTRATIONS, No. 1
PS 1, 43
NPNF XIII, 352

ST. AUGUSTINE

337
(1650)

All those Catholic expounders of the divine Scriptures, both Old and New, whom I have been able to read, who have written before me concerning the Trinity, Who is God, have purposed to teach, according to the Scriptures, this doctrine, that the Father, and the Son, and the Holy Spirit intimate a divine unity of one and the same substance in an indivisible equality; and therefore that they are not three Gods, but one God: although the Father has begotten the Son, and so the Son is begotten by the Father, and so He who is the Son is not the Father; and the Holy Spirit is neither the Father nor the Son, but only the Spirit of the Father and of the Son, Himself also co-equal with the Father and the Son, and pertaining to the unity of the Trinity.

ON THE TRINITY, Bk. 1, Ch. 4
ML 42, 824
NPNF III, 20

63. *Against Arianism the later Fathers appealed to this constant tradition.*

ST. ATHANASIUS

And concerning the everlasting co-existence of the Word with the Father, and that He is not of another essence or subsistence, but proper to the Father's, as the Bishops in the Council said, you may hear again from the labour-loving Origen also . . . for let him understand well who dares to say, 'Once the Son was not,' that he is saying, 'Once Wisdom was not,' and 'Word was not,' and 'Life was not.' . . . See, we are proving that this view has been transmitted from father to father; but you, O modern Jews and disciples of Caiaphas, how many fathers can you assign to your phrases? Not one of the understanding and wise; for all abhor you, but the devil alone; only he is your father in this apostasy. . . . For the faith which the Council has confessed in writing, that is the faith of the Catholic Church; to assert this, the blessed Fathers so expressed themselves while condemning the Arian heresy.

338
(757)

DEFENSE OF THE NICENE DEFINITION, Ch. 27
MG 25, 465
NPNF IV, 168

ST. EPIPHANIUS

[The Antiochenes] confess the Father and the Son and the Holy Spirit to be consubstantial, three hypostases, one essence, one divinity. That is the true faith which has been handed down by the fathers and is prophetic and evangelical and apostolic, which our fathers and bishops professed, who were gathered together in the Council of Nicea when the great and blessed Constantine was Emperor.

339
(1107)

AGAINST THE HERESIES OF THE PANARIANS, 73
MG 42, 468

64. *Father, Son, and Holy Spirit are distinct, and yet One.*

THE SHEPHERD OF HERMAS

Let me tell you the parable I have in mind relative to fasting. A man had a field and numerous servants. One part of the field he planted as a vineyard. Then he chose a dependable, respected, and honest servant,

340
(89)

summoned him and said: 'Take this vineyard I planted and fence it in till I come. Do not do anything else to the vineyard. Do this and you will receive from me your freedom.' Then the master of that slave went off to a foreign country. After a while the master of the slave and of the field returned to his vineyard. When he saw that the vineyard had been fenced in properly and, over and above this, had been dug and cleared of weeds and that the vines were flourishing, he was exceedingly glad at the work of his slave. So, he summoned his beloved son who was his heir and his friends who were his advisers and told them what he had ordered his slave to do and what he found. They, also, were happy at the master's testimony in favor of the slave. The latter said to them: 'I promised freedom to this slave, if he observed the order I gave him. He has kept my order and besides, to my great pleasure, has done a good work in the vineyard. So, as a reward for this, I wish to make him joint heir with my son.'

I shall elucidate for you the parable of the field and all the other points that follow, so you can make them known to everybody. 'Listen,' he said, 'and understand this. The field is this world. The Lord of the field is the One who has created everything, and fitted things together, and given them strength. The servant is the Son of God, while the vines are the people He engendered. The fences are the holy angels of the Lord who support His people. The weeds plucked from the vineyard are iniquities of the servants of God. The food He sent are the commandments He gave to His people through His Son. The friends and advisers are the holy angels, His first creation. The departure of the master for a foreign land is the time left over before His coming.'

God planted the vineyard, that is to say, created His people and gave them over to His Son. The Son appointed the angels to watch over them. He Himself cleansed their sins away by undergoing innumerable toils and labors, for, nobody can dig without toil and labor. By cleansing their sins in person, He showed them the ways of life and gave them the law which He received from His Father. 'So you see,' he said, 'that He Himself is Lord of His people, because He has all power from His Father. Now, let me tell you why the Lord took His Son and the glorious angels as advisers in the question of the slave's inheritance. The Holy Ghost, the Pre-existent, the Creator of all creation, was made by God to dwell in the flesh of His choice. This flesh, then, in which the Holy Spirit dwelt, was beautifully subject to the Spirit, and walked in holiness and purity, and sullied the Spirit in absolutely nothing. Therefore, the flesh was guided with beauty and purity by the Spirit, and shared His toil and labor in everything.

Because the flesh had conducted itself with strength and courage, He associated it with the Holy Spirit, for He was pleased with the career of this flesh, which had not been sullied while holding the Spirit on earth. Therefore, He took the Son and the glorious angels as advisors, in order that the flesh might have some place of abode for its blameless subjection to the Spirit and might not seem to have lost the reward of its services. For, all flesh that has been found unsullied and spotless, in which the Holy Spirit has had His abode, will receive a reward.'

SIMILITUDES, 5, 6
MG 2, 957, 961
FC I, 292–293, 296–298

I want to point out to you what the Holy Spirit has shown you while speaking to you in the form of the Church. For that Spirit is the Son of God. 341 (91)

SIMILITUDES, 9
MG 2, 979
FC I, 316–317

ST. THEOPHILUS OF ANTIOCH
See No. 185.

TERTULLIAN
See No. 201.

ST. CYPRIAN
See No. 334.

ST. GREGORY THAUMATURGUS
See No. 335.

ST. ATHANASIUS

'I am in the Father, and the Father in Me' (Jn. 14:10). For the Son is in the Father, as it is allowed us to know, because the whole Being of the Son is proper to the Father's essence, as radiance from light, and stream from fountain; so that whoever sees the Son, sees what is proper to the Father, and knows that the Son's Being, because from the Father is therefore in the Father. For the Father is in the Son, since the Son is what is from the Father and proper to Him, as in the radiance the sun, and in the word the thought, and in the stream the fountain; for who- 342 (768) soever thus contemplates the Son, contemplates what is proper to the Father's Essence, and knows that the Father is in the Son. For whereas the Form and Godhead of the Father is the Being of the Son, it follows that the Son is in the Father and the Father in the Son. On this account and reasonably, having said before, 'I and the Father are One' (Jn. 10:30), He added, 'I am in the Father and the Father in Me,' by way of showing the identity of Godhead and the unity of Essence. For they are one, not as one thing divided into two parts, and these nothing but one, nor as one thing twice named, so that the same becomes at one time Father, at another His own Son, for since Sabellius held this he was judged a heretic. But They are two, because the Father is Father and is not also Son, and the Son is Son and not also Father; but the nature is one; (for the offspring is not unlike its parent, for it is his image), and all that is the Father's is the Son's. Wherefore neither is the Son another God, for He was not procured from without, else there would be many, if a godhead be procured foreign from the Father's; for if the Son be other, as an Offspring, still He is the Same as God; and He and the Father are one in propriety and peculiarity of nature, and in the identity of the one Godhead, as has been said.

FOUR DISCOURSES AGAINST THE ARIANS, No. 3:3, 4
MG 26, 328
NPNF IV, 395

343
(776)

For the Word, being Son of the One God, is referred to Him of whom He is; so that Father and Son are two, yet the Monad of the Godhead is indivisible and inseparable. And thus too we preserve One Beginning of Godhead and not two Beginnings, whence there is strictly a Monarchy. And of this very Beginning the Word is by nature Son, not as if another beginning, subsisting by Himself, nor having come into being externally to that Beginning, lest from that diversity a Dyarchy and Polyarchy should ensue; but of the one Beginning He is *Son, Wisdom, Word,* existing from It.

FOUR DISCOURSES AGAINST THE ARIANS, No. 4:1
MG 26, 468
NPNF IV, 433

ST. BASIL
See No. 272.

344
(915)

[To his brother Gregory] Since, then, the Holy Spirit, from Whom all the supply of good things for creation has its source, is attached to the Son, and with Him is inseparably apprehended, and has Its being

184

attached to the Father, as cause from Whom also It proceeds; It has this note of Its peculiar hypostatic nature, that It is known after the Son and together with the Son, and that It has Its subsistence of the Father. The Son, Who declares the Spirit proceeding from the Father through Himself and with Himself, shining forth alone and by only-begetting from the unbegotten light, so far as the peculiar notes are concerned, has nothing in common either with the Father or with the Holy Spirit. He alone is known by the stated signs. But God, Who is over all, alone has, as one special mark of His own hypostasis, His being Father, and His deriving His hypostasis from no cause; and through this mark He is peculiarly known. . . . He who perceives the Father, and perceives Him by Himself, has at the same time mental perception of the Son; and he who receives the Son does not divide Him from the Spirit, but, in consecution so far as nature is concerned, expresses the faith commingled in himself in the three together. He who makes mention of the Spirit alone, embraces also in this confession Him of whom He is the Spirit. And since the Spirit is Christ's and of God, as says Paul, then just as he who lays hold on one end of the chain pulls the other to him, so he who 'draws the Spirit,' as says the prophet, by this means draws to him at the same time both the Son and the Father. And if any one verily receives the Son, he will hold Him on both sides, the Son drawing towards him on the one His own Father, and on the other His own Spirit. . . . For it is in no wise possible to entertain the idea of severance or division, in such a way as that the Son should be thought of apart from the Father, or the Spirit be disjoined from the Son. But the communion and the distinction apprehended in Them are, in a certain sense, ineffable and inconceivable, the continuity of nature being never rent asunder by the distinction of the hypostases, nor the notes of proper distinction confounded in the community of essence.

LETTERS, 38
MG 32, 329
NPNF VIII, 138–139

ST. AMBROSE

The Substance of the Trinity is, so to say, a common Essence in that 345 which is distinct, an incomprehensible, ineffable Substance. We hold (1269) the distinction, not the confusion of Father, Son, and Holy Spirit; a distinction without separation; a distinction without plurality; and

185

thus we believe in Father, Son, and Holy Spirit as each existing from and to eternity in this divine and wonderful Mystery: not in two Fathers, nor in two Sons, nor in two Spirits. . . . We know the fact of distinction, we know nothing of the hidden mysteries; we pry not into the causes, but keep the outward signs intact.

TO GRATIAN, ON THE CHRISTIAN FAITH, Bk. 4, Ch. 8
ML 16, 634
NPNF X, 274

ST. AUGUSTINE

346
(1672)

But that is the right purpose which starts from faith. For a certain faith is in some way the starting-point of knowledge; but a certain knowledge will not be made perfect, except after this life, when we shall see face to face. (1 Cor. 13:12) . . . As regards this question, then, let us believe that the Father, and the Son, and the Holy Spirit is one God, the Creator and Ruler of the whole creature; and that the Father is not the Son, nor the Holy Spirit either the Father or the Son, but a trinity of persons mutually interrelated, and a unity of an equal essence. And let us seek to understand this, praying for help from Himself, whom we wish to understand.

ON THE TRINITY, Bk. 9, Ch. 1
ML 42, 961
NPNF III, 125

65. *There are three Persons in the unity of one nature.*

TERTULLIAN
See Nos. 201 and 330.

ST. BASIL
See No. 272.

347
(920)

The Father, the Son and the Holy Spirit alike hallow, quicken, enlighten, and comfort. No one will attribute a special and peculiar operation of hallowing to the operation of the Spirit, after hearing the Saviour in the Gospel saying to the Father about His disciples, 'Father, sanctify them in Your name' (Jn. 17:17). In like manner all other operations are equally performed, in all who are worthy of them, by the Father and by the Son and by the Holy Spirit; every grace and virtue, guidance, life, consolation, change into the immortal, the passage into freedom and all other good things which come down to man. . . . Identity of operation in the case of Father and of Son and of Holy Spirit clearly proves the invariability of nature. It follows that, even if the name of Godhead does signify nature, the community of essence proves that this title is very properly applied to the Holy Spirit.

LETTERS, No. 189:7
MG 32, 693
NPNF VIII, 231

The distinction between ousía and hypostasis is the same as that between the general and the particular; as, for instance, between the animal and the particular man. Wherefore, in the case of the Godhead, we confess one essence or substance so as not to give a variant definition of existence, but we confess a particular hypostasis, in order that our conception of Father, Son and Holy Spirit may be without confusion and clear. If we have no distinct perception of the separate characteristics, namely, fatherhood, sonship, and sanctification, but for our conception of God from the general idea of existence, we cannot possibly give a sound account of our faith. We must, therefore, confess the faith by adding the particular to the common. The Godhead is common; the fatherhood particular. We must therefore combine the two and say, 'I believe in God the Father.' The like course must be pursued in the confession of the Son; we must combine the particular with the common and say, 'I believe in God the Son,' so in the case of the Holy Spirit we must make our utterance conform to the appellation and say 'in God the Holy Spirit.' Hence it results that there is a satisfactory preservation of the unity by the confession of the one Godhead, while in distinction of the individual properties regarded in each there is the confession of the peculiar properties of the Persons.

LETTERS, No. 236:6
MG 32, 884
NPNF VIII, 278

348
(926)

Thus the way of the knowledge of God lies from One Spirit through the One Son to the One Father, and conversely the natural Goodness and the inherent Holiness and the royal Dignity extend from the Father through the Only-begotten to the Spirit. Thus there is both

349
(953)

acknowledgment of the hypostases and the true dogma of the Monarchy is not lost.*

ON THE HOLY SPIRIT, Ch. 18:47

MG 32, 153

NPNF VIII, 29

ST. GREGORY NAZIANZEN

350
(996)

'. . . The Holy Spirit, which proceeds from the Father'; (Jn. 15:26) Who, inasmuch as He proceeds from That Source, is no Creature; and inasmuch as He is not Begotten is no Son; and inasmuch as He is between the Unbegotten and the Begotten is God. . . . What then is Procession? Do you tell me what is the Unbegottenness of the Father, and I will explain to you the physiology of the Generation of the Son and the Procession of the Spirit, and we shall both of us be frenzy-stricken for prying into the mystery of God. . . . What then, say they, is there lacking to the Spirit which prevents His being a Son, for if there were not something lacking He would be a Son? We assert that there is nothing lacking—for God has no deficiency. But the difference of manifestation, if I may so express myself, or rather of their mutual relations one to another, has caused the difference of their Names. For indeed it is not some deficiency in the Son which prevents His being Father (for Sonship is not a deficiency), and yet He is not Father. According to this line of argument there must be some deficiency in the Father, in respect of His not being Son. For the Father is not Son, and yet this is not due to either deficiency or subjection of Essence; but the very fact of being Unbegotten or Begotten, or Proceeding has given the name of Father to the First, or the Son to the Second, and of the Third, Him of Whom we are speaking, of the Holy Spirit that the distinction of the Three Persons may be preserved in the one nature and dignity of the Godhead. For neither is the Son Father, for the Father is One, but He is what the Father is; nor is the Spirit Son

* The great objection which the Eastern Church makes to the *Filioque* is that it implies the existence of two *archai* in the Godhead; and if we believe in two *anarchoi,* we in effect believe in two Gods. The unity of the Godhead can only be maintained by acknowledging the Father to be the sole *Arché* or *pégé theótetos,* who from all eternity has communicated his Own Godhead to His coeternal and consubstantial Son and Spirit. This reasoning is generally true. But, as the doctrine of the Procession of the Spirit from the Father and the Son presupposes the eternal generation of the Son from the Father, it does not follow that the doctrine impugns the Catholic belief in the *mía arché.*

because He is of God, for the Only-begotten is One, but He is what the Son is. The Three are One in Godhead, and the One Three in properties; so that neither is the Unity a Sabellian one, nor does the Trinity countenance the present evil distinction. What then? Is the Spirit God? Most certainly. Well then, is He Consubstantial? Yes, if He is God.

> ORATIONS, No. 31
> *MG* 36, 141
> *NPNF* VII, 320–321

What is our quarrel and dispute with both? To us there is One God, for the Godhead is One, and all that proceeds from Him is referred to One, though we believe in Three Persons. For one is not more and another less God; nor is One before and another after; nor are They divided in will or parted in power; nor can you find here any of the qualities of divisible things; but the Godhead is, to speak concisely, undivided in separate Persons; and there is one mingling of Light, as it were of three suns joined to each other.

351
(997)

> ORATIONS, No. 31
> *MG* 36, 148
> *NPNF* VII, 322

But [the faithful] worship the Father and the Son and the Holy Spirit, One Godhead; God the Father, God the Son and (do not be angry) God the Holy Spirit, One Nature in Three Personalities, intellectual, perfect, Self-existent, numerically separate, but not separate in Godhead.

352
(999)

> ORATIONS, No. 33
> *NPNF* VII, 334

And when I speak of God you must be illumined at once by one flash of light and by three. Three in Individualities or Hypostases, if any prefer so to call them, or persons, for we will not quarrel about names so long as the syllables amount to the same meaning; but one in respect of the Substance—that is, the Godhead. For they are divided without division, if I may so say; and they are united in division. For the Godhead is one in three, and the three are one, in whom the Godhead is, or to speak more accurately, Who are the Godhead.

353
(1008)

> ORATIONS, No. 39
> *MG* 36, 236
> *NPNF* VII, 355

354
(1017)

If anyone does not believe that Holy Mary is the Mother of God, he is severed from the Godhead. If anyone should assert that He passed through the Virgin as through a channel, and was not at once divinely and humanly formed in her (divinely, because without the intervention of a man; humanly, because in accordance with the laws of gestation), he is in like manner godless. If any assert that the Manhood was formed and afterward was clothed with the Godhead, he too is to be condemned. For this were not a Generation of God, but a shirking of generation. . . . And (if I am to speak concisely) the Saviour is made of elements which are distinct from one another (for the invisible is not the same with the visible, nor the timeless with that which is subject to time), yet He is not two Persons. God forbid! For both natures are one by the combination, the Deity being made Man, and the Manhood deified or however one should express it. And I say different Elements, because it is the reverse of what is the case in the Trinity; for there we acknowledge different Persons so as not to confound the persons; but not different Elements, for the Three are One and the same in Godhead.

LETTERS, No. 101
MG 37, 117
NPNF VII, 439

ST. GREGORY OF NYSSA

355
(1029)

And so one who diligently studies the depths of the mystery, receives secretly in his spirit, indeed, a moderate amount of apprehension of the doctrine of God's nature, yet he is unable to explain clearly in words the ineffable depth of this mystery. As, for instance, how the same thing is capable of being numbered and yet rejects numeration, how it is observed with distinctions yet is apprehended as a monad, how it is separate as to personality yet is not divided as to subject matter.

THE GREAT CATECHISM, Ch. 3
MG 45, 17
NPNF V, 403

ST. AUGUSTINE
See No. 337.

356
(1668)

For that which must be understood of persons according to our usage, this is to be understood of substances according to the Greek usage;

for they say three substances, one essence, in the same way as we say three persons, one essence or substance.

ON THE TRINITY, Bk. 7, Ch. 4
ML 42, 941

See No. 287.

NPNF III, 110

ST. JOHN OF DAMASCUS

In the case, therefore, of the Godhead we confess that there is but one nature, but hold that there are three subsistences actually existing, and hold that all things that are of nature and essence are simple, and recognise the difference of the subsistences only in the three properties of independence of cause and Fatherhood, of dependence on cause and Sonship, of dependence on cause and procession. And we know further that these are indivisible and inseparable from each other and united into one, and interpenetrating one another without confusion. . . . In the very same way, then, in the case of the divine and ineffable dispensation, exceeding all thought and comprehension, I mean the Incarnation of the One God the Word of the Holy Trinity, and our Lord Jesus Christ, we confess that there are two natures, one divine and one human, joined together with one another and united in subsistence, so that one compound subsistence is formed out of the two natures: but we hold that the two natures are still preserved, even after the union, in the one compound subsistence, that is, in the one Christ, and that these exist in reality and have their natural properties; for they are united without confusion, and are distinguished and enumerated without being separable. And just as the three subsistences of the Holy Trinity are united without confusion, so in the same way the natures of Christ also, although they are united, yet are united without confusion. . . . For Christ, indeed, is one perfect both in divinity and in humanity.

357
(2362)

EXPOSITION OF THE ORTHODOX FAITH, Bk. 3, Ch. 5
MG 94, 1000
NPNF IX, 49

66. *The most holy Trinity is a mystery.*

ST. IRENAEUS

But inflated beyond reason [with your own wisdom], you presumptuously maintain that you are acquainted with the unspeakable mysteries of God; while even the Lord, the very Son of God, allowed that the

358
(204)

Father alone knows the very day and hour of judgment, when He plainly declares, 'But of that day and that hour knows no man, neither the Son, but the Father only' (Mk. 13:32). If, then, the Son was not ashamed to ascribe the knowledge of that day to the Father only, but declared what was true regarding the matter, neither let us be ashamed to reserve for God those greater questions which may occur to us. For no man is superior to his master (Mt. 10:24; Lk. 6:40). If any one, therefore says to us, 'How then was the Son produced by the Father?' we reply to him, that no man understands that production, or generation, or calling, or revelation, or by whatever name one may describe His generation, which is in fact altogether indescribable. Neither Valentinus, nor Marcion, nor Saturninus, nor Basilides, nor angels, nor archangels, nor principalities, nor powers [possess this knowledge], but the Father only who begat, and the Son who was begotten. Since therefore His generation is unspeakable, those who strive to set forth generations and productions cannot be in their right mind, inasmuch as they undertake to describe things which are indescribable.

AGAINST HERESIES, Bk. 2, Ch. 28
MG 7, 808
ANF I, 401

LACTANTIUS

359
(632)

For we especially testify that [Christ] was twice born, first in the spirit, and afterwards in the flesh. Whence it is thus spoken by Jeremiah: 'Before I formed You in the womb I knew You' (Jer. 1:5). And likewise by the same: 'Who was blessed before He was born'; which was the case with no one else but Christ. For though He was the Son of God from the beginning, He was born again a second time according to the flesh: . . . In what manner, then, did [the Father] beget Him? First of all, divine operations cannot be known or declared by any one; but nevertheless the sacred writings teach us, in which it is laid down that this Son of God is the speech, or even the reason of God, and also that the other angels are spirits of God. For speech is breath sent forth with a voice signifying something. But, however, since breath and speech are sent forth from different parts, inasmuch as breath proceeds from the nostrils, speech from the mouth, the difference between the Son of God and the other angels is great. For they proceeded from God as silent spirits, because they were not created to teach the knowledge of God, but for His service. But though He is Himself also a spirit, yet He proceeded from the mouth of God with voice and sound, as the

Word, on this account indeed, because He was about to make use of His voice to the people; that is, because He was about to be a teacher of the knowledge of God, and of the heavenly mystery to be revealed to man: which word also God Himself first spoke, that through Him He might speak to us, and that He might reveal to us the voice and will of God.

With good reason, therefore, is He called the Speech and the Word of God, because God, by a certain incomprehensible energy and power of His majesty, enclosed the vocal spirit proceeding from His mouth, which he had not conceived in the womb, but in His mind, within a form which has life through its own perception and wisdom, and He also fashioned other spirits of His into angels. . . . Our expressions, although they are mingled with the air, and fade away, yet generally remain comprised in letters; how much more must we believe that the voice of God both remains for ever, and is accompanied with perception and power, which it has derived from God the Father as a stream from its fountain! But if any one wonders that God could be produced from God by a putting forth of the voice and breath, if he is acquainted with the sacred utterances of the prophets he will cease to wonder.

THE DIVINE INSTITUTES, Bk. 4, Ch. 8
ML 6, 465
ANF VII, 106–107

ST. CYRIL OF JERUSALEM

Believe also in the Son of God, One and Only, our Lord Jesus Christ, Who was begotten God of God, begotten Life of Life, begotten Light of Light, Who is in all things like to Him that begat, Who received not His being in time, but was before all ages eternally and incomprehensibly begotten of the Father: The Wisdom and the Power of God, and His Righteousness personally subsisting: Who sits on the right hand of the Father before all ages.

360
(816)

CATECHESES, 4:7
MG 33, 461
NPNF VII, 20–21

And the Father indeed gives to the Son; and the Son shares with the Holy Spirit. For it is Jesus Himself, not I, who says, 'All things are delivered unto Me of My Father' (Mt. 11:27); and of the Holy Spirit He says, 'When He, the Spirit of Truth, shall come,' and the rest. . . . 'He shall glorify Me; for He shall receive of Mine, and shall

361
(834)

193

show it unto you' (Jn. 16:13 ff.). The Father through the Son, with the Holy Spirit, is the giver of all grace; the gifts of the Father are none other than those of the Son, and those of the Holy Spirit; for there is one Salvation, one Power, one Faith; One God, the Father; One Lord, His only-begotten Son; One Holy Spirit, the Comforter. And it is enough for us to know these things; but inquire not curiously into His nature or substance: for had it been written, we would have spoken of it; what is not written, let us not venture on; it is sufficient for our salvation to know, that there is Father, and Son, and Holy Spirit.

CATECHESES, 16:24
MG 33, 952
NPNF VII, 121

ST. HILARY

362
(859)

I must undertake something that cannot be limited and venture upon something that cannot be comprehended, so that I may speak about God who cannot be accurately defined. He fixed the names of the nature—the Father, the Son, and the Holy Spirit. Whatever is sought over and above this transcends the meaning of words, the limits of perception, and the concepts of understanding. It may not be expressed, attained, or grasped. The nature of this subject exhausts the meaning of words, an impenetrable light darkens the vision of the mind, and whatever is without limits is beyond the capacity of our power of reasoning.

ON THE TRINITY, Bk. 2, Ch. 5
ML 10, 54
FC XXV, 39

363
(878)

Just as from the fact that Your Only-begotten was born from You all ambiguity in language and difficulty in understanding are at an end and only one thing remains, that He was born, so, too, in my consciousness I hold fast to the fact that your Holy Spirit is from You, although I do not grasp it with my understanding.

ON THE TRINITY, Bk. 12, Ch. 56
ML 10, 470
FC XXV, 542–543

ST. BASIL
See No. 344.

194

ST. GREGORY NAZIANZEN
See No. 356.

ST. GREGORY OF NYSSA
See No. 355.

ST. AMBROSE
See No. 345.

ST. AUGUSTINE
See No. 346.

THE PERSONS OF THE TRINITY

67. The Father alone does not proceed.

ST. CLEMENT OF ALEXANDRIA

[The Gnostic] accordingly judges all excellence to be honorable accord-   364
ing to its worth; and judges that among the objects perceived by our   (431)
senses, we are to esteem rulers, and parents, . . . and among intellectual
ideas, what is oldest in origin, the timeless and unoriginated First
Principle, and Beginning of existences—the Son—from whom we are
to learn the Remoter Cause, the Father, of the universe, the most ancient
and the most beneficent of all.

STROMATA, Bk. 7:1:2
MG 9, 404
ANF II, 523

ORIGEN
See No. 333.

LACTANTIUS

Therefore the Most High God, and Parent of all, when He had pur-   365
posed to transfer His religion, sent from heaven a teacher of righteous-   (634)
ness, that in Him or through Him He might give a new law to new

worshippers; not as He had before done, by the instrumentality of man. Nevertheless it was His pleasure that He should be born as a man, that in all things He might be like His supreme Father. For God the Father Himself, who is the origin and source of all things, inasmuch as He is without parents, is most truly named by Trismegistus 'fatherless' and 'motherless,' because He was born from no one. For which reason it was befitting that the Son also should be twice born, that He also might become 'fatherless' and 'motherless.' For in His first nativity, which was spiritual, He was 'motherless,' because He was begotten by God the Father alone, without the office of a mother. But in His second, which was in the flesh, He was born of a virgin's womb without the office of a father, that, bearing a middle substance between God and man, He might be able, as it were, to take by the hand this frail and weak nature of ours, and raise it to immortality. He became both the Son of God through the Spirit, and the Son of man through the flesh, —that is, both God and man.

THE DIVINE INSTITUTES, Bk. 4, Ch. 13
ML 6, 482
ANF VII, 111–112

ST. BASIL
See Nos. 344 and 202.

ST. GREGORY NAZIANZEN

366
(1009)

The Father is Father, and is Unoriginate, for He is of no one; the Son is Son, and is not unoriginate, for He is of the Father. But if you take the word Origin in a temporal sense, He too is Unoriginate, for He is the Maker of Time, and is not subject to Time. The Holy Spirit is truly Spirit, coming forth from the Father indeed, but not after the manner of the Son, for it is not by Generation but by Procession (since I must coin a word for the sake of clearness); for neither did the Father cease to be Unbegotten because of His begetting something, nor the Son to be begotten because He is of the Unbegotten (how could that be?), nor is the Spirit changed into Father or Son because He proceeds, or because He is God—though the ungodly do not believe it. For Personality is unchangeable; else how could Personality remain, if it were changeable, and could be removed from one to another?

ORATIONS, 39, 12
MG 36, 348
NPNF VII, 356

ST. AUGUSTINE

But the Father is not said to be sent, when from time to time He is apprehended by any one, for He has no one of whom to be, or from whom to proceed; since Wisdom says, 'I came out of the mouth of the Most High' (Eccles. 24:5), and it is said of the Holy Spirit, 'He proceeds from the Father' (Jn. 15:26), but the Father is from no one.

367
(1657)

ON THE TRINITY, Bk. 4, Ch. 20
ML 42, 908
NPNF III, 83

For if the Son has of the Father whatever He has, then certainly He has of the Father, that the Holy Spirit proceeds also from Him. . . . For the Father alone is not from another, and therefore He alone is called unbegotten, not indeed in the Scriptures, but in the usage of disputants, who employ such language as they can on so great a subject. And the Son is born of the Father; and the Holy Spirit proceeds from the Father principally, the Father giving the procession without any interval of time, yet in common from both (Father and Son). But He would be called the Son of the Father and of the Son, if—a thing abhorrent to the feeling of all sound minds—both had *begotten* Him. Therefore the Spirit of both is not begotten of both, but proceeds from both.

368
(1681)

ON THE TRINITY, Bk. 15, Ch. 26
ML 42, 1094
NPNF III, 225

ST. JOHN OF DAMASCUS

[We believe] in one Father, the beginning, and cause of all: begotten of no one: without cause or generation, alone subsisting: creator of all: but Father of one only by nature, His Only-begotten Son and our Lord and God and Saviour Jesus Christ, and Producer of the most Holy Spirit. . . . For there never was a time when the Father was and the Son was not, but always the Father and always the Son, Who was begotten of Him, existed together. For He could not have received the name Father apart from the Son.

369
(2342)

EXPOSITION OF THE ORTHODOX FAITH, Bk. 1, Ch. 8
MG 94, 809
NPNF IX, 6

197

370
(2348)
The Father is the source and cause of the Son and the Holy Spirit: Father of the Son alone and producer of the Holy Spirit. The Son is Son, Word, Wisdom, Power, Image, Effulgence, Impress of the Father and derived from the Father. But the Holy Spirit is not the Son of the Father but the Spirit of the Father as proceeding from the Father. For there is no impulse without Spirit. And we speak also of the Spirit of the Son, not as though proceeding from Him, but as proceeding through Him from the Father. For the Father alone is cause.

EXPOSITION OF THE ORTHODOX FAITH, Bk. 1, Ch. 12
MG 94, 849
NPNF IX, 15

68. *The Son was not made.*

ST. CLEMENT OF ALEXANDRIA

371
(442)
What therefore [John] says, 'from the beginning' (1 Jn. 1:1), the Presbyter explained to this effect, that the beginning of generation is not separated from the beginning of the Creator. For when he says, 'That which was from the beginning,' he touches upon the generation without beginning of the Son, who is co-existent with the Father. There was, then, a Word importing an unbeginning eternity; as also the Word itself, that is, the Son of God, who being, by equality of substance, one with the Father, is eternal and uncreated. That He was always the Word, is signified by saying, 'In the beginning was the Word' (Jn. 1:1). •

ADUMBRATIONES IN 1 JNO. 1:1
MG 9, 734
ANF II, 574

ST. ATHANASIUS
See No. 270.

372
(758)
This then being the force of such titles, in like manner let a man call God unoriginated, if it so please him; not however as if the Word were of originated things, but because, as I said before, God not only is not originated, but through His proper Word is He the maker of things which are so. For though the Father be called such, still the Word is the Father's Image, and one in essence with Him; and being His Image, He must be distinct from things originated, and from everything; for whose Image He is, His property and likeness He has; so that he who

198

calls the Father unoriginated and almighty, perceives in the Unoriginated and the Almighty, His Word and His Wisdom, which is
the Son.

DEFENSE OF THE NICENE DEFINITION, No. 30

MG 25, 472

NPNF IV, 171

But, observe, say they, God was always a Maker, nor is the power of
framing adventitious to Him; does it follow then, that, because He is
the Framer of all, therefore His works also are eternal, and is it wicked
to say of them too, that they were not before origination? . . . However, not to leave even a weak argument unnoticed, they must be told,
that although God always had the power to make, yet the things
originated had not the power of being eternal. For they are out of
nothing, and therefore were not before they originated; but things which
were not before their origin, how could these co-exist with the everlasting God? Wherefore God, looking to what was good for them,
then made them all when He saw that, when originated, they were
able to abide. . . . But the Son, not being a work, but proper to
the Father's offspring, always is; for, whereas the Father always is, so
what is proper to His essence must always be; and this is His Word
and His Wisdom. And that creatures should not be in existence, does
not disparage the Maker; for He has the power of framing them, when
He wills; but for the offspring not to be ever with the Father, is a
disparagement of the perfection of His essence. Wherefore His works
were framed, when He would, through His Word; but the Son is ever
the proper offspring of the Father's essence.

FOUR DISCOURSES AGAINST THE ARIANS, No. 1:29

MG 26, 72

NPNF IV, 323

373
(761)

For how, if, as you hold, He is come of nothing, is He able to frame
things that are nothing into being? or if He, a creature, none the less
frames a creature, the same will be conceivable in the cases of every
creature, viz. the power to frame others. And if this pleases you, what
is the need of the Word, seeing that things inferior can be brought
to be by things superior? or at all events, every thing that is brought
to be could have heard in the beginning God's words, 'Become' and
'be made,' and so would have been framed. But this is not so written,

374
(764)

199

nor could it be. For none of the things which are brought to be is an efficient cause, but all things were made through the Word: who would not have wrought all things, were He Himself in the number of the creatures. For neither would the Angels be able to frame, since they too are creatures, though Valentinus, and Marcion, and Basilides think so, and you are their copyists.

FOUR DISCOURSES AGAINST THE ARIANS, No. 2:21
MG 26, 189
NPNF IV, 359

375
(765)

For, though no works had been created, still 'the Word' of God 'was,' and 'the Word was God.' And His becoming man would not have taken place, had not the need of men become a cause. The Son then is not a creature. For had He been a creature, He would not have said, 'He begets me,' for the creatures are from outside, and are works of the Maker; but the Offspring is not from outside nor a work, but from the Father, and proper to His Essence. Wherefore they are creatures; this God's Word and Only-begotten Son.

FOUR DISCOURSES AGAINST THE ARIANS, No. 2:56
MG 26, 268
NPNF IV, 378

ST. HILARY

376
(866)

First of all, I raise the question: What new element could the birth have introduced into the nature of the Son so that He is not God? The judgment of the human mind rejects this opinion, that anything by its birth is distinct from the nature of its origin. . . . Since these things are so in these corporeal processes and occurrences, what madness is it, I ask, to connect the birth of the only-begotten God with a spurious nature, since birth comes only from the essence of the nature, and there will no longer be a birth if the essence of the nature is not in the birth?

Hence, the purpose of all that heat and fury is that there may not be a birth but a creation in the Son of God, and that He who subsists may not preserve the origin of His nature, but may receive from non-existing matter a different nature from God. . . . The Son of God, however, does not begin to be God from nothing, but was born, nor was He anything else before He was God. Thus, He who is born into God did not begin to be, nor did He develop into that which God is. The birth, therefore, maintains the nature from which it subsists,

200

and the Son of God does not subsist as anything else than that which
God is.

ON THE TRINITY, Bk. 7, Ch. 14
ML 10, 210
FC XXV, 237–238

69. *The Son was truly born of the Father.*

TATIAN

God was in the beginning; but the beginning, we have been taught, is
the power of the Logos. For the Lord of the universe, who is Himself
the necessary ground ($ὑπόστασις$) of all being, inasmuch as no creature
was yet in existence, was alone; but inasmuch as He was all power,
Himself the necessary ground of things visible and invisible, with Him
were all things; with Him, by Logos-power ($λογικῆς δυνάμεως$) the Logos
Himself also, who was in Him, subsists. And by His simple will the
Logos springs forth; and the Logos, not coming forth in vain, becomes
the first-begotten work of the Father. Him [the Logos] we know to be
the beginning of the world. But He came into being by participation,
not by abscission; for what is cut off is separated from the original
substance, but that which comes by participation, making its choice
of function, does not render him deficient from whom it is taken. For
just as from one torch many fires are lighted, but the light of the first
torch is not lessened by the kindling of many torches, so the Logos,
coming forth from the Logos-power of the Father, has not divested of
the Logos-power Him who begat Him.

377
(153)

ORATION AGAINST THE GREEKS, Ch. 5
MG 6, 813
ANF II, 67

TERTULLIAN

This is the perfect nativity of the Word, when He proceeds forth from
God—formed by Him first to devise and think out [all things] under
the name of Wisdom ('The Lord created [or formed] me as the beginning of His ways') (Prov. 8:22); then afterwards begotten, to carry
all into effect ('When He prepared the heaven, I was present with
Him') (ib. 27). Thus does He make Him equal to Him; for by
proceeding from Himself He became His first-begotten Son, because
begotten before all things; and His only-begotten also, because alone

378
(373)

201

begotten of God, in a way peculiar to Himself, from the womb of His own heart, —even as the Father Himself testifies: 'My heart,' says He, 'has emitted my most excellent Word' (Ps. 44:2).

AGAINST PRAXEAS, Ch. 7
ML 2, 161
ANF III, 601

ST. HIPPOLYTUS

379
(391)
God, subsisting alone, and having nothing contemporaneous with Himself, determined to create the world. . . . Beside Him there was nothing; but He, while existing alone, yet existed in plurality. For He was neither without reason, nor wisdom, nor power, nor counsel. And all things were in Him, and He was the All. When He willed, and as He willed, He manifested His word in the times determined by Him, and by Him He made all things. . . . He made them, then, as He pleased, for He was God. And as the Author, and fellow-Counsellor, and Framer of the things that are in formation, He begat the Word; and as He bears this Word in Himself, and that, too, as [yet] invisible to the world which is created, He makes Him visible; [and] uttering the voice first, and begetting Him as Light of Light, He set Him forth to the world as its Lord, [and] His own mind. . . .

AGAINST THE HERESY OF NOETUS, Ch. 10
MG 10, 817
ANF V, 227

ST. ATHANASIUS
See No. 375.

ST. CYRIL OF JERUSALEM
See No. 360.

380
(823)
God then is in an improper sense the Father of man, but by nature and in truth of One only, the Only-begotten Son, our Lord Jesus Christ; not having attained in course of time to being a Father, but being ever the Father of the Only-begotten. Not that being without a Son before, He has since by change of purpose become a Father: but before every substance and every intelligence, before times and all ages, God has the dignity of Father.

CATECHESES, 7:5
MG 33, 609
NPNF VII, 45

But the Father, having begotten the Son, remained the Father, and is not changed. He begat Wisdom, yet lost not wisdom Himself; and begat Power, yet became not weak: He begat God, but lost not His own Godhead: and neither did He lose anything Himself by diminution or change; nor has He who was begotten anything wanting. Perfect is He who begat, Perfect that which was begotten: God was He who begat, God He who was begotten; God of all Himself, yet entitling the Father His own God.

381
(826)

> CATECHESES, 11:18
> *MG* 33, 713
> *NPNF* VII, 69

ST. HILARY
See No. 376.

ST. AMBROSE

But the Arians think that they must oppose hereto the fact that He had said, 'I live by the Father' (Jn. 6:58). Of a certainty (suppose that they conceive the words as referring to His Godhead) the Son lives by the Father, because He is the Son begotten of the Father, —by the Father, because He is of one Substance with the Father, —by the Father, because He is the Word given forth from the heart of the Father (Ps. 44:1), because He came forth from the Father, because He is begotten of the 'bowels of the Father,' because the Father is the Fountain and Root of the Son's being.

382
(1271)

> TO GRATIAN ON THE CHRISTIAN FAITH, Bk. 4, Ch. 10
> *ML* 16, 642
> *NPNF* X, 279

ST. JOHN OF DAMASCUS

The terms, 'Word' and 'effulgence,' then, are used because He is begotten of the Father without the union of two, or passion, or time, or flux, or separation: and the terms 'Son' and 'impress of the Father's subsistence,' because He is perfect and has subsistence and is in all respects similar to the Father, save that the Father is not begotten: and the term 'Only-begotten' because He alone was begotten alone of the Father alone. For no other generation is like to the generation of the Son of God, since no other is Son of God. For though the Holy Spirit proceeds from the Father, yet this is not generative in character but

383
(2343)

processional. This is a different mode of existence, alike incomprehensible and unknown, just as is the generation of the Son. Wherefore all the qualities the Father has are the Son's save that the Father is unbegotten, and this exception involves no difference in essence nor dignity, but only a different mode of coming into existence.

EXPOSITION OF THE ORTHODOX FAITH, Bk. 1, Ch. 8
MG 94, 816
NPNF IX, 8

70. *The Son is coeternal with the Father.*

ST. JUSTIN MARTYR
See No. 247.

384
(137)

'I shall give you another testimony, my friends,' said I, 'from the Scriptures, that God begat before all creatures a Beginning, [who was] a certain rational power [proceeding] from Himself, who is called by the Holy Spirit, now the Glory of the Lord, now the Son, again Wisdom, again an Angel, then God, and then Lord and Logos; and on another occasion He calls Himself Captain, when He appeared in human form to Joshua the son of Nave (Nun). For He can be called by all those names, since He ministers to the Father's will, and since He was begotten of the Father by an act of will; just as we see happening among ourselves: for when we give out some word, we beget the word; yet not by abscission, so as to lessen the word [which remains] in us, when we give it out: and just as we see also happening in the case of a fire, which is not lessened when it has kindled [another], but remains the same; and that which has been kindled by it likewise appears to exist by itself, not diminishing that from which it was kindled.

DIALOGUE WITH TRYPHO, Ch. 61
MG 6, 613
ANF I, 227

ST. IRENAEUS

385
(200)

[There are those who] transfer the generation of the word to which men gave utterance to the eternal Word of God, assigning a beginning and a course of production [to Him], even as they do their own word. And in what respect will the Word of God—yea, rather God Himself, since He is the Word—differ from the word of men, if He follows the same order and process of generation?

AGAINST HERESIES, Bk. 2, Ch. 13
MG 7, 747
ANF I, 375

ST. HIPPOLYTUS
See No. 379.

What Son of His own, then, did God send through the flesh but the Word, whom He addressed as Son because He was to become such [or be begotten] in the future? And He takes the common name for tender affection among men in being called the Son. For neither was the Word, prior to incarnation and when by Himself, yet perfect Son, although He was perfect Word, only-begotten. Nor could the flesh subsist by itself apart from the Word, because it has its subsistence in the Word. Thus, then, one perfect Son of God was manifested. . . . But let us also look at the subject in hand, —namely, the question, brethren, that in reality the Father's power, which is the Word, came down from heaven, and not the Father Himself.

386
(393)

AGAINST THE HERESY OF NOETUS, Ch. 15
MG 10, 824
ANF V, 229

ST. CLEMENT OF ALEXANDRIA

This Word, then, the Christ, the cause of both our being at first (for He was in God) and of our well-being, this very Word has now appeared as man, —the Author of all blessings to us; by whom we, being taught to live well, are sent on our way to life eternal. . . . This is the New Son, the manifestation of the Word that was in the beginning, and before the beginning. The Saviour, who existed before, has in recent days appeared. He, who is in Him that truly is, has appeared; for the Word, who 'was with God,' and by whom all things were created, has appeared as our Teacher. The Word, who in the beginning bestowed on us life as Creator when He formed us, taught us to live well when He appeared as our Teacher; that as God He might afterwards conduct us to the life which never ends.

387
(401)

EXHORTATION TO THE HEATHEN, Ch. 1, 7:1
MG 8, 61
ANF II, 173

388
(431)
[The Gnostic] accordingly judges all excellence to be honorable according to its worth; and judges that among the objects perceived by our senses, we are to esteem rulers, and parents, . . . and among intellectual ideas, what is oldest in origin, the timeless and unoriginated First Principle, and Beginning of existences—the Son—from whom we are to learn the Remoter Cause, the Father, of the universe, the most ancient and the most beneficent of all.

> STROMATA, Bk. 7, Ch. 1
> *MG* 9, 404
> *ANF* I, 539

ST. DIONYSIUS OF ALEXANDRIA

389
(609)
There certainly was not a time when God was not the Father. . . . [The Son] being the brightness of eternal Light, He Himself also is absolutely eternal. For since light is always in existence, it is manifest that its brightness also exists, because light is perceived to exist from the fact that it shines, and it is impossible that light should not shine. . . . Since, therefore, the Father is eternal, the Son also is eternal, Light of Light. For where there is the begetter, there is also the offspring. And if there is no offspring, how and of what can He be the begetter? But both are, and always are.

> ELENCHUS AND APOLOGY, Bk. 1
> *MG* 25, 501

ST. GREGORY THAUMATURGUS
See No. 335.

ST. ATHANASIUS

390
(760)
'If there never was, when the Son was not,' say they, 'but He is eternal, and coexists with the Father, you call Him no more the Father's Son, but brother.' O insensate and contentious! For if we said only that He was eternally with the Father, and not His Son, their pretended scruple would have some plausibility; but if, while we say that He is eternal, we also confess Him to be Son from the Father, how can He that is begotten be considered brother of Him who begets? ∴ . . . For the Father, and the Son were not generated from some pre-existing origin, that we may account Them brothers, but the Father is the Origin of the Son and begat Him; and the Father is Father, and not born the Son of any; and the Son is Son, and not brother. Further, if He is called the eternal offspring of the Father, He is rightly so called. For never

was the essence of the Father imperfect, that what is proper to it should be added afterwards; nor as man from man, has the Son been begotten, so as to be later than His Father's existence, but He is God's offspring, and as being proper Son of God, who is ever, He exists eternally. For, whereas it is proper to men to beget in time, from the imperfection of their nature, God's offspring is eternal, for His nature is ever perfect.

> FOUR DISCOURSES AGAINST THE ARIANS, Or. 1:14
> *MG* 26, 40

See No. 373.   *NPNF* IV, 314

ST. CYRIL OF JERUSALEM

If you too have sincere piety, the Holy Ghost comes down on you also, and a Father's voice sounds over you from high—not, 'This is My Son' (Mt. 3:17), but, 'This has now been made My Son'; for the 'is' belongs to Him alone, because 'In the beginning was the Word, and the Word was with God, and the Word was God' (Jn. 1:1). To Him belongs the 'is' since He is always the Son of God; but to you 'has now been made': since you have not the sonship by nature, but you receive it by adoption.

391
(813)

> CATECHESES, No. 4:4
> *MG* 33, 444

See Nos. 360 and 380.   *NPNF* VII, 17

ST. HILARY

Hence, [the Son] was and is, because He is from Him who always is what He is. To be from Him, that is to say, to be from the Father, is the birth. To be always from Him who always is is eternity—an eternity not from Himself, but from Him who is eternal. From Him who is eternal nothing else comes except what is eternal. If that is not eternal, then neither is the Father eternal who is the author of the generation. Since it is proper for Him to be always the Father and for Him to be always His Son, and since eternity is implied in that which is, so in the case of Him to whom it is also proper to be that which is, it is also proper that He be eternal.

392
(877)

> ON THE TRINITY, Bk. 12, Ch. 25
> *ML* 10, 448
> *FC* XXV, 518

ST. GREGORY NAZIANZEN
See Nos. 366 and 297.

ST. AUGUSTINE

393
(1460)
If the Son of God was born of the Father, then the Father has now ceased to beget; and if He ceased, He began; but if He began to beget, there was a time when He was without the Son. But He never was without the Son, because His Son is His wisdom, which is the brightness of eternal light. Therefore, the Father begets from all eternity and the Son is born from all eternity.

> LETTERS, No. 238
> *ML* 33, 1047
> *FC* XXXII, 206

394
(1816)
As, in fact, you have in your heart the word that you speak, and as it is with you, and is none other than the spiritual conception itself... so God gave out His Word, that is, begat the Son. And you, indeed, beget the word even in your heart according to time; God without time begat the Son by whom He created all times.

> ON THE GOSPEL OF ST. JOHN, Tr. 14:7
> *ML* 35, 1506
> *NPNF* VII, 96

ST. JOHN OF DAMASCUS
See No. 383.

71. The Son is consubstantial with the Father.

TATIAN
See No. 377.

TERTULLIAN

395
(277)
The holy voices which warned [the Jews] of this fate all insisted always on the same points: that the day would come in the last cycles of Time when God would select for Himself worshippers from every race and people and place—worshippers much more faithful, to whom He would transfer His favor in fuller measure because they were receptive of a fuller doctrine.

Consequently, there came the One who God had foretold would

come to renew and shed light upon the doctrine; namely, Christ, the Son of God. It was proclaimed beforehand that the Lord and Master of this grace and doctrine, the Enlightener and Guide of the human race, would be the Son of God, yet His birth was not such that He must blush at the name of son or the thought of paternal seed. . . . But the Son of God has no mother in any sense which involves the violation of her purity; in fact, she who is regarded as His mother did not marry [that is, consummate her marriage]. But, let me discuss His nature first; then the manner of His birth will be understood. We have already said that God fashioned this whole world by His Word, His reason, His power. . . . Moreover, we, too, ascribe Spirit as its proper substance to that Word, Reason, and Power by which, as we have said, God made everything. For, in Spirit giving utterance, there would be the Word; with Spirit arranging all things, Reason would cooperate; and in Spirit perfecting all things, Power would be present. This, as we have been taught, has been uttered by God and begotten by this utterance, and is, therefore, called the Son of God and God on account of the unity of nature; for God, too, is Spirit. When a ray is shot forth from the sun, a part is taken from the whole; but there will be sun in the ray because it is a sun ray; its nature is not separated, but extended. Thus, spirit proceeds from spirit and God from God just as light is kindled from light. The source of the substance remains whole and unimpaired, although you may borrow from it many offshoots of its quality. Thus, too, what proceeds from God is God and the Son of God, and both are one; similarly, Spirit proceeds from Spirit and God from God, making two by the measure of existence, plurality by gradation, but not by condition; He has not separated from, but proceeded from the producing cause.

This ray of God, then, as was ever foretold in the past, descended into a certain virgin and, becoming flesh in her womb, was born as one who is man and God united. The flesh, provided with a soul, is nourished, matures, speaks, teaches, acts, and *is* Christ.

APOLOGY, Ch. 21
ML 1, 394
FC X, 62–64

See No. 330.

ST. HIPPOLYTUS

And thus there appeared another beside Himself. But when I say another, I do not mean that there are two gods, but that it is only as light of light, or as water from a fountain, or as a ray from the sun.

396
(392)

For there is but one power, which is from the All; and the Father is All, from whom comes this Power, the Word. And this is the mind which came forth into the world, and was manifested as the Son of God.

AGAINST THE HERESY OF NOETUS, Ch. 11
MG 10, 817
ANF V, 227

ST. CLEMENT OF ALEXANDRIA

397
(409)

There is nothing in existence for which God is not the cause. It must be, then, that there is nothing that God hates, nothing that the Word hates. Both are one, and both are God, because Scripture says: 'In the beginning was the Word, and the Word was in God, and the Word was God' (Jn. 1:1).

CHRIST THE EDUCATOR, Bk. 1, Ch. 8
MG 8, 325
FC XXIII, 57

ST. ATHANASIUS

398
(755)

Since the generation of the Son from the Father is not according to the nature of men, and not only like, but also inseparable from the essence of the Father, and He and the Father are one, as He has said Himself, and the Word is ever in the Father and the Father in the Word, as the radiance stands towards the light (for this the phrase itself indicates), therefore the Council, as understanding this, suitably wrote, 'one in essence,' that they might both defeat the perverseness of the heretics, and show that the Word was other than originated things.

DEFENSE OF THE NICENE DEFINITION, Ch. 20
MG 25, 452
See Nos. 270 and 372. *NPNF* IV, 164

399
(767)

'Yet,' they say, 'though the Saviour were a creature, God was able to speak the word only and undo the curse.' And so another will tell them in like manner, 'Without His coming among us at all, God was able just to speak and undo the curse'; but we must consider what was expedient for mankind, and not what simple is possible with God.... He could too, without Moses, have spoken the word only and have brought the people out of Egypt; but it profited to do it through Moses. . . . The Saviour too might have come among us from the beginning, or on His coming might not have been delivered to Pilate; but He came 'at the fullness of the ages,' and when sought for said, 'I am He' (Jn.

18:5). For what He does, that is profitable for men, and was not fitting in any other way; and what is profitable and fitting, for that He provides. . . . If God had but spoken, because it was in His power, and so the curse would have been undone, the power had been shown of Him who gave the word, but man had become such as Adam was before the transgression, having received grace from without, and not having it united to the body; (for he was such when he was placed in Paradise) nay, perhaps had become worse, because he had learned to transgress. Such then being his condition, had he been seduced by the serpent, there would have been fresh need for God to give command and undo the curse; and thus the need would have become interminable, and men would have remained under guilt not less than before, as being enslaved to sin. Again, if the Son were a creature, man would have remained mortal as before, not being joined to God; for a creature would not have joined creatures to God, as seeking itself one to join it; nor would a portion of the creation have been the creation's salvation, as needing salvation itself. To provide against this also, He sends His own Son, and He becomes Son of Man, by taking created flesh; that, since all were under sentence of death, He, being other than them all, might Himself for all offer to death His own body; and that henceforth, as if all had died through Him, the word of that sentence might be accomplished (for all died in Christ), and all through Him might thereupon become free from sin and from the curse which came upon it, and might truly abide for ever, risen from the dead and clothed in immortality and incorruption. For, the Word being clothed in the flesh, as has many times been explained, every bit of the serpent began to be utterly staunched from out of it; and whatever evil sprung from the motions of the flesh, to be cut away, and with these death also was abolished, the companion of sin.

FOUR DISCOURSES AGAINST THE ARIANS, 2:68
MG 26, 292
See No. 342.   *NPNF* IV, 385–386

Nor is this Form of the Godhead partial merely, but the fulness of   400
the Father's Godhead is the Being of the Son, and the Son is whole   (769)
God. Therefore also, being equal to God, He 'thought it not a prize to
be equal to God' (Phil. 2:6); and again since the Godhead and the
Form of the Son is none other than the Father's, this is what He says,
'I in the Father' (Jn. 14:10). Thus 'God was in Christ reconciling the

world unto Himself' (2 Cor. 5:19); for the propriety of the Father's Essence is that Son, in whom the creation was then reconciled with God. Thus what things the Son then wrought are the Father's works, for the Son is the Form of that Godhead of the Father, which wrought the works. And thus he who looks at the Son, sees the Father; for in the Father's Godhead is and is contemplated the Son; and the Father's Form which is in Him shows in Him the Father; and thus the Father is in the Son.

FOUR DISCOURSES AGAINST THE ARIANS, 3:6

MG 26, 332

NPNF IV, 396

401
(787)

And again, if, as we have said before, the Son is not such by participation, but, while all things originated have by participation the grace of God, He is the Father's Wisdom and Word of which all things partake; it follows that He, being the deifying and enlightening power of the Father, in which all things are deified and quickened, is not alien in essence from the Father, but coessential. For by partaking of Him, we partake of the Father; because the Word is the Father's own. Whence, if He was Himself too from participation, and not from the Father His essential Godhead and Image, He would not deify, being deified Himself.

ON THE COUNCILS OF ARIMINUM AND SELEUCIA, Ch. 51

MG 26, 784

NPNF IV, 477

ST. HILARY
   See No. 376.

402
(868)

He who has seen me has seen also the Father (Jn. 14:9). . . . God is recognized in Him, if, indeed, He will be recognized by anyone at all, by the power of His nature, and when God the Son is perceived He allows us to perceive the Father, while He is the image in such a manner that He does not differ in nature, but manifests His author. . . . The Son is the living image of the living One, and He who has been born from Him does not have a different nature, and He who does not differ in anything preserves the power of His nature from whom He does not differ. That He is the image, therefore, proceeds from the fact that the birth of the only-begotten God points to God the Father, but it points to Him in such a manner that He Himself is the form and the image of the invisible God; hence, He does not lose the united similarity of the nature, because He is not lacking in the power of the nature.

ON THE TRINITY, Bk. 7, Ch. 37
ML 10, 230
FC XXV, 265–266

ST. BASIL

We in accordance with the true doctrine speak of the Son as neither like, nor unlike the Father. Each of these terms is equally impossible, for like and unlike are predicated in relation to quality, and the divine is free from quality. We, on the contrary, confess identity of nature and accepting the consubstantiality, and rejecting the composition of the Father, God in substance, Who begat the Son, God in substance. From this the consubstantiality is proved.

403
(912)

LETTERS, No. 8
MG 32, 249
NPNF VIII, 116–117

Worshipping as we do God of God, we both confess the distinction of the Persons, and at the same time abide by the Monarchy. We do not fritter away the theology in a divided plurality, because one Form, so to say, united in the invariableness of the Godhead, is beheld in God the Father, and in God the Only begotten. For the Son is in the Father and the Father in the Son; since such as is the latter, such is the former, and such as is the former, such is the latter; and herein is the Unity. So that according to the distinction of Persons, both are one and one, and according to the community of Nature, one. How, then, if one and one, are there not two Gods? Because we speak of a king, and of the king's image, and not of two kings. The majesty is not cloven in two, nor the glory divided. The sovereignty and authority over us is one, and so the doxology ascribed by us is not plural but one; because the honor paid to the image passes on to the prototype. Now what in the one case the image is by reason of imitation, that in the other case the Son is by nature.

404
(952)

ON THE HOLY SPIRIT, 18:45
MG 32, 149
NPNF VIII, 28

ST. GREGORY NAZIANZEN

In my opinion He is called Son because He is identical with the Father in Essence; and not only for this reason, but also because He is of Him.

405
(994)

And He is called Only-begotten, not because He is the only Son and of the Father alone, and only a Son; but also because the manner of His Sonship is peculiar to Himself and not shared by bodies. And He is called the Word, because He is related to the Father as Word to Mind; not only on account of His passionless Generation, but also because of the Union, and of His declaratory function.

ORATIONS, 30:20
MG 36, 128
NPNF VII, 316

ST. JOHN CHRYSOSTOM

406
(1168)

'If any one has seen Me, he has seen the Father' (Jn. 14:9), He says Now had He been of a different Essence, He would not have spoken thus. But to make use of a grosser argument, no man that knows not what gold is, can discern the substance of gold in silver.

HOMILIES ON ST. JOHN, No. 74:1
MG 59, 401
NPNF XIV, 272

ST. AMBROSE

407
(1264)

Further, that none may fall into error, let a man attend to those signs vouchsafed us by holy Scripture, whereby we may know the Son. He is called the Word, the Son, the Power of God, the Wisdom of God. The Word, because He is without blemish; the Power, because He is perfect; the Son, because He is begotten of the Father; the Wisdom, because He is one with the Father, one in eternity, one in Divinity. Not that the Father is one Person with the Son; between Father and Son is the plain distinction that comes of generation; so that Christ is God of God, Everlasting of Everlasting, Fulness of Fulness.

TO GRATIAN ON THE CHRISTIAN FAITH, Bk. 1, Ch. 2
ML 16, 532
NPNF X, 203–204

408
(1271)

But the Arians think that they must oppose hereto the fact that He had said, 'I live by the Father' (Jn. 6:58). Of a certainty (suppose that they conceive the words as referring to His Godhead) the Son lives by the Father, because He is the Son begotten of the Father, —by the Father, because He is the Word given forth from the heart of the Father, because He came forth from the Father, because He is begotten of the 'bowels of the Father,' because the Father is the Fountain and Root of the Son's being.

TO GRATIAN, ON THE CHRISTIAN FAITH, Bk. 4, Ch. 10
ML 16, 642
NPNF X, 279

ST. AUGUSTINE

But if the Son is said to be sent by the Father on this account, that the one is the Father, and the other the Son, this does not in any manner hinder us from believing the Son to be equal, and consubstantial, and coeternal with the Father, and yet to have been sent as Son by the Father. Not because the one is greater, the other less; but because the one is Father, the other Son; the one begetter, the other begotten; the one He who is from Him who sends.

409
(1656)

ON THE TRINITY, Bk. 4, Ch. 20
ML 42, 906
NPNF III, 83

The Word of God, then, the only-begotten Son of the Father, in all things like and equal to the Father, God of God, Light of Light, Wisdom of Wisdom, Essence of Essence, is altogether that which the Father is, yet is not the Father, because the one is Son, the other is Father. And hence He knows all that the Father knows; but to Him to know, as to be, is from the Father, for to know and to be is there one. And therefore, as to be is not to the Father from the Son, so neither is to know. Accordingly, as though uttering Himself, the Father begat the Word equal to Himself in all things; for He would not have uttered Himself wholly and perfectly, if there were in His Word anything more or less than in Himself.

410
(1677)

ON THE TRINITY, Bk. 15, Ch. 14
ML 42, 1076
NPNF III, 213

ST. CYRIL OF ALEXANDRIA
See No. 438.

72. *The Holy Spirit is God.*

TERTULLIAN

See No. 330.

ST. BASIL
  See No. 348.

ST. GREGORY NAZIANZEN
  See Nos. 350 and 352.

ST. AUGUSTINE

411
(1670)

We have said elsewhere that those things are predicated specially in the Trinity as belonging severally to each Person, which are predicated relatively the one to the other, as Father and Son, and the gift of both, the Holy Spirit; for the Father is not the Trinity, nor the Son the Trinity, nor the gift the Trinity: but that whenever each is singly spoken of in respect to themselves, then they are not spoken of as three in the plural number, but one, the Trinity itself, as the Father God, the Son God, and the Holy Spirit God; the Father good, the Son good, and the Holy Spirit good; and the Father omnipotent, the Son omnipotent, and the Holy Spirit omnipotent: yet neither three Gods, nor three goods, nor three omnipotents, but one God, good, omnipotent, the Trinity itself; and whatsoever else is said of them not relatively in respect to themselves. For they are thus spoken of according to essence, since in them to be is the same as to be great, as to be good, as to be wise, and whatever else is said of each person individually therein, or of the Trinity itself, in respect to themselves. And that therefore they are called three persons, or three substances, not in order that any difference of essence may be understood, but that we may be able to answer by some one word, should any one ask what three, or what three things? And that there is so great an equality in that Trinity, that not only the Father is not greater than the Son, as regards divinity, but neither are the Father and Son together greater than the Holy Spirit; nor is each individual person, whichever it be of the three, less than the Trinity Itself.

ON THE TRINITY, Bk. 8, Proemium
ML 42, 946
NPNF III, 115

73. *That the Holy Spirit is God is proved by His operation.*

ST. BASIL
  See No. 347.

ST. AMBROSE

Who, then, can dare to say that the Holy Spirit is separated from the Father and the Son, since through Him we attain to the image and likeness of God, and through Him, as the Apostle Peter says (2 Pet. 1:4), are partakers of the divine nature?

412
(1283)

ON THE HOLY SPIRIT, Bk. 1, Ch. 6:80
ML 16, 723
NPNF X, 103

By footstool (Is. 66:1) is understood earth, but by the earth the Flesh of Christ, which we this day also adore in the mysteries, and which the apostles, as we said above, adored in the Lord Jesus; for Christ is not divided but is one; nor, when He is adored as the Son of God, is He denied to have been born of the Virgin. Since, then, the mystery of the Incarnation is to be adored, and the Incarnation is the work of the Spirit . . . without doubt the Holy Spirit also is to be adored, since He Who according to the flesh was born of the Holy Spirit is adored. And let no one divert this to the Virgin Mary; Mary was the temple of God, not the God of the temple. And therefore He alone is to be worshipped Who was working in His temple.

413
(1285)

ON THE HOLY SPIRIT, Bk. 3, Ch. 11:79
ML 16, 794
NPNF X, 146

ST. AUGUSTINE

With respect to the Holy Spirit, however, there has not been as yet, on the part of learned and distinguished investigators of the Scriptures, a discussion of the subject full enough or careful enough to make it possible for us to obtain an intelligent conception of what also constitutes His special individuality [proprium]: in virtue of which special individuality it comes to be the case that we cannot call Him either the Son or the Father, but only the Holy Spirit; excepting that they predicate Him to be the Gift of God, so that we may believe God not to give a gift inferior to Himself.

414
(1561)

ON FAITH AND THE CREED, Ch. 9:19
ML 40, 191
NPNF III, 329

74. *The Holy Spirit is consubstantial with the Father and the Son.*

ST. BASIL

415
(914)

You say that the Holy Spirit is a creature. And every creature is a servant of the Creator, for 'all are your servants' (Ps. 118:91). If then He is a servant, His holiness is acquired; and everything of which the holiness is acquired is receptive of evil; but the Holy Spirit being holy in essence is called 'fount of holiness' (cf. Rom. 1:4). Therefore the Holy Spirit is not a creature. If He is not a creature, He is of one essence and substance with the Father.

LETTERS, No. 8:10
MG 32, 261
NPNF VIII, 120

ST. GREGORY NAZIANZEN
See No. 350.

ST. AMBROSE
See No. 182.

ST. AUGUSTINE
See No. 337.

75. *The Holy Spirit proceeds from the Father and the Son.*

ST. AMBROSE

416
(1284)

Learn now that as the Father is the Fount of Life, so, too, many have stated that the Son is signified as the Fount of Life; so that, he says, with You, Almighty God, Your Son is the Fount of Life. That is the Fount of the Holy Spirit, for the Spirit is Life, as the Lord says: 'The words which I speak unto you are Spirit and Life' (Jn. 6:64), for where the Spirit is, there also is Life; and where Life is, is also the Holy Spirit.

ON THE HOLY SPIRIT, Bk. 1, Ch. 15
ML 16, 739
NPNF X, 113

ST. AUGUSTINE

If, therefore, that also which is given has him for a beginning by whom it is given, since it has received from no other source that which proceeds from him; it must be admitted that the Father and the Son are a Beginning of the Holy Spirit, not two Beginnings; but as the Father and Son are one God, and one Creator, and one Lord relatively to the creature, so are they one Beginning relatively to the Holy Spirit. But the Father, the Son, and the Holy Spirit is one Beginning in respect to the creature, as also one Creator and one God.

417
(1662)

ON THE TRINITY, Bk. 5, Ch. 14
ML 42, 921

See No. 368.   *NPNF* III, 95

Why, then, should we not believe that the Holy Spirit proceeds also from the Son, seeing that He is likewise the Spirit of the Son? For did He not so proceed, He could not, when showing Himself to His disciples after the resurrection, have breathed upon them, and said, 'Receive the Holy Spirit' (Jn. 20:22). For what else was signified by such a breathing upon them, but that from Him also the Holy Spirit proceeds?

418
(1839)

ON THE GOSPEL OF ST. JOHN, Tr. 99:7
ML 35, 1889
NPNF VII, 383–384

But from Him, of Whom the Son has it that He is God (for He is God of God), He certainly has it that from Him also the Holy Spirit proceeds: and in this way the Holy Spirit has it of the Father Himself, that He should also proceed from the Son, even as He proceeds from the Father. In connection with this, we come also to some understanding of the further point, that is, so far as it can be understood by such beings as ourselves, why the Holy Spirit is not said to be born, but to proceed: since, if He also were called by the name of Son, He could not avoid being called the Son of both, which is utterly absurd. For no one is a son of two, unless of a father and mother. But it would be utterly abhorrent to entertain the suspicion of any such intervention between God the Father and God the Son.

419
(1840)

ON THE GOSPEL OF ST. JOHN, Tr. 99:8
ML 35, 1890
NPNF VII, 384

76. *The divine Persons are distinguished among themselves only by relations.*

ST. HILARY

420
(867)

The apostolic faith, therefore, does not have two gods, because it does not have two fathers and two sons. When it acknowledges the Father it has acknowledged the Son. When it believes in the Son it has also believed in the Father, because the name of the Father likewise contains the name of the Son in itself. There is no father except through a son; the designation of a son reveals the father to us because there is no son except from a father. There is not one person, therefore, in the confession of the one God, while the Son also completes the Father and the birth of the Son is from the Father. Let him also ascribe a different nature to the two who does not know that in our teaching the Father and the Son are one! Let the heretics suppress the statement of the Son about Himself in the Gospel: 'I in the Father and the Father in me' (Jn. 10:38) so that they may teach either that there are two gods or a unique God! For, there are no designations of natures in the proper meaning of one nature, nor does the truth of God from God result in two gods, nor does the birth of God admit of a unique God, nor are they not one who are interchangeable. But they are interchangeable since the one is from the one.

ON THE TRINITY, Bk. 7, Ch. 31
ML 10, 226
FC XXV, 260–261

ST. BASIL
· See Nos. 344 and 348.

ST. GREGORY NAZIANZEN

421
(990)

Father is not a name either of an essence or of an action, most clever sirs. But it is the name of the relation in which the Father stands to the Son, and the Son to the Father. For as with us these names make known a genuine and intimate relation, so, in the case before us too, they denote an identity of nature between Him That is begotten and Him That begets.

ORATIONS, No. 29
MG 36, 96
See Nos. 350 and 366.
NPNF VII, 307

ST. GREGORY OF NYSSA
See No. 382.

ST. AMBROSE
See No. 407.

ST. AUGUSTINE
See Nos. 275, 411, 346, and 266.

ST. JOHN OF DAMASCUS
See No. 383.

The Father, the Son, and the Holy Spirit are one in all respects, save those of not being begotten, of birth and of procession. But it is by thought that the difference is perceived. For we recognize one God: but only in the attributes of Fatherhood, Sonship, and Procession, both in respect of cause and effect and perfection of subsistence, that is, manner of existence, do we perceive difference. For with reference to the un-circumscribed Deity we cannot speak of separation in space, as we can in our own case. For the subsistences dwell in one another, in no wise confused but cleaving together, according to the word of the Lord, 'I am in the Father, and the Father in Me' (Jn. 14:11) nor can one admit difference in will or judgment or energy or power or anything else whatsoever which may produce actual and absolute separation in our case. . . . For the Deity is undivided amongst things divided, to put it concisely: and it is just like three suns cleaving to each other without separation and giving out light mingled and conjoined into one.

422
(2344)

EXPOSITION OF THE ORTHODOX FAITH, Bk. 1, Ch. 8
MG 94, 828
NPNF IX, 10

Therefore all these names must be understood as common to deity as a whole, and as containing the notions of sameness and simplicity and indivisibility and union: while the names Father, Son and Spirit, and causeless and caused, and unbegotten and begotten, and procession contain the idea of separation; for these terms do not explain His essence, but the mutual relationship and manner of existence.

423
(2346)

EXPOSITION OF THE ORTHODOX FAITH, Bk. 1, Ch. 10
MG 94, 837

See No. 357.

NPNF IX, 12

77. *Operations outside are common to the three Persons.*

ST. IRENAEUS
See No. 327.

ST. ATHANASIUS
See No. 400.

ST. CYRIL OF JERUSALEM
See No. 361.

ST. BASIL
See No. 347.

424
(949)

And in the creation [of angels] think first, I pray you, of the original cause of all things that are made, the Father; of the creative cause, the Son; of the perfecting cause, the Spirit; so that the ministering spirits subsist by the will of the Father, are brought into being by the operation of the Son, and perfected by the presence of the Spirit. Moreover, the perfection of angels is sanctification and continuance in it. And let no one imagine me either to affirm that there are three original hypostases or to allege the operation of the Son to be imperfect. For the first principle of existing things is One, creating through the Son and perfecting through the Spirit. The operation of the Father who works all in all is not imperfect, neither is the creating work of the Son incomplete if not perfected by the Spirit. The Father, who creates by His sole will, could not stand in any need of the Son, but nevertheless He wills through the Son; nor could the Son, who works according to the likeness of the Father, need cooperation, but the Son too wills to make perfect through the Spirit.

ON THE HOLY SPIRIT, Ch. 16:38
MG 32, 136
NPNF VIII, 28

ST. GREGORY OF NYSSA

425
(1037)

Every operation which extends from God to the Creation, and is named according to our variable conceptions of it, has its origin from the Father, and proceeds through the Son, and is perfected in the Holy

222

Spirit. For this reason the name derived from the operation is not divided in the multitude of operations [of those who fulfill it].

ON "NOT THREE GODS"
MG 45, 125

See No. 382.   NPNF V, 334

ST. JOHN CHRYSOSTOM

Neither Angel nor Archangel can do anything with regard to what is given from God; but the Father, the Son, and the Holy Ghost, dispenses all, while the priest lends his tongue and affords his hand. For neither would it be just that through the wickedness of another, those who come in faith to the symbols of their salvation should be harmed.

HOMILIES ON ST. JOHN, 86:4
MG 59, 472
NPNF XIV, 326

426
(1169)

He who has the Spirit not only is called Christ's, but even has Christ Himself. For it cannot but be that where the Spirit is, there Christ is also. For wheresoever one Person of the Trinity is, there the whole Trinity is present. For It is undivided in Itself, and has a most entire Oneness.

HOMILIES ON ROMANS, 13:8
MG 60, 519
NPNF XI, 436

427
(1186)

ST. AUGUSTINE

When we say, both that the Father is the Beginning, and that the Son is the Beginning, we do not speak of two beginnings of the creature; since both the Father and the Son together is one beginning in respect to the creature, as one Creator, as one God.

ON THE TRINITY, Bk. 5, Ch. 13
ML 42, 920

See No. 417.   NPNF III, 89

428
(1661)

78. *Creation takes place through the Word.*

LETTER TO DIOGNETUS

The Almighty Creator of the Universe, the invisible God Himself, scattered from heaven among them the seed of truth and of holy

429
(98)

thought which is higher than men's minds, and He made it take firm root in their hearts. He did not send a servant (whether angel or principality, whether of those that direct the affairs of earth or of those entrusted with arrangements in heaven), but He sent the very Artificer and Maker of the cosmos, by whom He created the heavens, Him by Whom He enclosed the ocean in its proper bounds—He sent Him to them. Do you really think—as might be humanly supposed—that He sent Him to impose His power with fear and terror? Certainly not. He came in gentleness and humility. He sent Him as a King would send a son and king; He sent Him as God for the sake of men. In sending Him, He acted as a Savior, appealing to persuasion and not to power—for it is not like God to use compulsion.

Ch. 7:2
MG 2, 1176
FC I, 360–361

ST. JUSTIN MARTYR
See No. 247.

TATIAN
See No. 377.

430
(156)
For the heavenly Logos, a spirit emanating from the Father and a Logos from the Logos-power, in imitation of the Father who begat Him made man an image of immortality, so that, as incorruption is with God, in like manner, man, sharing in a part of God, might have the immortal principle also. The Logos, too, before the creation of men, was the Framer of angels. And each of these two orders of creatures was made free to act as it pleased, not having the nature of good, which again is with God alone, but is brought to perfection in men through their freedom of choice, in order that the bad man may be justly punished, having become depraved through his own fault, but the just man be deservedly praised for his virtuous deeds, since in the exercise of his free choice he refrained from transgressing the will of God.

ORATION AGAINST THE GREEKS, Ch. 7
MG 6, 820
ANF II, 67

ST. THEOPHILUS OF ANTIOCH
See No. 185.

ST. IRENAEUS

See No. 278.

But how can [the heretics] be consistent with themselves, [when they say] that the bread over which thanks have been given is the body of their Lord, and the cup His blood, if they do not call Himself the Son of the Creator of the world, that is, His Word, through whom the wood fructifies, and the fountains gush forth, and the earth gives 'first the blade, then the ear, then the full corn in the ear.'

431
(234)

Then, again, how can they say that the flesh, which is nourished with the body of the Lord, and with His blood, goes to corruption, and does not partake of life? Let them, therefore, either alter their opinion, or cease from offering the things just mentioned. But our opinion is in accordance with the Eucharist, and the Eucharist in turn establishes our opinion. For we offer to Him His own, announcing consistently the fellowship and union of the flesh and Spirit. For as the bread, which is produced from the earth, when it receives the invocation of God, is no longer common bread, but the Eucharist, consisting of two realities, earthly and heavenly; so also our bodies, when they receive the Eucharist, are no longer corruptible, having the hope of the resurrection to eternity.

AGAINST HERESIES, Bk. 4, Ch. 18
MG 7, 1027
ANF I, 486

See No. 327.

TERTULLIAN

See Nos. 395, 53, and 201.

ST. HIPPOLYTUS

See No. 379.

Let us believe then, dear brethren, according to the tradition of the Apostles, that God the Word came down from heaven, [and entered] into the holy Virgin Mary, in order that, taking the flesh from her, and assuming also a human, by which I mean a rational soul, and becoming thus all that man is with the exception of sin, He might save fallen man, and confer immortality on men who believe on His name. In all, therefore, the word of truth is demonstrated to us, that the Father is One, whose word is present [with Him], by whom He made all things;

432
(394)

whom also, as we have said above, the Father sent forth in later times for the salvation of men. This [Word] was preached by the law and the prophets as destined to come into the world. And even as He was preached then, in the same manner also did He come and manifest Himself, being by the Virgin and the Holy Spirit made a new man; for in that He had the heavenly [nature] of the Father, as the Word and the earthly [nature], as taking to Himself the flesh from the old Adam by the medium of the Virgin, He now, coming forth into the world, was manifested as God in a body, coming forth too as a perfect man. For it was not in mere appearance or by conversion, but in truth, that He became man.

AGAINST THE HERESY OF NOETUS, Ch. 17

MG 10, 825

ANF V, 230

ST. CLEMENT OF ALEXANDRIA
See Nos. 387 and 332.

ORIGEN
See No. 333.

ST. ATHANASIUS
See Nos. 372 and 374.

ST. BASIL

433
(943)

Whenever [Christ] instructs us about His Father, He is in the habit of using terms of personal authority, saying, 'I will; be clean' (Mt. 8:3); and 'Peace, be still' (Mk. 4:39); and 'But I say unto you' (Mt. 5:22); and 'You dumb and deaf spirit, I charge you' (Mk. 9:25); and all other expressions of the same kind, in order that by these we may recognize our Master and Maker, and by the former may be taught the Father of our Master and Creator. Thus on all sides is demonstrated the true doctrine that the fact that the Father creates through the Son neither constitutes the creation of the Father imperfect nor exhibits the active energy of the Son as feeble, but indicates the unity of the will; so the expression 'through whom' contains a confession of an antecedent Cause, and is not adopted in objection to the efficient Cause.

ON THE HOLY SPIRIT, Ch. 8:21

MG 32, 105

NPNF VIII, 14–15

See No. 424.

ST. AUGUSTINE
See No. 394.

ST. JOHN OF DAMASCUS

[The angels] are secondary intelligent lights derived from that first light which is without beginning, for they have the power of illumination; they have no need of tongue or hearing, but without uttering words they communicated to each other their own thoughts and counsels.

Through the Word, therefore, all the angels were created, and through the sanctification by the Holy Spirit were they brought to perfection, sharing each in proportion to his worth and rank in brightness and grace.

434
(2352)

EXPOSITION OF THE ORTHODOX FAITH, Bk. 2, Ch. 3
MG 94, 868
NPNF IX, 19

79. *Sanctification takes place through the Holy Spirit.*

ST. HIPPOLYTUS
See No. 298.

ST. GREGORY THAUMATURGUS
See No. 335.

ST. ATHANASIUS
See No. 401.

ST. CYRIL OF JERUSALEM

Then having sanctified ourselves by these spiritual Hymns, we beseech the merciful God to send forth His Holy Spirit upon the gifts lying before Him; that He may make the Bread the Body of Christ, and the Wine the Blood of Christ; for whatsoever the Holy Spirit has touched, is surely sanctified and changed.

435
(850)

CATECHESES, No. 23:7
MG 33, 1113
NPNF VII, 154

ST. BASIL
See No. 344.

227

ST. AMBROSE

436
(1282)

If, then, there be any grace in the water, it is not from the nature of the water, but from the presence of the Holy Spirit. . . . We were then sealed with the Spirit by God. For as we die in Christ, in order to be born again, so, too, we are sealed with the Spirit, that we may possess His brightness and image and grace, which is undoubtedly our spiritual seal. For although we were visibly sealed in our bodies, we are in truth sealed in our hearts, that the Holy Spirit may portray in us the likeness of the heavenly image.

ON THE HOLY SPIRIT, Bk. 1, Ch. 6
ML 16, 723
NPNF X, 103

ST. JOHN OF DAMASCUS
See No. 434.

THE MISSION OF THE DIVINE PERSONS

80. The Son is sent by the Father.

TERTULLIAN
See No. 330.

ST. HIPPOLYTUS
See No. 432.

ST. AUGUSTINE
See No. 409.

81. The Holy Spirit is also sent by the Son.

TERTULLIAN
See No. 53.

ST. HILARY

437
(871)

'When that Advocate has come, whom I will send you from the Father, the Spirit of truth who proceeds from the Father, He will bear witness concerning me' (Jn. 15:26). The Advocate will come and the Son will send Him from the Father, and He is the Spirit of truth who proceeds from the Father. . . . He who sends manifests His power in that which He sends. . . . Nor will I now infringe upon anyone's liberty of thought in this matter, whether they may regard the Paraclete Spirit as coming from the Father or from the Son. The Lord has left nothing uncertain, since He spoke as follows in the same discourse: 'Many things yet I have to say to you,' etc. (Jn. 16:12–15). Consequently, He receives from the Son who has been sent by Him and who proceeds from the Father. And I raise the question whether it is the same to receive from the Son as to proceed from the Father? But, if we must hold that there is a difference between receiving from the Son and proceeding from the Father, then, certainly, we shall have to admit that it is one and the same to receive from the Son as it is to receive from the Father.

ON THE TRINITY, Bk. 8, Ch. 19
ML 10, 250
FC XXV, 289

ST. CYRIL OF ALEXANDRIA

We believe in one God the Father Almighty, maker of all things visible and invisible. And in One Lord Jesus Christ His Son, naturally born of Him before the world and time. For He is at once coeternal with His Father before all time, His Father having no principle. The Son is endowed with equal glory and of the same rank, with every equality. For His face is the Splendor of His Substance. We believe likewise in the Holy Spirit whom we do not reckon apart from the divine nature; for He is naturally from the Father, infused through the Son. For so we understand the One and Consubstantial and Holy in the identity of glory and adorable Trinity.

438
(2126)

ON THE TRUE FAITH, Or. 1:3
MG 76, 1204

VI.

Creation

Anything which exists apart from God was produced by God out of nothing. Nor has God any need of anything, since He is totally sufficient in Himself, and all creation is His free act, designed solely to manifest His goodness. Revelation tells us that God alone creates according to the divine ideas, and it is through them that He knows all created things. It follows therefore that all creatures are good insofar as they participate in existence, for every being is derived from God. He it is who conserves all created things in their existence and coöperates immediately in every act they perform.

That God created all things is asserted by virtually all of the Church Fathers, and that everything was created out of nothing is repeated again and again by Tertullian in his *Against Hermogenes*. That God alone creates seems to be explicitated only by St. Athanasius and St. Augustine, although others certainly concur in this implicitly. It is their common doctrine that God creates freely and out of his goodness; only St. Augustine seems to resort explicitly to the divine ideas. Against some of the Gnostics it is necessary to affirm that the world is not eternal, and that God is not the author of evil just because He creates matter.

That there are angels created by God is testified to by as early a writer as St. Clement of Rome at the end of the first century. The Shepherd of Hermas, St. Justin Martyr, Tatian, and Athenagoras are second century witnesses, Origen and Tertullian in the third. Tertullian is more fascinated by the demons, and under what conditions angels may assume flesh. Lactantius, at the beginning of the fourth century, devotes considerable space to angels in *The Divine Insti-*

tutes, and St. Augustine advances the argument, which comes to full bloom in the *Dialogues* of St. Gregory the Great. The angels were created with free will, St. Justin Martyr tells us, and this is treated at some length by other second century writers such as Tatian and St. Irenaeus. Angels are able to communicate with one another and are distinguished in different orders. Some have already attained eternal beatitude, indeed many of them, and they are already confirmed in the good. The good angels are ministers of God and aid men in the business of salvation, and this is discussed at some length by the third century writer, Origen. Tertullian reminds us, however, that many angels, having committed grave sin, rushed into eternal damnation. All of this is admirably summarized by St. Augustine, notably in his classic *The City of God.*

Man himself is made in the image of God. He is composed of a body and of a soul which is distinct from his body and is immortal. Each man's soul is endowed with intellect and will, the freedom to choose good and avoid evil. Upon these all-important choices man's salvation depends. All men are descended from a single pair of parents. These first parents possessed utmost happiness, great knowledge, and self-control of all their natural powers, as well as freedom from death. Most of all, they had sanctifying grace which permitted them to share in God's own divine life. This made them children of God and heirs to the kingdom of heaven.

St. Justin Martyr, Tatian, and Athenagoras (second century writers) are the first to explicitate the body-soul composition of man. That the human soul is incorporeal is an important point with St. Irenaeus at the end of the second century and Tertullian in the third. As we might expect, the latter stresses the more dramatic aspects of the situation, such as the possibility of the incorporeal soul being tortured in hell by corporeal fire (*On the Soul*). The immortality of the human soul is especially pointed out by St. Justin Martyr, and all of these ideas are synthesized by both St. Augustine in the fifth century and St. John of Damascus in the eighth.

Possessing one immortal soul which has been created by God, man is endowed with free will, a point emphasized by all the major writers including Tatian and St. Theophilus of Antioch in the late second century. St. Justin Martyr affirms it; so do St. Irenaeus,

Tertullian, and Origen, and, of course, St. Augustine. Along with Origen, St. Gregory Nazianzen, and St. Hilary, St. Augustine feels that man's soul did not exist before his body and hence is not traduced by generation.

St. Irenaeus, Tertullian, and Aphraates affirm that God's creation of man is immediate.

Before the fall, our first parents were endowed with gifts of nature not due them. St. Irenaeus expatiates at some length on original justice, along with St. Cyprian (mid-third century) and St. Basil. St. Irenaeus is likewise impressed by our first parents' immunity to concupiscence. On the freedom from death St. Methodius has something to say in *The Banquet of the Ten Virgins,* as does St. Athanasius in the mid-fourth century in his *Treatise on the Incarnation of the Word.* Nor should we neglect the contributions of the great St. Augustine on these points. St. Cyril of Alexandria (fifth century) is impressed with the outstanding quality of Adam's knowledge, and St. Augustine reminds us that our first parents lived a life of the utmost happiness.

That God conserves all things in his divine government is mentioned by St. Theophilus of Antioch, St. Irenaeus, Origen, St. Gregory Nazianzen, and St. John of Damascus; and St. Jerome adds that God concurs in all the acts of His creatures.

82. *God created all things.*

ST. CLEMENT OF ROME

By the word of His majesty He has set up all things, and by a word He can overturn them.

439
(14)

LETTER TO THE CORINTHIANS, Ch. 27:4
MG 1, 268
FC I, 31

THE LETTER TO DIOGNETUS
See No. 429.

TERTULLIAN
See Nos. 243 and 87.

TATIAN
See No. 229.

440
(154)

For matter is not, like God, without beginning, nor, as having no beginning, is of equal power with God; it is created, and not produced by any other being, but brought into existence by the Framer of all things alone.

ORATION AGAINST THE GREEKS, Ch. 5
MG 6, 817
ANF II, 67

ST. THEOPHILUS OF ANTIOCH
See No. 277.

ST. IRENAEUS
See Nos. 211 and 278.

441
(267)

Inasmuch as certain men, impelled by what considerations I know not, remove from God the half of His creative power, by asserting that He is merely the cause of quality resident in matter, and by maintaining that matter itself is uncreated, —come, now, let us put the question, What is at any time, . . . is immutable. Matter, then, is immutable. But if matter be immutable, and the immutable suffers no change in regard to quality, it does not form the substance of the world. For which reason it seems to them superfluous, that God has annexed qualities to matter, since indeed matter admits of no possible alteration, it being in itself an uncreated thing. But further, if matter be uncreated, it has been made altogether according to a certain quality, and this immutable, so that it cannot be receptive of more qualities, nor can it be the thing of which the world is made. But if the world be not made from it, [this theory] entirely excludes God from exercising power on the creation [of the world].

FRAGMENT, No. 33
MG 7, 1248
ANF 573–574

TERTULLIAN

442
(326)

The very 'beginning' when God made the heaven and the earth, [some] will construe as if it meant something substantial and embodied, to

234

be regarded as Matter. We, however, insist on the proper signification of every word, [and say] that principium means beginning, —being a term which is suitable to represent things which begin to exist. For nothing which has to come into being is without a beginning, nor can this its commencement be at any other moment than when it begins to have existence. Thus principium, or beginning, is simply a term of inception, not the name of a substance.

AGAINST HERMOGENES, Ch. 19

ML 2, 214

ANF III, 486

ST. CLEMENT OF ALEXANDRIA
See Nos. 281 and 397.

ORIGEN
See No. 212.

And I cannot understand how so many distinguished men have been of opinion that this matter, which is so great, and possesses such properties as to enable it to be sufficient for all the bodies in the world which God willed to exist, and to be the attendant and slave of the Creator for whatever forms and species He wished in all things, receiving into itself whatever qualities He desired to bestow upon it, was uncreated, that is, not formed by God Himself, Who is the creator of all things, but that its nature and power were the result of chance. And I am astonished that they should find fault with those who deny either God's creative power or His providential administration of the world, and accuse them of impiety for thinking that so great a work as the world could exist without an architect or overseer; while they themselves incur a similar charge of impiety in saying that matter is uncreated, and co-eternal with the uncreated God.

443
(459)

ON FIRST PRINCIPLES, Bk. 2, Ch. 1:4

MG 11, 185

ANF IV, 269

ST. METHODIUS
See No. 233.

ST. HILARY
See No. 336.

ST. ATHANASIUS

444
(748)

But others, including Plato, who is in such repute among the Greeks, argue that God has made the world out of matter previously existing and without beginning. For God could have made nothing had not the material existed already; just as the wood must exist ready at hand for the carpenter, to enable him to work at all. . . . Thus do they vainly speculate. But the godly teaching and the faith according to Christ brands their foolish language as godlessness. For it knows that it was not spontaneously, because forethought is not absent; nor of existing matter, because God is not weak; but that out of nothing, and without its having any previous existence, God made the universe to exist through His Word, as He says firstly through Moses: 'In the beginning God created the heaven and the earth' (Gen. 1:1).

TREATISE ON THE INCARNATION OF THE WORD, Ch. 2
MG 25, 100
NPNF IV, 37

ST. GREGORY NAZIANZEN
See No. 297.

ST. CYRIL OF ALEXANDRIA
See No. 438.

83. God created all things out of nothing.

ST. JUSTIN MARTYR

445
(114)

For as in the beginning [God] created us when we were not, so do we consider that, in like manner, those who choose what is pleasing to Him are, on account of their choice, deemed worthy of incorruption and of fellowship with Him. For the coming into being at first was not in our own power; and in order that we may follow those things which please Him, choosing them by means of the rational faculties He has Himself endowed us with, He both persuades us and leads us to faith.

FIRST APOLOGY, Ch. 10
MG 6, 341
ANF I, 165

ST. JUSTIN'S HORTATORY ADDRESS TO THE GREEKS

And I think it necessary to attend to this also, that Plato never names him the creator, but the fashioner of the gods, although, in the opinion of Plato, there is considerable difference between these two. For the creator creates the creature by his own capability and power, being in need of nothing else; but the fashioner frames his production when he has received from matter the capability for his work.

446
(150)

Ch. 22
MG 6, 281
ANF I, 282

ST. THEOPHILUS OF ANTIOCH

But Plato and those of his school acknowledge indeed that God is uncreated, and the Father and Maker of all things; but then they maintain that matter as well as God is uncreated, and aver that it is coeval with God. But if God is uncreated and matter uncreated, God is no longer, according to the Platonists, the Creator of all things, nor, so far as their opinions hold, is the monarchy of God established. And further, as God, because He is uncreated, is also unalterable; so if matter, too, were uncreated, it also would be unalterable, and equal to God; for that which is created is mutable and alterable, but that which is uncreated is immutable and unalterable. And what great thing is it if God made the world out of existent materials? For even a human artist, when he gets material from some one, makes of it what he pleases. But the power of God is manifested in this, that out of things that are not He makes whatever He pleases; just as the bestowal of life and motion is the prerogative of no other than God alone.

447
(178)

TO AUTOLYCUS, Bk. 2, Ch. 4
MG 6, 1052
ANF II, 95

See No. 185.

ST. IRENAEUS
See No. 278.

While men, indeed, cannot make anything out of nothing, but only out of matter already existing, yet God is in this point pre-eminently superior to men, that He Himself called into being the substance of His creation, when previously it had no existence.

448
(199)

AGAINST HERESIES, Bk. 2, Ch. 10
MG 7, 736
ANF I, 370

TERTULLIAN

See Nos. 9, 53, and 279.

449
(324)

I cannot tell how Hermogenes is to escape from my conclusion; for he supposes that God cannot be the author of evil, in what way soever He created evil out of Matter, whether it was of His own will, or of necessity, or from the reason [of the case]. If, however, He is the author of evil, who was the actual Creator, Matter being simply associated [with Him] by reason of its furnishing Him with substance, you now do away with the cause of [your] introducing Matter. For it is not the less [true], that it is by means of matter that God shows himself the author of evil, although Matter has been assumed [by you] expressly to prevent God's seeming to be the author of evil. Matter being therefore excluded, since the cause of it is excluded, it remains that God, without doubt, must have made all things out of nothing. Whether evil things were among them we shall see, when it shall be made clear what are evil things, and whether those things are evil which you at present deem to be so. For it is more worthy of God that He produced even these of His own will, by producing them out of nothing, than from the predetermination of another, [which must have been the case] if He had produced them out of Matter. Liberty, not necessity, suits the character of God. I would much rather that He should have even willed to create evil of Himself, than that He should have lacked ability to hinder its creation.

AGAINST HERMOGENES, Ch. 16
ML 2, 211
ANF III, 486

See No. 280.

450
(327)

This authority of Scriptures I claim for myself even from this circumstance, that while it shows me the God Who created, and the works He created, it does not in like manner reveal to me the source from which He created. For since in every operation there are three principal things, He who makes, and that which is made, and that of which it is made, there must be three names mentioned in a correct narrative of the operation—the person of the maker, the sort of thing which is made, [and] the material of which it is formed. If the material is not mentioned, while the work and the maker of the work are both mentioned, it is manifest that He made the work out of nothing. For if He had had anything to operate upon, it would have been mentioned as well as [the other two particulars].

AGAINST HERMOGENES, Ch. 20
ML 2, 215
ANF III, 489

For I maintain that, even if the Scripture has not expressly declared that all things were made out of nothing—just as it abstains [from saying that they were formed] out of Matter—there was no such pressing need for expressly indicating the creation of all things out of nothing, as there was of their creation out of Matter, if that had been their origin. Because, in the case of what is made out of nothing, the very fact of its not being indicated that it was made of any particular thing shows that it was made of nothing; and there is no danger of its being supposed that it was made of anything, when there is no indication at all of what it was made of. . . . Then, if God had been unable to make all things of nothing, the Scripture could not possibly have added that He had made all things out of nothing. But it must by all means have informed us that He had made all things out of Matter, since Matter must have been the source; because the one case was quite to be understood, if it were not actually stated, whereas the other case would be left in doubt unless it were stated.

AGAINST HERMOGENES, Ch. 21
ML 2, 216
ANF III, 489

451
(328)

Firmly believe, therefore, that He produced it wholly out of nothing [the world], and then you have found the knowledge of God, by believing that He possesses such mighty power. But some persons are too weak to believe all this at first, owing to their views about Matter. They will rather have it [after the philosophers], that the universe was in the beginning made by God out of underlying matter. Now, even if this opinion could be held in truth, since He must be acknowledged to have produced in His reformation of matter far different substances and far different forms from those which Matter itself possessed, I should maintain, with no less persistence, that He produced these things out of nothing, since they absolutely had no existence at all previous to His production of them. Now, where is the difference between a thing's being produced out of nothing or out of something, if so be that what existed not comes into being, when even to have had no existence is tantamount to having been nothing? The

452
(363)

contrary is likewise true; for having once existed amounts to having been something. If, however, there *is* a difference, both alternatives support my position. For if God produced all things whatever out of nothing, He will be able to draw forth from nothing even the flesh which had fallen into nothing; or if He moulded other things out of matter, He will be able to call forth the flesh too from somewhere else, into whatever [abyss] it may have been engulfed. And surely He is most competent to re-create who created, inasmuch as it is a far greater work to have produced than to have reproduced, to have imparted a beginning than to have maintained a continuance. On this principle, you may be quite sure that the restoration of the flesh is easier than its first formation.

ON THE RESURRECTION OF THE FLESH, Ch. 11
ML 2, 809
ANF III, 553

ORIGEN
See No. 212.

453
(478)
A beginning may be that out of which a thing comes, the underlying matter from which things are formed. This, however, is the view of those who hold matter itself to be uncreated, a view which we believers cannot share, since we believe God to have made the things that are out of the things which are not, as the mother of the seven martyrs in the Maccabees teaches, and as the angel of repentance in the Shepherd inculcated.

COMMENTARY ON ST. JOHN, Bk. 1, Ch. 18
MG 14, 53

ST. METHODIUS

454
(615)
For man will exist even without the art of building, but it will have no existence unless man be previously in being. Whence we must say that it is in the nature of things for arts to be produced in men out of what has no existence. If, then, we have shown that this is so in the case of men, why was it improper to say that God is able to make not only qualities, but also substances, out of that which has no existence? For as it appears possible for something to be produced out of what exists not, it is evident that this is the case with substances.

ON FREE WILL
MG 18, 256
ANF VI, 360

ST. ATHANASIUS
See Nos. 444, 258, and 373.

ST. GREGORY NAZIANZEN
See No. 297.

ST. JOHN OF DAMASCUS

Since, then, God, Who is good and more than good, did not find satis- 455
faction in self-contemplation, but in His exceeding goodness wished (2349)
certain things to come into existence which would enjoy His benefits
and share in His goodness, He brought all things out of nothing into
being and created them, both what is invisible and what is visible.
Yes, even man, who is a compound of the visible and the invisible. And
it is by thought that He creates, and thought is the basis of the work,
the Word filling it and the Spirit perfecting it.

EXPOSITION OF THE ORTHODOX FAITH, Bk. 2, Ch. 2
MG 94, 864
NPNF IX, 18

84. *God creates freely.*

ATHENAGORAS

But God can neither have made man in vain, for He is wise, and no *456
work of wisdom is in vain; nor for His own use, for He is in want of (168)
nothing. But to a Being absolutely in need of nothing, no one of His
works can contribute anything to His own use. Neither, again, did He
make man for the sake of any of the other works which He has made.
For nothing that is endowed with reason and judgment has been
created, or is created, for the use of another, whether greater or less
than itself, but for the sake of the life and continuance of the being
itself so created. . . . Therefore, if man has been created neither without cause and in vain (for none of God's works is in vain, so far at
least as the purpose of their Maker is concerned), nor for the use of
the Maker Himself, or of any of the works which have proceeded from
Him, it is quite clear that although, according to the first and more
general view of the subject, God made man for Himself, and in pur-
suance of the goodness and wisdom which are conspicuous throughout
the creation, yet, according to the view which more nearly touches

the beings created, He made him for the sake of the life of those created, which is not kindled for a little while and then extinguished.

THE RESURRECTION OF THE DEAD, Ch. 12

MG 6, 996

ANF II, 155

ST. IRENAEUS

457
(196)

Nor was [God] influenced by any one, but of His own free will created all things, since He is the only God, the only Lord, the only Creator, the only Father, alone containing all things, and Himself commanding all things into existence.

AGAINST HERESIES, Bk. 2, Ch. 1

MG 7, 710

See No. 327.

ANF I, 359

ST. HIPPOLYTUS
See No. 379.

ST. ATHANASIUS
See No. 444.

ST. AUGUSTINE — *God creates freely & is good.*

458
(1751)

And by the words, 'God saw that it was good' (Gen. 1:10), it is sufficiently intimated that God made what was made not from any necessity, nor for the sake of supplying any want, but solely from His own goodness, that is, because it was good.

THE CITY OF GOD, Bk. 11, Ch. 24

ML 41, 338

NPNF II, 219

85. *God created out of His goodness.*

ST. ATHENAGORAS
See No. 456.

ST. IRENAEUS

459
(231)

In the beginning, therefore, did God form Adam, not as if He stood in need of man, but that He might have [some one] upon whom to confer His benefits. For not alone antecedently to Adam, but also be-

242

fore all creation, the Word glorified His Father, remaining in Him; and was Himself glorified by the Father, as He did Himself declare, 'Father, glorify Me with the glory which I had with You before the world was' (Jn. 17:5). Nor did He stand in need of our service when He ordered us to follow Him; but He thus bestowed salvation upon ourselves.

AGAINST HERESIES, Bk. 4, Ch. 14
MG 7, 1010
ANF I, 478

ORIGEN

We have frequently shown, by those declarations which we were able to produce from the holy Scriptures, that God, the Creator of all things, is good, and just, and all-powerful. When He in the beginning created those beings which He desired to create, that is, rational natures, He had no other reason for creating them than on account of Himself, that is, His own goodness.

460
(462)

ON FIRST PRINCIPLES, Bk. 2, Ch. 9
MG 11, 230
ANF IV, 291

ST. GREGORY NAZIANZEN

But since this movement of self-contemplation alone could not satisfy Goodness, but Good must be poured out and go forth beyond Itself to multiply the objects of Its beneficence, for this was essential to the highest Goodness, He first conceived the Heavenly and Angelic Powers. And this conception was a work fulfilled by His Word, and perfected by His Spirit. And so the secondary Splendours came into being, as the Ministers of the Primary Splendor; whether we are to conceive of them as intelligent Spirits, or as Fire of an immaterial and incorruptible kind, or as some other nature approaching this as near as may be.

461
(1005)

ORATIONS, No. 38:9
MG 36, 320
NPNF VII, 347

ST. AUGUSTINE
See No. 458.

ST. JOHN OF DAMASCUS
See No. 455.

86. *The world (matter) is not eternal.*

ST. JUSTIN MARTYR

462
(151)

So that Plato seems to grant an empty and impossible prerogative to his 'maker,' when he propounds that those who were once perishable because made from matter, which, according to Plato's opinion, is un-created, and contemporary and coaeval with the maker, should resist his will. For he who has not created has no power, in respect of that which is uncreated, so that it is not possible that it [matter], being free, can be controlled by any external necessity.

HORTATORY ADDRESS TO THE GREEKS, Ch. 23
MG 6, 284
ANF I, 282

TATIAN
See No. 440.

ST. THEOPHILUS OF ANTIOCH
See Nos. 447 and 185.

ST. IRENAEUS

463
(207)

For as the heaven which is above us, the firmament, the sun, the moon, the rest of the stars, and all their grandeur, although they had no previous existence, were called into being, and continue throughout a long course of time according to the will of God, so also any one who thinks thus respecting souls and spirits, and, in fact, respecting all created things, will not by any means go far astray, inasmuch as all things that have been made had a beginning when they were formed, but endure as long as God wills that they should have an existence and continuance.

AGAINST HERESIES, Bk. 2, Ch. 34
MG 7, 836

See No. 441.

ANF I, 411

TERTULLIAN
See No. 280.

ST. HIPPOLYTUS
See No. 379.

ORIGEN

This also is a part of the church's teaching, that the world was made and took its beginning at a certain time, and is to be destroyed on account of its wickedness. But what existed before this world, or what will exist after it, has not become certainly known to the many, for there is no clear statement regarding it in the teaching of the church.

ON FIRST PRINCIPLES, Bk. 1, Praef., 7
MG 11, 119
ANF IV, 240

464
(447)

As no one can be a father without having a son, nor a master without possessing a servant, so even God cannot be called omnipotent unless there exist those over whom He may exercise His power; and therefore, that God may be shown to be almighty, it is necessary that all things should exist. For if any one would have some ages or portions of time, or whatever else he likes to call them, to have passed away, while those things which were afterwards made did not yet exist, he would undoubtedly show that during those ages or periods God was not omnipotent, but became so afterwards, namely from the time that He began to have persons over whom to exercise power; and in this way He will appear to have received a certain increase, and to have risen from a lower to a higher condition; since there can be no doubt that it is better for Him to be omnipotent than not to be so.

ON FIRST PRINCIPLES, Bk. 1, Ch. 2
MG 11, 138
ANF IV, 249–250

465
(454)

ST. METHODIUS
See No. 233.

ST. ATHANASIUS
See No. 373.

ST. AUGUSTINE *the world is not eternal*

And if the sacred and infallible Scriptures say that 'in the beginning God created the heavens and the earth' (Gen. 1:1), in order that it may be understood that He had made nothing previously, —for if He had made anything before the rest, this thing would rather be said to have been made 'in the beginning,'—then assuredly the world was made, not in time, but simultaneously with time.

THE CITY OF GOD, Bk. 11, Ch. 6
ML 41, 321
NPNF II, 208

466
(1747)

245

467
(1757)
I own that I do not know what ages passed before the human race was created, yet I have no doubt that no created thing is co-eternal with the Creator.

THE CITY OF GOD, Bk. 12, Ch. 16
ML 41, 365
NPNF II, 236

ANGELS

87. There exist angels created by God.

ST. CLEMENT OF ROME

468
(17)
Let our glorying and our confidence be in Him; let us be subject to His will. Let us consider the whole multitude of angels, how they stand and minister to His will.

LETTER TO THE CORINTHIANS, Ch. 34
MG 1, 276
FC I, 179

THE SHEPHERD OF HERMAS

469
(83)
In answer I said to her: 'Lady, this is a great and marvellous thing. But, lady, the young men, the six who are building, who are they?' 'These are the holy angels of God, the first to be created, to whom He has committed His whole creation, to give increase, and to build, and to have complete control of creation. By their agency the building of the tower will be perfected.' 'Who are the others who are dragging along stones?' 'These also are God's holy angels, but the former six are superior to them. With their help, then, the tower will be perfected and all together will rejoice around the tower and give glory to God because the building of the tower has been perfected.'

VISION 3, 4:1
MG 2, 901
FC I, 244

ST. JUSTIN MARTYR

470
(113)
Hence are we called atheists. And we confess that we are atheists, so far as gods of this sort are concerned, but not with respect to the most true God, the Father of righteousness and temperance and the other

virtues, who is free from all impurity. But both Him, and the Son (who came forth from Him and taught us these things, and the host of the other good angels who follow and are made like to Him), and the prophetic Spirit, we worship and adore, knowing them in reason and truth, and declaring without grudging to every one who wishes to learn, as we ourselves have been taught.

FIRST APOLOGY, Ch. 6
MG 6, 336
ANF I, 164

See No. 354.

TATIAN
See No. 430.

ATHENAGORAS
See No. 325.

ORIGEN

This also is a part of the teaching of the church, that there are certain angels of God, and certain good influences, which are His servants in accomplishing the salvation of men. When these, however, were created, or of what nature they are, or how they exist, is not clearly stated.

471
(448)

ON FIRST PRINCIPLES, Bk. 1, Preface, 10
MG 11, 120
ANF IV, 241

ST. AUGUSTINE

For it is [God] Himself who in the beginning created the world full of all visible and intelligible beings, among which He created nothing better than those spirits whom He endowed with intelligence, and made capable of contemplating and enjoying Him. . . . It is He Who gave to this intellectual nature free-will of such a kind, that if he wished to forsake God, i.e., his blessedness, misery should at once result.

472
(1782)

THE CITY OF GOD, Bk. 22, Ch. 1
ML 41, 751
NPNF II, 475

ST. JOHN OF DAMASCUS

He is Himself the Maker and Creator of the angels: for He brought them out of nothing into being and created them after His own image, an incorporeal race, a sort of spirit or immaterial fire: in the words of

473
(2350)

the divine David, 'He makes His angels spirits, and His ministers a flame of fire' (Ps. 103:4).

EXPOSITION OF THE ORTHODOX FAITH, Bk. 2, Ch. 3

MG 94, 865

NPNF IX, 18

88. *Many angels, having attained eternal beatitude, have already been confirmed in the good.*

ST. GREGORY NAZIANZEN
See No. 285.

ST. AUGUSTINE

474
(1955)
At that time, therefore, God had given to man a good will, because in that will He had made him, since He had made him upright. He had given help without which he could not continue therein if he would; but that he should will, He left in his free will. He could therefore continue if he would, because the help was not wanting whereby he could, and without which he could not, perseveringly hold fast the good which he would. But that he willed not to continue is absolutely the fault of him whose merit it would have been if he had willed to continue; as the holy angels did, who, while others fell by free will, themselves by the same free will stood, and deserved to receive the due reward of this continuance—namely such a fulness of blessing that by it they might have the fullest certainty of always abiding in it. . . . Because by this grace of God there is caused in us, in the reception of good and in the persevering hold of it, not only to be able to do what we will, but even to will to do what we are able. But this was not the case in the first man; for the one of these things was in him, but the other was not.

ON GRACE AND FREE WILL, Bk. 11, Ch. 32

ML 44, 935

NPNF V, 484–485

89. *Many angels, however, having committed grave sin, rushed into eternal damnation.*

TERTULLIAN

475
(356)
But Christ, they say, bore [the nature of] an angel. For what reason? The same which induced Him to become man? Christ, then, was

actuated by the motive which led Him to take human nature. Man's salvation was the motive, the restoration of that which had perished. Man had perished; his recovery had become necessary. No such cause, however, existed for Christ's taking on Him the nature of angels. For although there is assigned to angels also perdition in 'the fire prepared for the devil and his angels' (Mt. 25:41), yet a restoration is never promised to them. No charge about the salvation of angels did Christ ever receive from the Father; and that which the Father neither promised nor commanded, Christ could not have undertaken.

ON THE FLESH OF CHRIST, Ch. 14
ML 2, 777
ANF III, 533

ST. AUGUSTINE

Thus the true cause of the blessedness of the good angels is found to be this, that they cleave to Him who supremely is. And if we ask the cause of the misery of the bad, it occurs to us, and not unreasonably, that they are miserable because they have forsaken Him who supremely is, and have turned to themselves who have no such essence. . . . For when the will abandons what is above itself, and turns to what is lower, it becomes evil—not because that is evil to which it turns, but because the turning itself is wicked. Therefore it is not an inferior thing which has made the will evil, but it is itself which has become so by wickedly and inordinately desiring an inferior thing. For if two men, alike in physical and moral constitution, see the same corporeal beauty, and one of them is excited by the sight to desire an illicit enjoyment while the other steadfastly maintains a modest restraint of his will, what do we suppose brings it about, that there is an evil will in the one and not in the other? . . . If both are tempted equally and one yields and consents to the temptation while the other remains unmoved by it, what other account can we give of the matter than this, that the one is willing, the other unwilling, to fall away from chastity? And what causes this but their own wills, in cases at least such as we are supposing, where the temperament is identical?

THE CITY OF GOD, Bk. 12, Ch. 6
ML 41, 353
NPNF II, 229

476
(1753)

See No. 474.

90. *The good angels are ministers of God and aid men in the business of salvation.*

THE SHEPHERD OF HERMAS
See Nos. 469 and 340.

ORIGEN

477
(446)

After these points, also, the apostolic teaching is that the soul, having a substance, and life of its own, shall, after its departure from the world, be rewarded according to its deserts, being destined to obtain either an inheritance of eternal life and blessedness, if its actions shall have procured this for it, or to be delivered up to eternal fire and punishments, if the guilt of its crimes shall have brought it down to this: and also, that there is too a time of resurrection from the dead, when this body, which now 'is sown in dishonor will rise in glory' (1 Cor. 15:42). This also is clearly defined in the teaching of the church, that every rational soul is possessed of free-will and volition; that it has a struggle to maintain with the devil and his angels, and opposing influences, because they strive to burden it with sins; but if we live rightly and wisely, we should endeavour to shake ourselves free of a burden of that kind. From which it follows, also, that we understand ourselves not to be subject to necessity, so as to be compelled by all means, even against our will, to do either good or evil. For if we are our own masters, some influences perhaps may impel us to sin, and others help us to salvation; we are not forced, however, by any necessity either to act rightly or wrongly, which those persons think is the case who say that the courses and movements of the stars are the cause of human actions, not only of those which take place beyond the influence of the freedom of the will, but also of those which are placed within our own power. But with respect to the soul, whether it is derived from the seed by a process of traducianism, so that the reason or substance of it may be considered as placed in the seminal particles of the body themselves, or whether it has any other beginning; and this beginning itself, whether it be by birth or not, or whether bestowed upon the body from outside or not, is not distinguished with sufficient clearness in the teaching of the church.

ON FIRST PRINCIPLES, Bk. 1, Praef. 5
MG 11, 118
ANF IV, 240

See No. 471.

ST. JOHN CHRYSOSTOM

This is the office of angels, to minister to God for our salvation. So
that it is an angelical work, to do all for the salvation of the brethren:
or rather it is the work of Christ Himself, for He indeed saves as
Lord, but they as servants.

478
(1217)

HOMILIES ON HEBREWS, 3:4
MG 63, 30
NPNF XIV, 377

ST. JOHN OF DAMASCUS

They are mighty and prompt to fulfill the will of God, and their
nature is endowed with such celerity that wherever the Divine glance
bids them there they are straightway found. They are the guardians of
the divisions of the earth: they are set over nations and regions,
allotted to them by their Creator: they govern all our affairs and bring
us help.

479
(2354)

EXPOSITION OF THE ORTHODOX FAITH, Bk. 2, Ch. 3
MG 14, 128
NPNF IX, 19

MAN

91. Man is composed of body and soul.

ST. JUSTIN MARTYR

But, in truth, [God] has even called the flesh to the resurrection, and
promises to it everlasting life. For where He promises to save man,
there He gives the promise to the flesh. For what is man but the
reasonable animal composed of body and soul? Is the soul by itself
man? No; but the soul of man. Would the body be called man? No,
but it is called the body of man. If, then, neither of these is by itself
man, but that which is made up of the two together is called man, and
God has called man to life and resurrection, He has called not a part,
but the whole, which is the soul and the body.

480
(147)

FRAGMENTS OF THE LOST WORK ON THE RESURRECTION, Ch. 8
MG 6, 1585
ANF I, 297

TATIAN

481
(159)

But further, it becomes us now to seek for what we once had, but have lost, to unite the soul with the Holy Spirit, and to strive after union with God. . . . The perfect God is without flesh; but man is flesh. The bond of the flesh is the soul; that which encloses the soul is the flesh. Such is the nature of man's constitution; and, if it be like a temple, God is pleased to dwell in it by the spirit, His representative; but, if it be not such a habitation, man excels the wild beasts in articulate language only, —in other respects his manner of life is like theirs, as one who is not a likeness of God.

ORATION AGAINST THE GREEKS, Ch. 15
MG 6, 837
ANF II, 71

ATHENAGORAS

482
(170)

For if the whole nature of men in general is composed of an immortal soul and a body which was fitted to it in the creation, and if neither to the nature of the soul by itself, nor to the nature of the body separately, has God assigned such a creation or such a life and entire course of existence as this, but to men compounded of the two, in order that they may, when they have passed through their present existence, arrive at one common end, with the same elements of which they are composed at their birth and during life, it unavoidably follows, since one living-being is formed from the two, experiencing whatever the soul experiences and whatever the body experiences, doing and performing whatever requires the judgment of the senses or of the reason, that the whole series of these things must be referred to some one end, in order that they all, and by means of all, —namely man's creation, man's nature, man's life, man's doings and sufferings, his course of existence, and the end suitable to his nature, —may concur in one harmony and the same common experience.

THE RESURRECTION OF THE DEAD, Ch. 15
MG 6, 1004
ANF II, 157

ST. AUGUSTINE ― Man Composed of Body / Soul

483
(1563)

And inasmuch as there are three things of which man consists, —namely, spirit, soul, and body—which again are spoken of as two, because frequently the soul is named along with the spirit; for a certain

252

rational position of the same, of which beasts are devoid, is called spirit: the principal part in us is the spirit.

ON FAITH AND THE CREED, Ch. 10:23
ML 40, 193
NPNF III, 331

ST. JOHN OF DAMASCUS
See No. 455.

92. *The human soul is immortal.*

ST. JUSTIN MARTYR

But if the world is begotten, souls also are necessarily begotten; and perhaps at one time they were not in existence, for they were made on account of men and other living creatures, if you will say that they have been begotten wholly apart, and not along with their respective bodies.

'This seems to be correct.'

'They are not, then, immortal?'

'No; since the world has appeared to us to be begotten.'

'But I do not say, indeed, that all souls die; for that would truly be a piece of good fortune to the evil. What then? The souls of the pious remain in a better place, while those of the unjust and wicked are in a worse, waiting for the time of judgment. Thus some which have appeared worthy of God never die; but others are punished so long as God wills them to exist and to be punished. . . . For those things which exist after God, or shall at any time exist, these have the nature of decay, and are such as may be blotted out and cease to exist; for God alone is unbegotten and incorruptible, and therefore He is God, but all other things after Him are created and corruptible. For this reason souls both die and are punished.'

DIALOGUE WITH TRYPHO, Ch. 5
MG 6, 488
ANF I, 197

484
(132)

The soul either is or has life. If then, it is life, it would cause something else, and not itself, to live, even as motion would move something else than itself. Now, that the soul lives, no one would deny. But if it lives, it lives not as being life, but as the partaker of life; but that

485
(133)

which partakes of anything, is different from that of which it does partake. Now the soul partakes of life, since God wills it to live. Thus, then, it will not even partake [of life] when God does not will it to live.

DIALOGUE WITH TRYPHO, Ch. 6
MG 6, 489
ANF I, 198

TATIAN

486
(157)

The soul is not in itself immortal, O Greeks, but mortal. Yet it is possible for it not to die. If, indeed, it knows not the truth, it dies, and is dissolved with the body, but rises again at last at the end of the world with the body, receiving death by punishment in immortality. But, again, if it acquires the knowledge of God, it dies not, although for a time it be dissolved.

ORATION AGAINST THE GREEKS, Ch. 13
MG 6, 833
ANF II, 70

ATHENAGORAS
See No. 456.

APHRAATES

487
(683)

Therefore, my beloved, we also have received of the Spirit of Christ, and Christ dwells in us, as it is written that the Spirit said this through the mouth of the Prophet: I will dwell in them and will walk in them. Therefore let us prepare our temples for the Spirit of Christ, and let us not grieve it that it may not depart from us. . . . For from baptism do we receive the Spirit of Christ. For in that hour in which the priests invoke the Spirit, the heavens open and it descends and moves upon the waters. And those that are baptized are clothed in it; for the Spirit stays aloof from all that are born of the flesh, until they come to the new birth by water, and then they receive the Holy Spirit. For in the first birth they are born with an animal soul which is created within man and is not thereafter subject to death, as he said: Adam became a living soul. But in the second birth, that through baptism, they received the Holy Spirit from a particle of the Godhead, and it is not again subject to death. For when men die, the animal spirit is buried with the body, and sense is taken away from it, but the heavenly spirit that they receive goes according to its nature to Christ.

254

And both these the Apostle has made known, for he said: The body is buried in animal wise, and rises again in spiritual wise. . . . And whatever man there is that receives the Spirit from the water [of baptism] and grieves it, it departs from him until he dies, and returns according to its nature to Christ, and accuses that man of having grieved it.

DEMONSTRATIONS, No. 6:14
PS 1, 291
NPNE XIII, 371–372

93. *Man is free* (see under heading 102).

ST. JUSTIN MARTYR

We have learned from the prophets, and we hold it to be true, that punishments, and chastisements, and good rewards, are rendered according to the merit of each man's actions. Since if it be not so, but all things happen by fate, neither is anything at all in our own power. For if it be fated that this man, e.g., be good, and this other evil, neither is the former meritorious nor the latter to be blamed. And again, unless the human race have the power of avoiding evil and choosing good by free choice, they are not accountable for their actions, of whatever kind they be. But that it is by free choice they both walk uprightly and stumble, we thus demonstrate. We see the same man making a transition to opposite things. . . . For neither would [man] be worthy of reward or praise did he not of himself choose the good, but were created for this end; nor, if he were evil, would he be worthy of punishment, not being evil of himself, but being able to do nothing else than what he was made.

488
(123)

FIRST APOLOGY, Ch. 43
MG 6, 392
ANF I, 177

TATIAN
See No. 430.

ST. THEOPHILUS OF ANTIOCH

But some one will say to us, Was man made by nature mortal? Certainly not. Was he, then, immortal? Neither do we affirm this. But one will say, Was he, then, nothing? Not even this hits the mark. He was by nature neither mortal nor immortal. For if [God] had made him

489
(184)

immortal from the beginning, He would have made him God. Again, if He had made him mortal, God would seem to be the cause of his death. Neither, then, immortal nor yet mortal did He make him, but, as we have said above, capable of both; so that if he should incline to the things of immortality, keeping the commandment of God, he should receive as reward from Him immortality, and should become God; but if, on the other hand, he should turn to the things of death, disobeying God, he should himself be the cause of death to himself. For God made man free, and with power over himself.

TO AUTOLYCUS, Bk. 2, Ch. 27
MG 6, 1093
ANF II, 105

TERTULLIAN

490
(335)
I find, then, that man was by God constituted free, master of his own will and power; indicating the presence of God's image and likeness in him by nothing so well as by this constitution of his nature. For it was not by his face, and by the lineaments of his body, though they were so varied in his human nature, that he expressed his likeness to the form of God. . . . This his state was confirmed even by the very law which God then imposed upon him. For a law would not be imposed upon one who had it not in his power to render that obedience which is due to law; nor, again, would the penalty of death be threatened against sin, if a contempt of the law were impossible to man in the liberty of his will.

AGAINST MARCION, Bk. 2, Ch. 5
ML 2, 290
ANF III, 301

ORIGEN
See No. 477.

491
(466)
This too, I think, should next be inquired into, viz. what are the reasons why a human soul is acted on at one time by good [spirits], and at another by bad: . . . To all which instances, those who maintain that everything in the world is under the administration of divine providence (as is also our own belief), can, as it appears to me, give no other answer, so as to show that no shadow of injustice rests upon the divine government, than by holding that there were certain causes of prior existence, in consequence of which the souls, before their

birth in the body, contracted a certain amount of guilt in their sensitive nature, or in their movements, on account of which they have been judged worthy by Divine Providence of being placed in this condition. For a soul is always in possession of free-will, as well when it is in the body as when it is without it.

ON FIRST PRINCIPLES, Bk. 3, Ch. 3
MG 11, 318
ANF IV, 336

94. *The human soul is created by God.*

APHRAATES
See No. 487.

ST. JEROME

I ask whence Cain and Abel, who were the first-born of our first parents, had their souls? And the whole human race downwards, what are we to think was the origin of their souls? Did they come by propagation, like brute beasts? So that, as body springs from body, so soul from soul? Or is God daily making souls—He, with whom to will is to do, and who never ceases to be a Creator?

492
(1385)

TO PAMMACHIUS AGAINST JOHN OF JERUSALEM, Ch. 22
ML 23, 372
NPNF VI, 434

ST. AUGUSTINE

These things being so, it is necessary still to investigate and to make known the reason why, if souls are created new for every individual at his birth, those who die in infancy without the sacrament of Christ are doomed to perdition; for that they are doomed to this if they so depart from the body is testified both by Holy Scripture and by the Holy Church. Wherefore, as to that opinion of yours concerning the creation of new souls, if it does not contradict this firmly grounded article of faith, let it be mine also; but if it does, let it be no longer yours.

493
(1441)

LETTERS, No. 166:8:25
ML 33, 731
FC IX, 28

494
(1559)

I say that the soul was made by God as all other things that were made by God; and that among the things that God Almighty made the principal place was given to the soul. But if you ask whence God made the soul, remember that you and I agree in confessing that God is almighty.

DISPUTATION AGAINST FORTUNATUS, Ch. 13
ML 42, 117
NPNF IV, 116

495
(1879)

Since, then, I am now speaking to a catholic, whence I pray you tell me, do you suppose that the soul, I will not say your soul or my own soul, but the soul of the first man, was given to him? If you admit that it came from nothing, made, however, and inbreathed into him by God, then your belief tallies with my own.

ON THE SOUL AND ITS ORIGIN, Bk. 2, Ch. 3
ML 44, 497
NPNF V, 333

ST. LEO THE GREAT

496
(2181)

Men's souls did not exist until they were breathed into their bodies, and they were not there implanted by another than God, Who is the Creator both of the souls and of the bodies. And because through the transgression of the first man the whole stock of the human race was tainted, no one can be set free from the state of the old Adam save through Christ's sacrament of baptism.

LETTERS, No. 15:10
ML 54, 683
NPNF XII, 23

THE FIRST MAN

95. Before the fall, our first parents were endowed with gifts of nature not due them: original justice.

ST. IRENAEUS

497
(225)

Resisting the erring, the lustful propensity of his flesh (since he had lost his natural disposition and child-like mind, and had come to the knowledge of evil things), he girded a bridle of continence upon himself and his wife, fearing God, and waiting for His coming, and indicating, as it were, some such thing: —Inasmuch as, he says, I have by disobedience lost that robe of sanctity which I had from the Spirit, I do now also acknowledge that I am deserving of a covering of this nature, which affords no gratification, but which gnaws and frets the body.

AGAINST HERESIES, Bk. 3, Ch. 23
MG 7, 963
ANF I, 457

And again, those persons who are not bringing forth the fruits of righteousness, and are, as it were, covered over and lost among brambles, if they use diligence, and receive the word of God as a graft, arrive at the pristine nature of man—that which was created after the image and likeness of God. But as the engrafted wild olive does not certainly lose the substance of its wood, but changes the quality of its fruit, and receives another name, being now not a wild olive, but a fruit-bearing olive, and is called so; so also, when man is grafted in by faith and receives the Spirit of God, he certainly does not lose the substance of flesh, but changes the quality of the fruit [brought forth, that is,] of his works, and receives another name, showing that he has become changed for the better, being now not [mere] flesh and blood, but a spiritual man, and is called such.

498
(253)

AGAINST HERESIES, Bk. 5, Ch. 10
MG 7, 1148
ANF I, 536

ST. CYPRIAN

The devil bore with impatience the fact that man was made to the image of God, and for this reason was the first to perish and cause to perish. Adam, in violation of the heavenly command, was incapable of resisting the desire of the deadly food and fell into the death of sin; he did not preserve, under the guardianship of patience, the grace received from God.

499
(567)

THE GOOD OF PATIENCE, Ch. 19
ML 4, 634
FC XXXVI, 281

ST. BASIL

500
(973)
Man was made after the image and likeness of God; but sin marred the beauty of the image by dragging the soul down to passionate desires. Now, God, who made man, is the true life. Therefore, when man lost his likeness to God, he lost his participation in the true life; separated and estranged from God as he is, it is impossible for him to enjoy the blessedness of the divine life. Let us return, then, to the grace [which was ours] in the beginning and from which we have alienated ourselves by sin, and let us again adorn ourselves with the beauty of God's image, being made like to our Creator through the quieting of our passions.

ASCETICAL WORKS, Ch. 1
MG 31, 869
FC IX, 207

ST. LEO THE GREAT

501
(2192)
If, dearly beloved, we comprehend faithfully and wisely the beginning of our creation, we shall find that man was made in God's image, to the end that he might imitate his Creator, and that our race attains its highest natural dignity, by the form of the Divine goodness being reflected in us, as in a mirror. And assuredly to this form the Saviour's grace is daily restoring us, so long as that which in the first Adam fell, is raised up again in the second.

SERMONS, No. 12:1
ML 54, 168
NPNF XII, 121

96. Our first parents were free from concupiscence.

ST. IRENAEUS

502
(224)
And even as she [Eve], having indeed a husband, Adam, but being nevertheless as yet a virgin (for in Paradise 'they were both naked, and were not ashamed') (Gen. 2:25), inasmuch as they, having been created a short time previously, had no understanding of the procreation of children: (for it was necessary that they should first come to adult age, and then multiply from that time onward), having become disobedient, was made the cause of death, both to herself and to the entire human race; so also did Mary having a man betrothed [to her],

260

and being nevertheless a virgin, by yielding obedience, become the cause of salvation, both to herself and the whole human race. And on this account does the law term a woman betrothed to a man, the wife of him who had betrothed her, although she was as yet a virgin; thus indicating the back-reference from Mary to Eve, because what is joined together could not otherwise be put asunder than by inversion of the process by which these bonds of union had arisen; so that the former ties be cancelled by the latter, that the latter may set the former again at liberty. . . . And thus also it was that the knot of Eve's disobedience was loosed by the obedience of Mary. For what the virgin Eve had bound fast through unbelief, this did the virgin Mary set free through faith.

AGAINST HERESIES, Bk. 3, Ch. 22
MG 7, 959
ANF I, 455

ST. AUGUSTINE - *Parents free of concupiscence*

In Paradise, then, man lived as he desired so long as he desired what God had commanded. He lived in the enjoyment of God, and was good by God's goodness; he lived without any want, and had it in his power so to live eternally. He had food that he might not hunger, drink that he might not thirst, the tree of life that old age might not waste him. There was in his body no corruption, nor seed of corruption, which could produce in him any unpleasant sensation. He feared no inward disease, no outward accident. Soundest health blessed his body, absolute tranquillity his soul. As in Paradise there was no excessive heat or cold, so. its inhabitants were exempt from the vicissitudes of fear and desire.

THE CITY OF GOD, Bk. 14, Ch. 26
ML 41, 434
NPNF II, 281

503
(1762)

What then? Did not Adam have the grace of God? Yes, truly, he had it largely, but of a different kind. He was placed in the midst of benefits which he had received from the goodness of his Creator; for he had not procured those benefits by his own deservings; in which benefits he suffered absolutely no evil. But saints in this life, to whom pertains this grace of deliverance, are in the midst of evils out of which they cry to God, 'Deliver us from evil' (Mt. 6:13). He in those benefits needed not the death of Christ: these, the blood of that Lamb

504
(1952)

absolves from guilt, as well inherited as their own. He had no need to that assistance which they implore when they say, 'I see another law in my members' (Rom. 7:23–5). . . . . He, however, tempted and disturbed in no such conflict concerning himself against himself, in that position of blessedness enjoyed his peace with himself.

ON REBUKE AND GRACE, Ch. 11:29
ML 44, 933
NPNF V, 482

97. *Our first parents were immune from the necessity of dying.*

ST. THEOPHILUS OF ANTIOCH
See No. 489.

ST. CYPRIAN

505
(566)

For since in that first transgression of God's command strength of body departed with immortality, and infirmity entered the body by death, and since strength cannot be regained except when immortality shall have been regained, it is necessary to keep struggling and contending in this state of bodily weakness and infirmity.

THE GOOD OF PATIENCE, Ch. 17
ML 4, 633
FC XXXVI, 279–280

ST. METHODIUS

506
(612)

For [Adam] also was created without corruption, that he might honor the king and maker of all things, responding to the shouts of the melodious angels which came from heaven. But when it came to pass that, by transgressing the commandment [of God], he suffered a terrible and destructive fall, being thus reduced to a state of death, for this reason the Lord says that He came from heaven into [a human] life, leaving the ranks and the armies of angels. . . . For it remained that man should be included in this catalogue and number, the Lord lifting him up and wrapping him round, that he might not again, as I said, be overflowed and swallowed up by the waves of deceit. For with this purpose the Word assumed the nature of man, that, having overcome the serpent, He might by Himself destroy the condemnation which had come into being along with man's ruin. For it was fitting that the Evil One should be overcome by no other, but by him whom he had deceived, and whom he was boasting that he held in subjection, because no otherwise was it possible that sin and condemnation should be destroyed, unless that same man on whose account it had been said, 'Dust you are, and unto dust you shall return' (Gen. 3:19), should be created anew, and undo the sentence which for his sake had gone forth on all, that 'as in Adam' at first 'all die, even so' again 'in Christ,' who assumed the nature and position of Adam should 'all be made alive.'

THE BANQUET OF THE TEN VIRGINS, Ch. 3:6
MG 18, 69
ANF VI, 318

ST. ATHANASIUS

Men, having despised and rejected the contemplation of God, and devised and contrived evil for themselves (as was said in the former treatise), received the condemnation of death with which they had been threatened; and from thenceforth no longer remained as they were made, but were being corrupted according to their devices; and death had the mastery over them as king. For transgression of the command-ment was turning them back to their natural state, so that just as they have had their being out of nothing, so also, as might be expected, they might look for corruption into nothing in the course of time.

507
(749)

TREATISE ON THE INCARNATION OF THE WORD, Ch. 4
MG 25, 104
NPNF IV, 38

For God has not only made us out of nothing; but He gave us freely, by the Grace of the Word, a life in correspondence with God. But men, having rejected things eternal, and, by counsel of the devil, turned to the things of corruption, became the cause of their own corruption in death, being, as I said before, by nature corruptible, but destined, by the grace following from partaking of the Word, to have escaped their natural state, had they remained good. For because of the Word dwelling with them, even their natural corruption did not come near them.

508
(750)

TREATISE ON THE INCARNATION OF THE WORD, Ch. 5
MG 25, 104
NPNF IV, 40–41

ST. AUGUSTINE

509
(1760)

And therefore it is agreed among all Christians who truthfully hold the Catholic faith, that we are subject to the death of the body, not by the law of nature, by which God ordained no death for man, but by His righteous infliction on account of sin.

THE CITY OF GOD, Bk. 13, Ch. 15

ML 41, 387

See No. 468.

NPNF II, 252

510
(1956)

On which account we must consider with diligence and attention in what respect those pairs differ from one another, —to be able not to sin, and not to be able to sin; to be able not to die, and not to be able to die; to be able not to forsake good, and not to be able to forsake good. For the first man was able not to sin, was able not to die, was able not to forsake good. . . . Therefore the first liberty of the will was *to be able not to sin,* the last will be much greater, *not to be able to sin;* the first immortality was to be able not to die, the last will be much greater, not to be able to die; the first was the power of perseverance, to be able not to forsake good—the last will be the felicity of perseverance, not to be able to forsake good.

ON REBUKE AND GRACE, Ch. 12:33

ML 44, 942

NPNF V, 485

VII.

Sin

Sin is a turning away from God and a turning towards creatures. After the angels were created by the goodness of God out of nothing they were subjected to a moral testing. The good angels who passed the test were rewarded with the beatific vision; the bad angels were rejected and through their own fault merited consignment to hell. Our first parents underwent a similar testing, but sinned seriously and lost both the preternatural gifts of great knowledge, self-control, freedom from suffering and death, and the supernatural gifts of sanctifying grace and the infused virtues of faith, hope, and charity. As a result, every person born into this world is born with original sin, the deprivation of grace caused by the free act of sin committed by the head of the race, for original sin is transmitted by natural generation. Those who die in the state of original sin are excluded from the beatific vision of God. Adam's fall, however, did not destroy man's free will, as some of the Reformers vigorously maintained. There can be no sin unless there first be free consent, for all sin has a voluntary aspect. Sins may be serious or venial; something of sin remains even after the sinful act has already taken place, and if there is grave sin on the soul at the time of death that soul is eternally lost.

All of these ideas find their fullest development in the writings of St. Augustine, although they are not all to be found in any one place. In the *Reply to Faustus the Manichaean,* we learn that sin is a turning from God and a conversion to creatures, and *The City of God* reminds us that sin is not something positive, but rather a negation. But this is not to say that he is the sole commentator on

265

this dreary subject. St. Justin Martyr, Athenagoras, St. Irenaeus, and Minucius Felix in the second century, and Tertullian in the third, also remind us that there are such sins as merely internal sins, but it is still primarily the Bishop of Hippo who distinguishes grave sins from those which are merely venial. Nor are all grave sins equal, St. Jerome tells us.

St. Justin Martyr, St. Irenaeus, and Tertullian will not admit of sin without free consent. Once again it is St. Augustine who is most articulate and precise with regard to this doctrine. He also assures us that God is not the author of sin, but only permits it, but sin indeed inflicts death in the soul and something of sin remains even after the sinful act has already taken place.

With regard to original sin, and the sin of our first parents, there is ample testimony. St. Irenaeus, St. Cyprian, and Tertullian discuss it, the latter expounding at great length on the effect of Adam's sin, which is death. St. Hippolytus in the early third century, as well as St. Cyprian and St. Methodius, also discusses this subject. The fourth century is represented by selections from St. Athanasius and St. Cyril of Jerusalem. St. Theophilus of Antioch, St. Irenaeus, and St. Ephraem testify along with St. Augustine that Adam through sin lost his other free gifts as well.

In spite of all this, free will has been preserved even though all have been corrupted by the sin of Adam. St. Irenaeus and Tertullian insist on this point, and in the mid-third century St. Cyprian and a century later St. Athanasius follow suit. Particularly eloquent is St. John Chrysostom in the latter part of the fourth century. And of course we must never forget St. Augustine. His doctrine is fully expounded at several points in *On Marriage and Concupiscence*. He even advances the theory at one point that in natural generation original sin is passed down from the father. In this he has the support of St. Leo the Great. All of this has a relationship to the question of concupiscence, but only St. Augustine clearly distinguishes between concupiscence and original sin.

With only two notable exceptions St. Augustine is the only writer who puzzles for a long time over the fate of infants dying without baptism. How can they be saved if they are contaminated by original sin as they surely must be? But how can they be lost if it be not through their own fault? St. Gregory Nazianzen seems to think they will be neither glorified nor punished, and St. Prosper of Aquitaine suggests that infants are lost or saved because the divine Omnipotence can tell what would have happened to them later on in life. If these solutions seem somewhat somber and perhaps not altogether satisfactory, we must remember that the struggle with the Pelagians and Semi-Pelagians no doubt colored the rather austere thinking of St. Augustine, and when a solution was finally reached at the Second Council of Orange in 529, it was a solution based with some exceptions on his essential doctrine.

PERSONAL SIN

98. *Sin is a turning from God and a conversion to creatures.*

ST. AUGUSTINE

Sin, then, is any transgression in deed, or word, or desire, of the eternal law. And the eternal law is the divine order or will of God, which requires the preservation of the natural order, and forbids the breach of it. But what is this natural order in man? Man, we know, consists of soul and body; but so does a beast. Again, it is plain that in the order of nature the soul is superior to the body. Moreover, in the soul of man there is reason, which is not in a beast. Therefore, as the soul is superior to the body, so in the soul itself the reason is superior by the law of nature to the other parts which are found also in beasts.

511
(1605)

REPLY TO FAUSTUS THE MANICHAEAN, Bk. 22, Ch. 27
ML 42, 418
See No. 476. *NPNF* IV, 283

Because man was made upright, that he might not live according to himself, but according to Him that made him—in other words, that he might do His will and not his own; and not to live as he was made to live, that is a lie. For he certainly desires to be blessed even by not

512
(1761)

living so that he may be blessed. And what is a lie if this desire be not? Wherefore it is not without meaning said that all sin is a lie.

THE CITY OF GOD, Bk. 14, Ch. 4
ML 41, 407
NPNF II, 264

ORIGINAL SIN

99. *Our first parents, having committed grave sin, lost original justice.*

ST. IRENAEUS
See No. 497.

TERTULLIAN

513
(286)

Finally, in every instance of annoyance and in every expression of contempt and detestation, you utter the word 'Satan.' This is the one whom we call the angel of wickedness, the artificer of every error, the corrupter of the whole world; through him, man was deceived from the beginning so that he transgressed the commandment of God and, therefore, having been given unto death, made the whole human race, which was infected by his seed, the transmitter of condemnation.

THE TESTIMONY OF THE SOUL, Ch. 3
ML 1, 613
FC X, 136

ST. CYPRIAN
See No. 499.

100. *Death is the effect of Adam's sin.*

ST. THEOPHILUS OF ANTIOCH

514
(183)

So also for the first man, disobedience procured his expulsion from Paradise. Not, therefore, as if there were any evil in the tree of knowledge; but from his disobedience did man draw, as from a fountain, labor, pain, grief, and at last fall a prey to death.

TO AUTOLYCUS, Ch. 2:25
MG 6, 1092
ANF II, 104

TERTULLIAN

Now in this very point, which is called the resurrection of the dead, it is requisite that the proper force of the words should be accurately maintained. The word *dead* expresses simply what has lost the vital principle, by means of which it used to live. Now the body is that which loses life, and as the result of losing it becomes dead. To the *body,* therefore, the term dead is only suitable. Moreover, as resurrection accrues to what is dead, and dead is a term applicable only to a body, therefore the body alone has a resurrection incidental to it. So again the word 'resurrection,' or [rising again], embraces only that which has fallen down. 'To rise,' indeed, can be predicated of that which has never fallen down, but had already been always lying down. But 'to rise again' is predicable only of that which has fallen down; because it is by rising *again,* in consequence of its having fallen down, that it is said to have *re*-risen. For the syllable *re* always implies iteration [or happening *again*]. We say, therefore, that the body falls to the ground by death, as indeed facts themselves show, in accordance with the law of God. For to the body it was said, [till you return to the ground, for out of it were you taken; for] dust you are, and unto dust shall you return' (Gen. 3:19). That, therefore, which came from the ground shall return to the ground. Now that falls down which returns to the ground; and that rises again which falls down. 'Since by man came death, by man came also the resurrection' (1 Cor. 15:21). Here in the word *man,* who consists of bodily substance, as we have often shown already is presented to me the body of Christ. But if we are all so made alive in Christ, as we die in Adam, it follows of necessity that we are made alive in Christ as a bodily substance, since we died in Adam as a bodily substance. The similarity, indeed, is not complete, unless our revival in Christ concur in identity of substance with our mortality in Adam. But at this point [the apostle] has made a parenthetical statement concerning Christ, which, bearing as it does on our present discussion, must not pass unnoticed. For the resurrection of the body will receive all the better proof, in proportion as I shall succeed in showing

515
(345)

269

that Christ belongs to that God who is believed to have provided this resurrection of the flesh in His dispensation.

AGAINST MARCION, Bk. 5, Ch. 9
ML 2, 491
ANF III, 447–448

ST. HIPPOLYTUS

516
(395)

We therefore believe that the body also is raised. For if it become corrupt, it is not at least destroyed. For the earth receiving its remains preserves them, and they, becoming as it were seed, and being wrapped up with the richer part of earth, spring up and bloom. And that which is sown is sown indeed bare grain; but at the command of God the Artificer it buds, and is raised arrayed and glorious, but not until it has first died, and been dissolved, and mingled with earth. Not, therefore, without good reason do we believe in the resurrection of the body. Moreover, if it is dissolved in its season on account of the primeval transgression, and is committed to the earth as to a furnace, to be moulded again anew, it is not raised the same as it is now, but pure and no longer corruptible. And to every body its own proper soul will be given again; and the soul, being endued again with it, shall not be grieved, but shall rejoice together with it, abiding itself pure with it also pure. And as it now sojourns with it in the world righteously, and finds it in nothing now a traitor, it will receive it again [the body] with great joy. But the unrighteous will receive their bodies unchanged, and unransomed from suffering and disease, and unglorified, and still with all the ills in which they died. And whatever manner of persons they [were when they] lived without faith, as such they shall be faithfully judged.

AGAINST THE GREEKS (PLATO), Ch. 2
MG 10, 800
ANF V, 222

ST. CYPRIAN
See Nos. 505 and 499.

ST. METHODIUS
See No. 506.

ST. ATHANASIUS
See Nos. 507 and 508.

For since the first man Adam altered, and through sin death came into 517
the world, therefore it became the second Adam to be unalterable; that, (763)
should the Serpent again assault, even the Serpent's deceit might be
baffled, and, the Lord being unalterable and unchangeable, the Serpent
might become powerless in his assaults against all. For as when Adam
had transgressed, his sin reached unto all men, so, when the Lord had
become man and had overthrown the Serpent, that so great strength
of His is to extend through all men, so that each of us may say, 'For
we are not ignorant of his devices' (2 Cor. 2:11). Good reason then
that the Lord, whoever is in nature unalterable, loving righteousness
and hating iniquity, should be anointed and Himself sent, that, He,
being and remaining the same, by taking this alterable flesh, 'might
condemn sin in it,' and might secure its freedom, and its ability henceforth 'to fulfil the righteousness of the law' in itself, so as to be able to
say, 'But we are not in the flesh but in the Spirit, if so be that the
Spirit of God dwells in us' (Rom. 8:9).

FOUR DISCOURSES AGAINST THE ARIANS, Or. 1:51
MG 26, 117
NPNF IV, 336

ST. CYRIL OF JERUSALEM

And wonder not that the whole world was ransomed; for it was no 518
mere man, but the only-begotten Son of God, who died on its behalf. (829)
Moreover one man's sin, even Adam's had power to bring death to the
world; but if by the trespass of the one death reigned over the world
(Rom. 5:17), how shall not life much rather reign by the righteousness of the One? And if because of the tree of good they were then cast
out of Paradise, shall not believers now more easily enter into Paradise
because of the Tree of Jesus? If the first man formed out of the earth
brought in universal death, shall not He Who formed him out of the
earth bring in eternal life, being Himself the Life? If Phinees, when
he waxed zealous and slew the evil-doer, stayed the wrath of God
(Num. 25:8), shall not Jesus, who slew not another, but gave up
Himself for a ransom, put away the wrath which is against mankind?

CATECHESES, 13:2
MG 33, 773
NPNF VII, 82

ST. AUGUSTINE
See No. 509.

101. Through sin Adam lost the other free gifts.

ST. THEOPHILUS OF ANTIOCH
See No. 514.

ST. IRENAEUS
See No. 497.

ST. EPHRAEM

519
(703)

Adam sinned and earned all sorrows; —likewise the world after his example, all guilt. —And instead of considering how it should be restored, —considered how its fall should be pleasant for it. Glory to Him Who came and restored it! This cause summoned Him that is pure, —that He should come and be baptized, even He with the defiled, —Heaven for His glory was rent asunder. —That the purifier of all might be baptized with all, —He came down and sanctified the water for our baptism.

HYMNS FOR THE FEAST OF THE EPIPHANY, No. 10:1
L 1, 98
NPNF XIII, 280

ST. AUGUSTINE

520
(1727)

As therefore our first parents, by their subsequent return to righteous living, by which they are supposed to have been released from the worst penalty of their sentence through the blood of the Lord, were still not deemed worthy to be recalled to Paradise during their life on earth, so in like manner our sinful flesh, even if a man lead a righteous life in it after the remission of his sins, does not deserve to be immediately exempted from that death which it has derived from its propagation of sin.

ON THE MERITS AND REMISSION OF SINS, AND ON THE
BAPTISM OF INFANTS, Bk. 2: 34:55
MG 11, 828
NPNF V, 66

But who of us will say that by the sin of the first man free will perished from the human race? Through sin freedom indeed perished, but it was that freedom which was in Paradise, to have a full righteousness with immortality; and it is on this account that human nature needs divine grace.

521
(1883)

AGAINST TWO LETTERS OF THE PELAGIANS, Bk. 1, Ch. 2
ML 44, 552
NPNF V, 378

102. Adam's sin has passed on to all men.

ST. IRENAEUS
See No. 502.

[God] we had indeed offended in the first Adam, when he did not perform His commandment. In the second Adam, however, we are reconciled, being made obedient even unto death. For we were debtors to none other but to Him Whose commandment we had transgressed at the beginning.

522
(255)

AGAINST HERESIES, Bk. 5, Ch. 16
MG 7, 1148
ANF I, 544

TERTULLIAN
See No. 513.

ST. CYPRIAN

If even to the greatest sinners, and to those who had sinned much against God, when they subsequently believed, remission of sins is granted—and nobody is hindered from baptism and from grace—how much rather ought we to shrink from hindering an infant, who, being lately born, has not sinned, except in that, being born after the flesh according to Adam, he has contracted the contagion of the ancient death at its earliest birth, who approaches the more easily on this very account to the reception of the forgiveness of sins—that to him are remitted, not his own sins, but the sins of another.

523
(586)

LETTERS, No. 64:5
ML 3, 1018
ANF V, 354

APHRAATES
See No. 487.

ST. ATHANASIUS
See No. 517.

ST. JOHN CHRYSOSTOM

524
(1184)

But what means, 'for that all have sinned' (Rom. 5:12)? This; he having once fallen, even they that had not eaten of the tree did from him, all of them, become mortal. . . . From whence it is clear, that it was not this sin, the transgression, that is, of the Law, but that of Adam's disobedience, which marred all things. Now what is the proof of this? The fact that even before the Law all died: for 'death reigned,' he says, 'from Adam to Moses, even over them that had not sinned' (ib. 14). How did it reign? 'After the similitude of Adam's transgression, who is the figure of Him that was to come' (ib.). Now this is why Adam is a type of Christ. . . . When the Jew says to you, How came it that by the well-doing of this one Person, Christ, the world was saved? you might be able to say to him, How by the disobedience of this one person, Adam, came it to be condemned?

LETTER TO THE ROMANS, Ch. 10:1
MG 60, 474
NPNF XI, 401

525
(1185)

For we were at once freed from punishment, and put off all iniquity, and were also born again from above and rose again with the old man buried, and were redeemed, justified, led up to adoption, sanctified, made brothers of the Only-begotten, and joint heirs and of one Body with Him, and counted for His Flesh, and even as a Body with the Head, so were we united unto Him! All these things then Paul calls a 'superabundance' of grace (Rom. 5:17), showing that what we received was not a medicine only to counterbalance the wound, but even health, and comeliness, and honor, and glory and dignities far transcending our natural state. And of these each in itself was enough to do away with death, but when all manifestly run together in one, there is not the least vestige of it left, nor can a shadow of it be seen, so entirely is it done away. . . . For Christ has paid down far more than we owe, yes as much more as the illimitable ocean is than a little drop. . . . 'Therefore as by the offence of one judgment came upon all men to condemnation; even so by the righteousness of One the free

274

gift came upon all men unto justification of life' (Rom. 5:19). . . .
What then does the word 'sinners' mean here? To me it seems to mean
liable to punishment and condemned to death.

LETTER TO THE ROMANS, Ch. 10:2

MG 60, 476

NPNF XI, 403–404

ST. AUGUSTINE - *a. sin passed to all men.*

All His saints, also, imitate Christ in the pursuit of justice; whence the
same apostle, whom we have already quoted, says: 'Be imitators of me,
as I am also of Christ' (1 Cor. 11:1). But besides this imitation, His
grace works within us our illumination and justification, by that operation concerning which the same preacher of His [name] says: 'Neither
is he that plants anything nor he that waters, but God that gives the
increase' (ib. 3, 7). For by this grace He engrafts into His body even
baptized infants, who certainly have not yet become able to imitate
anyone. And therefore He, in Whom all are made alive, besides offering
Himself as an example of righteousness to those who imitate Him,
gives also to those who believe on Him the hidden grace of His Spirit,
which He secretly infuses even into infants; so likewise he, in whom
all die, besides being an example for imitation to those who wilfully
transgress the commandment of the Lord, depraved also in his own
person all who come of his stock by the hidden corruption of his own
carnal concupiscence. . . . This indicates propagation, not imitation.

526
(1715)

ON THE MERITS AND REMISSION OF SINS, AND ON THE

BAPTISM OF INFANTS, Bk. 1:9

ML 44, 114

NPNF V, 19

This grace, however, of Christ, without which neither infants nor
adults can be saved, is not rendered for any merits, but is given *gratis,*
on account of which it is also called grace. 'Being justified,' says the
apostle, 'freely through His blood' (Rom. 3:24). Whence they, who
are not liberated through grace, either because they are not yet able to
hear, or because they are unwilling to obey; or again because they did
not receive, at the time when they were unable on account of youth to
hear, that bath of regeneration, which they might have received and
through which they might have been saved, are indeed justly condemned; because they are not without sin, either that which they have
derived from their birth, or that which they have added from their own

527
(1791)

misconduct. 'For all have sinned'—whether in Adam or in themselves—'and come short of the glory of God' (ib. 23).

ON NATURE AND GRACE, Ch. 4:4
ML 44, 249
NPNF V, 122

528   Concupiscence which is cleansed only by the sacrament of regenera-
(1871) tion, does undoubtedly, by means of natural birth, pass on the bond of
sin to a man's posterity, unless they are themselves loosed from it by
regeneration. In the case, however, of the regenerate, concupiscence is
not itself sin any longer, whenever they do not consent to it for
illicit works, and when the members are not applied by the presiding
mind to perpetrate such deeds. . . . Inasmuch, however, as by a certain
manner of speech it is called sin, since it arose from sin, and, when it
has the upper hand, produces sin, the guilt of it prevails in the natural
man; but this guilt, by Christ's grace through the remission of all sins,
is not suffered to prevail in the regenerate man, if he does not yield
obedience to it whenever it urges him to the commission of evil.

ON MARRIAGE AND CONCUPISCENCE, Bk. 1, Ch. 23
ML 44, 428
NPNF V, 274

529   The very embrace which is lawful and honourable cannot be effected
(1872) without the ardour of lust, so as to be able to accomplish that which
appertains to the use of reason and not of lust. . . . This carnal concupiscence is the daughter of sin; and whenever it yields assent to the
commission of shameful deeds, it becomes also the mother of many
sins. Now from this concupiscence whatever comes into being by
natural birth is bound by original sin, unless, indeed, it be born again
in Him Whom the Virgin conceived without this concupiscence. Wherefore, when He vouchsafed to be born in the flesh, He alone was born
without sin.

ON MARRIAGE AND CONCUPISCENCE, Bk. 1, Ch. 24
ML 44, 429
NPNF V, 274

530   Marriage is not the cause of the sin which is transmitted in the
(1876) natural birth, and atoned for in the new birth; but the voluntary transgression of the first man is the cause of original sin. . . . What then is
[Julian's] object when he inquires of us, 'By what means sin may be
found in an infant, through the will, or through marriage, or through

its parents?' . . . Now, there is an answer for him to all these questions given by the apostle, who censures neither the infant's will, which is not yet matured in him for sinning, nor marriage, which, as such, has not only its institution, but its blessing also, from God; nor parents, so far as they are parents, who are united together properly and lawfully for the procreation of children; but he says, "By one man sin entered into the world, and death by sin; and so death passed upon all men, for in him all have sinned' (Rom. 5:12).

ON MARRIAGE AND CONCUPISCENCE, Bk. 2, Ch. 26
ML 44, 461
NPNF V, 300

'If,' says [Julian] 'sin comes from the will, it is an evil will that causes sin; if it comes from nature, then nature is evil.' I at once answer, Sin does come from the will. Perhaps he wants to know, whether original sin also. I answer, most certainly original sin also. Because it, too, was engendered from the will of the first man; so that it both existed in him, and passed on to all. 531
(1877)

ON MARRIAGE AND CONCUPISCENCE, Bk. 2, Ch. 28
ML 44, 464

See No. 303.   *NPNF* V, 302

ST. LEO THE GREAT
See No. 496.

103. *On the fate of infants dying without baptism.*

ST. GREGORY NAZIANZEN

And so also in those who fail to receive the Gift [baptism], some are altogether animal or bestial, according as they are either foolish or wicked; and this, I think, has to be added to their other sins, that they have no reverence at all for this Gift, but look upon it as a mere gift— to be acquiesced in if given them, and if not given them, then to be neglected. Others know and honor the Gift, but put it off; some through laziness, some through greediness. Others are not in a position to receive it, perhaps on account of infancy, or some perfectly involuntary circumstance through which they are prevented from receiving it, even if they wish. . . . And I think that the first will have to suffer punishment, as for all their sins, so for their contempt of baptism; and that 532
(1012)

the second will also have to suffer, but less, because it was not so much through wickedness as through folly that they wrought their failure; and that the third will neither be glorified nor punished by the righteous Judge, as unsealed and yet not wicked, but persons who have suffered rather than done wrong.

> ORATIONS, No. 40:23
> *MG* 36, 389
> *NPNF* VII, 367

ST. AUGUSTINE
See No. 493.

533
(1878)
Let no one promise for the case of unbaptized infants, between damnation and the kingdom of heaven, some middle place of rest and happiness, such as he pleases' and where he pleases. For this is what the heresy of Pelagius promised them.

> ON THE SOUL AND ITS ORIGIN, Bk. 1, Ch. 9
> *ML* 44, 481

See No. 302.
> *NPNF* V, 292

534
(1908)
Who can doubt that non-baptized infants, having only original sin and no burden of personal sins, will suffer the lightest condemnation of all? I cannot define the amount and kind of their punishment, but I dare not say it were better for them never to have existed than to exist there.

> AGAINST JULIAN, Bk. 5, Ch. 11
> *ML* 44, 809
> *FC* 286

535
(1924)
And, of course, the mildest punishment of all will fall upon those who have added no actual sin, to the original sin they brought with them; and as for the rest who have added such actual sins, the punishment of each will be the more tolerable in the next world, according as his iniquity has been less in this world.

> ON FAITH, HOPE, AND LOVE (ENCHIRIDION), Ch. 93
> *ML* 40, 275

See Nos. 311 and 315.
> *NPNF* III, 267

VIII.

Actual Grace

Grace is a supernatural gift which God of His free benevolence bestows on rational creatures for their eternal salvation. For every salutary act God's internal supernatural grace is absolutely necessary, even for the beginning of faith and of salvation. Indeed, special help is needed if the just are to persevere to the end in justification, for even they cannot avoid all sins during their entire life without the special privilege of the grace of God. Against the Pelagians who maintained that Adam's sin had affected only himself, and that everyone could work out his salvation through good moral conduct, the Church insisted that supernatural grace was both a free gift and a necessity. But this did not mean (as the extreme Augustinians and some of the Reformers held) that men could not posit certain naturally good acts. Grace does not destroy free will, and yet it is essentially gratuitous and surpasses all the exigencies of nature. It enables man to participate in the divine life of God, and ultimately to attain and enjoy the beatific vision.

It is of course St. Augustine who dominates the field of grace, but while he did much in his struggle against the Pelagians and Semi-Pelagians to explicitate the Church's doctrine of grace, it would be incorrect to say that he was the sole influence—even granting that he was certainly the chief influence. For example, the idea that every good salutary work requires grace as an absolute necessity is discovered as early as the second century in the writings of St. Irenaeus in his *Against Heresies,* and shortly after in Tertullian's *On the Soul.* In the third century it appears in St. Cyprian, in the fourth in St. Gregory Nazianzen and St. Chrysostom. But by conservative estimate it appears specifically in St. Augustine's writings at least in twenty different places, notably in his *On the Gospel of St. John* and *On Grace and Free Will.* This is not to say that without grace man cannot place certain acts naturally good, for God does not command the impòssible. Yet in some sense, the acts of sinners and of the infidels are sins, for without grace man cannot keep the law for any length of time.

Even for the beginning of faith and conversion grace is necessary as St. Justin Martyr points out in the second century, and in the fourth this is echoed by St. Cyril of Jerusalem, St. Basil, and St. John Chrysostom, in any number of places in his homilies. St. Augustine hammers the point repeatedly in his *On the Predestination of the Saints,* and it can be found in later writers such as St. Prosper of Aquitaine and St. John Cassian. St. Cyprian reminds us that without grace man cannot resist for long concupiscence and grave temptations, and Origen adds that no one can be completely immune from concupiscence and small sins without a special privilege of grace. St. Augustine makes the same point a dozen different times in his writings against the Pelagians, adding that grace is necessary even for the man already perfectly justified. And final perseverance, he goes on to say, is a great gift of God.

St. Cyril of Jerusalem points out that grace is a certain internal motion, consisting in an illumination of the mind according to St. Clement of Alexandria and St. Ephraem, as well as an inspiration of the will (St. Ignatius of Antioch, St. Cyprian, and St. John Chrysostom). But only St. Augustine seems actually to refer to grace as coming before salutary acts as prevenient, calling, or exciting, while denominating the grace which aids the performance of salutary acts as helping, cooperating, and subsequent. But he does not monopolize the idea that grace so coöperates with the human will that man can thus do no good which God does not do at the same time. One finds this in the second century in both Origen and St. Cyprian, and St. Ephraem, St. Gregory Nazianzen, and St. John Chrysostom teach it in the fourth.

The idea of "sufficient grace" (*gratia sufficiens*)—grace which truly suffices to produce its effect, but nevertheless does not actually produce it, —is discussed by the second-century writer St. Irenaeus, and also by Arnobius; St. John Chrysostom also dwells on it some-what in the fourth century. "Efficacious grace" (*gratia efficax*)—the grace which effectively moves the will—is discussed by both Tertullian and St. Cyprian, writing in the third century. All of this, of course, receives masterful treatment at the hands of St. Augustine.

But while emphasizing the necessity of grace, it is also important not to destroy freedom of the will; hence a large number of writers such as St. Irenaeus and Origen, St. Ephraem and St. Gregory of Nyssa, St. John Chrysostom and St. Augustine vigorously defend man's human liberty. So with an equal grace, one person can give consent and another dissent. Yet St. Augustine reminds us that God infallibly knows beforehand in what way free will is to make use of the aid of grace.

Grace is a free gift of God and surpasses all the exigencies of nature—here all of the quotations are almost entirely from St. Augustine, but St. Prosper of Aquitaine reminds us of God's grace to the most hardened sinners, and St. Caesar of Arles asserts that God never deserts a man unless He is first deserted by him.

The prickly problem of grace and free will as opposites to be reconciled does not become a major concern until the fourth century, and even then it is St. Augustine who is the most articulate. Yet the idea that God denies sufficient grace for faith and salvation to no one, not even the unfaithful, appears in as early a writer as St. Clement of Rome. Arnobius has it, as well as St. John Chrysostom and St. Jerome, and it occurs in such post-Augustinian writers as St. Prosper of Aquitaine and St. Hilary of Arles. The controversies flare up again during the Reformation and continue on into the seventeenth century, but at bottom the fundamental mystery remains, probably incapable of a really satisfactory solution.

THE NECESSITY OF GRACE

104. For every good salutary work grace is absolutely necessary.

ST. IRENAEUS

536
(220)

The Lord also promised to send the comforter, who should join us to God (Jn. 16:7). For as a compacted lump of dough cannot be formed of dry wheat without fluid matter, nor can a loaf possess unity, so, in like manner, neither could we, being many be made one in Christ Jesus without the water from heaven. And as dry earth does not bring forth unless it receive moisture, in like manner we also, being originally a dry tree, could never have brought forth fruit unto life without the voluntary rain from above. For our bodies have received unity among themselves by means of that laver which leads to incorruption; but our souls by means of the Spirit. Wherefore both are necessary, since both contribute towards the life of God.

AGAINST HERESIES, Bk. 3, Ch. 17
MG 7, 930
ANF I, 444–445

TERTULLIAN

537
(348)

The evil tree will never bear good fruit unless the good branch be grafted onto it, and the good tree will bear evil fruit unless it be cultivated. And stones will become sons to Abraham, if they are formed in the faith of Abraham; a generation of vipers will bring forth fruits of repentance if they will but spit out the poison of their wickedness. Such is the power of Divine Grace, stronger than nature itself, that it can even make subject to itself the faculty of free will which is generally said to be master of itself. Now, since this faculty is naturally changeable, it varies; and so does nature.

ON THE SOUL, Ch. 21
ML 2, 685
ANF III, 202

ST. CYPRIAN

538
(558)

We also say in addition: 'Your will be done in heaven as it is on earth' (Mt. 6:10), not that God may do what He wishes, but that

282

we may be able to do what God wishes. For who stands in the way of God's doing what He wishes? But since the devil stands in the way of our mind and action obeying God in all things, we pray and petition that God's will be done in us. That it may be done in us, there is need of God's will, that is, of His help and protection, because no one is strong in his own strength, but is safe by the indulgence and mercy of God.

THE LORD'S PRAYER, Ch. 14
ML 4, 528
FC XXXVI, 138–139

ST. GREGORY NAZIANZEN

For when you hear, Not of him that wills, nor of him that runs, but of God that shows mercy, I counsel you to think the same. For since there are some who are so proud of their successes that they attribute all to themselves and nothing to Him that made them and gave them wisdom and supplied them with good; such are taught by this word that even to wish well needs help from God; or rather that even to choose what is right is divine and a gift of the mercy of God. For it is necessary both that we should be our own masters and also that our salvation should be of God. This is why He says not of him that wills; that is, not of him that wills only, nor of him that runs only, but also of God. That shows mercy. Next; since to will also is from God, He has attributed the whole to God with reason. However much you may run, however much you may wrestle, yet you need one to give the crown.

ORATIONS, No. 37:13
MG 36, 297
NPNF VII, 342

539
(1003)

ST. JOHN CHRYSOSTOM

All depends indeed on God, but not so that our free-will is hindered. 'If then it depend on God, [one says], 'why does He blame us?' On this account I said, 'so that our free-will is not hindered.' It depends then on us, and on Him. For we must first choose the good; and then He leads us to His own. He does not anticipate our choice, lest our free-will should be outraged. But when we have chosen, then great is the assistance He brings to us. . . . For it is ours to choose and to wish; but God's to complete and to bring to an end. Since therefore the

540
(1219)

greater part is of Him, he says all is of Him, speaking according to the custom of men. . . . Even should you run, even should you be very earnest, do not consider that the will doing is your own. For if you obtain not the impulse that is from above, all is to no purpose. Nevertheless that you will attain that which you earnestly strive after is very evident; so long as you run, so long as you will.

HOMILIES ON HEBREWS, 12:3
MG 63, 99
NPNF XIV, 425

ST. AUGUSTINE

541
(1455)
As strongly as we could, we urged on them, as on your and our brothers, to persevere in the Catholic faith, which neither denies free will whether for a bad life or a good one, nor allows it so much effect that it can do anything without the grace of God, whether to convert the soul from evil to good, or to persevere and advance in good, or to attain eternal good, where there is no more fear of falling away.

LETTER TO VALENTINUS, No. 215:4
ML 33, 873
FC XXXII, 64–65

542
(1719)
Now for the commission of sin we get no help from God: but we are not able to do justly, and to fulfill the law of righteousness in every part thereof, unless we are helped by God. For as the bodily eye is not helped by the light to turn away therefrom shut or averted, but is helped by it to see, and cannot see at all unless it help it; so God, Who is the light of the inner man, helps our mental sight, in order that we may do some good, not according to our own, but according to His righteousness.

ON THE MERITS AND REMISSION OF SINS, AND ON THE
BAPTISM OF INFANTS, Bk. 2, Ch. 5
ML 44, 153
See No. 527. *NPNF* V, 45

543
(1832)
And besides, this is the apostolic declaration, 'No one says, "Lord Jesus" but in the Holy Spirit' (1 Cor. 12:3): and who is it that calls Him Lord Jesus but he that loves Him, if he so call Him in the way the apostle intended to be understood? For many call Him so with their lips, but deny Him in their hearts and works. . . . No one, therefore,

says, 'Lord Jesus,' in mind, in word, in deed, with the heart, the lips, the labor of the hands, —no one says, Lord Jesus but in the Holy Spirit.

ON THE GOSPEL OF ST. JOHN, 74:1
ML 35, 1827
NPNF VII, 333

Let no one think that the branch can bear at least some little fruit of itself, after saying, 'the same brings forth much fruit' (Jn. 15:5). His next words are not, Without me you can do little, but 'you can do nothing' (ib.). Whether then it be little or much, without Him it is impracticable; for without Him nothing can be done.

544
(1835)

ON THE GOSPEL OF ST. JOHN, 81:3
ML 35, 1841
See No. 521.   *NPNF* VII, 346

'No man can come to me, except the Father who has sent me draw him' (Jn. 6:44)! For He does not say, 'except He lead him,' so that we can thus in any way understand that his will precedes. For who is 'drawn,' if he was already willing? And yet no man comes unless he is willing. Therefore he is drawn in wondrous ways to will, by Him who knows how to work within the very hearts of men. Not that men who are unwilling should believe, which cannot be, but that they should be made willing from being unwilling.

545
(1890)

AGAINST TWO LETTERS OF THE PELAGIANS, Bk. 1, Ch. 19
ML 44, 568
NPNF V, 389

Most bitter enemies of grace, you offer us examples of ungodly men who, you say, 'though without faith, abound in virtues where there is, without the aid of grace, only the good of nature even though shackled by superstitions.' Such men, by the mere powers of their inborn liberty, are often merciful, and modest, and chaste, and sober. When you say this you have already removed what you thought to attribute to the grace of God: namely, effectiveness of will. . . . If it pleases you so much to praise the ungodly that you say they abound in true virtues —as though you did not hear the Scripture saying: 'They that say to the wicked man: You are just, shall be accursed by the people, and the tribes shall abhor them' (Prov. 24:24)—it were much better for you,

546
(1902)

who say they abound in virtues, to confess that these are gifts of God in them.

AGAINST JULIAN, Bk. 4, Ch. 3:16
ML 44, 744
FC XXXV, 179

547
(1903)

But God forbid there be true virtues in anyone unless he is just, and God forbid he be truly just unless he lives by faith, for 'He who is just lives by faith' (Rom. 1:17). Who of those wishing to be considered Christians, except the Pelagians alone, or perhaps, you alone among the Pelagians, will call an unbeliever just, and an ungodly man just, and say a just man is in bondage to the Devil?

AGAINST JULIAN, Bk. 4, Ch. 3:17
ML 44, 745
FC XXXV, 181

548
(1914)

Surely, if no Christian will dare to say this, 'It is not of God that shows mercy, but of man that wills,' lest he should openly contradict the apostle, it follows that the true interpretation of the saying, 'It is not of him that wills, nor of him that runs, but of God that shows mercy' (Rom. 9:16), is that the whole work belongs to God, Who both makes the will of man righteous, and thus prepares it for assistance, and assists it when it is prepared. For the man's righteousness of will precedes many of Gods gifts, but not all; and it must itself be included among those which it does not precede. We read in Holy Scripture, both that God's mercy 'shall meet me' (Ps. 58:11), and that His mercy 'shall follow me' (Ps. 22:6). It goes before the unwilling to make him willing; it follows the willing to make his will effectual.

ON FAITH, HOPE, AND LOVE (ENCHIRIDION), Ch. 32
ML 40, 248
NPNF III, 248

549
(1936)

Lest the will itself should be deemed capable of doing any good thing without the grace of God, after saying, 'His grace within me was not in vain, but I have labored more abundantly than they all,' he immediately added the qualifying clause, 'Yet not I, but the grace of God which was with me' (1 Cor. 15:10). In other words, Not I alone, but the grace of God with me. And thus, neither was it the grace of God alone, nor was it he himself alone, but it was the grace of God with him. For his call, however, from heaven and his conversion by that great and most effectual call, God's grace was alone, because his merits, though great, were yet evil (cf. Acts 9:1 ff.).

ON GRACE AND FREE WILL, Ch. 5:12
ML 44, 889
NPNF V, 448–449

'There is henceforth laid up for me,' he says, 'a crown of righteousness, which the Lord, the righteous Judge, shall give me at that day' (2 Tim. 4:8). Now, to whom should the righteous Judge award the crown, except to him in whom the merciful Father had bestowed grace? And how could the crown be one 'of righteousness,' unless the grace had preceded which 'justifies the ungodly'?

550
(1937)

ON GRACE AND FREE WILL, Ch. 6:14
ML 44, 890
NPNF V, 449

'I have fought,' says [Paul] 'the good fight; I have finished my course; I have kept the faith' (2 Tim. 4:7). Now, in the first place, these good works were nothing, unless they had been preceded by good thoughts. Observe, therefore what he says concerning these very thoughts. His words, when writing to the Corinthians, are: 'Not that we are sufficient of ourselves to think anything as of ourselves; but our sufficiency is of God' (2 Cor. 3:5).

551
(1938)

ON GRACE AND FREE WILL, Ch. 7:16
ML 44, 891
NPNF V, 450

The first man had not that grace by which he should never will to be evil; but assuredly he had that in which if he willed to abide he would never be evil, and without which, moreover, he could not by free will be good, but which, nevertheless, by free will he could forsake. God, therefore, did not will even him to be without His grace, which He left in his free will; because free will is sufficient for evil, but is too little for good, unless it is aided by Omnipotent Good. And if that man had not forsaken that assistance of his free will, he would always have been good; but he forsook it, and he was forsaken. Because such was the nature of the aid, that he could forsake it when he would, and that he could continue in it if he would; but not such that it could be brought about that he would.

552
(1954)

ON REBUKE AND GRACE, Ch. 11:31
ML 44, 935
NPNF V, 484

ST. JOHN OF DAMASCUS
See No. 296.

105. Without grace man can place certain acts naturally good.

ST. JOHN CHRYSOSTOM

553 Thus, if you bear with meekness and gentleness, you will be able to reprove your enemy, to shame him, to weary him of being angry. No man cures evil with evil, but evil with good. These rules of wisdom some of the heathen give; now, if there be such wisdom among the foolish heathen, let us be ashamed to show ourselves inferior to them. Many of them have been injured and have borne it; many have been maliciously accused and not defended themselves; have been plotted against and have repaid by benefits. And there is no small fear lest some of them be found in their lives to be greater than we, and so render our punishment severer.

HOMILIES ON ST. JOHN, 51:3
MG 59, 286
NPNF XIV, 186

ST. AUGUSTINE

554
(1809) No one has anything of his own except falsehood and sin. But if man has any truth and justice, it is from that fountain after which we ought to thirst in this desert, so that being, as it were, bedewed by some drops from it, and comforted in the meantime in this pilgrimage, we may not fail by the way, but reach His rest and satisfying fullness.

ON THE GOSPEL OF ST. JOHN, Tr. 5:1
ML 35, 1414
NPNF VII, 31

555
(1905) The thoughts of the unfaithful will defend them on the day of judgment thus: that they may receive a more tolerable punishment, because in some way they did naturally the works of the Law, having the work of the Law written in their hearts (Rom. 2:14f.) to the extent that they did not do to others what they did not want done to themselves. But those men without faith sinned in that they did not refer their works to the end to which they should be referred.

AGAINST JULIAN, Bk. 4, Ch. 3
ML 44, 751
FC XXXV, 190

106. *Without grace man cannot keep the Law for any length of time.*

ST. JOHN CHRYSOSTOM
See No. 553.

ST. AUGUSTINE
See No. 542.

Without His assisting grace, the law is 'the letter which kills'; but when the life-giving spirit is present, the law causes that to be loved as written within, which it once caused to be feared as written without.

556
(1731)

> ON THE SPIRIT AND THE LETTER, Ch. 19:32
> *ML* 44, 220
> *NPNF* V, 97

It is certain that it is we that *will* when we will, but it is He Who makes us will what is good, of whom it is said, 'The will is prepared by the Lord' (Prov. 8:35 LXX). Of the same Lord it is said, 'The steps of a man are ordered by the Lord, and his way does He will.' Of the same Lord again it is said, 'It is God who works in you, even to will!' It is certain that it is we that act when we act; but it is He who makes us act, by applying efficacious powers to our will.

557
(1941)

> ON GRACE AND FREE WILL, Ch. 16:32
> *ML* 44, 900
> *NPNF* V, 457

107. *Even for the beginning of faith and conversion grace is necessary.*

ST. JUSTIN MARTYR
See No. 445.

ST. CYRIL OF JERUSALEM

For as those who are going to make a levy for war examine the ages and the bodies of those who are taking service, so also the Lord in enlisting souls examines their purpose: and if any has a secret hypocrisy, He rejects the man as unfit for His true service; but if He

558
(808)

finds one worthy, to him He readily gives His grace. He gives not holy things to the dogs; but where He discerns the good conscience, there He gives the Seal of salvation, that wondrous Seal, which devils tremble at, and Angels recognize; . . . For as a writing-reed or a dart has need of one to use it, so grace also has need of believing minds.... It is God's to grant grace, but yours to receive and guard it. Despise not the grace because it is freely given, but receive and treasure it devoutly.

CATECHESES, 1:3
MG 33, 372
NPNF VII, 6–7

ST. JOHN CHRYSOSTOM

559
(1165)

'No man can come unto Me, except the Father Who has sent Me draw him' (Jn. 6:44). The Manichaeans spring upon these words, saying, 'that nothing lies in our own power'; yet the expression shows that we are masters of our will. 'For if a man comes to Him,' says some one, 'what need is there of drawing?' But the words do not take away our free will, but show that we greatly need assistance. And He implies not an unwilling comer, but one enjoying much succor.

HOMILIES ON ST. JOHN, No. 46:1
MG 59, 257
NPNF XIV, 164

560
(1177)

Because although to be called and to be cleansed was of grace, yet, when called and clothed in clean garments, to continue keeping them so, this is of the diligence of them that are called. The being called was not of merit, but of grace.

HOMILIES ON ST. MATTHEW, No. 69:2
MG 62, 212
NPNF X, 423

561
(1207)

The Offering is the same, whether a common man, or Paul or Peter offer it. It is the same which Christ gave to His disciples, and which the Priests now minister. This is nowise inferior to that, because it is not men that sanctify even this, but the Same who sanctified the one sanctifies the other also. For as the words which God spoke are the same which the Priest now utters, so is the Offering the same, and the Baptism, that which He gave. Thus the whole is of faith. The Spirit immediately fell upon Cornelius (Acts 10:44), because he had previously fulfilled his part, and contributed his faith. And this is His Body, as well as that. And he who thinks the one inferior to the other, knows not that Christ even now is present, even now operates.

HOMILIES ON SECOND TIMOTHY, 2:4

MG 62, 612

See No. 540. *NPNF* XIII, 483

ST. AUGUSTINE

God acts upon us by the incentives of our perceptions, to will and to believe, either externally by evangelical exhortations, where even the commands of the law also do something, if they so far admonish a man of his infirmity that he betakes himself to the grace that justifies by believing; or internally, where no man has in his own control what shall enter into his thoughts, although it appertains to his own will to consent or to dissent. Since God, therefore, in such ways acts upon the reasonable soul in order that it may believe in Him (and certainly there is no ability whatever in free will to believe, unless there be persuasion or summons towards works in man the willing to believe, and in all things prevents us with his mercy. To yield our consent, indeed, to God's summons, or to withhold it, is (as I have said) the function of our own will.

562 (1736)

ON THE SPIRIT AND THE LETTER, Ch. 34:60

ML 44, 240

See No. 549. *NPNF* V, 110

Now if faith is simply of free will, and is not given by God, why do we pray for those who will not believe, that they may believe? This it would be absolutely useless to do, unless we believe, with perfect propriety, that Almighty God is able to turn to belief wills that are perverse and opposed to faith.

563 (1940)

ON GRACE AND FREE WILL, Ch. 14:29

ML 44, 898

NPNF V, 455

Thus there is here no departure from that opinion which Pelagius himself was constrained to condemn in the judgment of the bishops of Palestine, as is testified in the same Proceedings, 'That the grace of God is given according to our merits, if it is not of God's grace that we begin to believe, but rather that on account of this beginning an addition is made to us of a more full and perfect belief; and so we

564 (1978)

291

first give the beginning of our faith to God, that His supplement may also be given to us again, and whatever else we faithfully ask.

ON THE PREDESTINATION OF THE SAINTS, Ch. 2:3
ML 44, 961
NPNF V, 499

565
(1979)

The apostle says, 'Unto you it is given in the behalf of Christ not only to believe on Him, but also to suffer for His sake' (Phil. 1:29). He shows that both are the gifts of God, because he said that both were given. And he does not say, 'to believe on Him more fully and perfectly,' but, 'to believe on Him.' Neither does he say that he himself had obtained mercy to be more faithful, but 'to be faithful' (1 Cor. 7:25), because he knew that he had not first given the beginning of his faith to God, and had its increase given back to him again by Him; but that he had been made faithful by God, who also had made him an apostle. For the beginnings of his faith are recorded, and they are very well known by being read in the church on an occasion calculated to distinguish them: how, being turned away from the faith which he was destroying, and being vehemently opposed to it, he was suddenly by a more powerful grace converted to it.

ON THE PREDESTINATION OF THE SAINTS, Ch. 2:4
ML 44, 962
NPNF V, 499

566
(1981)

'For what have you that you have not received? And if you have received it, why do you boast as if you had not received it?' (1 Cor. 4:7). And it was chiefly by this testimony that I myself also was convinced when I was in a similar error, thinking that faith whereby we believe on God is not God's gift, but that it is in us from ourselves, and that by it we obtain the gifts of God, whereby we may live temperately and righteously and piously in this world.

ON THE PREDESTINATION OF THE SAINTS, Ch. 3:7
ML 44, 964
NPNF V, 500

567
(1982)

Accordingly, the capacity to have faith, as the capacity to have love, belongs to men's nature; but to have faith, even as to have love, belongs to the grace of believers. That nature, therefore, in which is given to us the capacity of having faith, does not distinguish man from man, but faith itself makes the believer to differ from the unbeliever. And thus, when it is said, 'For who makes you to differ? and what have

292

you that you have not received' (1 Cor. 4:7) if any one dares to say, 'I have faith of myself, I did not, therefore, receive it,' he directly contradicts this most manifest truth, —not because it is not in the choice of man's will to believe or not to believe, but because in the elect the will is prepared by the Lord (Prov. 8:35 LXX).

> ON THE PREDESTINATION OF THE SAINTS, Ch. 5:10
> ML 44, 968
> NPNF V, 503

Faith, then, as well in its beginning as in its completion, is God's gift; and let no one have any doubt whatever, unless he desires to resist the plainest sacred writings, that this gift is given to some, while to some it is not given. But why it is not given to all ought not to disturb the believer, who believes that from one all have gone into condemnation, which undoubtedly is most righteous; so that even if none were delivered therefrom, there would be no just cause for finding fault with God.

568
(1984)

> ON THE PREDESTINATION OF THE SAINTS, Ch. 8:16
> ML 44, 972
> NPNF V, 506

Let those, however, to whom in their love for me, I ought not to be ungrateful, who profess that they embrace, over and above that which comes into the argument, all my views, as you write, —let those, I say, see whether, in the latter portions of the first book of those two which I wrote in the beginning of my episcopate, before the appearance of the Pelagian heresy, to Simplicianus, the bishop of Milan, there remained anything whereby it might be called in question that God's grace is not given according to our merits; and whether I have not there sufficiently argued that even the beginning of faith is God's gift; and whether from what is there said it does not by consequence result, although it is not expressed, that even perseverance to the end is not given, except by Him who has predestinated us to His kingdom and glory.

569
(2005)

> ON THE GIFT OF PERSEVERANCE, Ch. 21:55
> ML 45, 1027
> NPNF V, 548

'God has sent the Spirit of His Son into our hearts, crying, Abba, Father!' (Gal. 4:6). And here what is the meaning of 'crying,' but 'making to cry,' by that figure of speech whereby we call a day that makes people glad, a glad day? . . . when we understand that this is

570
(2006)

also itself the gift of God, that with a true heart and spiritually we cry to God. Let them, therefore, observe how they are mistaken who think that our seeking, asking, knocking is of ourselves, and is not given to us.

ON THE GIFT OF PERSEVERANCE, Ch. 23:64
ML 45, 1032
NPNF V, 551

ST. PROSPER OF AQUITAINE

571
(2045)

This evidence from Scripture—and we could gather many other texts—demonstrates abundantly, I think, that faith which justifies a sinner cannot be had except for God's gift, and that it is not a reward for previous merits. Rather is it given that it may be a source of merit, and while it is itself given unprayed for, the prayers it inspires obtain all other favors.

THE CALL OF ALL NATIONS, Bk. 1, Ch. 24
ML 51, 679
ACW, 76

ST. JOHN CASSIAN

572
(2052)

[God] when He sees in us some beginnings of a good will, at once enlightens it and strengthens it and urges it on towards salvation, increasing that which He Himself implanted or which He sees to have arisen from our own efforts.

CONFERENCES, No. 13:8
ML 49, 912
NPNF XI, 426

573
(2053)

For neither does anyone enjoy good health whenever he will, nor is he at his own will and pleasure set free from disease and sickness. But what good is it to have desired the blessing of health, unless God, who grants us the enjoyments of life itself, grant also vigorous and sound health? But that it may be still clearer that through the excellence of nature which is granted by the goodness of the Creator, sometimes the first beginnings of a good will arise, which however cannot attain to the complete performance of what is good unless it is guided by the Lord, the Apostle bears witness and says, 'For to will is present with me, but to perform what is good I find not' (Rom. 7:18).

CONFERENCES, No. 13:9
ML 49, 919
NPNF XI, 427

108. *Without grace man cannot resist for long concupiscence and grave temptations.*

ST. CYPRIAN

For as I myself was held entangled by the very many errors of my previous life, of which I did not believe that I could divest myself, so I was disposed to give in to my clinging vices, and in my despair of better things I indulged my sins as if now proper and belonging to me. But afterwards, when the stain of my past life had been washed away by the aid of the water of regeneration, a light from above poured itself upon my chastened and pure heart; afterwards when I had drunk of the Spirit from heaven a second birth restored me into a new man; immediately in a marvelous manner doubtful matters clarified themselves, the closed opened, the shadowy shone with light, what seemed impossible was able to be accomplished, so that it was possible to acknowledge that what formerly was born of the flesh and lived submissive to sins was earthly, and what the Holy Spirit already was animating began to be of God.

574
(548)

TO DONATUS, Ch. 4
ML 4, 200
FC XXXVI, 9–10

ST. JOHN CHRYSOSTOM

'God is faithful, Who will not suffer you to be tempted above what you are able' (1 Cor. 10:13). There are therefore temptations which we are not able to bear. And what are these? All, so to speak. For the ability lies in God's gracious influence; a power which we draw down by our own will. Wherefore that you may know and see that not only those which exceed our power, but not even these which are 'common to man' is it possible without assistance from God easily to bear, he added 'But will with the temptation also make the way of escape, that you may be able to endure it' (ib.).

575
(1191)

HOMILIES ON FIRST CORINTHIANS, No. 24:1
MG 61, 198
NPNF XII, 138

ST. AUGUSTINE

To Your grace also I attribute whatsoever of evil I have not committed; for what might I not have committed, loving as I did the sin for the

576
(1592)

sin's sake? Yes, all I confess to have been pardoned me, both those which I committed by my own perverseness, and those which, by Your guidance, I committed not. Where is he who, reflecting upon his own infirmity, dares to ascribe his chastity and innocency to his own strength, so that he should love You the less, as if he had been in less need of Your mercy, whereby You forgive the transgressions of those that turn to You?

CONFESSIONS, Bk. 2, Ch. 7:15
ML 32, 681
NPNF I, 59

577
(1718)
Now these people [the Pelagians] imagine that they are sharp (as if none among us knew it) when they say, that 'if we have not the will, we commit no sin; nor would God command man to do what was impossible for human volition.' But they do not see, that in order to overcome certain things, which are the objects either of an evil desire or an ill-conceived fear, men need the strenuous efforts, and sometimes even all the energies, of the will; and that we should only imperfectly employ these in every instance.

ON THE MERITS AND REMISSION OF SINS, AND ON THE
BAPTISM OF INFANTS, Bk. 2, Ch. 3
ML 44, 152
NPNF V, 44–45

109. No one can be completely immune from concupiscence and small sins without a special privilege of grace.

ORİGEN

578
(527)
God the Word was sent, indeed, as a physician to sinners. . . . But Celsus asks, 'Why was he not sent to those who were without sin? What evil is it not to have committed sin?' To which we reply, that if by those 'who were without sin' he means those who sin no more, then our Saviour Jesus was sent even to such, but not as a physician. While if by those 'who were without sin' he means such as have never at any time sinned, —for he made no distinction in his statement, —we reply that it is impossible for man thus to be without sin. And this we say, excepting, of course, the man understood to be in Christ Jesus, who 'did no sin' (1 Pet. 2:22).

AGAINST CELSUS, Bk. 3, Ch. 62
MG 11, 1001
ANF IV, 488

ST. GREGORY NAZIANZEN

Let us be assured that to do no wrong is really superhuman, and belongs to God alone.

579
(981)

ORATIONS, 16:15
MG 35, 953
NPNF VII, 252

ST. AUGUSTINE

For the sake of all sins was Baptism provided; for the sake of light sins, without which we cannot be, was prayer provided. What has the Prayer? 'Forgive us our debts, as we also forgive our debtors' (Mt. 6:12). Once for all we have washing in Baptism, every day we have washing in prayer. Only, do not commit those things for which you must needs be separated from Christ's body: which be far from you! For those whom you have seen doing penance, have committed heinous things, either adulteries or some enormous crimes: for these they do penance. Because if theirs had been light sins, to blot out these daily prayer would suffice. . . . In three ways then are sins remitted in the Church; by Baptism, by prayer, by the greater humility of penance.

580
(1536)

ON THE CREED: A SERMON TO THE CATECHUMENS, 1:7:15
ML 40, 636
NPNF III, 374–375

Now, if I were asked, Whether it be possible for a man in this life to be without sin, I should allow the possibility, through the grace of God and the man's own free will; not doubting that the free will itself is ascribable to God's grace, in other words, to the gifts of God, —not only as to its existence, but also as to its being good, that is, to its conversion to doing the commandments of God. Thus it is that God's grace not only shows what ought to be done, but also helps to the possibility of doing what it shows. . . . I cannot doubt that God has laid no impossible command on man; and that, by God's aid and help, nothing is impossible, by which is wrought what He commands. In this way may a man, if he pleases, be without sin by the assistance of God. If, however, I am asked the second question which I have suggested, —whether there be a sinless man, —I believe there is not.

581
(1720)

ON THE MERITS AND REMISSION OF SINS, AND ON THE
BAPTISM OF INFANTS, Bk. 2, Ch. 6
ML 44, 155
NPNF V, 46

582
(1722)

Since by divine grace assisting the human will, man may possibly exist in this life without sin, why does he not? To this question I might very easily and truthfully answer: Because men are unwilling. But if I am asked why they are unwilling, we are drawn into a lengthy statement. And yet, without prejudice to a more careful examination, I may briefly say this much: Men are unwilling to do what is right, either because what is right is unknown to them, or because it is unpleasant to them. . . . But that what was hidden may come to light, and what was unpleasant may be made agreeable, is of the grace of God which helps the wills of men; and that they are not helped by it, has its cause likewise in themselves, not in God, whether they be predestinated to condemnation, on account of the iniquity of their pride, or whether they are to be judged and disciplined contrary to their very pride, if they are children of mercy.

ON THE MERITS AND REMISSION OF SINS, AND ON THE
BAPTISM OF INFANTS, Bk. 2, Ch. 17
ML 44, 167
NPNF V, 55

583
(1737)

See how an instance of perfect righteousness is unexampled among men, and yet is not impossible. For it might be achieved if there were only applied so much of will as suffices for so great a thing. There would, however, be so much will, if there were hidden from us none of those conditions which pertain to righteousness; and at the same time these so delighted our mind, that whatever hindrance of pleasure or pain might else occur, this delight in holiness would prevail over every rival affection. And that this is not realized, is not owing to any intrinsic impossibility, but to God's judicial act.

ON THE SPIRIT AND THE LETTER, Ch. 35:63
ML 44, 242
NPNF V, 112

584
(1794)

We must except the holy Virgin Mary, concerning whom I wish to raise no question when it touches the subject of sins, out of honor to the Lord; for from Him we know what abundance of grace for overcoming sin in every particular was conferred upon her who had the merit to conceive and bear Him who undoubtedly had no sin. Well, then, if, with this exception of the Virgin, we could only assemble together all the forementioned holy men and women, and ask them whether they lived without sin while they were in this life, what can we suppose would be their answer? Would it be in the language of

298

our author [Pelagius] or in the words of the Apostle John? I put it to you, whether, on having such a question submitted to them, however excellent might have been their sanctity in this body, they would not have exclaimed with one voice: 'If we say we have no sin, we deceive ourselves, and the truth is not in us' (1 Jn. 1:8)?

ON NATURE AND GRACE, Ch. 36:42
ML 44, 267
NPNF V, 135

Finally, if it be asserted that there either have been, or are in this present life, any persons, with the sole exception of our Great Head, 'the Saviour of His body,' who are righteous, without any sin, —and this, either by not consenting to the lusts thereof, or because that must not be accounted as any sin which is such that God does not impute it to them by reason of their godly lives (although the blessedness of being without sin is a different thing from the blessedness of not having one's sin imputed to him (Ps. 31:2)—I do not deem it necessary to contest the point over-much. I am quite aware that some hold this opinion, whose views on the subject I have not the courage to censure, although, at the same time, I cannot defend them. But if any man says that we ought not to use the prayer, 'Lead us not into temptation' (and he says as much who maintains that God's help is unnecessary to a person for the avoidance of sin, and that human will, after accepting only the law, is sufficient for the purpose), then I do not hesitate at once to affirm that such a man ought to be removed from the public ear, and to be anathematized by every mouth.

585
(1801)

MAN'S PERFECTION IN RIGHTEOUSNESS, Ch. 21:44
ML 44, 316
NPNF V, 176

Many baptized believers are without crime, but I should say that no one in this life is without sin, —however much the Pelagians are inflated, and burst asunder in madness against me because I say this: not because there remains anything of sin which is not remitted in baptism; but because by us who remain in the weakness of this life such sins do not cease daily to be committed, as are daily remitted to those who pray in faith and work in mercy.

586
(1888)

AGAINST TWO LETTERS OF THE PELAGIANS, Bk. 1, Ch. 14
ML 44, 563
NPNF V, 386

587
(1894)

Let us, then, see that third point, which in these men is not less shocking to every member of Christ and to His whole body, —that they contend that there are in this life, or that there have been, righteous men having absolutely no sin. In which presumption they most manifestly contradict the Lord's Prayer, wherein, with truthful heart and with daily words, all members of Christ cry aloud, 'Forgive us our debts' (Mt. 6:21).

AGAINST TWO LETTERS OF THE PELAGIANS, Bk. 4, Ch. 10
ML 44, 629
NPNF V, 429

588
(1921)

Now the daily prayer of the believer makes satisfaction for those daily sins of a momentary and trivial kind which are necessary incidents of this life. For he can say, 'Our Father which art in heaven' (Mt. 6:9), seeing that to such a Father he is now born again of water and of the Spirit, (Jn. 3:5). And this prayer certainly takes away the very small sins of daily life.

ON FAITH, HOPE, AND LOVE (ENCHIRIDION), Ch. 71
ML 40, 265
NPNF III, 260

110. Final perseverance is a great gift of God.

ST. AUGUSTINE

589
(1958)

And thus God willed that His saints should not—even concerning perseverance in goodness itself—glory in their own strength, but in Himself, who not only gives them aid such as He gave to the first man, without which they cannot persevere if they will, but causes in them also the will; . . . Therefore aid is brought to the infirmity of human will, so that it might be unchangeably and invincibly influenced by divine grace; and thus, although weak, it still might not fail, nor be overcome by any adversity.

ON REBUKE AND GRACE, Ch. 12:38
ML 44, 939
NPNF V, 487

590
(1992)

I assert, therefore, that the perseverance by which we persevere in Christ even to the end is the gift of God; and I call that the end by which is finished that life wherein alone there is peril of falling. There-

300

fore it is uncertain whether any one has received this gift so long as he is still alive. For if he fall before he dies, he is, of course, said not to have persevered; and most truly is it said. . . . But lest any one should object to this, and say, If from the time at which any one become a believer he has lived—for the sake of the argument—ten years, and in the midst of them has fallen from the faith, has he not persevered for five years? I am not contending about words. If it be thought that this should be called perseverance, as it were for so long as it lasts, assuredly he is not to be said to have had in any degree that perseverance of which we are now discoursing, by which one perseveres in Christ even to the end.

ON THE GIFT OF PERSEVERANCE, Ch. 1
ML 45, 993
NPNF V, 526

For we are speaking of that perseverance whereby one perseveres   591
unto the end, and if this is given, one does persevere unto the end; but   (1993)
if one does not persevere unto the end, it is not given. . . . But since no
one has perseverance to the end, many people have it, but none can lose
it. For it is not to be feared that perchance when a man has persevered
unto the end, some evil will may arise in him, so that he does not
persevere unto the end. This gift of God, therefore, may be obtained by
prayer, but when it has been given, it cannot be lost by contumacy.

ON THE GIFT OF PERSEVERANCE, Ch. 6:10
ML 45, 999
See Nos. 306 and 567.   *NPNF* V, 529

*111. There is some grace which truly suffices to produce its ef-
fect, but nevertheless does not actually produce it (gratia
sufficiens).*

ST. IRENAEUS

For creation is an attribute of the goodness of God; but to be created   592
is that of human nature. If, then, you deliver up to Him what is   (247)
yours, that is, faith towards Him and subjection, you will receive His
handiwork, and will be a perfect work of God. If, however, you will
not believe in Him, and will flee from His hands, the cause of imperfection shall be in you who did not obey, but not in Him who
called [you]. For He commissioned [messengers] to call people to the

marriage, but they who did not obey Him deprived themselves of the royal supper. The skill of God, therefore is not defective, for He has power of the stones to raise up children to Abraham; but the man who does not obtain it, is the cause to himself of his own imperfection. Nor, [in like manner], does the light fail because of those who have blinded themselves; but while it remains the same as ever, those who are [thus] blinded are involved in darkness through their own fault. The light never enslaves any one by necessity; nor, again, does God exercise compulsion upon any one unwilling to accept the exercise of His skill. Those persons, therefore, who have apostatized from the light given by the Father, and transgressed the law of liberty, have done so through their own fault, since they have been created free agents, and possessed of power over themselves.

AGAINST HERESIES, Bk. 4, Ch. 39
MG 7, 1110
ANF I, 523

ARNOBIUS

593
(622)

But, [my opponents ask] if Christ came as the Saviour of men, as you say, why does He not with uniform benevolence, free all without exception? I reply, does not He free all alike who invites all alike? or does He thrust back or repel any one from the kindness of the Supreme who gives to all alike the power of coming to Him, —to men of high rank, to the meanest slaves, to women, to boys? To all, He says, the fountain of life is open, and no one is hindered or kept back from drinking. If you are so fastidious as to spurn the kindly offered gift, nay, more, if your wisdom is so great that you term those things which are offered by Christ ridiculous and absurd, why should He keep on inviting *you,* while His only duty is to make the enjoyment of His bounty depend upon your own free choice?

AGAINST THE NATIONS, Bk. 2, Ch. 64
ML 5, 910
ANF VI, 458–459

ST. JOHN CHRYSOSTOM

594
(1158)

If He 'enlightens every man that comes into the world' (Jn. 1:9), how is it that so many continue unenlightened? for not all have known the majesty of Christ. How then does He 'light every man'? He enlightens all as far as in Him lies. But if some, wilfully closing the eyes of their mind, would not receive the rays of that Light, their darkness arises not from the nature of the Light, but from their own wickedness, who wilfully deprive themselves of the gift.

HOMILIES ON ST. JOHN, 8:1
MG 59, 65
NPNF XIV, 29

And if by grace, it will be said, how came we all not to be saved? Because you would not. For grace, though it be grace, saves the willing, not those who will not have it, and turn away from it, who persist in fighting against it, and opposing themselves to it.

595
(1188)

EPISTLE TO THE ROMANS, 18:5
MG 60, 579
NPNF XI, 483

ST. AUGUSTINE
See Nos. 476, 474, and 510.

112. *However there is another grace which efficaciously moves the will (gratia efficax).*

TERTULLIAN
See No. 537.

ST. CYPRIAN
See No. 538.

ST. AUGUSTINE
See No. 545.

And, moreover, who will be so foolish and blasphemous as to say that God cannot change the evil wills of men, whichever, whenever, and wheresoever He chooses, and direct them to what is good? But when He does this, He does it of mercy.

596
(1926)

ON FAITH, HOPE, AND LOVE (ENCHIRIDION), Ch. 98
ML 40, 277

See Nos. 561 and 587.

NPNF III, 268

It is not, then, to be doubted that men's wills cannot, so as to prevent His doing what He wills, withstand the will of God, 'who has done all things whatsoever He pleased in heaven and in earth' (Ps.

597
(1963)

134:6), and who also 'has done those things that are to come' (Is. 45:11 **LXX**); since He does even concerning the wills themselves of men what He will, when He will . . . because He beyond doubt had the most omnipotent power of inclining men's hearts whither it pleased Him.

ON REBUKE AND GRACE, Ch. 14:5

ML 44, 943

See No. 563.   *NPNF* V, 489

598
(1996)

For not to say how possible it may be for God to convert the wills of men averse and opposed to His faith, and to operate on their hearts so that they yield to no adversities, and are overcome by no temptation so as to depart from Him, —since He also can do what the apostle says, namely, not allow them to be tempted above that which they are able; —not, then, to say this, God foreknowing that they would fall, was certainly able to take them away from this life before that fall should occur. Are we to return to that point of still arguing how absurdly it is said that dead men are judged even for those sins which God foreknew that they would have committed if they had lived? which is so abhorrent to the feelings of Christians, or even of human beings, that one is even ashamed to rebut it.

ON THE GIFT OF PERSEVERANCE, Ch. 9:22

ML 45, 1005

NPNF V, 533

GRACE AND FREEDOM

113. Grace does not destroy free will.

ORIGEN
   See No. 477.

ST. GREGORY OF NYSSA

599
(1034)

Yet, even in their reply to this, or the like, they are not at a loss for a contentious rejoinder. For they assert that God, if He had been so pleased, might have forcibly drawn those, who were not inclined to yield, to accept the Gospel message. But where then would have been their free will? Where their virtuous merit? Where their meed of praise from their moral directors? It belongs only to inanimate or irrational creatures to be brought round by the will of another to his purpose.

THE GREAT CATECHISM, Ch. 31
MG 45, 77
NPNF V, 499

ST. JOHN CHRYSOSTOM
See Nos. 557, 593, and 540.

ST. AUGUSTINE

The freedom of the will is not destroyed by being helped, it is rather helped because it is not destroyed. He who says to God: 'Be my helper' (Ps. 26:9), confesses that he wishes to carry out what is commanded, but asks help of Him who gave the command so that he may be able to do it.

600
(1436)

LETTER TO HILARY, No. 157, 2:10
ML 33, 677
FC XX, 325

See No. 580.

We may not so defend grace as to seem to take away free will, or, on the other hand, so assert free will as to be judged ungrateful to the grace of God, in our arrogant impiety.

601
(1723)

ON THE MERITS AND REMISSION OF SINS, AND ON THE
BAPTISM OF INFANTS, Bk. 2, Ch. 18
ML 44, 168
NPNF V, 56

See No. 560.

See how the Father draws: he delights by teaching, not by imposing a necessity. Behold how He draws.

602
(1823)

ON THE GOSPEL OF ST. JOHN. Tr. 26:7
ML 35, 1610
NPNF VII, 170

Inasmuch, however, as the discussion about free will and God's grace has such difficulty in its distinctions, that when free will is maintained, God's grace is apparently denied; while when God's grace is asserted, free will is supposed to be done away with, —Pelagius can

603
(1856)

so involve himself in the shades of this obscurity as to profess agreement with all that we have quoted from St. Ambrose, and declare that such is, and always has been, his opinion also.

ON THE GRACE OF CHRIST AND ON ORIGINAL SIN, Ch. 47:52
ML 44, 383

See Nos. 545, 552, and 474.   *NPNF* V, 235

604
(1961)
For so to will or not to will is in the power of Him who wills or wills not, as not to hinder the divine will nor overcome the divine power. For even concerning those who do what He wills not, He Himself does what He will.

ON REBUKE AND GRACE, Ch. 14:43
ML 44, 942
NPNF V, 489

ST. JOHN OF DAMASCUS
See No. 296.

114. *God infallibly knows beforehand in what way free will is to make use of the aid of grace.*

ST. AUGUSTINE
See No. 293.

605
(1830)
'They could not believe' (Jn. 12:39; Is. 6:10), because Isaiah the prophet foretold it; and the prophet foretold it because God foreknew that such would be the case. But if I am asked why they could not, I reply at once, because they would not; for certainly their depraved will was foreseen by God, and foretold through the prophet by Him from Whom nothing that is future can be hid. But the prophet, you say, assigns another cause than that of their will. What cause does the prophet assign? That 'God has given them the spirit of remorse, eyes that they should not see, and ears that they should not hear; and has blinded their eyes, and hardened their heart' (Is. 6:9, 10). This also, I reply, their will deserved. For God thus blinds and hardens, simply by letting alone and withdrawing His aid: and God can do this by a judgment that is hidden, although not by one that is unrighteous.

ON THE GOSPEL OF ST. JOHN, Tr. 53:6
ML 35, 1776

See No. 304.   *NPNF* VII, 293

GRATUITY

115. *Grace surpasses all the exigencies of nature.*

ST. AUGUSTINE

Will not nature be grace? For this, too, the Pelagians have been bold enough to aver, that grace is the nature in which we were created, so as to possess a rational mind, by which we are enabled to understand, —formed as we are in the image of God, so as to have dominion over the fish of the sea, and over the fowl of the air, and over every living thing that creeps upon the earth. This, however, is not the grace which the apostle commends to us through the faith of Jesus Christ. For it is certain that we possess this nature in common with ungodly men and unbelievers; whereas the grace which comes through the faith of Jesus Christ belongs only to them to whom the faith itself appertains.

606
(1939)

ON GRACE AND FREE WILL, Ch. 13:25
ML 44, 896
NPNF V, 454

See No. 565.

116. *Grace is essentially gratuitous.*

ST. CYRIL OF JERUSALEM
See No. 558.

ST. AUGUSTINE

If we say that prayer produces antecedent merit so that the gift of grace may follow, it is true that prayer, by asking and obtaining whatever it does obtain, shows clearly that it is God's gift when a man does not think that he has grace of himself, because if it were in his own power, he would assuredly not ask for it. But, lest we should think that even the merit of prayer is antecedent to grace, in which case it would not be a free gift—and then it would not be grace because it would be the reward which was due—our very prayer itself is counted among the gifts of grace.

607
(1451)

LETTERS, No. 194:4:16
ML 33, 879
FC XXX, 311

608
(1452)   What merit, then, has man before grace which could make it possible
for him to receive grace, when nothing but grace produces good merit
in us; and what else but His gifts does God crown when He crowns our
merits?

LETTERS, No. 194:4:16
ML 33, 880
FC XXX, 313

609
(1473)   Grace is given freely. For if it were not free it would not be grace.
Moreover since it is grace freely given, nothing of yours preceded it in
order for you to accept it. For if any of your good works had preceded
it, you would receive a reward, not something free. And the reward
which was owed to us was punishment.

EXPOSITION ON THE PSALMS, 70:2:1
See No. 527.   *ML* 36, 891

610
(1807)   What is grace? That which is freely given. What is 'freely given'?
Given, not paid. If it was due, wages were given, not grace bestowed;
but if it was really due, you were good; but if, as is true, you were evil,
but did believe on Him who justifies the ungodly (Rom. 4:5) (What
is, Who justifies the ungodly? Of the ungodly makes pious), consider
what did by right hang over you by the law, and what you have obtained by grace. But having obtained that grace of faith, you shall be
just by faith (for the just lives by faith); and you will obtain favor
of God by living by faith. And having obtained favor from God by
living by faith, you will receive immortality as a reward, and life
eternal. And that is grace. For because of what merit do you receive
life eternal? Because of grace.

ON THE GOSPEL OF ST. JOHN, Tr. 3:9
ML 35, 1400
See No. 310.   *NPNF* VII, 21–22

611
(1851)   For the very name of grace, and the thing that is meant by it, is
taken away, if it is not bestowed gratuitously, but he only receives it
who is worthy of it. Will anybody say that I do the apostle wrong,
because I do not admit him to have been worthy of grace? Nay, I should
indeed rather do him wrong, and bring on myself a punishment, if I
refused to believe what he himself says. Well, now, has he not pointedly
so defined *grace* as to show that it is so called because it is bestowed

gratuitously? These are his own very words: 'And if by grace, then is it no more of works; otherwise grace is no more grace' (Rom. 11:6).

ON THE PROCEEDINGS OF PELAGIUS, Ch. 14:33
ML 44, 340
NPNF V, 198

See No. 569.

ST. PROSPER OF AQUITAINE

Now turn your attention to the case of sinners who after a long life-time of shame and crime receive new life in the sacrament of Christ's baptism just before they depart from this world. Without any good works to plead for them they are admitted to the communion of the kingdom of heaven. How will you understand this judgment of God? You can only confess unhesitatingly that God's gifts are unmerited. There are no crimes so hateful that can prevent the gift of grace, just as there can be no good works so excellent that can claim as their just reward what God gives gratuitously.

612
(2044)

Suppose that justification, which is the work of grace, were due to previous merits; suppose it were like the pay of a laborer rather than the gift of a Donor: would not then our Redemption in the blood of Christ be debased, and the initiative claimed by human works refuse to yield to God's mercy?

THE CALL OF ALL NATIONS, Bk. 1, Ch. 17
ML 51, 669
ACW, 60

See No. 571.

117. *To no one, not even the unfaithful, does God deny grace sufficient for faith and for salvation.*

ST. CLEMENT OF ROME

Let us fix our gaze on the blood of Christ and realize how precious it is to His Father, seeing that it was poured out for our salvation and brought the grace of conversion to the whole world. Let us look back over all the generations, and learn that from generation to generation the Lord has given an opportunity of repentance to all who would return to Him.

613
(12)

LETTER TO THE CORINTHAINS, Ch. 7:4
MG 1, 224
FC I, 15

ARNOBIUS
See No. 593.

ST. JOHN CHRYSOSTOM
See No. 594.

ST. AUGUSTINE

614
(1461)
'And there is none that may hide himself from His heat' (Ps. 18:7).
But whereas, 'the Word was even made flesh, and dwelt in us' (Jn.
1:14) assuming our mortality, He permitted no man to excuse himself
from the shadow of death; for the heat of the Word penetrated even
it.

EXPOSITIONS ON THE PSALMS, 18:7
ML 36, 155
See No. 527.   NPNF VIII, 55

ST. PROSPER OF AQUITAINE

615
(2046)
It may be true that, just as we know that in former times some peoples
were not admitted to the fellowship of the sons of God, so also today
there are in the remotest parts of the world some nations who have not
yet seen the light of the grace of the Saviour. But we have no doubt
that in God's hidden judgment, for them also a time of calling has been
appointed, when they will hear and accept the Gospel which now
remains unknown to them. Even now they receive that measure of
general help which heaven has always bestowed on all men.

THE CALL OF ALL NATIONS, Bk. 2, Ch. 17
ML 51, 704
ACW, 121

616
(2047)
Certainly, as we have proved abundantly, God's manifold and ineffable goodness always provided and still provides for all mankind in
such a way that not one of the reprobate can find an excuse as though
he had been refused the light of truth, and that no one can rightly
boast of his own justice. The one group perishes by reason of its own
malice, while it is God's grace that leads the other into glory.

THE CALL OF ALL NATIONS, Bk. 2, Ch. 29
ML 51, 715
ACW, 142

IX.

Habitual Grace

When a man is "made right" in the sight of God he receives the infused gift of habitual grace which blots out his sins and renews him internally. He now becomes a temple of the Holy Spirit, a friend of God, His adopted son, a sharer of the divine nature and an heir to the heavenly kingdom. While all grace is God's free gift, man must dispose himself through faith as well as by acts of the other virtues. Habitual grace is lost by mortal sin and man can never really be certain of his justification. Although a righteous man cannot merit this justification itself, nevertheless the just can have true merit and an increase of sanctifying grace, and they can merit eternal life itself. Conditions for meriting this eternal life rest on the state of grace, man's own free will, and the promises of God Himself.

The distinction between the natural and the supernatural order is made by a number of writers, such as St. Irenaeus in the second century, Origen in the third, and St. Cyril of Jerusalem, St. Basil, St. Gregory of Nyssa, and St. John Chrysostom in the fourth. The notion that in justification there is infused a permanent supernatural gift (known as habitual grace although not specifically called that) appears as early as St. Irenaeus, and in the third century in both Origen and St. Cyprian. St. Ambrose and St. Augustine also speak of it.

What is important is that sins are truly blotted out—St. Justin Martyr assures us of that along with St. Clement of Alexandria (St. Ambrose and St. Gregory the Great are later writers), and the

311

Letter to Barnabas states that man is renewed internally. This internal renewal is affirmed by St. Irenaeus and St. Cyprian, Novatian, the three Cappadocian Fathers along with St. John Chrysostom, and St. Leo the Great. The indwelling of the Holy Spirit is specifically mentioned as early as the *Letter to Barnabas* and Hermas, and subsequent writers are almost too numerous to mention (Tatian, St. Irenaeus, Origen, Novatian, Aphraates, St. Athanasius, St. Cyril of Jerusalem, St. Hilary, St. Basil, and St. John Chrysostom). Akin to this idea is that man becomes a sharer of the divine nature: so say St. Ignatius of Antioch early in the second century, and later St. Clement of Alexandria and St. Methodius, and in the fourth, St. Athanasius, St. Cyril of Jerusalem, St. Basil, St. Ambrose, St. Augustine, and St. Leo the Great. All of this is quite Pauline, but it is interesting to see how many different writers are impressed by it. The notion of man as the adoptive son of God occurs in St. Clement of Alexandria, and then in the fourth century in St. Athanasius, St. Cyril of Jerusalem, St. Basil, St. John Chrysostom, St. Ambrose, and St. Augustine.

Man must dispose himself for justification through faith as well as through the acts of the other virtues. This we hear from St. Clement of Rome in the first century, from St. Clement of Alexandria in the third, and from St. John Chrysostom and St. Augustine a century later.

Mortal sin destroys habitual grace—so Tatian, Aphraates, St. Athanasius, and St. Basil; and St. Augustine adds that man can, after all, never be certain of his righteousness.

The question of merit which agitated the Reformers in the sixteenth century, and the belief that the just man can have true merit finds ample discussion among the early Fathers. St. Ignatius of Antioch and St. Justin Martyr, and later St. Irenaeus (all in the second century) all hold for it; so do Tertullian and St. Cyprian, so also do St. Cyril of Jerusalem, St. Jerome, and St. Augustine. St. Theophilus of Antioch (late second century) and St. Hippolytus at about the same time, along with St. Cyprian, declare that the just can merit eternal life, but St. Augustine reminds us that while the just man can merit an increase of grace he cannot merit justification itself. St. Augustine adds that the conditions of merit depend upon

312

the promise of God, the freedom of the will, and the necessity of being in the state of grace. In mentioning the freedom of the will as a necessary requisite, he is joined by St. Justin Martyr, Tatian, and St. Jerome.

THE SUPERNATURAL ORDER

118. Among the gifts which God has bestowed on His creatures, some are natural, others are supernatural.

ST. IRENAEUS
See No. 498.

ORIGEN

And if we must press the force of words, we would say that, in comparison with what is generally understood as 'nature,' there *are* certain
things which are beyond its power, which God could at any time do;
as, e.g.: on raising man above the level of human nature, and causing
him to pass into a better and more divine condition, and preserving
him in the same, so long as he who is the object of His care shows by
his actions that he desires [the continuance of His help].

617
(529)

AGAINST CELSUS, Bk. 5, Ch. 23
MG 11, 1217
ANF IV, 553

ST. CYRIL OF JERUSALEM
See No. 391.

ST. GREGORY OF NYSSA

Man is esteemed as nothing, as ashes and grass and vanity among the
things that exist, yet he becomes akin to this great Majesty that can
neither be seen nor heard nor thought; he is received as a son by the
God of the universe. How can one give thanks worthily for such a
gift? With what words, what thoughts that move our mind can we
praise this abundance of grace? Man transcends his own nature, he who

618
(1027)

was subject to corruption in his mortality, becomes immune from it in his immortality, eternal from being fixed in time—in a word, a god from a man. For if he is made worthy of becoming a son of God, he will possess in himself the dignity of the Father and be made heir of all the Father's goods. How munificent is this rich Lord! How generously He opens His hands wide to give us His ineffable treasures!

ON THE BEATITUDES, Ch. 7
MG 44, 1280
NPNF V, 403

ST. JOHN CHRYSOSTOM
See No. 525.

ST. AUGUSTINE

619
(1433)

[To Honoratus] This is the grace of the New Testament, which lay hid in the Old, yet was constantly prophesied and foretold by veiled figures, so that the soul might recognize its God and be reborn to Him, by His grace. This is truly a spiritual birth, therefore not of blood, nor of the will of man, nor of the will of the flesh, but of God. This is called adoption. For we were something before we were the sons of God, and we received the benefit of becoming what we were not, just as the one who is adopted, before adoption, was not yet the son of the one who adopts him; still, he was one who could be adopted. From this begetting by grace we distinguish that son who, although He was the Son of God, came that He might become the son of man, and might give us, who were sons of man, the power to become the sons of God.

LETTERS, No. 140:3:9
ML 33, 541
FC XX, 64

ST. JOHN OF DAMASCUS
See No. 296.

JUSTIFICATION

119. In justification there is infused a permanent supernatural gift, habitual grace.

ST. IRENAEUS

Those, then, are the perfect who have had the Spirit of God remaining in them, and have preserved their souls and bodies blameless, holding fast the faith of God, that is, that faith which is [directed] towards God, and maintaining righteous dealings with respect to their neighbors. Whence also he says, that this handiwork is 'the temple of God,' thus declaring: 'Know you not that you are the temple of God, and that the Spirit of God dwells in you? If any man, therefore, will defile the temple of God, him will God destroy: for the temple of God is holy, which [temple] you are' (1 Cor. 3:16 f.). Here he manifestly declares the body to be the temple in which the Spirit dwells.

620
(251)

AGAINST HERESIES, Bk. 5, Ch. 6:1

MG 7, 1138

See No. 498.

ANF I, 532

ORIGEN

And since many saints participate in the Holy Spirit, He cannot therefore be understood to be a body, which being divided into corporeal parts, is partaken of by each one of the saints; but He is manifestly a sanctifying power, in which all are said to have a share who have deserved to be sanctified by His grace.

621
(449)

ON FIRST PRINCIPLES, Bk. 1, Ch. 1

MG 11, 122

ANF IV, 242

ST. CYPRIAN

Buy for yourself a white garment, that you, who according to Adam had been naked and were before frightful and unseemly, may be clothed in the white raiment of Christ. And you who are a rich and wealthy matron anoint your eyes not with the stibium of the devil but with the

622
(564)

eye-salve of Christ, that you can come to see God, when you merit God by character and good works.

WORKS AND ALMSGIVING, Ch. 14
ML 4, 612
FC XXXVI, 240

ST. AMBROSE
See No. 436.

ST. AUGUSTINE
See No. 526.

623
(1730)

His words are, 'The righteousness of God is manifested' (Rom. 3:21): he does not say, the righteousness of man, or the righteousness of his own will, but 'the righteousness of God,'—not that whereby He is Himself righteous, but that with which He endows man when He justifies the ungodly.

ON THE SPIRIT AND THE LETTER, Ch. 9
ML 44, 209
NPNF V, 89

120. Sins are truly blotted out.

ST. JUSTIN MARTYR

624
(146)

So that if they repent, all who wish for it can obtain mercy from God: and the Scripture foretells that they shall be blessed, saying, 'Blessed is the man to whom the Lord imputes not sin' (Ps. 31:2); that is, having repented of his sins, that he may receive remission of them from God; and not as you deceive yourselves, and some others who resemble you in this, who say, that even though there be sinners, but know God, the Lord will not impute sin to them.

DIALOGUE WITH TRYPHO, Ch. 141
MG 6, 797
ANF I, 270

ST. CLEMENT OF ALEXANDRIA

625
(407)

Is it, then, that [Christ] was made perfect only in the sense of being washed, and that He was consecrated by the descent of the Holy Spirit? Yes, that is the true explanation. This is what happens with us, whose model the Lord made Himself. When we are baptized, we are enlightened; being enlightened, we become adopted sons; becoming adopted sons, we are made perfect; and becoming perfect, we are made divine. 'I have said,' it is written, 'you are gods and all of you the sons of the most High'. (Ps. 81:6).

This ceremony is often called 'free gift,' 'enlightenment,' 'perfection,' and 'cleansing'—'cleansing,' because through it we are completely purified in our sins; 'free gift,' because by it the punishments due to our sins are remitted; 'enlightenment,' since by it we behold the wonderful holy light of salvation, that is, it enables us to see God clearly; finally, we call it 'perfection' as needing nothing further, for what more does he need who possesses the knowledge of God? It would indeed be out of place to call something that was not fully perfect a gift of God.

CHRIST THE EDUCATOR, Bk. 1, Ch. 6:25:3

MG 8, 280

FC XXIII, 26

ST. AMBROSE

[To Horontianus] 'Who is a God like you, who takes away iniquity and passes by wickedness?' (Mic. 7:18). You have not been mindful of Your wrath, but have cast all our iniquities into the sea, like Egyptian lead, and graciously have restored us to mercy which You gave with two-fold generosity, forgiving and hiding our sins. . . . the expression, 'pardoning sins,' applies to their forgiveness, for He takes them away altogether, and what He remembers not are as though they did not exist.

626
(1256)

LETTERS, No. 70

ML 16, 1240

FC XXVI, 240

ST. AUGUSTINE

I say that baptism gives remission of all sins, and takes away guilt, and does not shave them off; and that the roots of all sins are not retained in the evil flesh, as if of shaved hair on the head, whence the sins may grow to be cut down again.

627
(1886)

AGAINST TWO LETTERS OF THE PELAGIANS, Bk. 1, Ch. 13

ML 44, 562

NPNF V, 385

628
(1910)

You state untruly that I said: 'Grace does not perfectly renew man.' Note what I actually said: 'Grace perfectly renews man, since it brings him even to immortality of body and full happiness.' It perfectly renews man now, also, as regards deliverance from all sins, but not as regards deliverance from all evils, nor from every ill of mortality by which the body is now a load upon the soul.

AGAINST JULIAN, Bk. 6, Ch. 13
ML 44, 809
FC XXXV, 346

ST. GREGORY THE GREAT

629
(2298)

Whoever says, then, that sins are not entirely put away in baptism, let him say that the Egyptians did not really die in the Red Sea. But, if he acknowledges that the Egyptians really died, he must needs acknowledge that sins die entirely in baptism, since surely the truth avails more in our absolution than the shadow of the truth.

LETTERS, Bk. 11:45
ML 77, 1162
NPNF XIII, 66

121. Man is renewed internally.

LETTER TO BARNABAS

630
(32)

Since then he has renewed us by the forgiveness of sins, He made us another product, and we have the souls of children, as though He were creating us again.

Ch. 6:11
MG 2, 741
FC I, 200

631
(36)

'But it shall be built in the name of the Lord.' Now, make sure that the temple of the Lord be built gloriously. How? I shall tell you. When we received forgiveness of sins, and put our hope in the Name [of Jesus] we were renewed, totally recreated; and so God truly dwells in us as in His habitation.

Ch. 16:8
MG 2, 773
FC I, 218

ST. IRENAEUS

And again, giving to the disciples the power of regeneration into God, He said to them, 'Go and teach all nations, baptizing them in the name of the Father, and of the Son, and of the Holy Spirit' (Mt. 28:19). For [God] promised, that in the last times He would pour [Him] the Spirit upon [His] servants and handmaids, that they might prophesy (Jl. 2:28); wherefore He did also descend upon the Son of God, made the Son of man, becoming accustomed in fellowship with Him to dwell in the human race, to rest with human beings, and to dwell in the workmanship of God, working the will of the Father in them, and renewing them from their old habits into the newness of Christ.

632
(219)

AGAINST HERESIES, Bk. 3, Ch. 17
MG 7, 929
ANF I, 444

ST. CYPRIAN
See No. 574.

NOVATIAN

[The Holy Spirit] it is who effects with water the second birth, as a certain seed of divine generation, and a consecration of a heavenly nativity, the pledge of a promised inheritance, and as it were a kind of handwriting of eternal salvation; who can make us God's temple, and fit us for His house; who solicits the divine hearing for us with groanings that cannot be uttered; filling the offices of advocacy, and manifesting the duties of our defence, —an inhabitant given for our bodies and an effector of their holiness.

633
(607)

ON THE TRINITY, Ch. 29
ML 3, 944
ANF V, 641

ST. CYRIL OF JERUSALEM

The water however flows round the outside only, but the Spirit baptizes also the soul within, and that completely. And why do you wonder? Take an example from matter; poor indeed and common, yet useful for the simpler sort. If the fire passing in through the mass of the iron makes the whole of it fire, so that what was cold becomes burning and what was black is made bright, —if fire which is a body thus penetrates

634
(835)

and works without hindrance in iron which is also a body, why wonder that the Holy Spirit enters into the very inmost recesses of the soul?

CATECHESES, 17:14
MG 33, 985
NPNF VII, 127

ST. BASIL
See No. 500.

ST. GREGORY NAZIANZEN

635
(1011)

Just as [God] gave existence to that which did not exist [us], so He gave new creation to that which did exist, a diviner creation and a loftier than the first, which is to those who are beginning life a Seal, and to those who are more mature in age both a gift and a restoration of the image which had fallen through sin.

ORATIONS, 40:7
MG 36, 365
NPNF VII, 361

ST. JOHN CHRYSOSTOM

636
(1203)

And he who praises and marvels at the grace displayed towards himself will thus be more devoted and more earnest. 'Which He freely bestowed on us,' he says. He does not say, 'Which He has graciously given us' (ἧς ἐχαρίσατο), but, 'wherein He has shown grace to us' (ἐχαρίτωσέν). That is to say, He has not only released us from our sins, but has also made us fitting objects of His love. It is as though one were to take a leper, wasted by distemper, and disease, by age, and poverty and famine, and were to turn him all at once into a graceful youth, surpassing all mankind in beauty, shedding a bright lustre from his cheeks, and eclipsing the sun-beams with the glances of his eyes; and then were to set him in the very flower of his age, and after that array him in purple and a diadem and all the attire of royalty. It is thus that God has arrayed and adorned this soul of ours, and clothed it with beauty, and rendered it an object of His delight and love.

LETTER TO THE EPHESIANS, Ch. 1:3
MG 62, 13
NPNF XIII, 52

ST. LEO THE GREAT

637
(2193)

Let us then, dearly beloved, give thanks to God the Father, through His Son, in the Holy Spirit, Who 'for His great mercy, wherewith He

320

has loved us,' has had pity on us: and 'when we were dead in sins, has quickened us together in Christ' (Eph. 2:5), that we might be in Him a new creation and a new production. Let us put off then the old man with his deeds: and having obtained a share in the birth of Christ let us renounce the works of the flesh. Christian, acknowledge your dignity, and becoming a partner in the Divine nature, refuse to return to the old baseness by degenerate conduct. Remember the Head and the Body of which you are a member. Recollect that you were rescued from the power of darkness and brought into God's light and kingdom.

SERMONS, No. 21:3
ML 54, 192
NPNF XII, 129

122. *The Holy Spirit dwells in man.*

LETTER TO BARNABAS
See No. 631.

THE SHEPHERD OF HERMAS.
See No. 340.

TATIAN

Now, in the beginning the spirit was a constant companion of the soul, but the spirit forsook it because it was not willing to follow. Yet, retaining as it were a spark of its power, though unable by reason of the separation to discern the perfect, while seeking for God it fashioned to itself in its wandering many gods, following the sophistries of the demons. But the Spirit of God is not with all, but taking up its abode with those who live justly, and intimately combining with the soul, by prophecies it announced hidden things to other souls.

638
(158)

ORATION AGAINST THE GREEKS, Ch. 13
MG 6, 833
See No. 481.   ANF II, 71

ST. IRENAEUS

And again, giving to the disciples the power of regeneration into God, He said to them, 'Go and teach all nations, baptizing them in the

639
(219)

name of the Father, and of the Son, and of the Holy Spirit' (Mt. 28:19). For [God] promised, that in the last times He would pour the Spirit upon [His] servants and handmaids, that they might prophesy; wherefore He did also descend upon the Son of God, made the Son of man, becoming accustomed in fellowship with Him to dwell in the human race, to rest with human beings, and to dwell in the workmanship of God, working the will of the Father in them, and renewing them from their old habits into the newnes of Christ.

AGAINST HERESIES, Bk. 3, Ch. 17

MG 7, 929

ANF I, 444

See No. 620.

ORIGEN
See No. 621.

NOVATIAN
See No. 633.

APHRAATES
See No. 487.

ST. CYRIL OF JERUSALEM
See No. 391.

ST. BASIL

640
(944)

So, too, is the Spirit to every one who receives It, as though given to him alone, and yet It sends forth grace sufficient and full for all mankind, and is enjoyed by all who share It, according to the capacity, not of Its power, but of their nature. . . . Shining upon those that are cleansed from every spot, He makes them spiritual by fellowship with Himself. Just as when a sunbeam falls on bright and transparent bodies, they themselves become brilliant too, and shed forth a fresh brightness from themselves, so souls wherein the Spirit dwells, illuminated by the Spirit, themselves become spiritual and send forth their grace to others. Hence . . . abiding in God, the being made like to God, and, highest of all, the being made God.

ON THE HOLY SPIRIT, Ch. 9:22

MG 32, 109

NPNF VIII, 15

ST. JOHN CHRYSOSTOM
See No. 427.

123. Man becomes a sharer of the divine nature.

ST. IGNATIUS OF ANTIOCH
See No. 320.

ST. CLEMENT OF ALEXANDRIA

But the man in whom reason dwells does not keep shifting, makes no false pretenses, retains the form dictated by reason, is like God and possesses true beauty with no need of artificial beauty. Beauty is what is true, for it is in fact God. Such a man becomes God because God wills it. Heraclitus said well: 'Men are gods and gods are men, for reason is the same'—manifestly a mystery.

641
(412)

CHRIST THE EDUCATOR, Bk. 3, Ch. 1

MG 8, 556

FC XXIII, 200

ST. METHODIUS

For I think that the Church is here said to give birth to a male; since the enlightened receive the features, and the image, and the manliness of Christ, the likeness of the form of the Word being stamped upon them, and begotten in them by a true knowledge and faith, so that in each one Christ is spiritually born. And, therefore, the Church swells and travails in birth until Christ is formed in us, so that each of the saints, by partaking of Christ, has been born a Christ. According to which meaning it is said in a certain scripture, 'Touch not my anointed, and do my prophets no harm' (Ps. 104:15), as though those who were baptized into Christ had been made Christs by communication of the Spirit, the Church contributing here their clearness and transformation into the image of the Word.

642
(613)

THE BANQUET OF THE TEN VIRGINS, Ch. 8:8

MG 18, 149

ANF VI, 337

ST. CYRIL OF JERUSALEM
See No. 391.

ST. BASIL
See No. 641.

ST. AMBROSE
See No. 412.

ST. AUGUSTINE

643
(1468)

It is evident then, that He has called men gods, that are deified by His Grace, not born of His Substance. For He justifies who is just through His own self, and not of another; and He deifies who is God through Himself, not by the partaking of another. But He that justifies deifies Himself, in that by justifying He makes sons of God. 'For He has given them power to become the sons of God' (Jn. 1:12). If we have been made sons of God, we have also been made gods: but this is the effect of Grace adopting, not of nature generating.

EXPOSITIONS ON THE PSALMS, Ps. 49:2
ML 36, 565
NPNF VIII, 178

ST. LEO THE GREAT
See No. 637.

124. Man becomes the adoptive son of God.

ST. CLEMENT OF ALEXANDRIA
See No. 635.

ST. ATHANASIUS

644
(766)

But this is God's kindness to man, that of whom He is Maker, of them according to grace He afterwards becomes Father also; becomes, that is, when men, His creatures, receive into their hearts, as the Apostle says, 'the Spirit of His Son, crying, Abba, Father' (Gal. 4:6). And these are they who, having received the Word, gained power from Him to become sons of God; for they could not become sons, being by nature creatures, otherwise than by receiving the Spirit of the natural

324

and true Son. Wherefore, that this might be, 'The Word became flesh' (Jn. 1:14), that He might make man capable of Godhead.

FOUR DISCOURSES AGAINST THE ARIANS, Or. 2:59
MG 26, 273
NPNF IV, 380

ST. CYRIL OF JERUSALEM
See No. 391.

ST. BASIL

Through the Holy Spirit comes our restoration to paradise, our ascension into the kingdom of heaven, our return to the adoption of sons, our liberty to call God our Father, our being made partakers of the grace of Christ, our being called children of light, our sharing in eternal glory, and, in a word, our being brought into a state of all 'fullness of blessing,' both in this world and in the world to come, of all the good gifts that are in store for us, by promise whereof, through faith, beholding the reflection of their grace as though they were already present, we await the full enjoyment.

645
(948)

ON THE HOLY SPIRIT, Ch. 15:36
MG 32, 132
NPNF VIII, 22

ST. JOHN CHRYSOSTOM

Being Son of the Unoriginate God, and His true Son, He suffered Himself to be called also Son of David, that He might make you Son of God. He suffered a slave to be father to Him, that He might make the Lord Father to you a slave. Do you see at once from the beginning of what nature are the Gospels? If you doubt concerning the things that pertain to you, from what belongs to Him believe these also. For it is far more difficult, judging by human reason, for God to become man, than for a man to be declared a Son of God. When therefore you are told that the Son of God is Son of David and of Abraham, doubt not any more that you too, the son of Adam, shall be son of God. For not at random, nor in vain did He abase Himself so greatly, only He was minded to exalt us. Thus He was born after the flesh, that you might be born after the Spirit; He was born of a woman, that you might cease to be the son of a woman.

646
(1171)

HOMILIES ON MATTHEW, 2:2
MG 57, 25
NPNF X, 9–10

ST. AMBROSE

647
(1273)

Can men indeed be loved by God as the Son is, in Whom the Father is well-pleased? He is well-pleasing in Himself; we through Him. For those in whom God sees His own Son after His own likeness, He admits through His son into the favor of sons. So that as we go through likeness unto likeness, so through the Generation of the Son are we called unto adoption. The eternal love of God's nature is one thing, that of grace is another.

TO GRATIAN ON THE CHRISTIAN FAITH, Bk. 5, Ch. 7
ML 16, 666
NPNF X, 295

ST. AUGUSTINE
See Nos. 619 and 643.

648
(1777)

There is but one Son of God by nature, who in His compassion became Son of man for our sakes, that we, by nature sons of men, might by grace become through Him sons of God. . . . For as by the sin of one man we have fallen into a misery so deplorable, so by the righteousness of one Man, who also is God, shall we come to a blessedness inconceivably exalted.

THE CITY OF GOD, Bk. 21, Ch. 15
ML 41, 729
NPNF II, 465

125. *Man must dispose himself for justification through faith.*

ST. CLEMENT OF ROME

649
(16)

And we also, having been called through His will in Christ Jesus are not justified by ourselves, or by our own wisdom or understanding or piety or the works we have done in holiness of heart, but through the faith, by which the Almighty God has justified all men from the beginning; to whom be glory for all ages. Amen. What, then, shall we do, brothers? Shall we slacken from doing good and abandon charity? May the Lord never allow this to happen to us, but let us be diligent to accomplish every good work (Tit. 3:1) with earnestness and zeal.

LETTER TO THE CORINTHIANS, Ch. 32:4
MG 1, 272
FC I, 34–35

ST. CLEMENT OF ALEXANDRIA

Such a change, then, from unbelief to faith—and to trust in hope and fear, is divine. And, in truth, faith is discovered by us to be the first movement towards salvation; after which fear, and hope, and repentance, advancing in company with temperance and patience, lead us to love and knowledge.

650
(419)

> STROMATA, Bk. 2, Ch. 6
> *MG* 8, 965
> *ANF* II, 354

ST. JOHN CHRYSOSTOM

'Who believes in the Son, has eternal life' (Jn. 3:36). . . . 'Is it then enough,' says one, 'to believe on the Son, that one may have eternal life?' By no means. And hear Christ Himself declaring this, and saying, 'Not every one that says to Me, Lord, Lord, shall enter into the kingdom of heaven' (Mt. 7:21); and the blasphemy against the Spirit is enough of itself to cast a man into hell. But why speak I of a portion of doctrine? Though a man believe rightly on the Father, the Son, and the Holy Spirit, yet if he lead not a right life, his faith will avail nothing towards his salvation.

651
(1163)

> HOMILIES ON ST. JOHN, 31:1
> *MG* 59, 175
> *NPNF* XIV, 106

ST. AUGUSTINE

Let no one say to himself: 'If it is of faith, how is it freely given? (Rom. 5:1; 3:24). If faith earns it, why is it not rather paid than given?' Let the faithful man not say that because, when he says: 'I have faith that I may earn justification,' he is answered: 'What have you that you have not received?' (1 Cor. 4:7). Therefore, since faith asks for and receives justification, 'according as God has divided to every one the measure of faith' (Rom. 12:3), no human merit precedes the grace of God, but grace itself merits an increase, and the increase merits perfection, with the will accompanying it, not going before it; followed behind it, not pointing out the way.

652
(1446)

> LETTERS, No. 186:3:10
> *ML* 33, 819
> *FC* XXX, 198

653
(15)

126. Man also disposes himself for justification through the acts of the other virtues.

ST. CLEMENT OF ROME

Why was our father Abraham blessed? Was it not because he performed justice and truth through faith?

LETTER TO THE CORINTHIANS, Ch. 31
MG 1, 272
See No. 649.
FC I, 34

ST. CLEMENT OF ALEXANDRIA
See No. 221.

654
(428)

So that when we hear, 'Your faith has saved you' (Mt. 9:22; Mk. 5:34; Lk. 8:48), we do not understand Him to say absolutely that those who have believed in any way whatever shall be saved, unless also works follow. But it was to the Jews alone that He spoke this utterance, who kept the law and lived blamelessly, who wanted only faith in the Lord.

STROMATA, Bk. 6, Ch. 14
MG 9, 329
ANF II, 505

ST. JOHN CHRYSOSTOM
See No. 651.

ST. AUGUSTINE

655
(1590)

For certainly it very rarely happens, indeed, I should rather say, never, that any one approaches us with the wish to become a Christian who has not been smitten with some sort of fear of God. For if it is in the expectation of some advantage from men whom he deems himself unlikely to please in any other way, or with the idea of escaping any disadvantage at the hands of men of whose displeasure or hostility he is seriously afraid, that a man wishes to become a Christian, then his wish to become one is not so earnest as his desire to feign one.

ON CATECHIZING THE UNINSTRUCTED, Ch. 5:9
ML 40, 316
NPNF II, 288

127. Habitual grace is lost by mortal sin.

TATIAN

Now, in the beginning the spirit was a constant companion of the soul, but the spirit forsook it because it was not willing to follow. Yet, retaining as it were a spark of its power, though unable by reason of the separation to discern the perfect, while seeking for God it fashioned to itself in its wandering many gods, following the sophistries of the demons. But the Spirit of God is not with all, but taking up its abode with those who live justly, and intimately combining with the soul, by prophecies it announced hidden things to other souls.

ORATION AGAINST THE GREEKS, Ch. 13
MG 6, 833
ANF II, 71

656
(158)

APHRAATES
See No. 487.

ST. BASIL
See No. 500.

ST. AUGUSTINE

If, however, being already regenerate and justified, he relapses of his own will into an evil life, assuredly he cannot say, 'I have not received,' because of his own free choice to evil he has lost the grace of God, that he had received.

ON REBUKE AND GRACE, Ch. 6:9
ML 44, 921
NPNF V, 475

657
(1944)

128. Man can never be certain of his righteousness.

ST. AUGUSTINE

For however great a man's righteousness may be, he ought to reflect and think, lest there should be found something blameworthy, which has escaped indeed his own notice, when that righteous King shall sit upon His throne, whose cognizance no sins can possibly escape, not

658
(1800)

329

even those of which it is said, 'Who understands his transgressions?' (Ps. 18:13).

MAN'S PERFECTION IN RIGHTEOUSNESS, Ch. 15:33

ML 44, 309

NPNF V, 171

MERIT

129. *The just can have true merit.*

ST. IGNATIUS OF ANTIOCH

659
(68)

Please the leader under whom you serve, for from him you receive your pay. May none of you turn out a deserter. Let your baptism be ever your shield, your faith a helmet, your charity a spear, your patience a panoply. Let your works be deposits, so that you may receive the sum that is due to you. In humility be patient with one another, as God is with you.

LETTER TO POLYCARP, Ch. 6

MG 5, 724

FC I, 126

ST. JUSTIN MARTYR
See No. 488.

ST. IRENAEUS

660
(246)

We deem the crown precious, namely, that which is acquired by our struggle, but which does not encircle us of its own accord. And the harder we strive, so much is it the more valuable; while so much the more valuable it is, so much the more should we esteem it.

AGAINST HERESIES, Bk. 4, Ch. 37

MG 7, 1104

ANF I, 520

TERTULLIAN

A good deed has God as its debtor, just as an evil has too; for a judge is a rewarder of every cause.

661
(311)

ON PENANCE, Ch. 2
ML 1, 1230
ANF III, 658

ST. CYRIL OF JERUSALEM

The root of all good works is the hope of the Resurrection; for the expectation of the recompense nerves the soul to good works. For every laborer is ready to endure the toils, if he sees their reward in prospect; but when men weary themselves for nought, their heart soon sinks as well as their body. . . . He who believes that his body shall remain to rise again, is careful of his robe, and defiles it not with fornication; but he who disbelieves the Resurrection, gives himself to fornication, and misuses his own body, as though it were not his own. Faith therefore in the Resurrection of the dead, is a great commandment and doctrine of the Holy Catholic Church; great and most necessary, though contradicted by many, yet surely warranted by the truth.

662
(836)

CATECHESES, No. 18:1
MG 33, 1017
NPNF VII, 134

ST. JEROME

Now our work is, according to our different virtues, to prepare for ourselves a different future. . . . If we are all to be equal in heaven, in vain do we humble ourselves here that we may be greater there. . . . Why do virgins persevere? widows toil? Why do married women practise continence? Let us all sin, and when once we have repented, we shall be on the same footing as the apostles.

663
(1383)

AGAINST JOVINIANUS, Bk. 2, Ch. 32
ML 23:329
NPNF VI, 412

ST. AUGUSTINE

What merits of his own has the saved to boast of, when, if he received his just deserts, he would be damned? But, have the just no merits at all? Certainly they have, since they are just; only, there were no

664
(1449)

previous merits to make them just. They became just when they were justified.

LETTERS, No. 194:3:6

ML 33, 876

FC **XXX**, 305

See No. 608.

665
(1477)

[The Lord] has given grace, He will give glory. He is the giver of grace, the debtor of glory. But how is he a debtor? Has he received something? The Lord Himself has made Himself a debtor, not by receiving but by promising: it is not said to Him, Restore what You have received: but, Restore what You have promised.

EXPOSITIONS ON THE PSALMS, 83:16

ML 37, 1068

NPNF VIII, 404

ST. PROSPER OF AQUITAINE
See No. 571.

130. *The just can merit eternal life.*

ST. THEOPHILUS OF ANTIOCH
See No. 11.

666
(176)

But read the prophetic Scriptures, and they will make your way plainer for escaping the eternal punishments, and obtaining the eternal prizes of God. For He who gave the mouth for speech, and formed the ear to hear, and made the eye to see, will examine all things, and will judge righteous judgment, rendering merited awards to each. To those who by patient continuance in well-doing seek immortality, He will give life everlasting, joy, peace, rest, and abundance of good things, which neither has eye seen, nor ear heard, nor has it entered into the heart of man to conceive (1 Cor. 2:9). But to the unbelieving and despisers, who obey not the truth, but are obedient to unrighteousness, when they shall have been filled with adulteries and fornications, and filthiness, and covetousness, and unlawful idolatries, there shall be anger and wrath, tribulation and anguish, and at the last everlasting fire shall possess such men.

TO AUTOLYCUS, Ch. 1:14

MG 6, 1045

ANF II, 93

ST. HIPPOLYTUS

And being present at His judicial decision, all, both men and angels and demons, shall utter one voice, saying, 'Righteous is Your judgment' (Ps. 118:137). Of which voice the justification will be seen in the awarding to each that which is just; since to those who have done well shall be assigned righteously eternal bliss, and to the lovers of iniquity shall be given eternal punishment. And the fire which is unquenchable and without end awaits these latter, and a certain fiery worm which dies not, and which does not waste the body, but continues bursting forth from the body with unending pain. No sleep will give them rest; no night will soothe them; no death will deliver them from punishment; no voice of interceding friends will profit them. For neither are the righteous seen by them any longer, nor are they worthy of remembrance.

667
(396)

AGAINST THE GREEKS, Ch. 3
MG 10, 801
ANF V, 222

ST. CYPRIAN
See No. 622.

ST. AUGUSTINE

After he had said: 'The wages of sin is death' (Rom. 6:23), anyone would have agreed that he could have made a most consistent and logical conclusion if he had said: 'But the wages of justice is eternal life.' And it is true, because eternal life is awarded as if it were the wages which justice deserves, just as death is the wages which sin deserves.

668
(1453)

LETTERS, No. 194:5:20
ML 33, 881
FC XXX, 313–314

In that hire then shall we be all equal, and the first as the last, and the last as the first; because that denarius (Mt. 20:2) is life eternal, and in the life eternal all will be equal. For although through diversity of attainments [meritorum] the saints will shine, some more, some less; yet as to this respect, the gift of eternal life, it will be equal to all.

669
(1502)

SERMONS, No. 87:4:6
ML 38, 533
NPNF VI, 375

See Nos. 610 and 550.

X.

The Incarnate Word

"In the fulness of time God sent forth His Son" (Gal. 4:4). Jesus Christ is God's only-begotten Son, the second Person of the Blessed Trinity who assumed a true human nature and so became consubstantial with us. Hence Christ is both God and man. In assuming our nature the Word became flesh and dwelt among us in such a way that there was one person, Jesus Christ, with two distinct natures— one divine, the other human. These two natures are united by a personal union made at the time of conception and the union is inseparable. In Christ there are also two wills, one divine and the other human, but neither is opposed to the other. Christ was completely filled with grace and was all holy, and therefore He is to be adored as man. Free from original and personal sin as well as from sinful affections, He was not even capable of sinning. But His body was subject to passions, human weaknesses, and suffering, and His death was a free act of His own choice.

Against those who claimed that Jesus was a mere man, the ante-Nicene tradition testifies that Christ is true God. St. Clement of Rome, St. Ignatius of Antioch, and the *Letter to Barnabas* are the earliest witnesses; both the *Martyrdom of St. Ignatius* and the *Martyrdom* of *St. Polycarp* affirm it, as well as the *Epistle of Diognetus* and Aristides. The list is overwhelming: St. Justin Martyr, Tatian, St. Irenaeus, Tertullian, St. Clement of Alexandria, Origen, St. Cyprian, Arnobius, Lactantius—and we have not reached Nicea! All affirm that only the Son of God is incarnate, nor is He other than Jesus Christ. Against the Docetists and Gnostics, the Fathers affirm that Jesus assumed a true human nature, not one that was merely apparent. St. Ignatius of Antioch is most emphatic on this point, and Tertullian emphasizes it in his *On the Flesh of Christ*.

335

Testimony on this teaching is to be found especially in St. Athanasius, St. Cyril of Jerusalem, St. Hilary, St. Basil, St. John Chrysostom, St. Ambrose, and St. Leo, to mention only the more prominent writers. Thus it follows that Christ has a true body formed from the substance of Mary His mother.

Christ also had a rational soul (Origen discusses this at great length) and so He is consubstantial with us, being of the race of Adam. "What is not assumed is not healed" is the felicitous expression of St. Gregory Nazianzen, but the idea appears in St. Athanasius, St. Cyril of Jerusalem, St. Basil, as well as the Latin Fathers Ambrose and Augustine. The Damascene summarizes all of this beautifully. The Greek fathers remind us that the incarnation is a mystery, and after St. Augustine, St. John Cassian, St. Vincent of Lérins, and St. Leo reiterate this. St. John of Damascus expounds on it, of course. Tertullian reminds us at considerable length that the Word is not converted into the human nature, nor is it mixed with it, but rather that the Word assumed a human nature so that there are two natures truly distinct. A dozen different authors testify to this. Yet the two natures are somehow united, St. Irenaeus tells us, as do Novatian, St. Athanasius, St. Cyril of Jerusalem, St. Hilary, St. Gregory Nazianzen, St. Ambrose, and St. John of Damascus. St. Augustine in several passages states that the two natures of Christ are united by a personal union, and several writers echo him later on. This union of the two natures is inseparable, and in all of this one detects a direct attack on the Monophysite heresy of the fifth century. It is left to St. John of Damascus to refute the Monothelites of a later time by insisting on two wills in Christ which are not contrary to each other. There is abundant testimony to the fact of two operations in Christ, one divine, the other human; a number of writers affirm this, and St. Athanasius and St. Augustine go on to discuss the theandric operation. St. Cyril of Jerusalem has a great deal to say about the true communication of idioms, with several subsequent writers agreeing with him. The upshot of all this is that the man Christ is the natural Son of God, not the adopted Son. Hence He is to be adored as man, St. Athanasius tells the Arians.

Christ was free from original sin, from sinful affections, from personal sin: He was not even able to sin. Each of these points is dealt with by a few of the authors, freedom from personal sin receiving the most extended treatment.

Christ's capacity for suffering has a larger number of defenders, because of the various heretics who denied this. St. Ignatius of Antioch is most emphatic on this point, and St. Justin Martyr is not far behind. St. Irenaeus, Tertullian, St. Clement of Alexandria, and Origen all touch upon it, and St. Athanasius defends it vigorously as do St. Cyril of Jerusalem, St. Hilary, and St. Gregory Nazianzen. The Fathers remind us that Christ's body was subject to human weaknesses and passions. That He freely suffered and died is best expressed by the great St. Augustine. It is of interest that a good number of the Fathers seem puzzled by Mark 13:32 which seems to imply some sort of ignorance in Christ, and not a few of them attempt to explain the text to their satisfaction.

The purpose of Christ's incarnation, passion, and death was the salvation of men, and although God need not have saved man at all or could have redeemed the human race in another way, yet He chose to manifest His love to man by this free gift. So it was that Christ offered Himself freely on the cross as both priest and host by way of true vicarious sacrifice, a sacrifice paid not to the devil but to God. This satisfaction is both superabundant and universal and thus Christ is the great mediator between God and men. All grace flows through Him and it is He who has ascended into heaven from whence He will come to judge both the living and the dead.

St. Irenaeus, St. Athanasius, St. John Chrysostom, St. Augustine, and St. Leo the Great think that if Adam had not sinned, the incarnation would not have occurred. At any rate, God could indeed have effected the redemption of the human race in another way. Hence, the incarnation is a free gift of God, as the *Letter to Diognetus* states so beautifully. In one sense, however, the incarnation could be said to be necessary; following the *Letter to Barnabas* and St. Methodius, St. Athanasius discusses this in his *Treatise on the Incarnation of the Word*. So does St. Augustine in his work *On the Trinity*.

The purpose of the incarnation and passion of Christ is the salvation of men as well as a manifestation of love towards them; the *Letter to Diognetus* is a classic on these two points. So it was that

Christ desired to redeem men from sin and the servitude of the devil, and here we have an almost universal chorus of voices. The *Letter to Barnabas* and St. Ignatius of Antioch affirm this together with Hermas, St. Justin Martyr, and St. Irenaeus—who is the most persuasive on this point—Tertullian, St. Clement of Alexandria, and Origen; St. Athanasius, St. Basil, and St. Gregory Nazianzen; St. John Chrysostom, St. Ambrose, and St. Augustine, as well as St. Leo the Great and the Damascene. All implicitly agree that Christ wished to bestow on men grace and immortality and thus lead them back to the pristine state, lost through Adam's sin. The testimony on these points is universal and copious.

Christ effected the redemption in the manner of a true sacrifice to God on the cross as both priest and host. St. Justin Martyr and St. Cyprian assert this to be a true vicarious sacrifice, and this satisfaction is superabundant (so St. Cyril of Jerusalem) as well as universal (St. Basil and others). Thus Christ has become the mediator between God and men, and graces are therefore given to us through Christ and because of Him. Hence it is possible even for those under the old law to be justified through His superabundant satisfaction.

St. Irenaeus and St. Cyril of Jerusalem say that Christ's soul descended into hell, as does St. Leo the Great; St. Irenaeus and St. Augustine along with St. Leo affirm Christ's ascension; and the *Letter to Barnabas,* St. Clement of Rome, St. Justin Martyr, St. Irenaeus, Tertullian, St. Cyprian, Lactantius, and St. Gregory Nazianzen remind us that some day He will come to judge the living and the dead.

THE PERSON OF CHRIST

131. The ante-Nicene tradition testifies that Christ is true God (see under heading 71).

ST. CLEMENT OF ROME

670
(18)
This is the way, beloved, by which we found our Saviour, Jesus Christ, the high priest of our offerings, the protector and the helper of our

weakness. Through Him let us strain our eyes toward the heights of heaven; through Him we see mirrored His spotless and glorious countenance. Through Him the eyes of our heart have been opened; through Him our foolish and darkened understanding shoots up into the light; through Him the Lord willed that we should taste immortal knowledge, 'Who, being the brightness of His majesty is so much greater than the angels as He hath inherited a more excellent name' (Heb. 1:3, 4).

LETTER TO THE CORINTHIANS, Ch. 36

MG 1, 280

FC I, 38

LETTER TO BARNABAS

Moses says to Joshua, the son of Nun, after giving him this name, when he sent him to explore the land: 'Take a book in your hands, and write what the Lord says, that the Son of God shall in the last days tear up by the roots the whole house of Amalek' (Ex. 17:14). See again Jesus, not as son of man, but as Son of God, manifested by a type in the flesh. So, since they will say that Christ is David's son, David himself prophesies, fearing and realizing the error of sinners. 'The Lord said to my Lord, Sit at my right hand until I make your enemies your footstool' (Ps. 109:1). . . . See how David calls Him Lord and does not say 'Son.'

671
(35)

Ch. 12:9

MG 2, 764

FC I, 212

ST. IGNATIUS OF ANTIOCH

For our God Jesus Christ was, according to God's dispensation, the fruit of Mary's womb, of the seed of David; He was born and baptized in order that He might make the water holy by His passion.

672
(42)

LETTER TO THE EPHESIANS, Ch. 18

MG 5, 660

FC I, 94

THE MARTYRDOM OF ST. IGNATIUS

Trajan said, 'Do *we* not then seem to you to have the gods in our mind, whose assistance we enjoy in fighting against our enemies?' Ignatius answered, 'You are in error when you call the daemons of the

673
(69)

nations gods. For there is but one God, who made heaven, and earth, and the sea, and all that are in them (Ps. 145:6); and one Jesus Christ, the only-begotten Son of God, whose kingdom may I enjoy.' Trajan said, 'Do you mean Him who was crucified under Pontius Pilate?' Ignatius replied, 'I mean Him who crucified my sin, with him who was the inventor of it, and who has condemned (and cast down) all the deceit and malice of the devil under the feet of those who carry Him in their heart.' Trajan said, 'Do you then carry within you Him that was crucified?' Ignatius replied, 'Truly so, for it is written, "I will dwell in them, and walk among them" ' (2 Cor. 6:16).

Ch. 2:4
MG 5, 981
ANF I, 129

THE EPISTLE OF DIOGNETUS
See No. 429.

THE SO-CALLED SECOND LETTER OF ST. CLEMENT OF ROME TO THE CORINTHIANS

674
(101)
Brothers, we must think of Jesus Christ as of God—as the 'judge of the living and the dead' (Acts 10:42).

Ch. 1:1
MG 1, 329
FC I, 65

ARISTIDES
See No. 87.

ST. JUSTIN MARTYR
See Nos. 322 and 323.

675
(131)
For next to God, we worship and love the Word who is from the unbegotten and ineffable God, since also He became man for our sakes, that, becoming a partaker of our sufferings, He might also bring us healing.

THE SECOND APOLOGY, Ch. 13
MG 6, 465
ANF I, 193

676
(136)
But since I have certainly proved that this man is the Christ of God, whoever He be, even if I do not prove that He preexisted, and sub-

mitted to be born a man of like passions with us, having a body, according to the Father's will; in this last matter alone is it just to say that I have erred, and not to deny that He is the Christ, though it should appear that He was born a man of men, and [nothing more] is proved [than this], that He has become Christ by election. For there are some, my friends, I said, of our race, who admit that He is Christ, while holding Him to be man of men; with whom I do not agree, nor would I, even though most of those who have [now] the same opinions as myself should say so; since we were enjoined by Christ Himself to put no faith in human doctrines, but in those proclaimed by the blessed prophets and taught by Himself.

DIALOGUE WITH TRYPHO, Ch. 48

MG 6, 580

See No. 384.   *ANF* II, 219

TATIAN

We do not act as fools, O Greeks, nor utter idle tales, when we an-   677
nounce that God was born in the form of a man.   (160)

ORATION AGAINST THE GREEKS, Ch. 21

MG 6, 852

ANF II, 74

ST. IRENAEUS
See No. 211.

For if, in truth, the one suffered, and the other remained incapable of   678
suffering, and the one was born, but the other descended upon him who   (218)
was born, and left him again, it is not one, but two, that are shown
forth. . . . Do not err (Paul says to all): Jesus Christ, the Son of God,
is one and the same, who did by suffering reconcile us to God, and rose
from the dead; who is at the right hand of the Father, and perfect in
all things; . . . For He did Himself truly bring in salvation: since He
is Himself the Word of God, Himself the Only-begotten of the Father,
Christ Jesus our Lord.

AGAINST HERESIES, Bk. 3, Ch. 16

MG 7, 928

See No. 62.   *ANF* I, 443–444

It will be necessary for you, however, and all who may happen to   679
read this writing, to peruse with great attention what I have already   (248)
said, that you may obtain a knowledge of the subjects against which I

341

am contending. For it is thus that you will both controvert them (heretics in a legitimate manner), and will be prepared to receive the proofs brought forward against them, casting away their doctrines as filth by means of the celestial faith; but following the only true and steadfast Teacher, the word of God, our Lord Jesus Christ, who did, through His transcendent love, become what we are, that He might bring us to be even what He is Himself.

AGAINST HERESIES, Bk. 5, Praef.
MG 7, 1120
ANF I, 526

TERTULLIAN
See No. 395.

680
(336)

The Christ [of Marcion], therefore, in order to avoid all such deceits and fallacies, and the imputation, if possible, of belonging to the Creator, was not what he appeared to be, and feigned himself to be what he was not—incarnate without being flesh, human without being man, and likewise a divine Christ without being God! But why should he not have propagated also the phantom of God? Can I believe him on the subject of the internal nature, who was all wrong touching the external substance? How will it be possible to believe him true on a mystery, when he has been found so false on a plain fact? . . . On this principle, too, the sufferings of Christ will be found not to warrant faith in Him. For He suffered nothing who did not truly suffer; and a phantom could not truly suffer. God's entire work, therefore, is subverted.

AGAINST MARCION, Bk. 3, Ch. 8
ML 2, 331
ANF III, 327–328

681
(350)

God alone is without sin, and the only sinless man is Christ, since He is God.

ON THE SOUL, Ch. 41
ML 2, 720
ANF III, 221

See No. 331.

ST. CLEMENT OF ALEXANDRIA
See Nos. 387 and 54.

682
(406)

Isaac is another type, too (he can easily be taken in this other sense), this time of the Lord. He was a son, just as is the Son (he is the son of Abraham; Christ, of God); he was a victim, as was the Lord, but his sacrifice was not consummated, while the Lord's was. All he did was to carry the wood of his sacrifice, just as the Lord bore the wood of the Cross. Isaac rejoiced for a mystical reason, to prefigure the joy with which the Lord has filled us, in saving us from destruction through His blood. Isaac did not actually suffer, not only to concede the primacy of suffering to the Word, but also to suggest, by not being slain, the divinity of the Lord.

CHRIST THE EDUCATOR, Bk. 1, Ch. 5
MG 8, 277
See No. 388.   *FC* XXIII, 23

ORIGEN
See No. 212.

ST. CYPRIAN
See No. 334.

ARNOBIUS

'You worship one born a mere human being.' Even if that were   683
true . . . yet in consideration of the many liberal gifts which He has   (617)
bestowed on us, He ought to be called and be addressed as God. But
since He is God in reality and without any shadow of doubt, do you
think that we will deny that He is worshipped by us with all the fervor
we are capable of, and assumed as the guardian of our body? Is that
Christ of yours a god, then? some raving, wrathful, and excited man
will say. A god, we will reply, and *the* god of the inner powers.

AGAINST THE NATIONS, Bk. 1, Ch. 42
ML 5, 771
ANF VI, 424

LACTANTIUS
See No. 359 and 365.

APHRAATES

Yet it is a sure thing with us, that Jesus our Lord is God, the Son of   684
God, and the King, the King's Son, Light of Light, Creator and   (692)
Counsellor, and Guide, and the Way, and Redeemer, and Shepherd,
Gatherer, and the Door, and the Pearl, and the Lamp; and by man
(such names is He surnamed). But we shall leave aside all [the rest]

of them, and prove concerning Him, that He Who came from God is the Son of God, and [is] God.

DEMONSTRATIONS, 17:2

PS 1, 787

NPNF XIII, 387

132. Only the Son of God is incarnate, nor is He other than Jesus Christ.

ST. IGNATIUS OF ANTIOCH
See No. 107.

THE SHEPHERD OF HERMAS
See Nos. 340 and 341.

THE LETTER TO DIOGNETUS
See No. 429.

THE SO-CALLED SECOND LETTER OF ST. CLEMENT
OF ROME TO THE CORINTHIANS
See No. 674.

ST. JUSTIN MARTYR
See Nos. 61, 676, and 32.

ST. IRENAEUS
See Nos. 211, 34, and 678.

TERTULLIAN
See Nos. 53, 201, and 331.

ST. HIPPOLYTUS
See No. 386.

ST. CLEMENT OF ALEXANDRIA
See No. 387.

ORIGEN
See No. 56.

LACTANTIUS
See No. 359.

ST. AUGUSTINE

Let us rejoice, my brethren, let the nations exult and be glad because,   685
not the visible sun, but the invisible Creator of the sun has consecrated   (1518)
this day [Christmas] on which the Virgin, a true but inviolate Mother,
gave birth to Him who became visible for our sake and by whom she
herself was created. A virgin conceives, yet remains a virgin; a virgin
is heavy with child; a virgin brings forth her child, yet she is always
a virgin. . . . The same One who is Man is God, and the same One
who is God is Man, not by a confusion of nature but by a unity of
person. Finally, He who is the Son of God, being born of the Father,
is always co-eternal with His Father; He, being born of the Virgin,
became the Son of Man. Thus, humanity was added to the divinity
of the Son without producing a fourfold union of Persons; the Trinity
remains.

SERMONS, No. 186:1:1
ML 38, 999
FC XXXVIII, 9

ST. LEO THE GREAT

At the same time the only begotten of the eternal Father was born   686
eternal of the Holy Spirit and the Virgin Mary. And this nativity which   (2182)
took place in time took nothing from, and added nothing to that
divine and eternal birth, but expended itself wholly on the restoration
of man who had been deceived: in order that he might both vanquish
death and overthrow by his strength the Devil who possessed the power
of death. For we should not now be able to overcome the author of sin
and death unless He took our nature on Him and made it His own,
whom neither sin could pollute nor death retain. Doubtless then, He
was conceived of the Holy Spirit within the womb of His Virgin
Mother, who brought Him forth without the loss of her virginity,
even as she conceived Him without its loss. . . . But that birth so
uniquely wondrous and so wondrously unique, is not to be understood
in such wise that the properties of His kind were removed through the
novelty of His creation. For though the Holy Spirit imparted fertility
to the Virgin, yet a real body was received from her body; and, 'Wisdom building her a house' (Prov. 9:1), 'the Word became flesh and

dwelt in us' (Jn. 1:14), that is, in that flesh which He took from man and which He quickened with the breath of a higher life.

LETTERS, No. 28:2
ML 54, 759
NPNF XII, 39

TRUE HUMANITY

133. Jesus Christ assumed a true human nature, not one that was merely apparent.

ST. IGNATIUS OF ANTIOCH

687
(39)
There is one Doctor active in both body and soul, begotten and yet unbegotten, God in man, true life in death, son of Mary and Son of God, first able to suffer and then unable to suffer, Jesus Christ, our Lord.

LETTER TO THE EPHESIANS, Ch. 3
MG 5, 649
See Nos. 52 and 107.
FC I, 90

TERTULLIAN
See No. 680.

688
(343)
Then, having taken the bread and given it to His disciples, He made it His own body, by saying, 'This is my body' (Lk. 22:19), that is, the figure of my body. A figure, however, there could not have been, unless there were first a veritable body. An empty thing, or phantom, is incapable of a figure. If however (as Marcion might say), He pretended the bread was His body, because He lacked the truth of bodily substance, it follows that He might have given bread for us.

AGAINST MARCION, Bk. 4, Ch. 40
ML 2, 460
ANF III, 418

689
(357)
We maintain, moreover, that what has been abolished in Christ is not *carnem peccati*, 'sinful flesh,' but *peccatum carnis*, 'sin in the

346

flesh'—not the material thing, but its condition; not the substance, but its flaw; and (this we aver) on the authority of the apostle, who says, 'He abolished sin in the flesh' (Rom. 8:3). Now in another sentence he says that Christ was 'in the likeness of sinful flesh,' not, however, as if He had taken on Him 'the likeness of the flesh,' in the sense of a semblance of body instead of its reality; but he means us to understand likeness to the flesh which sinned, because the flesh of Christ, which committed no sin itself, resembled that which had sinned, —resembled it in its nature, but not in the corruption it received from Adam; whence we also affirm that there was in Christ the same flesh as that whose nature in man is sinful. In the flesh, therefore, [we say] that sin has been abolished, because in Christ that same flesh is maintained without sin, which in man was not maintained without sin.

ON THE FLESH OF CHRIST, Ch. 16
ML 2, 774
ANF III, 535

ST. HIPPOLYTUS
See No. 432.

ST. CLEMENT OF ALEXANDRIA
See No. 54.

But in the case of the Saviour, [the Gnostics say] it would be ludicrous [to suppose] that the body, as a body, demanded the necessary aids in order to keep alive. For He ate, not for the sake of the body, which was kept together by a holy energy, but in order that it might not enter into the minds of those who were with Him to entertain a different opinion of Him; in like manner as certainly some afterwards supposed that He appeared in phantasmal shape. But He was entirely impassible; inaccessible to any movement of feeling—either pleasure or pain.

690
(426)

STROMATA, Bk. 6, Ch. 9
MG 9, 292
ANF II, 496

NOVATIAN

Neither, therefore, do we acknowledge that that is a Christ of heretics who was—as it is said—in appearance and not in reality; for of those things which he did, he could have done nothing real, if he himself was a phantasm, and not reality. Nor him who wore nothing of our

691
(604)

body in himself, seeing 'he received nothing from Mary'; neither did he come to us, since he appeared 'as a vision, not in our substance.' Nor do we acknowledge that to be Christ who chose an ethereal or starry flesh, as some heretics have pretended. Nor can we perceive any salvation of ours in him, if in him we do not even recognise the substance of our body.

ON THE TRINITY, Ch. 10
ML 3, 902
ANF V, 619

ST. ATHANASIUS

692
(794)

The incorporeal Word made His own the properties of the Body, as being His own Body. Why, when the Body was struck by the attendant, as suffering Himself He asked, 'Why do you smite Me?' (Jn. 18:23).
. . . For what the human Body of the Word suffered, this the Word, dwelling in the body, ascribed to Himself, in order that we might be enabled to be partakers of the Godhead of the Word. And truly it is strange that He it was Who suffered and yet suffered not. Suffered, because His own Body suffered, and He was in it, which thus suffered; suffered not, because the Word, being by Nature God, is impassible. And while He, the incorporeal, was in the passible Body, the Body had in it the impassible Word, which was destroying the infirmities inherent in the Body. But this He did, and so it was, in order that He Himself taking what was ours and offering it as a sacrifice, He might do away with it. . . . Now this did not come to pass putatively, as some have supposed: far be the thought: but the Saviour having in very truth become Man, the salvation of the whole man was brought about. For if the Word were in the Body putatively, as they say, and by putative is meant imaginary, it follows that both the salvation and the resurrection of man is apparent only, as the most impious Manichaeus held. But truly our salvation is not merely apparent, nor does it extend to the body only, but the whole man, body and soul alike, has truly obtained salvation in the Word Himself. That then which was born of Mary was according to the divine Scriptures human by nature, and the Body of the Lord was a true one; but it was this, because it was the same as our body.

LETTER TO EPICTETUS, Ch. 6
MG 26, 1060
NPNF IV, 572

ST. CYRIL OF JERUSALEM

Believe then that this Only-begotten Son of God for our sins came down from heaven upon earth, and took upon Him this human nature of like passions with us, and was begotten of the Holy Virgin and of the Holy Ghost, and was made Man, not in seeming and mere show, but in truth; nor yet by passing through the Virgin as through a channel; but was of her made truly flesh, and did truly eat as we do, and truly drink as we do. For if the Incarnation was a phantom, salvation is a phantom also. The Christ was of two natures, Man in what was seen, but God in what was not seen; as Man truly eating like us, for He had the like feeling of the flesh with us; but as God feeding the five thousand from five loaves (Mt. 14:17 ff.).

693
(817)

CATECHESES, No. 4:9
MG 33, 465
NPNF VII, 21

ST. HILARY

He is completely unacquainted with his own life, he does not know, who is ignorant of the fact that Christ Jesus is the true God as well as the true man. And it is equally dangerous to deny that Christ Jesus is God the Spirit as it is to deny that He is flesh of our body. . . . [Christ] Himself has been appointed as the mediator in His own person for the salvation of the Church, and by the mystery itself of the mediator between God and man He alone is both, while He Himself, by reason of the two natures that are united in Him, is the same person in both natures, but in such a manner that He is not wanting in anything that belongs to either, so that He does not cease to be God by His birth as man, and again, He is man while He remains God. Hence, this is the true faith of human blessedness: to acknowledge Him as God and man, to proclaim Him as the Word and as the flesh, to know of God that He is man, and to know of the flesh that it is the Word.

694
(873)

ON THE TRINITY, Bk. 9, Ch. 3
ML 10, 282
FC XXV, 324–325

Hence, the man Jesus Christ, the only-begotten God, who through the flesh and the Word is the Son of Man as well as the Son of God, has assumed a true manhood according to the likeness of our manhood without sacrificing His divinity. Although a blow struck Him, or a

695
(876)

349

wound pierced Him, or ropes bound Him, or a suspension raised Him, the things indeed wrought the vehemence of the passion, but did not bring Him the pain of the passion. . . . Our Lord Jesus Christ truly suffers when He is struck, suspended, crucified, and dies. The suffering which rushes upon the body of the Lord was a suffering, but it does not manifest the nature of suffering, while on the one hand it rages with the function of pain, and on the other hand the divinity of the body receives the force of the pain rushing against it, but without feeling pain. . . . That flesh, that bread, is from heaven, and that man is from God. He certainly possessed a body to suffer and did suffer, but He does not possess a nature that could feel pain. That body had a nature peculiar and proper to it, that was transfigured on the mountain, drives away fevers by its touch and restores eyes by its spittle.*

ON THE TRINITY, Bk. 10, Ch. 23
ML 10, 361
FC XXV, 414–415

ST. BASIL

696
(928)

If, then, the sojourn of the Lord in flesh has never taken place, the Redeemer paid not the fine to death on our behalf, nor through Himself destroyed death's reign. For if what was reigned over by death was not that which was assumed by the Lord, death would not have ceased working his own ends, nor would the sufferings of the God-bearing flesh have been made our gain; He would not have killed sin in the flesh; we who have died in Adam should not have been made alive in Christ; the fallen to pieces would not have been framed again; the shattered would not have been set up again; that which by the serpent's trick had been estranged from God would never have been made once more His own.

LETTERS, No. 261:2
MG 32, 969
NPNF VIII, 300

ST. JOHN CHRYSOSTOM

697
(1160)

For since there are some who say that all the circumstances of the Dispensation were an appearance, a piece of acting, an allegory, at once

* Christ's human nature was 'peculiar and proper' to Him because it was not conceived according to the ordinary laws of human generation, was free from human defects, and was intimately united with a divine nature. But he possessed the defects that are common to mankind, as the capability of suffering, dying, etc.

350

to remove beforehand their blasphemy, he has put 'was made'; desiring to show thereby not a change of substance (away with the thought), but the assumption of true flesh. . . for by an Union and Conjoining God the Word and the Flesh are One, not by any confusion or obliteration of substances, but by a certain union ineffable, and past understanding. . . .

HOMILIES ON ST. JOHN, No. 11:2
MG 59, 79
NPNF XIV, 39

ST. AMBROSE

[We confess] the expression that just as in His nature as God He lacked nothing of the divine nature and fulness, so in the form of man He lacked nothing that would cause Him to be judged an imperfect man, for He came to save the whole man. It was not fitting that He who completed a good work in others should allow this to be imperfect in Himself. If He lacked anything as man, then He did not redeem all, and if He did not redeem all, He deceived us, since He said that He had come to save all men. But, since it is impossible for God to deceive, He did not deceive us. Therefore, since He came to redeem all men and save them, He certainly took upon Himself the whole of man's perfection.

LETTERS, No. 48
ML 16, 1153
FC XXVI, 126–127

698
(1254)

ST. LEO THE GREAT

For although the Lord's nativity according to the flesh has certain characteristics wherein it transcends the ordinary beginnings of man's being, both because He alone was conceived and born without concupiscence of a pure Virgin, and because He was so brought forth of His mother's womb that her fecundity bare Him without loss of virginity: yet His flesh was not of another nature to ours: nor was the soul breathed into Him from another source to that of all other men, and it excelled others not in difference of kind but in superiority of power. . . . His bodily senses were active without the law of sin, and the reality of His emotions being under the control of His Godhead and His mind, was neither assaulted by temptations nor yielded to injurious influences. . . . For He would not be 'the mediator between

699
(2184)

351

God and man,' unless God and man had coexisted in both natures forming one true Person.

LETTERS, No. 35:3

ML 54, 807

NPNF XII, 49

700
(2188)

But what reconciliation can there be, whereby God might be propitiated for the human race, unless the mediator between God and man took up the cause of all? And in what way could He properly fulfill His mediation, unless He who in the form of God was equal to the Father, were a sharer of our nature also in the form of a slave: so that the one new Man might effect a renewal of the old: and the bond of death fastened on us by one man's wrong-doing might be loosened by the death of the one Man who alone owed nothing to death. For the pouring out of the blood of the righteous on behalf of the unrighteous was so powerful in its effect, so rich a ransom, that, if the whole body of us prisoners only believed in their Redeemer, not one would be held in the tyrant's bonds. . . . What hope then do they, who deny the reality of the human person in our Saviour's body, leave for themselves in the efficacy of this mystery? Let them say by what sacrifice they have been reconciled, by what blood-shedding brought back. Who is He 'who gave Himself for us an offering and a victim to God for a sweet smell' (Eph. 5:22): or what sacrifice was ever more hallowed than that which the true High Priest placed upon the altar of the cross by the immolation of His own flesh?

LETTERS, No. 124:3

ML 54, 1064

NPNF XII, 91

134. Therefore Christ has a true body formed from the substance of Mary.

ST. IGNATIUS OF ANTIOCH
See Nos. 52 and 107.

ARISTIDES
See No. 87.

ST. JUSTIN MARTYR
See No. 676.

TERTULLIAN
See Nos. 395, 53, and 201.

ST. HIPPOLYTUS
See No. 298.

ST. ATHANASIUS

'In the beginning was the Word' (Jn. 1:1), the Virgin at the consummation of the ages conceived, and the Lord has become man. And He who is indicated by both statements is one Person, for 'the Word was made flesh' (ib. 14). But the expressions used about His Godhead, and His becoming man, are to be interpreted with discrimination and suitably to the particular context. And he that writes of the human attributes of the Word knows also what concerns His Godhead: and he who expounds concerning His Godhead is not ignorant of what belongs to His coming in the flesh: but discerning each as a skilled and 'approved moneychanger,' he will walk in the straight way of piety; when therefore he speaks of His weeping, he knows that the Lord, having become man, while He exhibits His human character in weeping, as God raises up Lazarus; and He knows that He used to hunger and thirst physically, while divinely He fed five thousand persons from five loaves; and knows that while a human body lay in the tomb, it was raised as God's body by the Word Himself.

701
(759)

ON THE OPINION OF DIONYSIUS, Ch. 9
MG 25, 492
NPNF IV, 179

ST. CYRIL OF JERUSALEM
See No. 693.

ST. GREGORY NAZIANZEN

[Christ] is called Man. . . that by Himself He may sanctify humanity, and be as it were a leaven to the whole lump; and by uniting to Himself that which was condemned may release it from all condemnation, becoming for all men all things that we are, except sin; —body, soul, mind and all through which death reaches—and thus He became Man, who is the combination of all these; God in visible form, because He retained that which is perceived by mind alone. He is Son of Man, both on account of Adam, and of the Virgin from Whom He came;

702
(995)

353

from the one as a forefather, from the other as His Mother, both in accordance with the law of generation, and apart from it. He is Christ, because of His Godhead. For this is the Anointing of His Manhood, and does not, as is the case with all other Anointed Ones, sanctify by its action, but by the Presence in His Fulness of the Anointing One; the effect of which is that That which anoints is called Man, and makes that which is anointed God. He is The Way, because He leads us through Himself.

ORATIONS, No. 30:21
MG 36, 132
NPNF VII, 317

ST. AUGUSTINE

703
(1578)

Let us not heed those who say that our Lord had a body like that of the dove which John the Baptist beheld coming down from heaven, as a symbol of the Holy Spirit, and resting upon Him. . . . Now, the reason why the Holy Spirit was not born of a dove, whereas Christ was born of a woman, is this: The Holy Spirit did not come to liberate doves, but to declare unto man innocence and spiritual love, which were outwardly symbolized in the form of a dove. The Lord Jesus Christ, having come to liberate human beings, including both men and women destined for salvation, was not ashamed of the male nature, for He took it upon Himself; or of the female, for He was born of a woman. Besides, there is the profound mystery that, as death had befallen us through a woman, Life should be born to us through a woman. By this defeat, the Devil would be tormented over the thought of both sexes, male and female, because he had taken delight in the defection of them both. The freeing of both sexes would not have been so severe a penalty for the Devil, unless we were also liberated by the agency of both sexes.

THE CHRISTIAN COMBAT, Ch. 22
ML 40, 302
FC II, 338–339

704
(1644)

And on this account, that one female, not only in the Spirit, but also in the flesh, is both a mother and a virgin. And a mother indeed in the Spirit, not of our Head, Which is the Saviour Himself, of Whom rather she was born after the Spirit: forasmuch as all, who have believed in Him, among whom is herself also, are rightly called 'children of the Bridegroom' (Mt. 9:15): but clearly the mother of His members, which are we: in that she wrought together by charity, that faithful ones should be born in the Church, who are members of That Head: but in the flesh, the mother of the Head Himself.

ON HOLY VIRGINITY, Ch. 6:6
ML 40, 399
NPNF III, 418–419

ST. VINCENT OF LÉRINS

There is one and the same Christ, God and man, the same uncreated and created, the same unchangeable and incapable of suffering, the same acquainted by experience with both change and suffering, the same equal to the Father and inferior to the Father, the same begotten of the Father before time (before the world), the same born of his mother in time ('in the world'), perfect God, perfect Man. In God supreme divinity, in man, perfect humanity. Perfect humanity, I say, forasmuch as it has both soul and flesh; the flesh, truly flesh; our flesh, his mother's flesh; the soul, intellectual, endowed with mind and reason. There is then in Christ the Word, the soul, the flesh; but the whole is one Christ, one Son of God, and one our Saviour and Redeemer: One, not I know not what corruptible confusion of Godhead and manhood, but by a certain entire and singular unity of Person. For the conjunction has not converted and changed the one nature into the other (which is the characteristic error of the Arians), but rather has in such wise compacted both into one, that while there always remains in Christ the singularity of one and the self-same Person, there abides eternally the characteristic property of each nature; whence it follows, that neither does God (the divine nature) ever begin to be body, nor does the body ever cease to be body. This may be illustrated in human nature: for not only in the present life, but in the future also, each individual man will consist of soul and body; nor will his body ever be converted into soul, or his soul into body; but while each individual man will live for ever, the distinction between the two substances will continue in each individual man forever. So likewise in Christ each substance will for ever retain its own characteristic property, yet without prejudice to the unity of Person.

COMMONITORY, Ch. 13
ML 50, 656
NPNF XI, 141

705
(2170)

355

706
(2171)
This unity of Person, then, in Christ was not effected after His birth of the Virgin, but was compacted and perfected in her very womb.... From this unity of Person it follows, by reason of a like mystery, that, since the flesh of the Word was born of an undefiled mother, God the Word Himself is most catholicly believed, most impiously denied to have been born of the Virgin; which being the case, God forbid that any one should seek to defraud Holy Mary of her prerogative of divine grace and her special glory. For by the singular gift of Him who is our Lord and God, and withal, her own son, she is to be confessed most truly and most blessedly—the mother of God 'Theotókos,' but not in the sense in which it is imagined by a certain impious heresy which maintains, that she is to be called the Mother of God for no other reason than because she gave birth to that man who afterwards became God, just as we speak of a woman as the mother of a priest, or the mother of a bishop. . . but rather, as was said before, because in her sacred womb was wrought that most sacred mystery whereby, on account of the singular and unique unity of Person, as the Word in flesh is flesh, so Man in God is God.

COMMONITORY, Ch. 15
ML 50, 658
NPNF XI, 142

ST. LEO THE GREAT
See No. 686.

707
(2183)
Therefore in consequence of this unity of person which is to be understood in both natures, we read of the Son of Man also descending from heaven, when the Son of God took flesh from the Virgin who bore Him. And again the Son of God is said to have been crucified and buried, although it was not actually in His Divinity whereby the Only-begotten is co-eternal and consubstantial with the Father, but in His weak human nature that He suffered these things. And so it is that in the Creed also we all confess that the Only-begotten Son of God was crucified and buried, according to that saying of the Apostle: 'for if they had known, they would never have crucified the Lord of glory' (1 Cor. 2:8).

LETTERS, No. 28:5
ML 54, 771
NPNF XII, 41

135. *Christ also has a rational soul.*

ST. HIPPOLYTUS
See No. 432.

ORIGEN

But neither, on the other hand, was it opposed to the nature of that soul, [Christ's] as a rational existence, to receive God, into whom, as stated above, as into the Word, and the Wisdom, and the Truth, it had already wholly entered. And therefore deservedly it is also called, along with the flesh which it had assumed, the Son of God, and the Power of God, the Christ, and the Wisdom of God, either because it was wholly in the Son of God, or because it received the Son of God wholly into itself. And again, the Son of God, through whom all things were created, is named Jesus Christ and the Son of man. For the Son of God also is said to have died—in reference, viz., to that nature which could admit of death; and He is called the Son of man, who is announced as about to come in the glory of God the Father, with the holy angels. And for this reason, throughout the whole of Scripture, not only is the divine nature spoken of in human words, but the human nature is adorned by appellations of divine dignity. More truly indeed of this than of any other can the statement be affirmed, 'They shall both be in one flesh, and are no longer two, but one flesh' (Gen. 2:24; Mk. 10:8). For the Word of God is to be considered as being more in one flesh with the soul than a man with his wife.

708
(460)

ON FIRST PRINCIPLES, Bk. 2, Ch. 6
MG 11, 211
ANF IV, 282

That the nature, indeed, of His soul was the same as that of all others cannot be doubted, otherwise it could not be called a soul were it not truly one. But since the power of choosing good and evil is within the reach of all, this soul which belonged to Christ elected to love righteousness, so that in proportion to the immensity of its love it clung to it unchangeably and inseparably, so that the firmness of purpose, and immensity of affection, and an inextinguishable warmth of love, destroyed all susceptibility [sensum] for alteration and change;

709
(461)

357

and that which formerly depended upon the will was changed by the power of long custom into nature; and so we must believe that there existed in Christ a human and rational soul, without supposing that it had any feeling or possibility of sin. . . . In this way, then, that soul which, like an iron in the fire, has been perpetually placed in the Word, and perpetually in the Wisdom, and perpetually in God, is all that it does, feels, and understands, and therefore can be called neither convertible nor mutable, inasmuch as, being incessantly heated, it possessed immutability from its union with the Word of God. To all saints, finally, some warmth from the Word of God must be supposed to have passed; and in this soul the divine fire itself must be believed to have rested, from which some warmth may have passed to others.

ON FIRST PRINCIPLES, Bk. 2, Ch. 6
MG 11, 213
ANF IV, 283

ST. GREGORY NAZIANZEN
See No. 702.

ST. AUGUSTINE

710
(1818)

Let Christ raise you by that which is man, lead you by that which is God-man, and guide you through to that which is God. And the whole preaching and dispensation by Christ is this, brethren, and there is not another, that souls may be raised again, and that bodies also may be raised again. For each of the two was dead; the body by weakness, the soul by iniquity. Because each was dead, each may rise again. What each? Soul and body. By what, then, can the soul rise again but by Christ God? By what body, but by the man Christ? For there was also in Christ a human soul, a whole soul; not merely the irrational part of the soul, but also the rational, which is called mind.

ON THE GOSPEL OF ST. JOHN, Tr. 23:6
ML 35, 1585
NPNF VII, 153

711
(1953)

God therefore took upon Him our nature—that is, the rational soul and flesh of the man Christ—by an undertaking singularly marvellous, or marvellously singular; so that with no preceding merits of His own righteousness He might in such wise be the Son of God from the beginning, in which He had begun to be man, that He and the Word which is without beginning, might be one person. . . . For it was in no wise to be feared that the human nature taken up by God the Word in that ineffable manner into a unity of person, would sin by free choice of will, since that taking up itself was such that the nature of man so taken up by God would admit into itself no movement of an evil will.

ON REBUKE AND GRACE, Ch. 11
ML 44, 934
NPNF V, 484

ST. VINCENT OF LÉRINS
See No. 705.

ST. LEO THE GREAT
See Nos. 686 and 699.

136. And so Christ is consubstantial with us, being of Adam's race.

NOVATIAN
See No. 691.

ST. ATHANASIUS
See No. 692.

ST. JOHN CHRYSOSTOM

[The Evangelists] attribute to [Christ] at the Passion much that is human, to show the reality of the Dispensation. And Matthew proves this by the Agony, the trouble, the trembling, and the sweat; but John by His sorrow. For had He not been of our nature, He would not once and again have been mastered by grief.

712
(1167)

HOMILIES ON ST. JOHN, Tr. 63:2
MG 59, 350
NPNF XIV, 233

ST. AUGUSTINE

For [Christ] was not conceived in iniquity, because not conceived of mortality; nor did His mother conceive Him in sin, whom the Virgin

713
(1808)

359

brought forth; because by faith she conceived, and by faith received Him. Therefore, 'Behold the Lamb of God' (Jn. 1:29). He is not a branch derived from Adam: flesh only did he derive from Adam, Adam's sin He did not assume.

ON THE GOSPEL OF ST. JOHN, Tr. 4:10
ML 35, 1410
NPNF VII, 28

ST. JOHN OF DAMASCUS

714
(2365)
Confessing, then, the same Jesus Christ, our Lord, to be perfect God and perfect man, we hold that the same has all the attributes of the Father save that of being ingenerate, and all the attributes of the first Adam, save only his sin, these attributes being body and the intelligent and rational soul; and further that He has, corresponding to the two natures, the two sets of natural qualities belonging to the two natures: two natural volitions, one divine and one human, two natural energies, one divine and one human, two natural free-wills, one divine and one human, and two kinds of wisdom and knowledge, one divine and one human.

EXPOSITION OF THE ORTHODOX FAITH, Bk. 3, Ch. 13
MG 94, 1033
NPNF IX, 57

137. *"What is not assumed is not healed."*

ST. ATHANASIUS
See No. 692.

ST. CYRIL OF JERUSALEM
See No. 693.

ST. BASIL
See No. 696.

ST. GREGORY NAZIANZEN

If anyone has put his trust in Him as a Man without a human mind, he is really bereft of mind, and quite unworthy of salvation. For that which He has not assumed He has not healed; but that which is united to His Godhead is also saved. If only half Adam fell, then that which Christ assumes and saves may be half also; but if the whole of his nature fell, it must be united to the whole nature of Him that was begotten, and so be saved as a whole.

715
(1018)

LETTERS, No. 101
MG 37, 181
NPNF VIII, 440

ST. AMBROSE

See No. 698.

ST. AUGUSTINE

See Nos. 703 and 710.

ST. JOHN OF DAMASCUS

Moreover we proclaim the holy Virgin to be in strict truth the Mother of God. For inasmuch as He who was born of her was true God, she who bare the true God incarnate is the true Mother of God. For we hold that God was born of her, not implying that the divinity of the Word received from her the beginning of its being, but meaning that God the Word Himself, Who was begotten of the Father timelessly before the ages, and was with the Father and the Spirit without beginning and through eternity, took up His abode in these last days for the sake of our salvation in the Virgin's womb, and was without change made flesh and born of her. For the holy Virgin did not bear mere man but true God: and not mere God but God incarnate, Who did not bring down His body from Heaven, not simply passed through the Virgin as channel, but received from her flesh of like essence to our own and subsisting in Himself. For if the body had come down from heaven and had not partaken of our nature, what would have been the use of His becoming man? For the purpose of God the Word becoming man was that the very same nature, which had sinned and fallen and become corrupted, should triumph over the deceiving tyrant and so be freed from corruption.

716
(2364)

EXPOSITION OF THE ORTHODOX FAITH, Bk. 3, Ch. 12
MG 94, 1028
NPNF IX, 55–56

THE UNION OF THE DIVINE AND HUMAN NATURES

138. The incarnation is a mystery.

ST. GREGORY NAZIANZEN
See No. 297.

ST. GREGORY OF NYSSA
See No. 69.

ST. JOHN CHRYSOSTOM
See No. 697.

ST. AUGUSTINE

717
(1430)
That very greatness of His power, which feels no narrowness in narrow quarters, enriched the Virgin's womb, not by an externally caused but by an intrinsic childbirth; that power took to itself a rational soul and thereby also a human body, and chose to better all mankind without suffering any diminution itself, deigning to take the name of humanity from man, while granting him a share in the divinity. That same power brought forth the body of the infant from the inviolate virginal womb of the mother, as afterward the Body of the Man penetrated closed doors. It will not be wondered at if an explanation is asked of this: it will not be remarkable if an example is demanded. Let us grant that God can do something which we confess we cannot fathom. In such matters the whole explanation of the deed is in the power of the Doer.

LETTERS, No. 137:2
ML 33, 519
FC III, 24

718
(1431)
But there are some who request an explanation of how God is joined to man so as to become the single person of Christ, as if they themselves could explain something that happens every day, namely, how the soul is joined to the body so as to form the single person of a man. For, as the soul makes use of the body in a single person to

form a man, so God makes use of a man in a single Person to form Christ.

LETTERS, No. 137:3

ML 33, 520

FC XX, 26

See No. 711.

ST. JOHN CASSIAN

And so you say, O heretic, whoever you may be, who deny that God was born of the Virgin, that Mary the Mother of our Lord Jesus Christ ought not to be called *Theotókos,* i.e., Mother of God, but *Christotókos,* i.e., only the Mother of Christ, not of God. For no one, you say, brings forth what is anterior in time. And of this utterly foolish argument whereby you think that the birth of God can be understood by carnal minds, and fancy that the mystery of His Majesty can be accounted for by human reasoning, we will, if God permits, say something later on. In the meanwhile we will now prove by Divine testimonies that Christ is God, and that Mary is the Mother of God.

719
(2054)

SEVEN BOOKS ON THE INCARNATION OF THE LORD, AGAINST NESTORIUS, Bk. 2:2

ML 50, 31

NPNF XI, 556

ST. VINCENT OF LÉRINS
See No. 706.

ST. LEO THE GREAT
See No. 686.

ST. JOHN OF DAMASCUS
See No. 357.

The body which is born of the holy Virgin is in truth body united with divinity, not that the body which was received up into the heavens descends, but that the bread itself and the wine are changed into God's body and blood. But if you enquire how this happens, it is enough for you to learn that it was through the Holy Spirit, just as the Lord took on Himself flesh that subsisted in Him and was born of the holy Mother of God through the Spirit. And we know nothing further save that the Word of God is true and energises and is omnipotent, but the manner of this cannot be searched out. But one

720
(2371)

can put it well thus, that just as in nature the bread by the eating and the wine and the water by the drinking are changed into the body and blood of the eater and drinker, and do not become a different body from the former one, so the bread of the table and the wine and water are supernaturally changed by the invocation and presence of the Holy Spirit into the body and blood of Christ, and are not two but one and the same. . . .

The bread and the wine are not merely figures of the body and blood of Christ (heaven forbid!) but the deified body of the Lord itself: for the Lord has said, 'This is My body, not, this is a figure of My body; and 'My blood,' not, a figure of My blood (Mt. 26:26, 28). . . .

But if some persons called the bread and the wine antetypes of the body and blood of the Lord, as did the divinely inspired Basil, they said so not after the consecration but before the consecration, so calling the offering itself. . . .

Further antetypes of future things are spoken of, not as though they were not in reality Christ's body and blood, but that now through them we partake of Christ's divinity, while then we shall partake mentally through the vision alone.

EXPOSITION OF THE ORTHODOX FAITH, Bk. 4, Ch. 13
ML 44, 1194
NPNF IX, 83

139. *The Word assumed a human nature so that there are two natures truly distinct.*

ST. IGNATIUS OF ANTIOCH
See No. 707.

ORIGEN

721
(453)
In the first place, we must note that the nature of that deity which is in Christ in respect of His being the only begotten Son of God is one thing, and that human nature which He assumed in these last times for the purposes of the dispensation [of grace] is another.

ON FIRST PRINCIPLES, Bk. 1, Ch. 2
MG 11, 130
ANF IV, 245

NOVATIAN

But lest, from the fact of asserting that our Lord Jesus Christ, the Son of God, the Creator, was manifested in the substance of the true body, we should seem either to have given assent to other heretics, who in this place maintain that He is man only and alone, and therefore desire to prove that He was a man bare and solitary; and lest we should seem to have afforded them any ground for objecting, we do not so express doctrine concerning the substance of His body, as to say that He is only and alone man, but so as to maintain by the association of the divinity of the Word in that very materiality, that He was also God according to the Scriptures.

722
(605)

ON THE TRINITY, Ch. 11
ML 3, 903
ANF V, 620

ST. JOHN CHRYSOSTOM
See No. 697.

ST. AMBROSE

As being man, therefore, [Christ] doubts; as man He is amazed. Neither His power nor His Godhead is amazed; but His Soul; He is amazed by consequence of having taken human infirmity upon Him. Seeing, then, that He took upon Himself a soul He also took the affections of a soul, for God could not have been distressed or have died in respect of His being God.

723
(1267)

TO GRATIAN, ON THE CHRISTIAN FAITH, Bk. 2, Ch. 7
ML 16, 571
NPNF X, 230

ST. JOHN CASSIAN

But in all the holy Scriptures He joins together and as it were incorporates in the Godhead, the Lord's manhood, so that no one can sever man from God in time, nor God from man at His Passion. For if you regard Him in time, you will find that the Son of man is ever with the Son of God. If you take note of His Passion, you will find that the Son of God is ever with the Son of man, and that Christ the Son of man and the Son of God is so one and indivisible, that, in the language of holy Scripture, the man cannot be severed in time from God, nor God from man at His Passion. . . . There was not then before the

724
(2057)

birth of a Virgin the same eternity belonging in the past to the manhood as to the Divinity, but because Divinity was united to manhood in the womb of the Virgin, it follows that when we use the name of Christ one cannot be spoken of without the other.

SEVEN BOOKS ON THE INCARNATION OF THE LORD,
AGAINST NESTORIUS, Bk. 6:22
ML 50, 185
NPNF XI, 602

ST. LEO THE GREAT

725
(2208)
The last discourse, dearly-beloved, of which we desire now to give the promised portion, had reached that point in the argument where we were speaking of that cry which the crucified Lord uttered to the Father: we bade the simple and unthinking hearer not to take the words 'My God, &c.' (Ps. 21:1), in a sense as if, when Jesus was fixed upon the wood of the cross, the Omnipotence of the Father's Deity had gone away from Him; seeing that God's and Man's Nature were so completely joined in Him that the union could not be destroyed by punishment nor by death. For while each substance retained its own properties, God neither held aloof from the suffering of His body nor was made passible by the flesh, because the Godhead which was in the Sufferer did not actually suffer.

SERMONS, No. 68:1
ML 54, 372
NPNF XII, 180

ST. JOHN OF DAMASCUS
See No. 714.

140. *The two natures are somehow united.*

ST. IRENAEUS

726
(221)
For if He did not truly suffer, no thanks to Him, since there was no suffering at all; and when we shall actually begin to suffer, He will seem as leading us astray, exhorting us to endure buffeting, and to turn the other cheek, if He did not Himself before us in reality suffer the same; and as He misled them by seeming to them what He was not, so does He also mislead us, by exhorting us to endure what He did not endure Himself.

Therefore, He caused man [human nature] to cleave to and to become one with God. For unless man had overcome the enemy of man, the enemy would not have been legitimately vanquished.

AGAINST HERESIES, Bk. 3, Ch. 18:6, 7

MG 7, 936

ANF I, 447

TERTULLIAN
See No. 395.

ORIGEN
See No. 708.

NOVATIAN

The Son of God descended, and that He, in taking up into Himself the Son of man, consequently made Him the Son of God, because the Son of God associated and joined Him to Himself. So that, while the Son of man cleaves in His nativity to the Son of God, by that very mingling He holds that as pledged and derived which of His own nature He could not possess. And thus by the word of the angel the distinction is made, against the desire of heretics, between the Son of God and man; yet with their association, by pressing them to understand that Christ the Son of man is man, and also to receive the Son of God and man the Son of God; that is, the Word of God as it is written as God; and thus to acknowledge that Christ Jesus the Lord, connected on both sides, so to speak, is on both sides woven in and grown together, and associated in the same agreement of both substances, by the binding to one another of a mutual alliance—man and God by the truth of the Scripture which declares this very thing.

ON THE TRINITY, Ch. 24

ML 3, 934

ANF V, 635

727
(606)

ST. ATHANASIUS
See No. 701.

For although 'the Word became flesh,' yet to the flesh are the affections proper; and though the flesh is possessed by God in the Word, yet to the Word belong the grace and the power. He did then the

728
(773)

Father's works through the flesh; and as truly contrariwise were the affections of the flesh displayed in Him; for instance, He inquired and He raised Lazarus, He chid His Mother, saying, 'My hour is not yet come' (Jn. 2:4), and then at once He made the water wine. For He was True God in the flesh, and He was true flesh in the Word. Therefore from His works He revealed both Himself as Son of God, and His own Father, and from the affections of the flesh He showed that He bore a true body, and that it was His own.

FOUR DISCOURSES AGAINST THE ARIANS, 3:41

MG 26, 409

NPNF IV, 416

ST. CYRIL OF JERUSALEM

729
(827)

For neither is it holy to worship the mere man, nor religious to say that He is God only without the Manhood. For if Christ is not God, as indeed He is, but took not human nature upon Him we are strangers to salvation. Let us then worship Him as God, but believe that He also was made Man. For neither is there any profit in calling Him man without Godhead, nor any salvation in refusing to confess the Manhood together with the Godhead. Let us confess the presence of Him who is both King and Physician. For Jesus the King when about to become our Physician, girded Himself with the linen of humanity, and healed that which was sick.

CATECHESES, 12:1

MG 33, 728

NPNF VII, 72

ST. HILARY

730
(874)

But, He who emptied Himself is not another person or a distinct person from Him who receives the form of a slave. To be able to receive does not belong to Him who does not exist, since to receive is characteristic of Him who subsists. Hence, the emptying of the form is not the destruction of the nature, because He who empties Himself is not wanting in His own nature and He who receives remains. And since it is He Himself who empties and receives, we find indeed a mystery in Him, because He empties Himself and receives Himself, but no destruction takes place so that He ceases to exist when He empties Himself or does not exist when He receives. Hence, the emptying brings it about that the form of a slave appears, but not that the Christ who was in the form of God does not continue to be Christ, since it is only Christ who has received the form of a slave. Since He who emptied Himself that the abiding Spirit Christ might be the same Man Christ, the change of the outer appearance in the body and the assumption of a nature did not remove the nature of the Godhead that remains, because it is one and the same Christ who changes and assumes the outward appearance.

ON THE TRINITY, Bk. 9, Ch. 14
ML 10, 293
FC XXV, 334–335

ST. GREGORY NAZIANZEN

What [Christ] was He laid aside; what He was not He assumed; not that He became two, but He deigned to be One made out of the two. For both are God, that which assumed, and that which was assumed; two Natures meeting in One, not two Sons (let us not give a false account of the blending).

731
(1001)

ORATIONS, No. 37:2
MG 36, 284
NPNF VII, 338

ST. AMBROSE
See No. 413.

ST. JOHN OF DAMASCUS

For we hold that the energies are not divided and that the natures do not energise separately, but that each conjointly in complete community with the other energises with its own proper energy. For the human part did not energise merely in a human manner, for He was not mere man; nor did the divine part energise only after the manner of God, for He was not simply God, but He was at once God and man. For just as in the case of natures we recognise both their union and their natural difference, so is it also with the natural wills and energies. Note, therefore that in the case of our Lord Jesus Christ, we speak sometimes of His two natures and sometimes of His one person: and the one or the other is referred to one conception. For the two natures are one Christ, and the one Christ is two natures. . . . This, then, the theandric energy makes plain that when God became man, that is when He became incarnate, both His human energy was divine,

732
(2366)

that is deified, and not without part in His divine energy, and His divine energy was not without part in His human energy, but either was observed in conjunction with the other.

EXPOSITION OF THE ORTHODOX FAITH, Bk. 3, Ch. 19
MG 94, 1080
NPNF IX, 68

141. The two natures of Christ are united by a personal union.

ST. HIPPOLYTUS
See No. 386.

ST. HILARY
See No. 694.

ST. GREGORY NAZIANZEN
See No. 354.

ST. AUGUSTINE

733
(1431)
But there are some who request an explanation of how God is joined to man so as to become the single person of Christ, as if they themselves could explain something that happens every day, namely, how the soul is joined to the body so as to form the single person of a man. For, as the soul makes use of the body in a single person to form a man, so God makes use of a man in a single Person to form Christ.

LETTERS, No. 137:3:11
ML 33, 520
See No. 685.
FC XX, 26

734
(1680)
Therefore also the Lord Jesus Christ Himself not only gave the Holy Spirit as God, but also received it as man, and therefore He is said to be full of grace, and of the Holy Spirit. And in the Acts of the Apostles it is more plainly written of Him, 'Because God anointed Him with the Holy Spirit' (Acts 10:38). Certainly not with visible oil but with the gift of grace which is signified by the visible oil ointment wherewith the Church anoints the baptized. And Christ was certainly not then anointed with the Holy Spirit, when He, as a dove, descended upon Him at His baptism (Mt. 3:16). For at that time He

deigned to prefigure His body, that is, His Church, in which especially the baptized receive the Holy Spirit. But He is to be understood to have been then anointed with that mystical and invisible unction, when the Word of God was made flesh (Jn. 1:14), that is, when human nature, without any precedent merits of good works, was joined to God the Word in the womb of the Virgin, so that with it it became one person.

ON THE TRINITY, Bk. 15, Ch. 26
ML 42, 1093
NPNF III, 224

'That they also may be sanctified in the truth' (Jn. 17:19). And what else is this but in me, in accordance with the fact that the truth is that Word in the beginning which is God? In whom also the Son of man was Himself sanctified from the beginning of His creation, when the Word was made flesh, for the Word and the man became one person. Then accordingly He sanctified Himself in Himself, that is, Himself the man in Himself the Word; for the Word and the man is one Christ, who sanctifies the manhood in the Word.

735
(1842)

ON THE GOSPEL OF ST. JOHN, Tr. 108:5
ML 35, 1916
NPNF VII, 405

Begotten and conceived, then, without any indulgence of carnal lust, and therefore bringing with Him no original sin, and by the grace of God joined and united in a wonderful and unspeakable way in one person with the Word, the Only-begotten of the Father, a son by nature, not by grace, and therefore having no sin of His own; nevertheless, on account of the likeness of sinful flesh in which He came, He was called sin, that He might be sacrificed to wash away sin. . . . [The apostle] says, 'Him who knew no sin,' that is, Christ, God to whom we are to be reconciled, 'has made to be sin for us' (2 Cor. 5:24), that is, has made Him a sacrifice for our sins, by which we might be reconciled to God. He, then, being made sin, just as we are made righteousness (our righteousness being not our own, but God's, not in ourselves, but in Him); He being made sin, not His own, but ours, not in Himself, but in us.

736
(1916)

ON FAITH, HOPE, AND LOVE (ENCHIRIDION), Ch. 41
ML 40, 252
NPNF III, 251

ST. JOHN CASSIAN

737
(2056)

'Making peace through the blood of His cross, both as to the things on earth and the things that are in heaven' (Col. 1:20). Surely he has made it as clear as possible of whom he was speaking, when he called Him the first-born from the dead. For are all things reconciled and brought into peace through the blood of the Word or Spirit? For no sort of passion can happen to nature that is impassible, nor can the blood of any but a man be shed, nor any but a man die: and yet the same Person who is spoken of in the following verses as dead, was above called the image of the invisible God. How then can this be? Because the apostles took every possible precaution that it might not be thought that there was any division in Christ, or that the Son of God being joined to a Son of man, might come by wild interpretations to be made into two Persons, and thus He who is in Himself but one might by wrongful and wicked notions of ours, be made into a double Person in one nature.

SEVEN BOOKS ON THE INCARNATION OF THE LORD,
AGAINST NESTORIUS, Bk. 5, Ch. 7
ML 50, 114
NPNF XI, 585

ST. VINCENT OF LÉRINS
See Nos. 705 and 706.

ST. LEO THE GREAT

738
(2183)

Therefore in consequence of this unity of person which is to be understood in both natures, we read of the Son of Man also descending from heaven, when the Son of God took flesh from the Virgin who bore Him. And again the Son of God is said to have been crucified and buried, although it was not actually in His Divinity whereby the Only-begotten is co-eternal and consubstantial with the Father, but in His weak human nature that He suffered these things. And so it is that in the Creed also we all confess that the Only-begotten Son of God was crucified and buried, according to that saying of the Apostle: 'for if they had known, they would never have crucified the Lord of glory' (1 Cor. 2:8).

LETTERS, No. 28:5
ML 54, 771
NPNF XII, 41

ST. JOHN OF DAMASCUS
See No. 357.

But those who hold that He progressed in wisdom and grace in the   739
sense of receiving some addition to these attributes, do not say that   (2368)
the union took place at the first origin of the flesh, nor yet do they
give precedence to the union in subsistence, but giving heed to the
foolish Nestorius they imagine some strange relative union and mere
indwelling, understanding neither what they say nor whereof they
affirm (1 Tim. 1:7). For if in truth the flesh was united with God the
Word from its first origin, or rather if it existed in Him and was
identical in subsistence with Him, how was it that it was not endowed
completely with all wisdom and grace? not that it might itself participate in the grace, nor share by grace in what belonged to the Word, but
rather by reason of the union in subsistence, since both what is human
and what is divine belong to the one Christ, and that He Who was
Himself at once God and man should pour forth like a fountain over
the universe His grace and wisdom and plenitude of every blessing.

EXPOSITION OF THE ORTHODOX FAITH, Bk. 3, Ch. 22
MG 94, 1088
NPNF IX, 69

*142. There are two operations in Christ: one divine, the other
human.*

TERTULLIAN
See No. 395.

ORIGEN

If, then, we consider Jesus in relation to the divinity that was in Him,   740
the things which He did in this capacity present nothing to offend our   (533)
ideas of God, nothing but what is holy; and if we consider Him as
man, distinguished beyond all other men by an intimate communion
with the Eternal Word, with absolute Wisdom, He suffered as one who
was wise and perfect, whatever it behoved Him to suffer who did all
for the good of the human race, yes, even for the good of all intelligent
beings. And there is nothing absurd in a man having died, and in His
death being not only an example of death endured for the sake of
piety, but also the first blow in the conflict which is to overthrow the

power of that evil spirit the devil, who had obtained dominion over the whole world.

AGAINST CELSUS, Bk. 7, Ch. 17

MG 11, 1445

ANF IV, 617

ST. ATHANASIUS

741
(771)

[Christ] being God, He had His own body, and using this as an instrument, He became man for our sakes. And on account of this, the properties of the flesh are said to be His, since He was in it, such as to hunger, to thirst, to suffer, to grow tired, and the like, of which the flesh is capable; while on the other hand the works proper to the Word Himself, such as to raise the dead, to restore sight to the blind, and to cure the woman with an issue of blood, He did through His own body. And the Word bore the infirmities of the flesh, as His own, for His was the flesh; and the flesh ministered to the works of the Godhead, because the Godhead was in it, for the body was God's.

FOUR DISCOURSES AGAINST THE ARIANS, Bk. 3, Ch. 31

MG 26, 389

NPNF IV, 410

See Nos. 728 and 692.

ST. CYRIL OF JERUSALEM
See No. 693.

ST. AMBROSE
See No. 723.

ST. JOHN OF DAMASCUS

742
(2361)

Moreover, the Word appropriates to Himself the attributes of humanity: for all that pertains to His holy flesh is His; and He imparts to the flesh His own attributes by way of communication in virtue of the interpenetration of the parts one with another, and the oneness according to subsistence, and inasmuch as He Who lived and acted both as God and as man, taking to Himself either form and holding intercourse with the other form, was one and the same. Hence it is that the Lord of Glory is said to have been crucified, although His divine nature never endured the Cross, and that the Son of Man is allowed to have been in heaven before the Passion, as the Lord Himself said. For the Lord of Glory is one and the same with Him Who is in nature and in truth the Son of Man, that is, Who became man, and both His wonders and His sufferings are known to us, although His wonders were worked in His divine capacity, and His sufferings endured as man.

EXPOSITION OF THE ORTHODOX FAITH, Bk. 3, Ch. 3

MG 94, 993

See Nos. 357, 714, and 732.   *NPNF* IX, 48

143. In Christ there is a true communication of idioms.

ORIGEN

See No. 708.

ST. ATHANASIUS

We do not worship a creature. Far be the thought! For such an error   743
belongs to heathens and Arians. But we worship the Lord of Creation,   (795)
Incarnate, the Word of God. For if the flesh also is in itself a part of
the created world, yet it has become God's body. And we neither
divide the body, being such, from the Word, and worship it by itself,
nor when we wish to worship the Word do we set Him far apart
from the Flesh, but knowing, as we said above, that 'the Word was
made flesh' (Jn. 1:14) we recognise Him as God also, after having
come in the flesh. Who, accordingly, is so senseless as to say to the
Lord: 'Leave the Body that I may worship Thee'?

LETTER TO ADELPHIUS, Ch. 3

MG 26, 1073

NPNF IV, 575

ST. CYRIL OF JERUSALEM

[Christ] gave not up His life by compulsion, nor was He put to   744
death by murderous violence, but of His own accord. Hear what He   (830)
says: 'I have power to lay down My life, and I have power to take it
again' (Jn. 10:18): I yield it of My own choice to My enemies; for
unless I chose, this could not be. He came therefore of His own set
purpose to His passion, rejoicing in His noble deed, smiling at the
crown, cheered by the salvation of mankind; not ashamed of the Cross,
for it was to save the world. For it was no common man who suffered,
but God in man's nature, striving for the prize of His patience.

CATECHESES, 13:6

MG 33, 780

NPNF VII, 83–84

745
(831)

These things the Saviour endured, and made peace through the Blood of His Cross, for things in heaven, and things in earth (Col. 1:20). For we were enemies of God through sin, and God had appointed the sinner to die. There must needs therefore have happened one of two things: either that God in His truth should destroy all men, or that in His loving-kindness He should cancel the sentence. But behold the wisdom of God; He preserved both the truth of His sentence, and the exercise of His loving-kindness. Christ took our sins in His body on the tree, that we by His death might die to sin, and live unto righteousness. Of no small account was He who died for us; He was not a literal sheep; He was not a mere man; He was more than an Angel; He was God made man. The transgression of sinners was not so great as the righteousness which He wrought also who laid down His life for us, —who laid it down when He pleased, and took it again when He pleased. And would you know that He laid not down His life by violence, nor yielded up the ghost against His will? He cried to the Father, saying, Father into your hands I commend My spirit (Lk. 23:46).

CATECHESES, No. 13:33
MG 33, 812
NPNF VII, 91

ST. HILARY
See No. 730.

ST. AMBROSE
See No. 723.

ST. JOHN CASSIAN
See No. 737.

ST. VINCENT OF LÉRINS
See No. 705.

ST. LEO THE GREAT
See No. 738.

ST. JOHN OF DAMASCUS
See No. 742.

THE RESULTS OF THIS UNION

*144. The man Christ is the natural Son of God, not the adopted
Son.*

ST. HILARY

Many of us are the sons of God, but not such as this Son. He is the
true and the proper Son, by origin, not by adoption; in truth, not in
name; by birth, not by creation.

746
(863)

ON THE TRINITY, Bk. 3, Ch. 11
ML 10, 82
FC XXV, 73

ST. AUGUSTINE
See No. 619.

It was fitting, then, that He should baptize who is God's only Son, not
His adopted Son. Adopted sons are the ministers of the only Son: the
only Son has power; the adopted, the ministry.

747
(1811)

ON THE GOSPEL OF ST. JOHN, Tr. 7:4
ML 35, 1439
NPNF VII, 49

Accordingly, when He says also of the Father, 'I abide in His love'
(Jn. 15:10), we are to understand it of that love which was borne
Him by the Father. But then, in this case also, is that love which the
Father bears to the Son referable to the same grace as that wherewith
we are loved of the Son: seeing that we on our part are sons, not by
nature, but by grace; while the Only-begotten is so by nature and not
by grace? Or is this even in the Son Himself to be referred to His
condition as man? Certainly so. For in saying, 'As the Father hath
loved me, so have I loved you,' He pointed to the grace that was His as
Mediator. For Christ Jesus is the Mediator between God and men, not
in respect to His Godhead, but in respect to His manhood (1 Tim.
2:5). And certainly it is in reference to this His human nature that
we read, 'And Jesus increased in wisdom and age, and in favor
[grace] with God and men' (Lk. 2:52).

748
(1836)

ON THE GOSPEL OF ST. JOHN, Tr. 82:4
ML 35, 1844
See No. 736. *NPNF* VII, 347

ST. CYRIL OF ALEXANDRIA
See No. 58.

145. Christ, completely filled with grace, had complete sanctity.

APHRAATES

749
(682)
Christ received the Spirit not by measure, but His Father loved Him and delivered all into His hands, and gave Him authority over all His treasure. For John said: Not by measure did the Father give the Spirit to His Son, but loved Him and gave all into His hands (Jn. 3:34 ff.).

DEMONSTRATIONS, 6:12
PS 1, 287
NPNF VIII, 371

ST. GREGORY NAZIANZEN
See No. 702.

ST. AUGUSTINE
See Nos. 734, 748, and 735.

ST. JOHN OF DAMASCUS
See No. 739.

146. Christ is to be adored as man.

ST. ATHANASIUS

750
(762)
For the Word was not impaired in receiving a body, that He should seek to receive a grace, but rather He deified that which He put on, and more than that, 'gave' it graciously to the race of man. For as He was ever worshipped as being the Word and existing in the form of God, so being what He ever was, though become man and called Jesus, He none the less has the whole creation under foot, and bending their knees to Him in this Name, and confessing that the Word's becoming flesh, and undergoing death in flesh, has not happened against the glory of His Godhead, but 'to the glory of God the Father.' For it is the Father's glory that man, made and then lost, should be found again; and when dead, that he should be made alive, and should become God's temple. For whereas the powers in heaven, both Angels

and Archangels, were ever worshipping the Lord, as they are now worshipping Him in the Name of Jesus, this is our grace and high exaltation, that even when He became man, the Son of God is worshipped, and the heavenly powers will not be astonished at seeing all of us, who are of one body with Him, introduced into their realms.

> FOUR DISCOURSES AGAINST THE ARIANS, 1:42
> *MG* 26, 100

See No. 743.   *NPNF* IV, 330–331

ST. CYRIL OF JERUSALEM
See No. 729.

ST. AMBROSE
See No. 413.

ST. JOHN OF DAMASCUS

Christ, therefore, is one, perfect God and perfect man: and Him we worship along with the Father and the Spirit, with one obeisance, adoring even His immaculate flesh and not holding that the flesh is not suited for worship: for in fact it is worshipped in the one subsistence of the Word, which indeed became subsistence for it. But in this we do not do homage to that which is created. For we worship Him, not as mere flesh, but as flesh united with divinity, and because His two natures are brought under the one person and one subsistence of God the Word. I fear to touch coal because of the fire bound up with the wood. I worship the twofold nature of Christ because of the divinity that is in Him bound up with the flesh.

751
(2363)

> EXPOSITION OF THE ORTHODOX FAITH, Bk. 3, Ch. 8
> *MG* 94, 1013
> *NPNF* IX, 52

147. *Christ was free from personal sin.*

TERTULLIAN
See No. 681.

ST. HIPPOLYTUS
See No. 432.

ORIGEN
See No. 578.

ST. GREGORY NAZIANZEN
See No. 702.

ST. JOHN CHRYSOSTOM

752
(1198)
How did [Christ] die at all for sinners, if He Himself were in sin? For he who dies for sinners ought himself to be without sin. Since if he himself also sin, how shall he die for other sinners? But if for others' sins He died, He died being without sin.

> HOMILIES ON FIRST CORINTHIANS, 38:3
> *MG* 61, 324
> *NPNF* XII, 228

ST. AUGUSTINE
See No. 736.

ST. LEO THE GREAT

753
(2213)
For if man, made after the image and likeness of God, had retained the dignity of his own nature, and had not been deceived by the devil's wiles into transgressing through lust the law laid down for him, the Creator of the world would not have become a Creature, the Eternal would not have entered the sphere of time, nor God the Son, Who is equal with God the Father, have assumed the form of a slave and the likeness of sinful flesh. But because 'by the devil's malice death entered into the world' (Wis. 2:24), and captive humanity could not otherwise be set free without His undertaking our cause, Who without loss of His majesty should both become true Man, and alone have no taint of sin, the mercy of the Trinity divided for Itself the work of our restoration in such a way that the Father should be propitiated, the Son should propitiate, and the Holy Ghost enkindle.

> LETTERS, No. 77:2
> *ML* 54, 412
> *NPNF* XII, 102

ST. JOHN OF DAMASCUS
See No. 714.

754
(2367)
We confess, then, that He assumed all the natural and innocent passions of man. For He assumed the whole man and all man's attributes

380

save sin. For that is not natural, nor is it implanted in us by the Creator, but arises voluntarily in our mode of life as the result of a further implantation by the devil, though it cannot prevail over us by force. For the natural and innocent passions are those which are not in our power, but which have entered into the life of man owing to the condemnation by reason of the transgression; such as hunger, thirst, weariness, labour, the tears, the corruption, the shrinking from death, the fear, the agony with the bloody sweat, the help at the hands of angels because of the weakness of the nature, and other such like passions which belong by nature to every man. All, then, He assumed that He might sanctify all.

EXPOSITION OF THE ORTHODOX FAITH, Bk. 3, Ch. 20

MG 94, 1081

NPNF IX, 68

148. *Christ had a body capable of suffering.*

ST. IGNATIUS OF ANTIOCH

Look for Him who is beyond all time, the Eternal, the Invisible who became visible for our sake, the Impalpable, the Impassible who suffered for our sake, who endured every outrage for our sake.

755

(66)

LETTER TO POLYCARP, Ch. 3:2

MG 5, 721

FC I, 125

ST. JUSTIN MARTYR

For the prophets have proclaimed two advents of His: the one, that which is already past, when He came as a dishonoured and suffering Man; but the second, when, according to prophecy, He shall come from heaven with glory, accompanied by His angelic host, when also He shall raise the bodies of all men who have lived, and shall clothe those of the worthy with immortality, and shall send those of the wicked, endued with eternal sensibility, into everlasting fire with the wicked devils.

756

(124)

APOLOGY I, Ch. 52

MG 6, 404

ANF I, 180

ST. IRENAEUS
See No. 726.

TERTULLIAN

See No. 680.

ST. CLEMENT OF ALEXANDRIA

See No. 690.

ORIGEN

See Nos. 212, 55, and 740.

ST. ATHANASIUS

757
(772)

And that one may attain to a more exact knowledge of the impassibility of the Word's nature and of the infirmities ascribed to Him because of the flesh, it will be well to listen to the blessed Peter; for he will be a trustworthy witness concerning the Saviour. He writes then in his Epistle thus: 'Christ then having suffered for us in the flesh' (1 Pet. 4:1). Therefore also when He is said to hunger and thirst and to toil and not to know, and to sleep, and to weep, and to ask, and to flee and to be born, and to deprecate the cup, and in a word to undergo all that belongs to the flesh, let it be said, as is congruous, in each case, Christ then hungering and thirsting 'for us in the flesh'; and saying He did not know and being buffeted, and toiling 'for us in the flesh'; and being exalted too, and born, and growing 'in the flesh'; and fearing and hiding 'in the flesh'; and saying, 'If it be possible let this cup pass from Me' (Mt. 26:39), and being beaten, and receiving, 'For us in the flesh'; and in a word all such things for us in the flesh. For on this account has the Apostle himself said, Christ then having suffered, not in His Godhead, but for us in the flesh, that these affections may be acknowledged as, not proper to the very Word by nature, but proper by nature to the very flesh.

FOUR DISCOURSES AGAINST THE ARIANS, 3:34
MG 26, 396

See Nos. 728 and 692.   *NPNF* IV, 412

ST. CYRIL OF JERUSALEM

758
(828)

So then after trial shown of our weakness, the Lord assumed that which man required: for since man required to hear from one of like countenance, the Saviour took on Him the nature of like affections, that men might be the more easily instructed. . . . The Lord took on Him from us our likeness, that He might save man's nature: He took

our likeness, that He might give greater grace to that which lacked; that sinful humanity might become partaker of God.

CATECHESES, No. 12:14

MG 33, 741

NPNF VII, 75

ST. HILARY
See No. 695.

ST. GREGORY NAZIANZEN
See No. 297.

149. Christ freely suffered and died.

ST. CYRIL OF JERUSALEM
See Nos. 744 and 745.

ST. AMBROSE

By the death of One the world was redeemed. For Christ, had He willed, need not have died, but He neither thought that death should be shunned as though there were any cowardice in it, nor could He have saved us better than by dying. And so His death is the life of all.

759
(1275)

ON THE DEATH OF HIS BROTHER SATYRUS, Bk. 2, Ch. 46

ML 16, 1327

NPNF X, 180

ST. AUGUSTINE

Hence [Christ] was pointed out to holy men of old; to the intent that they, through faith in His Passion to come, even as we through faith in that which is past, might be saved. For as man He was Mediator; but as the Word He was not between, because equal to God, and God with God, and together with the Holy Spirit one God. How have you loved us, O good Father, who spared not Your only Son, but delivered Him up for us wicked ones! (Rom. 8:32). How have You loved us, for whom He, who thought it no robbery to be equal with You, 'became obedient unto death, even the death of the cross' (Phil. 2:6,8); He alone 'free among the dead,' that had power to lay down His life, and power to take it again; for us was He unto You both Victor and Victim, and the Victor as being the Victim; for us was He unto You both

760
(1595)

383

Priest and Sacrifice, and Priest as being the Sacrifice; of slaves making us Your sons, by being born of You, and serving us.

CONFESSIONS, Bk. 10, Ch. 43
ML 32, 808
NPNF I, 162

761
(1654)

The spirit of the Mediator showed how it was through no punishment of sin that He came to the death of the flesh, because He did not leave it against His will, but because He willed, when He willed, as He willed.

ON THE TRINITY, Bk. 4, Ch. 13
ML 42, 898
NPNF III, 77

150. On the question of ignorance in Christ.

ST. IRENAEUS
See No. 358.

ST. ATHANASIUS

762
(774)

Certainly when He says in the Gospel concerning Himself in His human character, 'Father, the hour is come, glorify Thy Son' (Jn. 17:1), it is plain that He knows also the hour of the end of all things, as the Word, though as man He is ignorant of it, for ignorance is proper to man, and especially ignorance of these things. Moreover this is proper to the Saviour's love of man; for since He was made man, He is not ashamed, because of the flesh which is ignorant, to say 'I know not,' that He may show that knowing as God, He is but ignorant according to the flesh. And therefore He said not, 'no, not the Son of God knows,' lest the Godhead should seem ignorant, but simply, 'no, not the Son' (Mk. 13:32), that the ignorance might be the Son's as born from among men.

FOUR DISCOURSES AGAINST THE ARIANS, 3:43
MG 26, 413
NPNF IV, 417

ST. GREGORY NAZIANZEN

763
(992)

Their tenth objection is the ignorance, and the statement that, Of the last day and hour knows no man, not even the Son (Mk. 13:32) Himself, but the Father. And yet how can Wisdom be ignorant of anything?

. . . How then can you say that all things before that hour He knows accurately, and all things that are to happen about the time of the end, but of the hour itself He is ignorant? For such a thing would be like a riddle; as if one were to say that he knew accurately all that was in front of the wall, but did not know the wall itself; or that, knowing the end of the day, he did not know the beginning of the night—where knowledge of the one necessarily brings in the other. Thus everyone must see that He knows as God, and knows not as Man; —if one may separate the visible from that which is discerned by thought alone.

ON THE HOLY SPIRIT, Ch. 30:15
MG 36, 124
NPNF X, 463

ST. JOHN CHRYSOSTOM

But of that day and hour knows no man, no, not the angels of Heaven, neither the Son, but the Father" (Mt. 24:36). By saying, not the angels, He stopped their mouths, that they should not seek to learn what these angels know not; and by saying, "neither the Son," forbids them not only to learn, but even to inquire. . . . Therefore He refers it to His Father, both to make the thing awful, and to exclude that of which He had spoken from their inquiry. Since if it be not this, but He is ignorant of it, when will He know it? Will it be together with us? But who would say this? And the Father He knows clearly, even as clearly as He knows the Son; and of the day is He ignorant? . . . For this intent He tells them not, in order that they may watch, that they may be always ready; therefore He says, When you look not for it, then He will come, desiring that they should be anxiously waiting, and continually in virtuous action. But His meaning is like this: if the common sort of men knew when they were to die, they would surely strive earnestly at that hour.

764
(1178)

HOMILIES ON ST. MATTHEW, 77:1
MG 58, 702
NPNF X, 463

ST. JEROME

No man save Him who for our salvation has deigned to put on flesh has full knowledge and a complete grasp of the truth.

765
(1348)

LETTER TO POPE DAMASUS IN REPLY TO GEN. 27:23
ML 22, 459
NPNF VI, 47

ST. GREGORY THE GREAT

766
(2296)

But as to what your Sweetness has added in your letters, namely that you will continue to be urgent with me till I write that it has been revealed to me that your sins are forgiven, you have demanded a difficult, nay even an unprofitable thing; difficult indeed, because I am unworthy of having a revelation made to me; but unprofitable because you ought not to become secure about your sins, except when in the last day of your life you shall be able no longer to bewail them.

LETTER TO GREGORIA, Bk. 7:25
ML 77, 878
NPNF XII, 219

ST. JOHN OF DAMASCUS
See No. 739.

THE WORK OF CHRIST
THE PURPOSE OF THE INCARNATION

151. The purpose of the incarnation and passion of Christ is the salvation of men.

ST. CLEMENT OF ROME
See No. 613.

ST. IGNATIUS OF ANTIOCH
See Nos. 320 and 755.

ST. POLYCARP
See No. 210.

767
(75)

Without interruption, therefore, let us persevere by our hope and by the guarantee of our righteousness, which is Jesus Christ, who bore our sins in His own body on the tree (1 Pet. 2:24), who did no sin, nor was deceit found in His mouth (1 Pet. 2:22); but for our sake, that we might live in Him, He endured all things.

LETTER TO THE PHILIPPIANS, Ch. 8:1
MG 5, 1012
FC I, 140

ARISTIDES
See No. 87.

ST. JUSTIN MARTYR
See Nos. 24 and 675.

ST. HIPPOLYTUS
See No. 298.

ST. GREGORY NAZIANZEN
See No. 261.

ST. AUGUSTINE

Now it was not for the angels that Christ died. Yet what was done for the redemption of man through His death was in a sense done for the angels, because the enmity which sin had put between men and the holy angels is removed, and friendship is restored between them, and by the redemption of man the gaps which the great apostasy left in the angelic host are filled up.

768
(1917)

ON FAITH, HOPE, AND LOVE (ENCHIRIDION), Ch. 61
ML 40, 261
NPNF III, 257

152. The purpose of the incarnation and passion of Christ is a manifestation of love towards men.

LETTER TO DIOGNETUS
See No. 429.

ST. IRENAEUS
See No. 679.

ST. AUGUSTINE
See No. 760.

153. Christ Himself was both Priest and Host.

ST. AMBROSE

769
(1268)

It is a priest's duty to offer something, and, according to the Law, to enter into the holy places by means of blood; seeing, then, that God had rejected the blood of bulls and goats, this High Priest was indeed bound to make passage and entry into the holy of holies in heaven through His own blood, in order that He might be the everlasting propitiation for our sins. Priest and victim, then, are one; the priesthood and sacrifice are, however, exercised under the conditions of humanity, for He was led as a lamb to the slaughter, and He is a priest after the order of Melchisedech.

LETTER TO GRATIAN, ON THE CHRISTIAN FAITH, 3:11
ML 16, 607
NPNF X, 255

ST. AUGUSTINE
See No. 760.

770
(1608)

Whereas, then, Matthew had in view the kingly character, and Luke the priestly, they have at the same time both set forth preeminently the humanity of Christ: for it was according to His humanity that Christ was made both King and Priest. To Him, too, God gave the throne of His father David, in order that of His kingdom there should be no end (Lk. 1:32). And this was done with the purpose that there might be a mediator between God and men, the man Christ Jesus, to make intercession for us (1 Tim. 2:5).

THE HARMONY OF THE GOSPELS, Bk. 1, Ch. 3
ML 34, 1044
NPNF VI, 79

771
(1745)

Thus [Christ] is both the Priest who offers and the Sacrifice offered. And He designed that there should be a daily sign of this in the sacrifice of the Church, which, being His body, learns to offer herself through Him.

THE CITY OF GOD, Bk. 10, Ch. 20
ML 41, 298
NPNF II, 193

ST. JOHN OF DAMASCUS
See No. 751.

154. Christ offers Himself by way of true vicarious sacrifice.

ST. IGNATIUS OF ANTIOCH
See No. 107.

ST. JUSTIN MARTYR

For the whole human race will be found to be under a curse. . . . If, then, the Father of all wished His Christ for the whole human family to take upon Him the curses of all, knowing that, after He had been crucified and was dead, He would raise Him up, why do you argue about Him, who submitted to suffer these things according to the Father's will, as if He were accursed, and do not rather bewail yourselves? For although His father caused Him to suffer these things in behalf of the human family, yet you did not commit the deed as in obedience to the will of God. For you did not practise piety when you slew the prophets. And let none of you say: If His Father wished Him to suffer this, in order that by His stripes the human race might be healed, we have done no wrong. If, indeed, you repent of your sins, and recognise Him to be Christ, and observe His commandments, then you may assert this; for, as I have said before, remission of sins shall be yours.

772
(140)

DIALOGUE WITH TRYPHO, Ch. 95
MG 6, 701
ANF I, 247

ST. CYPRIAN

The Lord alone can have mercy. He alone can grant pardon for sins which were committed against Him, who bore our sins, who grieved for us, whom God delivered up for our sins. Man cannot be greater than God, nor can the servant by his own indulgence remit or forego what has been committed against the Lord by a more serious sin, lest to him still lapsed this too be added to his crime, if he does not know that it has been proclaimed: 'Cursed be the man that has hope in man' (Jer. 17:5). The Lord must be implored; the Lord must be placated by our own satisfaction, who said that He denied him who denied [Him], who alone received every judgment from the Father. We

773
(552)

believe indeed that the merits of the martyrs and the works of the righteous have very great power with the Judge, but [this will be] when the day of judgment shall come, when after the end of this age of the world His people shall stand before the tribunal of Christ.

THE LAPSED, Ch. 17
ML 4, 480
FC XXXVI, 72

774
(565)

Accordingly, [Christ's] every act right from the very outset of His coming is marked by an accompanying patience; for from the first moment of His descent from the sublimity of heaven to earthly things, He did not disdain, though the Son of God, to put on man's flesh, and although He Himself was not a sinner, to bear the sins of others.

THE GOOD OF PATIENCE, Ch. 6
ML 4, 626
FC XXXVI, 268

ST. ATHANASIUS
See No. 399.

ST. CYRIL OF JERUSALEM
See No. 745.

ST. AUGUSTINE
See No. 736.

155. Christ ascended into heaven according to His human nature.

ST. IRENAEUS
See No. 211.

156. Christ will judge the living and the dead.

ST. CLEMENT OF ROME
See No. 674.

ST. JUSTIN MARTYR
See No. 60.

ST. IRENAEUS
  See No. 211.

TERTULLIAN
  See No. 53.

ST. CYPRIAN
  See No. 773.

LACTANTIUS

Therefore the Son of the most high and mighty God shall come to
judge the living and the dead. . . . But He, when He shall have destroyed
unrighteousness, and executed His great judgment, and shall have
recalled to life the righteous, who have lived from the beginning, will
be engaged among men a thousand years, and will rule them with most
just command. . . . Then they who shall be alive in their bodies shall
not die, but during those thousand years shall produce an infinite
multitude, and their offspring shall be holy and beloved by God; . . .
About the same time also the prince of the devils, who is the contriver
of all evils, shall be bound with chains, and shall be imprisoned during
the thousand years of the heavenly rule in which righteousness shall
reign in the world, so that he may contrive no evil against the people
of God . . . the world itself shall rejoice, and all nature exult, being
rescued and set free from the dominion of evil and impiety, and guilt
and error. Throughout this time beasts shall not be nourished by
blood, nor birds by prey; but all things shall be peaceful and tranquil.
. . . But when the thousand years shall be completed, the world shall be
renewed by God, and the heavens shall be folded together, and the
earth shall be changed, and God shall transform men into the similitude
of angels, and they shall be white as snow; and they shall always be
employed in the sight of the Almighty, and shall make offerings to
their Lord, and serve Him forever. At the same time shall take place
that second and public resurrection of all, in which the unrighteous
shall be raised to everlasting punishments.

775
(647)

THE DIVINE INSTITUTES, Bk. 7, Ch. 24
ML 6, 808
ANF VII, 219

ST. GREGORY NAZIANZEN
  See No. 297.

XI.

Mary, Mother of God and Virgin

Mary is truly the mother of God (*theotókos*), and was herself conceived without stain of original sin and remained free from every personal sin during her whole life, thanks to a special privilege of grace from God. She was a virgin before, during, and after the birth of Christ. Mary conceived by the Holy Spirit without the coöperation of man and bore her Son without destroying her virginity in any way. Remaining a virgin her entire life she was finally assumed body and soul into heaven. As coöperator in the mystery of redemption she mediates all graces by her intercession in heaven. St. Irenaeus says, "As [Eve] who had Adam as her husband, but was nevertheless a virgin, was disobedient, and thereby became the cause of death to herself and to the whole of mankind, so also Mary, who had a pre-ordained husband, and was still a virgin, by her obedience became a cause of her own salvation and the salvation of the whole human race" (AGAINST HERESIES, Bk. 3, Ch. 22).

St. Ignatius of Antioch and St. Irenaeus in the second century as well as St. Gregory Nazianzen in the fourth and St. Cyril of Alexandria in the fifth declare that Mary was truly the mother of God, the expression "*theotókos*" appearing later in such writers as St. John Cassian, St. Vincent of Lérins, and St. John of Damascus. Aristides very early refers to the virgin birth and both St. Irenaeus and Tertullian dwell upon it at considerable length. We find it also in St. Hippolytus and Lactantius, and in the fourth century it occurs in St. Gregory Nazianzen and in St. Jerome's *The Perpetual Virginity of Blessed Mary*. In the post-Nicene period, the principal witnesses are St. Augustine, St. Peter Chrysologus, later St. Leo the Great, and finally St. John of Damascus. Tertullian is the first to emphasize that Mary was a virgin during Christ's birth, and the assertion is repeated later in the usual writers, St. Gregory Nazianzen, St. Augustine, St. Peter Chrysologus, St. Leo the Great, and St. John of Damascus. The same writers along with St. Jerome attest Mary's perpetual virginity.

Mary is the new Eve, coöperator in the mystery of redemption; this we find as early as the second century in St. Justin Martyr, and of course St. Irenaeus and Tertullian have it, along with St. Augustine. He as well as St. Basil attest to the completely singular nature of her sanctity, and the beautiful dogma of the immaculate conception receives classical expression in the twenty-seventh *Nisibene Hymn* of St. Ephraem. St. Augustine mentions it also; indeed all of these doctrines may be found somewhere in his voluminous writings.

The teaching that Mary's body was assumed into heaven seems to appear for the first time in the Gothic Missal some time in the sixth or seventh century.

157. Mary was truly the Mother of God.

ST. CYRIL OF ALEXANDRIA

776
(2064)

Christ, as I have said, was also God in his humanity, permitting human nature to use its laws while nonetheless conserving also the purity of divinity. For in this way and in no other is God to be understood both what was born by nature, and those things which the virgin mother produced not only of flesh and blood in the same way that other mothers do, but [the flesh and blood] of the Lord and of God imbued with our likeness.

PASCHAL HOMILIES, No. 17:2
MG 77, 776

THEOTÓKOS

ST. JOHN CASSIAN
See No. 719.

ST. VINCENT OF LÉRINS
See No. 706.

ST. JOHN OF DAMASCUS
See Nos. 716 and 7.

158. Mary was a virgin in conceiving.

ARISTIDES
See No. 87.

ST. IRENAEUS
See Nos. 211, 62, and 502.

TERTULLIAN
See No. 395.

For [Paul] writing to the Galatians says, 'God sent His own Son, made of a woman' (Gal. 4:4), who of course is admitted to have been a virgin, although Hebion* resists [this doctrine]. I recognise, too, the angel Gabriel as having been sent to 'a virgin.' But when he is blessing her, it is 'among women,' not among virgins, that he ranks her: Blessed art thou among women' (Lk. 1.28). For the angel knew that even a virgin is called a woman. . . . Here, at all events, there can be no semblance of speaking prophetically, as if the apostle should have named a future woman, that is, bride, in saying 'made of a woman.' For he could not be naming a posterior woman, from whom Christ had not to be born—that is, one who had known a man; but she who was then present, who was a virgin, was called a woman in consequence of the propriety of this name, —vindicated, in accordance with the primordial norm, [as belonging] to a virgin, and thus to the universal class of women.

777
(330)

ON THE VEILING OF VIRGINS, Ch. 6
ML 2, 897
ANF IV, 31

God recovered His own image and likeness, of which He had been robbed by the devil. For it was while Eve was yet a virgin, that the ensnaring word had crept into her ear which was to build the edifice

778
(358)

* I.e., Ebion, founder of the Ebionites.

of death. Into a virgin's soul, in like manner, must be introduced that Word of God which was to raise the fabric of life; so that what had been reduced to ruin by this sex, might by the selfsame sex be recovered to salvation. As Eve had believed the serpent, so Mary believed the angel. The delinquency which the one occasioned by believing, the other by believing effaced.

ON THE FLESH OF CHRIST, Ch. 17
ML 2, 782
ANF III, 325

779
(380)

For who was more worthily to perform the initiatory rite on the body of the Lord, than flesh similar in kind to that which conceived and give birth to that [body]? And indeed it was a virgin, about to marry once for all after her delivery, who gave birth to Christ, in order that each title of sanctity might be fulfilled in Christ's parentage, by means of a mother who was both virgin, and wife of one husband.

ON MONOGAMY, Ch. 8
ML 2, 939
ANF IV, 65

ST. HIPPOLYTUS
See No. 432.

LACTANTIUS

780
(633)

Therefore the Holy Spirit of God, descending from heaven, chose the holy Virgin, that He might enter into her womb. But she, being filled by the possession of the Divine Spirit, conceived; and without any intercourse with a man, her virgin womb was suddenly impregnated.

THE DIVINE INSTITUTES, Bk. 4, Ch. 12
ML 6, 478

See No. 365.   *ANF* VII, 110

ST. GREGORY NAZIANZEN
See Nos. 702 and 354.

ST. JEROME

781
(1361)

We believe that God was born of the Virgin, because we read it. That Mary was married after she brought forth, we do not believe, because we do not read it. Nor do we say this to condemn marriage. . . . for virginity itself is the fruit of marriage. . . . You say that Mary did not continue a virgin: I claim still more, that Joseph himself on account of Mary was a virgin, so that from a virgin wedlock a virgin son was born.

THE PERPETUAL VIRGINITY OF BLESSED MARY, Ch. 21
ML 23, 203
NPNF VI, 344

ST. AUGUSTINE
See Nos. 685 and 713.

ST. PETER CHRYSOLOGUS

Where are they who think that the Virgin's conception and giving birth to her child are to be likened to those of other women? For, this latter case is one of the earth, and the Virgin's is one from heaven. The one is a case of divine power; the other of human weakness. The one case occurs in a body subject to passion; the other in the tranquility of the divine Spirit and peace of the human body. The blood was still, and the flesh astonished; her members were put at rest, and her entire womb was quiescent during the visit of the Heavenly One, until the Author of flesh could take on His garment of flesh, and until He, who was not merely to restore the earth to man but also to give him heaven, could become a heavenly Man. The Virgin conceives, the Virgin brings forth her child, and she remains a virgin.

782
(2177)

SERMONS, No. 117
ML 52, 520
FC XVII, 200

ST. LEO THE GREAT
See No. 686.

And by a new nativity [Christ] was begotten, conceived by a Virgin, born of a Virgin, without paternal desire, without injury to the mother's chastity. . . . The origin is different but the nature like: not by intercourse with man but by the power of God was it brought about: for a Virgin conceived, a Virgin bare and a Virgin she remained.

783
(2194)

SERMONS, No. 22:2
ML 54, 195
NPNF XII, 130

ST. JOHN OF DAMASCUS

784
(2372)

But just as He who was conceived kept her who conceived still virgin, in like manner also He who was born preserved her virginity intact, only passing through her and keeping her closed. . . . For it was not impossible for Him to have come by this gate, without injuring her seal in any way. The ever-virgin One thus remains even after the birth still virgin, having never at any time up till death consorted with a man.

EXPOSITION OF THE ORTHODOX FAITH, Bk. 4, Ch. 14
MG 94, 1161
NPNF IX, 86

159. Mary was a virgin during Christ's birth.

TERTULLIAN
See No. 778.

ST. GREGORY NAZIANZEN
See No. 297.

ST. AUGUSTINE

785
(1430)

That very greatness of His power, which feels no narrowness in narrow quarters, enriched the Virgin's womb, not by an externally caused but by an intrinsic childbirth; that power took to itself a rational soul and thereby also a human body, and chose to better all mankind without suffering any diminution itself, deigning to take the name of humanity from man, while granting him a share in the divinity. That same power brought forth the body of the infant from the inviolate virginal womb of the mother, as afterward the Body of the Man penetrated closed doors. It will not be wondered at if an explanation is asked of this; it will not be remarkable if an example is demanded. Let us grant that God can do something which we confess we cannot fathom. In such matters the whole explanation of the deed is in the power of the Doer.

LETTERS, No. 137
ML 33, 519

See Nos. 685 and 713.
FC XX, 24

ST. PETER CHRYSOLOGUS
See No. 782.

ST. LEO THE GREAT
See Nos. 686, 699, and 783.

ST. JOHN OF DAMASCUS
See No. 784.

160. Mary remained a virgin after Christ's birth.

TERTULLIAN
See Nos. 777 and 779.

ST. JEROME
See No. 781.

ST. AUGUSTINE
See No. 685.

Thus Christ by being born of a virgin, who, before she knew Who was to be born of her, had determined to continue a virgin, chose rather to approve, than to command, holy virginity. And thus, even in the female herself, in whom He took the form of a servant, He willed that virginity should be free.

786
(1643)

ON HOLY VIRGINITY, Ch. 4:4
ML 40, 398
NPNF III, 418

ST. PETER CHRYSOLOGUS
See No. 782.

ST. LEO THE GREAT
See No. 783.

ST. JOHN OF DAMASCUS
See No. 784.

161. Mary was conceived immaculate.

ST. EPHRAEM

Truly you, Lord, and your mother are the only ones who are beautiful, completely so in every respect; for, Lord, there is no spot in you, nor

787
(719)

any spot at all in your mother. Even my babes are hardly similar to these two pulchritudes!

NISIBENE HYMNS, 27
BK 122

ST. AUGUSTINE
See No. 584.

162. Mary's body was assumed into heaven.

This appears in the Gothic Missal some time in the sixth or seventh century.

XII.

The Sacraments

Sacraments are sensible signs instituted by Christ to signify and effect the sanctification of man. The outward sign is some sensible thing or perceivable action and is the matter (and form) of the sacrament, the form is the words or signs by which the matter receives its proximate sacramental determination. Christ instituted the sacraments to confer grace from the power of the Holy Spirit and hence they are morally Christ's actions using the ministry of men. Of course, the sacraments do not depend on the moral character of the minister, nor do they confer grace when an obstacle is present, although they do confer more abundant grace on that recipient who is better disposed to receive them. The sacraments of baptism, confirmation, and orders imprint on the soul a spiritual and indelible character and they can never be repeated. Sacramentals are objects or actions which the Church uses, in imitation of the sacraments, to obtain favors, especially ones through her intercession.

St. Theophilus of Antioch (late second century) and Tertullian and St. Cyprian (third century) tell us that the sacraments are sensible signs which signify and at the same time confer grace; this is elaborated by St. Augustine in several different passages. He it is who distinguishes the things and words of the sacrament, opening the way for the matter-form interpretation. Tertullian, St. Cyprian, St. Basil, St. Ambrose, and St. Jerome emphasize the imposition of hands among the sacramental rites as signifying in a special manner the conferring of grace.

Sacramental theology was relatively late in developing, and was never fully treated nor systematized by the Fathers. Sometimes there is an adumbration of later scholastic terminology, but more frequently the approach is disparate, with one or two Fathers treating one point, and others another.

St. Cyril of Jerusalem, St. Gregory Nazianzen, St. Ambrose, and St. Augustine agree that the sacraments of baptism, confirmation, and orders imprint on the soul a spiritual and indelible sign, and Tertullian and St. Cyprian add that these cannot be repeated. A number of Fathers agree that the sacraments confer grace from the power of the Holy Spirit which is in the rite; Tertullian, Novatian, and Aphraates are in this group, as well as St. Cyril of Jerusalem, St. Basil, St. Ambrose, and St. Augustine, the latter asserting that Christ is the author of the sacraments and instituted all of them immediately. Hence they are morally His actions, using the ministry of men (St. John Chrysostom, St. Ambrose).

That the worth of the sacraments does not depend on either the faith or the probity of the minister is attested to by more than a few writers, while the valid, licit, and fruitful reception of the sacraments is stressed mainly by Origen and St. Augustine. The Fathers testify that there existed especially with regard to the sacraments a discipline of secret, and this is found in Tertullian, St. Basil, St. John Chrysostom, St. Augustine, and Theodoret.

By baptism we are spiritually reborn through washing with water and invocation of the Trinitarian formula. Anyone who has the right matter, form, and intention may baptize validly and even licitly in case of necessity. For adults the baptism of desire can take the place of the baptism of water, and for infants as well there is the possibility of the baptism of martyrdom. The effect of baptism is a spiritual regeneration which consists in the remission of every sin and punishment and the infusion of the first grace.

One of our very earliest sources, the *Didache,* tells us that baptism is a true sacrament instituted by Christ. This is confirmed by the *Letter to Barnabas* and St. Justin Martyr in the second century, by Tertullian in the third, and then by Aphraates, St. Ephraem, and St. Ambrose. The remote matter is natural water (*Didache* and Hermas), the proximate matter is the washing with water (*Didache,* St. Justin Martyr, Tertullian, and St. Ephraem). Immersion, infusion, or sprinkling were all valid forms of baptism, —the *Didache,* the *Letter to Barnabas,* and the Shepherd of Hermas being our earliest sources. It is essential that there be a distinct expression of God as one and three, and this is affirmed not only by the *Didache,* St. Justin Martyr, and Tertullian, but also by St. Cyprian, St. Hilary, St. Basil, St. Gregory Nazianzen, and St. Ambrose. Tertullian tells us that the bishop or priest is the usual minister of solemn baptism, but anyone in an emergency can licitly and validly baptize. Even heretics may perform the rite of baptism, as St. Cyprian was finally compelled to admit.

Baptism is necessary to all for salvation, both children and adults: there is good authority for this assertion, beginning with Tertullian, St. Cyprian, and St. Cyril of Jerusalem; Chrysostom is most insistent as are St. Ambrose and St. Augustine. But the baptism of desire or of martyrdom can take the place of water baptism. St. Cyprian speaks from experience here, but Tertullian, St. Cyril of Jerusalem, St. Gregory of Nazianzen, and St. Augustine are in full agreement. The Church has always recognized that even infants are capable of receiving baptism.

A dozen authors too numerous to mention assure us that the effect of baptism is a spiritual regeneration, which consists of the remission of every sin and punishment, and the infusion of the first grace.

Confirmation is the sacrament through which the Holy Spirit comes to us in a special way to impart His gifts and the effusion of grace. St. Theophilus of Antioch, Tertullian, St. Cyprian, St. Cyril of Jerusalem, St. Ambrose, St. Jerome, and St. Augustine assure us that it is a true sacrament. From the same authors we learn that the remote matter is blessed oil (chrism), and the proximate matter is its unction made on the forehead in the form of a cross; the ordinary minister is the bishop, the extraordinary minister is any priest (St. Gregory the Great), and its effect is a more abundant effusion of grace and of the gifts of the Holy Spirit.

The Eucharist commemorates Christ's passion and death. It nourishes and strengthens the spiritual life of our souls, unites us most intimately with Christ and His mystical body, the Church, increases sanctifying grace in us, weakens our evil inclinations, and confers on us a pledge of eternal life. The bread and wine are transformed into the body and blood of Christ through the words of consecration spoken by the priest, hence Christ is really present under each species, and each part of the species. The Mass is a representation of the sacrifice of the cross in which Christ Himself offers Himself as victim through the ministry of the priest. It is a propitiatory and impetrating sacrifice of worship and thanksgiving.

St. Justin Martyr in the second century declares that the sacrament of the Eucharist was instituted by Christ in memory of His passion and death. St. John Chrysostom and St. Ambrose comment on this, and also St. Augustine at some length. Not a few Fathers discuss the eucharistic promise given in John 6:48ff., and the testimony that Christ is really present in the Eucharist under the species of bread and wine is abundant. St. Justin Martyr, St. Irenaeus, and St. Cyril of Jerusalem, among others, remind us that the truth of the real Presence is evident from the words of institution, although a few like Tertullian interpret this less literally. That the bread and wine through the words of consecration are converted into the body and blood of Christ is the belief of at least St. Irenaeus, St. Cyril of Jerusalem, St. Gregory of Nyssa, St. Ambrose, St. Augustine, Theodoret, and the Damascene. Bread and wine are the traditional matter of the Eucharist (*Didache,* St. Justin Martyr, Abercius's *Epitaph,* St. Irenaeus, St. Cyprian, St. Cyril of Jerusalem, St. Augustine), and the form of the Eucharist the Fathers placed either in the words of Christ (St. Justin Martyr, St. John Chrysostom) or in *epiklesis* (St. Irenaeus, St. Cyril of Jerusalem, St. Basil, Theodoret, St. John of Damascus), or less precisely in the prayer or benediction (Origen, St. Gregory of Nyssa, St. Ambrose, St. Jerome, and St. Augustine). In the early Church the general custom was that communion be received under both species. The Eucharist is considered a pledge of the resurrection and of eternal life by many of the Fathers, and they assert that it also both signifies and procures the unity of the Church.

St. Irenaeus, St. Cyprian, and St. Cyril of Jerusalem speak of the Mass as a true sacrifice, along with St. Gregory Nazianzen, St. John Chrysostom, and St. Augustine; they see it as a re-presentation of the sacrifice of the cross, which was predicted in the Old Testament.

Penance is the sacrament in which the sins of a repentant sinner committed after baptism are forgiven by the absolution of a priest. By penance man detests and sorrows over sin, and intends to repair the injury done to God, and this is necessary to obtain the remission of sin. But although the guilt is remitted, the entire temporal punishment of the sin is not always remitted at the same time by God, and so after absolution there remains the obligation of satisfying the justice of God. The minister of the sacrament of penance is solely the priest.

Tertullian, Firmilian, Lactantius, St. John Chrysostom, St. Ambrose, St. Jerome, and St. Augustine all assure us that the Church received from Christ the power of remitting sins, which power extends to all sins committed after baptism (so St. Ignatius of Antioch and St. Polycarp). Adultery, apostasy, and murder are considered the worst sins, but readmission into the Church after sufficient penance becomes possible even for adultery in 220, for apostasy in 250, and for murder some time during the reign of Constantine. In the early Church a public penance was imposed for the most serious external crimes (Tertullian, Origen, St. Cyprian) and reconciliation was made by the imposition of hands, ordinarily by the bishop. Penance is necessary to obtain the remission of sin, Hermas tells us with Tertullian and St. Cyprian, but a contrite act of perfect charity in itself always and immediately justifies (St. Clement of Rome, St. Clement of Alexandria, St. Cyprian, and St. Augustine). Several authors insist that some confession of an external character is required for the remission of sins. The *Didache,* the *Letter to Barnabas,* and St. Irenaeus are most enlightening here, and Tertullian, St. Cyprian, St. John Chrysostom, and St. Ambrose also confirm the point. Tertullian reminds us that there remains after absolution the obligation of satisfying the justice of God. St. John Chrysostom has an eloquent passage on the minister of the sacrament of penance being the priest alone, and we are ultimately consoled by the fact that forgiven sins never return.

Holy orders is the sacrament by which spiritual power is conferred together with the grace to exercise properly the respective office. The matter of orders is the imposition of hands, and the form is the accompanying prayer. The minister of orders is only the bishop, and

405

the effect of orders is an increase of grace, a character, and spiritual power.

St. Basil, St. Augustine, and St. Leo the Great assure us that orders is a true sacrament; St. Clement of Rome indicates that in the Church, the clergy constitute a distinct order from the laity and this is affirmed by Tertullian, St. Clement of Alexandria, St. Athanasius, St. Basil, and St. Jerome. Episcopacy, priesthood, and diaconate constitute major orders, bishops being superior to priests. The *Constitutions of the Apostles* (ca. 400) delineate the various orders of clergy. The matter of orders (the imposition of hands) is described by St. Cyprian, the form (the consecrating prayer) by St. John Chrysostom. Tertullian, St. Jerome, and St. Gregory the Great declare that the ancient custom in the Church was that celibacy be imposed on clerics in major orders, or at least that they be prohibited from a second marriage.

Christian matrimony is a true sacrament according to St. Ignatius of Antioch, Tertullian, Origen, St. John Chrysostom, St. Ambrose, St. Augustine, St. Leo the Great, and St. John of Damascus. The Shepherd of Hermas declares that matrimony effects an indissoluble bond, and St. Justin Martyr, Tertullian, St. Clement of Alexandria, Origen, Lactantius, St. Basil, St. Gregory Nazianzen, St. Jerome, and St. Augustine agree. According to a few, even adultery cannot dissolve it. The sacrament effects an exclusive bond (Athenagoras, St. Theophilus of Antioch, Minucius Felix, St. John Chrysostom, and St. Leo the Great) and there is a general aversion to second marriages. St. John Chrysostom, St. Jerome, St. Augustine, and the Damascene insist that marriage is licit and good, but the tradition of the Church has constantly been that celibacy and especially virginity are however preferable to marriage, and this is explicitated in so many words by St. Ignatius of Antioch, St. Ambrose, St. Jerome, and St. John of Damascus.

Extreme unction is a true sacrament whose effect is to blot out the residue of sin and to increase the forces of the soul and body. Our sole source for this sacrament, but a forceful one, is the letter of St. Innocent I to Decentius some time at the beginning of the fifth century.

Against the Reformers of the sixteenth century, the Council of

Trent fixed the number of the sacraments at seven and attempted to delineate their character both in general and in particular. Thus a final form was given to the teachings of the Fathers and the work of the scholastic theologians of the twelfth and thirteenth centuries.

THE SACRAMENTS IN GENERAL

163. The sacraments are sensible signs which signify and at the same time confer grace.

ST. THEOPHILUS OF ANTIOCH

The things proceeding from the waters were blessed by God, that this also might be a sign of men's being destined to receive repentance and remission of sins, through the water and laver of regeneration (Tit. 3:5), —as many as come to the truth, and are born again, and receive blessing from God.

788
(181)

TO AUTOLYCUS, Ch. 2.16
MG 6, 1077
ANF II, 101

TERTULLIAN

All waters, therefore, in virtue of the pristine privilege of their origin, do, after invocation of God, attain the sacramental power of sanctification; for the Spirit immediately supervenes from the heavens, and rests over the waters, sanctifying them from Himself; and being thus sanctified, they imbibe at the same time the powers of sanctifying. Albeit the similitude may be admitted to be suitable to the simple act; that, since we are defiled by sins, as it were by dirt, we should be washed from those stains in waters.

789
(303)

ON BAPTISM, Ch. 4
ML 1, 1204
ANF III, 607

ST. CYPRIAN

790
(590)

You have asked also, dearest son, what I thought of those who obtain God's grace in sickness and weakness, whether they are to be accounted legitimate Christians, for that they are not to be washed, but sprinkled, with the saving water. In this point, my diffidence and modesty prejudges none, so as to prevent any from feeling what he thinks right, and from doing what he feels to be right. As far as my poor under-standing conceives it, I think that the divine benefits can in no respect be mutilated and weakened; nor can anything less occur in that case, where, with full and entire faith both of the giver and receiver, is ac-cepted what is drawn from the divine gifts. . . . In the sacraments of salvation, when necessity compels, and God bestows His mercy, the divine methods confer the whole benefit on believers; nor ought it to trouble any one that sick people seem to be sprinkled or affused, when they obtain the Lord's grace.

LETTERS, No. 69:12
ML 3, 1147
ANF V, 400–401

ST. JOHN CHRYSOSTOM
See No. 14.

ST. AUGUSTINE

791
(1432)

[To Marcellinus] God has no need of those sacrifices [of the Old Law], nor does He ever need any, but they are signs of divinely bestowed favors, intended either to endow the mind with virtues or to help in the attaining of eternal salvation. Their observance and performance are exercises of devotion, useful to us, not to God. It would take too long to discuss adequately the variety of signs which are called sacraments when they are applied to divine things.

LETTERS, No. 138
ML 33, 541
FC XX, 39–40

792
(1475)

For if we distinguish between the two Testaments, Old and New, there are not the same Sacraments nor the same promises; nevertheless the same commandments for the most part. . . . The Sacraments are not the same, for some Sacraments there are giving Salvation, others promising a Saviour. The Sacraments of the New Testament give salvation, the Sacraments of the Old Testament did promise a Saviour.

EXPOSITIONS ON THE PSALMS, 73:2
ML 36, 930
NPNF VIII, 342–343

There can be no religious society, whether the religion be true or false, without some sacrament or visible symbol to serve as a bond of union. The importance of these sacraments cannot be overstated, and only scoffers will treat them lightly. For if piety requires them, it must be impiety to neglect them.

793
(1601)

REPLY TO FAUSTUS THE MANICHAEAN, 19:11
ML 42, 355
NPNF IV, 243

The sacrament of chrism. . . is indeed holy as among the class of visible signs, like baptism itself, but yet can exist even among the worst of men, wasting their life in the works of the flesh, and never destined to possess the kingdom of heaven. . . . Separate therefore the visible holy sacrament, which exist both in the good and in the bad, —in the former for their reward, in the latter for judgment; separate it from the invisible unction of charity, which is the peculiar property of the good.

794
(1647)

AGAINST THE LETTERS OF PETILLIAN, THE DONATIST,
Bk. 2, Ch. 105
ML 43, 342
NPNF IV, 592

And the fact that the ancient church offered animal sacrifices, which the people of God now-a-days read of without imitating, proves nothing else than this, that those sacrifices signified the things which we do for the purpose of drawing near to God, and inducing our neighbor to do the same. A sacrifice, therefore, is the visible sacrament or sacred sign of an invisible sacrifice.

795
(1744)

THE CITY OF GOD, Bk. 10, Ch. 5
ML 41, 282
NPNF II, 183

'And you have an unction from the Holy One, that you may be manifest to your own selves' (1 Jn. 2:20). The spiritual unction is

796
(1847)

the Holy Spirit Himself, of which the Sacrament is in the visible unction.

TEN HOMILIES ON THE EPISTLE OF ST. JOHN TO THE PARTHIANS,
Tr. 3:5
ML 35, 2000

164. Physically the sacraments are constituted of things (matter) and words (form).

TERTULLIAN

See No. 789.

ST. AMBROSE

797
(1329)
What did you see? Water, certainly, but not water alone; you saw the deacons ministering there, and the bishop asking questions and hallowing. . . . Believe, then, that the presence of the Godhead is there. Do you believe the working, and not believe the presence? Whence should the working proceed unless the presence went before?

ON THE MYSTERIES, Ch. 3:8
ML 16, 391
NPNF X, 318

ST. AUGUSTINE

798
(1817)
What is the baptism of Christ? The washing of water by the Word (Eph. 5:26). Take away the water, it is no baptism; take away the Word, it is no baptism.

ON THE GOSPEL OF ST. JOHN, Tr. 15:4
ML 35, 1512
NPNF VII, 100

799
(1834)
'Now you are clean through the word which I have spoken unto you' (Jn. 15:3). Why does He not say, You are clean through the baptism wherewith you have been washed, but 'through the word which I have spoken unto you,' save only that in the water also it is the word that cleanses? Take away the word, and the water is neither more nor less than water. The word is added to the element, and there results the Sacrament, as if itself also a kind of visible word. For He

410

had said also to the same effect, when washing the disciples' feet, 'He that is washed needs not, save to wash his feet, but is completely clean' (Jn. 13:10). And whence has water so great an efficacy, as in touching the body to cleanse the soul, save by the operation of the word; and that not because it is uttered, but because it is believed? For even in the word itself the passing sound is one thing, the abiding efficacy another.

ON THE GOSPEL OF ST. JOHN, Tr. 80:3
ML 35, 1840
NPNF VII, 344

165. Among the sacramental rites the imposition of hands signifies in a special manner the conferring of grace.

TERTULLIAN

After this, when we have issued from the font, we are thoroughly anointed with a blessed unction, —[a practice derived] from the old discipline, wherein, on entering the priesthood, [men] were wont to be anointed with oil from a horn, ever since Aaron was anointed by Moses; whence Aaron is called 'Christ,' from the 'chrism,' which is 'the unction'; which, when made spiritual, furnished an appropriate name to the Lord, because He was "anointed" with the Spirit by God the Father; as [we have it] in the Acts; 'For truly they were gathered together in this city against Your Holy Son whom You have anointed' (Acts 4:27). Thus, too, in our case, the unction runs [down our flesh] carnally, but profits spiritually, in the same way as the act of baptism itself too is carnal, in that we are plunged in water; the effect spiritual, in that we are freed from sins. In the next place the hand is laid on us, invoking and inviting the Holy Spirit (through the words of benediction).

ON BAPTISM, Ch. 7, 8
ML 1, 1206
ANF III, 672

800
(304)

The flesh is the very condition on which salvation hinges. And since the soul is, in consequence of its salvation, chosen to the service of God, it is the flesh which actually renders it capable of such service. The flesh, indeed, is washed, in order that the soul may be cleansed; the

801
(362)

411

flesh is anointed, that the soul may be consecrated; the flesh is signed [with the cross], that the soul too may be fortified; the flesh is shadowed with the imposition of hands, that the soul also may be illuminated by the Spirit; the flesh feeds on the body and blood of Christ, that the soul likewise may fatten on [its] God. They cannot then be separated in their recompense, when they are united in their service.

ON THE RESURRECTION OF THE FLESH, Ch. 8
ML 2, 806
ANF III, 551

ST. CYPRIAN

802
(569)

For although in smaller sins sinners may do penance for a set time, and according to the rules of discipline come to public confession, and by imposition of the hand of the bishop and clergy receive the right of communion: now with their time still unfulfilled, while persecution is still raging, while the peace of the Church itself is not yet restored, they are admitted to communion, and their name is presented; and while the penance is not yet performed, confession is not yet made, the hands of the bishop and clergy are not yet laid upon them, the Eucharist is given to them; although it is written, 'Whosoever shall eat the bread and drink the cup of the Lord unworthily, shall be guilty of the body and blood of the Lord' (1 Cor. 11:27).

LETTERS, No. 16:2
ML 4, 251
ANF V, 290

803
(595)

And therefore, because [the Samaritans] had obtained a legitimate and ecclesiastical baptism, there was no need that they should be baptized any more, but only that which was needed was performed by Peter and John; viz., that prayer being made for them, and hands being imposed, the Holy Spirit should be invoked and poured out upon them (Acts 8:14 ff.), which now too is done among us, so that they who are baptized in the Church are brought to the prelates of the Church, and by our prayers and by the imposition of hands obtain the Holy Spirit, and are perfected with the Lord's seal.

LETTERS, No. 73:9
ML 3, 1115
ANF V, 381

ST. BASIL

Those who had separated themselves from the Church had no longer on them the grace of the Holy Spirit, for it ceased to be imparted when the continuity was broken. The first separatists had received their ordination from the Fathers, and possessed the spiritual gift by the laying on of their hands. But they who were broken off had become laymen, and, because they are no longer able to confer on others that grace of the Holy Spirit from which they themselves are fallen away, they had no authority either to baptize or to ordain.

804
(919)

LETTERS, No. 188:1
MG 32, 668
NPNF VIII, 224

ST. AMBROSE

Why, then, do you lay on hands, and believe it to be the effect of the blessing, if perchance some sick person recovers? Why do you assume that any can be cleansed by you from the pollution of the devil? Why do you baptize if sins cannot be remitted by man? If baptism is certainly the remission of all sins, what difference does it make whether priests claim that this power is given to them in penance or at the font? In each the mystery is one.

805
(1295)

ON REPENTANCE, Bk. 1, Ch. 8
ML 16, 477
NPNF X, 335

ST. JEROME

I do not deny that it is the practice of the Churches in the case of those who living far from the greater towns have been baptized by presbyters and deacons, for the bishop to visit them, and by the laying on of hands to invoke the Holy Spirit upon them. . . . The well-being of a Church depends upon the dignity of its chief-priest, and unless some extraordinary and unique functions be assigned to him, we shall have as many schisms in the Churches as there are priests. Hence it is that without ordination and the bishop's license neither presbyter nor deacon has the power to baptize. And yet, if necessity so be, we know that even laymen may, and frequently do, baptize. For as a man receives, so too he can give.

806
(1359)

THE DIALOGUE AGAINST THE LUCIFERIANS, Ch. 9
ML 23, 164
NPNF VI, 324

166. The sacraments confer more abundant grace on the recipient who is better disposed to receive.

ST. CYRIL OF JERUSALEM

807
(809)

Cleanse your vessel, that you may receive grace more abundantly. For though remission of sins is given equally to all, the communion of the Holy Ghost is bestowed in proportion to each man's faith. If you have labored little, you receive little; but if you have wrought much, the reward is great.

CATECHESES, 1:5
MG 33, 377
NPNF VII, 7

167. The sacraments do not confer grace when an obstacle is present, but when it is removed the sacraments revivify and grace is infused.

ST. AUGUSTINE
See Nos. 858, 848, and 850.

ST. FULGENTIUS
See No. 134.

168. The sacraments of baptism, confirmation, and orders imprint on the soul a spiritual and indelible sign.

ST. CYRIL OF JERUSALEM
See No. 558.

808
(847)

'You have anointed my head with oil' (Ps. 22:5). With oil he anointed your head upon your forehead, for the seal which you have from God; that you may be made the engraving of the signet, Holiness unto God.

CATECHESES, No. 22:7
MG 33, 1101
NPNF VII, 152

414

ST. GREGORY NAZIANZEN
See No. 635.

ST. AMBROSE
See No. 436.

ST. AUGUSTINE

Therefore the good of marriage throughout all nations and all men stands in the occasion of begetting, and faith of chastity: but, so far as pertains unto the People of God, also in the sanctity of the Sacrament, by reason of which it is unlawful for one who leaves her husband, even when she has been put away, to be married to another, so long as her husband lives, no not even for the sake of bearing children; and, whereas this is the lone cause, wherefore marriage takes place, not even where that very thing, wherefore it takes place, follows not, is the marriage bond loosed, save by the death of the husband or wife. In like manner as if there take place an ordination of clergy in order to form a congregation of people, although the congregation of people follow not, yet there remains in the ordained persons the Sacrament of Ordination; and if, for any fault, any be removed from his office, he will not be without the Sacrament of the Lord once for all set upon him, albeit continuing unto condemnation.

809
(1642)

ON THE GOOD OF MARRIAGE, Ch. 24:32

ML 40, 394

NPNF III, 412

169. *And so these sacraments of baptism, confirmation, and orders can never be repeated.*

TERTULLIAN
See No. 126.

These poisons of his [the devil's], therefore, God foreseeing, although the gate of forgiveness has been shut and fastened up with the bar of baptism, has permitted [it] still to stand somewhat open. In the vestibule He has stationed repentance the second to open to such as knock: but now once for all, because now for the second time; but never more, because the last time it had been in vain. For is not even this

810
(314)

once enough? You have what you now deserved not, for you had lost what you had received. . . . However, if any do incur the debt of a second repentance, his spirit is not to be forthwith cut down and undermined by despair. Let it by all means be irksome to sin again, but let not to repent again be irksome; irksome to imperil one's self again, but not to be again set free. Let none be ashamed. Repeated sickness must have repeated medicine. You will show your gratitude to the Lord by not refusing what the Lord offers you. You have offended, but can still be reconciled. You have One whom you may satisfy, and Him willing [to accept the satisfaction].

ON PENANCE, Ch. 7
ML 1, 1241
ANF III, 663

ST. CYPRIAN

811
(592a)

For I know not by what presumption some of our colleagues are led to think that they who have been dipped by heretics ought not to be baptized when they come to us, for the reason that they say that there is one baptism. . . . But we say that those who come thence are not re-baptized among us, but are baptized. . . . And they say that in this matter they follow ancient custom; although among the ancients these were as yet the first beginnings of heresy and schisms, so that those were involved in them who departed from the Church, having first been baptized therein; and these, therefore, when they returned to the Church and repented, it was not necessary to baptize. . . . Neither must we prescribe this from custom, but overcome opposite custom by reason. . . . Which thing, indeed, Agrippinus also, a man of worthy memory, with his other fellow-bishops, who at that time governed the Lord's Church in the province of Africa and Numidia, decreed, and by the well-weighed examination of the common council established: whose opinion, as being both religious and lawful and salutary, and in harmony with the Catholic faith and Church, we also have followed.

LETTERS, No. 71:1
ML 4, 409
ANF V, 377

812
(593)

You have written to me, dearest brother (Jubaianus), wishing that the impression of my mind should be signified to you, as to what I think concerning the baptism of heretics; who, placed outside, and established outside the Church, arrogate to themselves a matter neither within their right nor their power. This baptism we cannot consider as valid or legitimate, since it is manifestly unlawful among them; . . . And now also, when we had met together, bishops as well of the province of Africa as of Numidia, to the number of seventy-one, we established this same matter once more by our judgment, deciding that there is one baptism which is appointed in the Catholic Church; and that by this those are not re-baptized, but baptized by us, who at any time come from the adulterous and unhallowed water to be washed and sanctified by the truth of the saving water.

LETTERS, No. 73:1
ML 3, 1110
ANF V, 379

ST. FULGENTIUS
See No. 134.

170. *The sacraments confer grace from the power of the Holy Spirit which is in the rite.*

TERTULLIAN
See No. 789.

NOVATIAN
See No. 633.

APHRAATES
See No. 487.

ST. CYRIL OF JERUSALEM
See No. 634.

ST. BASIL

This then is what it is to be born again of water and of the Spirit, the being made dead being effected in the water, while our life is wrought in us through the Spirit. In three immersions, then, and with three invocations, the great mystery of baptism is performed, to the end that

813
(947)

417

the type of death may be fully figured, and that by the tradition of the divine knowledge the baptized may have their souls enlightened. It follows that if there is any grace in the water, it is not of the nature of the water, but of the presence of the Spirit.

ON THE HOLY SPIRIT, Ch. 15:35
MG 32, 129
NPNF VIII, 22

ST. AMBROSE
See Nos. 436 and 797.

ST. AUGUSTINE

814
(1423)
It is one Spirit that makes it possible for a man to be reborn through the agency of another's will when he is offered for baptism, and through Him the one offered is reborn. For it is not written: 'Unless a man be born again through the will of his parents' or: 'through the faith of his god-parents or the ministers,' but: 'Unless a man be born again of water and the Holy Spirit' (Jn. 3:5). The water, therefore, manifesting the sacrament of grace exteriorly, and the Spirit, effecting the benefit of grace interiorly, loosing the bond of guilt, restoring good to his nature, both regenerate in one Christ the man who was begotten of one Adam.

LETTERS, No. 98
ML 33, 360

See No. 799.   *FC* XVIII, 130

171. Christ is the author of the sacraments and instituted all of them immediately.

ST. AUGUSTINE
See No. 176.

815
(1814)
We are now permitted to seek Christ everywhere. . . . When Adam sleeps, Eve is formed from his side; when Christ is dead, the spear pierces His side, that the mysteries may flow forth whereby the Church is formed. Is it not evident to every man that in those things then done, things to come were foreshadowed, since the apostle says that

418

Adam himself was the figure of Him that was to come? 'Who is,' he says, 'the figure of Him that was to come' (Rom. 5:14).

ON THE GOSPEL OF ST. JOHN, Tr. 9:10
ML 35, 1463
NPNF VII, 66–67

172. The sacraments are morally Christ's actions, using the ministry of men.

ST. JOHN CHRYSOSTOM
See No. 426.

ST. AMBROSE

Damasus has not cleansed, Peter has not cleansed, Ambrose has not cleansed, Gregory has not cleansed; for the service is ours but the sacraments are yours. For it is not of human power to confer divine things, but it is your function, Lord, and that of the Father.

816
(1280)

ON THE HOLY SPIRIT, Prologue, 18
ML 16, 708
NPNF X, 96

ST. AUGUSTINE

'Howbeit, Jesus Himself baptized not, but His disciples' (Jn. 4:2). He, and not He: He by power, they by ministry; they performed the service of baptizing, the power of baptizing remained in Christ. His disciples, then, baptized, and Judas was still among his disciples: and were those, then, whom Judas baptized not again baptized; and those whom John baptized were they again baptized? Plainly there was a repetition, but not a repetition of the same baptism. For those whom John baptized, John baptized; those whom Judas baptized, Christ baptized. In like manner, then, they whom a drunkard baptized, those whom a murderer baptized, those whom an adulterer baptized, if it was the baptism of Christ, were baptized by Christ.

817
(1810)

ON THE GOSPEL OF ST. JOHN, Tr. 5:18
ML 35, 1424
NPNF VII, 38

419

173. The worth of the sacraments does not depend on the faith of the minister.

TERTULLIAN
See No. 126.

ST. CYPRIAN

818
(592)

It is also necessary that he should be anointed who is baptized; so that, having received the chrism, that is, the anointing, he may be anointed of God, and have in him the grace of Christ. Further, it is the Eucharist whence the baptized are anointed with the oil sanctified on the altar. But he cannot sanctify the creature of oil, who has neither an altar nor a church; whence also there can be no spiritual anointing among heretics, since it is manifest that the oil cannot be sanctified nor the Eucharist celebrated at all among them.

LETTERS, No. 70:2
ML 3, 1040
ANF V, 376

819
(594)

We perceive that only they who are set over the Church and established in the Gospel law, and in the ordinance of the Lord, are allowed to baptize and to give remission of sins; but that without, nothing can either be bound or loosed, where there is none who can either bind or loose anything.

LETTERS, No. 73:7
ML 3, 1114
ANF V, 381

FIRMILIAN
See No. 169.

ST. BASIL
See No. 804.

ST. AMBROSE

820
(1293)

[The power of binding and loosing.] It is plain and evident that either each is allowed or each is disallowed in the case of those to whom each has been given. Each is allowed to the Church, neither to heresy, for this power has been entrusted to priests alone.

ON REPENTANCE, Bk. 1, Ch. 2
ML 16, 468
NPNF X, 330

ST. JEROME

If he that baptized a person into our belief has had no injurious effect upon the person baptized, it follows that he who consecrates a bishop in the same faith causes no defilement to the person consecrated.

821
(1360)

THE DIALOGUE AGAINST THE LUCIFERIANS, Ch. 11
ML 23, 166
NPNF VI, 325

ST. AUGUSTINE
See No. 133.

ST. GREGORY THE GREAT

[Augustine's eighth question:] I ask whether, if length of way intervenes, and bishops are not able to assemble easily, a bishop should be ordained without the presence of other bishops. [Gregory's answer:] Indeed in the Church of the Angli, wherein you are so far the only bishop, you can not ordain a bishop otherwise than without bishops. (For when bishops shall come from Gaul, they will attend as witnesses for the ordination of a bishop.)

822
(2300)

LETTERS, Bk. 11, 64
ML 77, 1191
NPNF XIII, 76

174. The worth of the sacraments does not depend on the probity of the minister.

ST. JOHN CHRYSOSTOM
See No. 426.

For it may be that rulers are wicked and polluted, and their subjects good and virtuous; that laymen may live in piety, and priests in wickedness; and there could not have been either baptism, or the body of Christ, or oblation, through such, if in every instance grace required

823
(1189)

merit. But as it is, God uses to work even by unworthy persons, and in no respect is the grace of baptism damaged by the conduct of the priest; else would the receiver suffer loss.

HOMILIES ON FIRST CORINTHIANS, 8:2
MG 61, 69
NPNF XII, 44

ST. AUGUSTINE

824
(1645)

When, therefore, it shall be made clear to you that neither the man who administered baptism, nor the man who received it, had a pure conscience, will you give your judgment that he ought to be baptized afresh? You will assuredly neither say nor do anything of the sort. The purity therefore of baptism is entirely unconnected with the purity or impurity of the conscience either of the giver or the recipient.

AGAINST THE LETTERS OF PETILIAN,
THE DONATIST, Bk. 2, Ch. 35
ML 43, 288
NPNF IV, 551

175. To receive the sacraments licitly and with fruit, certain dispositions are required in an adult.

ORIGEN

825
(504)

That which is sanctified through the word of God and prayer (1 Tim. 4:5) does not, in its own nature, sanctify him who uses it, for, if this were so, it would sanctify even him who eats unworthily of the bread of the Lord, and no one on account of this food would become weak or sickly or asleep for something of this kind Paul represented in saying, 'For this cause many among you are weak and sickly and not a few asleep' (1 Cor. 11:30). And in the case of the bread of the Lord, accordingly, there is advantage to him who uses it, when with undefiled mind and pure conscience he partakes of the bread. . . . Now, if 'everything that enters into the mouth goes into the belly and is cast out into the draught' (Mt. 15:17), even the meat which has been sanctified through the word of God and prayer, in accordance with the fact that it is material, goes into the belly and is cast out into the draught, but in respect of the prayer which comes upon it, according to the proportion of the faith, becomes a benefit and is a means of clear vision to the mind which looks to that which is beneficial, and it is not the material of the bread but the word which is said over it which is of advantage to him who eats it not unworthily of the Lord. And these things indeed are said of the typical and symbolical body.

COMMENTARY ON MATTHEW, 11:14

MG 13, 948

ST. AUGUSTINE
See Nos. 824 and 794.

176. The holy Fathers knew of all of our sacraments.

TERTULLIAN

The next question will be, from whom is the interpretation of the sense of those words which contribute to heresies? Why, from the Devil, whose province it is to pervert the truth, who in the mysteries of idols, rivals even the very things of the mysteries of God. He too baptizes some, namely, his own believing and faithful people; he promises a putting away of sin by washing; and, if I yet remember right, Mithra there seals his soldiers in their foreheads: he celebrates also the oblation of bread, and introduces a representation of the resurrection, and purchases a crown under the sword. What shall we say also of his confining the chief priest to marriage with one only? He too has his virgins: he too has his self-restraining ones.

THE PRESCRIPTION OF HERETICS, Ch. 40

ML 2, 54

ANF III, 262

826
(299)

Indeed, up to the present time, [Christ] has not disdained the water which the Creator made wherewith he washes his people; nor the oil with which he anoints them; nor that union of honey and milk by which he gives them nourishment of children; nor the bread by which he represents his own proper body, thus requiring in his very sacraments the 'beggarly elements' of the Creator.

AGAINST MARCION, Bk. 1, Ch. 14

ML 2, 262

See No. 801.   *ANF* III, 281

827
(333)

ST. AUGUSTINE
See No. 176.

BAPTISM

177. Baptism is a true sacrament instituted by Christ.

THE DIDACHE

828
(4)
Regarding baptism, baptize thus. After giving the foregoing instructions, 'Baptize in the name of the Father, and of the Son, and of the Holy Spirit' (Mt. 28:19) in running water. But, if you have no running water, baptize in any other; and if you cannot in cold water, then in warm. But, if the one is lacking, pour the other three times on the head 'in the name of the Father, and Son, and Holy Spirit.' But before the baptism, let the one who baptizes and the one to be baptized fast, and any others who are able to do so. And you shall require the person being baptized to fast for one or two days.

Ch. 7
F 1, 16
FC I, 177

LETTER TO BARNABAS

829
(34)
This means that we go down into the water full of sins and foulness, and we come up bearing fruit in our hearts, fear and hope in Jesus in the Spirit.

Ch. 11:11
MG 2, 760
FC I, 210

ST. JUSTIN MARTYR
See No. 324.

TERTULLIAN
See No. 826.

830
(302)
Happy is the sacrament of our water, in that, by washing away the sins of our early blindness, we are set free, [and admitted] into eternal life! . . . But we, little fishes, after the example of our IXTHUS Jesus Christ, are born in water, nor have we safety in any other way than by permanently abiding in [that] water.

ON BAPTISM, Ch. 1
ML 1, 1197
ANF III, 669

See No. 801.

APHRAATES
See No. 336.

ST. EPHRAEM
See No. 519.

ST. AMBROSE

Things which are impossible with men are possible with God; and God   831
is able whensoever He wills to forgive us our sins, even those which   (1297)
we think cannot be forgiven. And so it is possible for God to give us
that which it seems to us impossible to obtain. For it seemed impossible
that water should wash away sin. . . . But that which was impossible
God made to be possible, Who gave us so great grace. In like manner
it seemed impossible that sins should be forgiven through repentance,
but Christ gave this power to His apostles, which has been transmitted
to the priestly office. That, then, has become possible which was
impossible.

ON REPENTANCE, Bk. 2, Ch. 2
ML 16, 499
NPNF X, 346

ST. AUGUSTINE
See No. 794.

178. *The remote matter is natural water.*

THE DIDACHE
See No. 828.

THE SHEPHERD OF HERMAS

A man is dead before he receives the Name of the Son of God, but,   832
when he receives the seal, he puts off death and receives life. The seal,   (92)
therefore is water. The dead go down into the water and come out of it
living.

SIMILITUDES, 9, 16:3
MG 2, 995
FC I, 333–334

425

ST. JUSTIN MARTYR
See No. 324.

TERTULLIAN
See No. 830.

ST. AMBROSE

833
(1330)

Therefore read that the three witnesses in baptism, the water, the blood, and the Spirit, are one (1 Jn. 5:8), for if you take away one of these, the Sacrament of Baptism does not exist. For what is water without the cross of Christ? A common element, without any sacramental effect. Nor, again, is there the Sacrament of Regeneration without water: 'For except a man be born again of water and of the Spirit, he cannot enter into the kingdom of God' (Jn. 3:5). Now, even the catechumen believes in the cross of the Lord Jesus, wherewith he too is signed; but unless he be baptized in the Name of the Father, and of the Son, and of the Holy Spirit, he cannot receive remission of sins nor gain the gift of spiritual grace.

ON THE MYSTERIES, Ch. 4:20
ML 16, 394
NPNF X, 319

ST. AUGUSTINE
See No. 798.

179. The proximate matter, however, is the washing with the water.

THE DIDACHE
See No. 828.

ST. JUSTIN MARTYR
See No. 324.

TERTULLIAN
See Nos. 329 and 827.

ST. EPHRAEM
See No. 519.

180. Baptism may be performed by immersion, infusion, or sprinkling.

THE DIDACHE
See No. 828.

THE LETTER TO BARNABAS
See No. 829.

THE SHEPHERD OF HERMAS
See No. 832.

TERTULLIAN
See No. 800.

ST. CYPRIAN
See No. 790.

ST. CYRIL OF JERUSALEM

For you go down into the water, bearing your sins, but the invocation of grace, having sealed your soul, suffers you not afterwards to be swallowed up by the terrible dragon. Having gone down dead in sins, you come up quickened in righteousness.

> CATECHESES, 3:12
> *MG* 33, 441
> *NPNF* VII, 17

834
(812)

And to you, after you had come up from the pool of the sacred streams, was given an Unction, the antetype of that wherewith Christ was anointed; and this is the Holy Spirit.

> CATECHESES, 21:3
> *MG* 33, 1089
> *NPNF* VII, 145–146

835
(841)

181. In the form of baptism, it is essential that there be a distinct expression of God as One and Three.

THE DIDACHE
See No. 828.

ST. JUSTIN MARTYR
See No. 324.

TERTULLIAN
See No. 329.

ST. CYPRIAN

836
(597)
Finally, when, after the resurrection, the apostles are sent by the Lord to the heathen, they are bidden to baptize the Gentiles 'in the name of the Father, and of the Son, and of the Holy Ghost.' How, then, do some say, that a Gentile baptized without, outside the Church, yes, and in opposition to the Church, so that it be only in the name of Jesus Christ, everywhere, and in whatever manner, can obtain remission of sin, when Christ Himself commands the heathen to be baptized in the full and united Trinity?

LETTERS, 73:18
ML 3, 1120
ANF V, 383

ST. GREGORY NAZIANZEN

837
(1000)
In whose name were you baptized? The Father? Good, but that is Jewish. The Son? Good, but Jewish still. The Holy Spirit? Fine. That is perfect.

ORATIONS, 33:17
MG 36, 236
NPNF VII, 334

ST. AMBROSE

838
(1281)
But baptism is complete if one confess the Father, the Son, and the Holy Spirit. If you deny One you overthrow the whole. And just as if you mention in words One only, either the Father or the Son, or the Holy Spirit, and in your belief do not deny either the Father, the Son, or the Holy Spirit, the mystery of the faith is complete, so, too, although you name the Father, Son, and Holy Spirit, and lessen the power of either the Father, the Son, or the Holy Spirit, the whole mystery is made empty.

ON THE HOLY SPIRIT, Bk. 1 Ch. 3
ML 16, 714

See No. 833.

NPNF X, 98

182. The minister of solemn baptism is the bishop and the priest, or, in case of necessity, a deacon.

ST. IGNATIUS OF ANTIOCH
See No. 117.

TERTULLIAN

For concluding our brief subject, it remains to put you in mind also of the due observance of giving and receiving baptism. Of giving it, the chief priest (who is the bishop) has the right: in the next place, the presbyters and deacons, yet not without the bishop's authority, on account of the honor of the church, which being preserved, peace is preserved. Beside these, even laymen have the right; for what is equally received can be equally given. Unless bishops, or priests, or deacons, be on the spot, [ordinary] disciples are called [to the work]. The Word of the Lord ought not to be hidden by any: in like manner, too, baptism, which is equally God's property, can be administered by all. But how much more is the rule of reverence and modesty incumbent on laymen —seeing that these [powers] belong [strictly] to their superiors—lest they assume to themselves the specific function of bishop! Emulation of the episcopal office is the mother of schisms. The most holy apostle has said, that 'all things are lawful, but not all expedient' (1 Cor. 6:12; 10:23). Let it suffice assuredly, in cases of necessity, to avail yourself [of that rule], if at any time circumstance either of place, or of time, or of person compels you [so to do]; for then the steadfast courage of the helper, when the situation of the endangered one is urgent, is exceptionally admissible; inasmuch as he will be guilty of a human creature's loss if he shall refrain from bestowing what he had free liberty to bestow.

839
(310)

ON BAPTISM, Ch. 17
ML 1, 1217
ANF III, 677

ST. CYPRIAN
See No. 819.

ST. CYPRIAN (?)

And thus, as our salvation is founded in the baptism of the Spirit, which for the most part is associated with the baptism of water, if indeed

840
(601)

baptism shall be given by us, let it be conferred in its integrity and with solemnity, and with all those means which are written; and let it be administered without any disconnection of anything. Or if, by the necessity of the case, it should be administered by an inferior cleric, let us await for the result, that it may either be supplied by us, or reserved to be supplied by the Lord.

ANONYMOUS TREATISE ON RE-BAPTISM, Ch. 10
ML 3, 1195
ANF V, 673

ST. JEROME
See No. 806.

183. Any man, using the right matter, form, and intention, baptizes validly, even licitly, in case of necessity.

TERTULLIAN
See No. 839.

841
(366)

It is the authority of the church, and the honor which has acquired sanctity through the joint session of the Order, which has established the difference between the Order and the laity. Accordingly, where there is no joint session of the ecclesiastical Order, you offer, and baptize, and are priest, alone for yourself. . . . Therefore, if you have the *right* of a priest in your own person, in cases of necessity, it behooves you to have likewise the *discipline* of a priest whenever it may be necessary to have the right of a priest. If you are a digamist, do you baptize? If you are a digamist, do you offer? How much more capital [a crime] is it for a digamist laic to act as a priest, when the priest himself, if he turn digamist, is deprived of the power of acting the priest! 'But to necessity,' you say, 'indulgence is granted.' No necessity is excusable which is avoidable. In a word, shun to be found guilty of digamy, and you do not expose yourself to the necessity of administering what a digamist may not lawfully administer. God wills us all to be so conditioned, as to be ready at all times and places to undertake [the duties of] His sacraments. There is 'one God, one faith,' one discipline too. So truly is this the case, that unless the laics as well observe the rules which are to guide the choice of presbyters, how will there be presbyters [at all], who are chosen to that office from among the laics? Hence we are bound to contend that the command to abstain

from second marriage relates *first* to the laic; so long as no other can
be a presbyter than a laic, provided he have been *once for all* a husband.

AN EXHORTATION TO CHASTITY, Ch. 7

ML 2, 922

ANF IV, 54

ST. JEROME
   See No. 806.

184. *And so, even heretics may validly baptize.*

TERTULLIAN
   See No. 126.

ST. CYPRIAN

[To Januarius and other Numidian Bishops, a. 255] We put forward our opinion, not as a new one, but we join with you in equal
agreement, in an opinion long since decreed by our predecessors,
and observed by us,—judging, namely, and holding it for certain
that no one can be baptized abroad outside the Church, since there is
one baptism appointed in the holy Church.

842
(591)

LETTERS, No. 70

ML 3, 1037

ANF V, 375

SEVENTH COUNCIL OF CARTHAGE

Cyprian of Carthage said: The letter which was written to our colleague
Jubaianus very fully expresses my opinion, that, according to evangelical and apostolic testimony, heretics, who are called adversaries of
Christ and Antichrists, when they come to the Church, must be
baptized with the one baptism of the Church, that they may be made
of adversaries, friends, and of Antichrists, Christians.

843
(600)

JUDGMENT OF EIGHTY-SEVEN BISHOPS UNDER ST. CYPRIAN

ML 3, 1074

See No. 840.   *ANF* V, 572

FIRMILIAN
   See No. 169.

431

ST. AMBROSE
See No. 838.

ST. JEROME
See No. 821.

ST. FULGENTIUS
See No. 134.

*185. Baptism is necessary for all for salvation, both children and
adults.*

TERTULLIAN

844
(306)

When, however, the prescript is laid down that 'without baptism, salvation is attainable by none' (chiefly on the ground of that declaration
of the Lord, who says, 'Unless one be born of water, he has not life')
(Jn. 3:5) ...

ON BAPTISM, Ch. 12
ML 1, 1213
ANF III, 674–675

ST. CYPRIAN
See No. 523.

ST. CYRIL OF JERUSALEM

845
(811)

If any man receive not Baptism, he has not salvation; except only
Martyrs, who even without the water receive the kingdom.

CATECHESES, 3:10
MG 33, 440
NPNF VII, 16

ST. JOHN CHRYSOSTOM

846
(1206)

Weep for the unbelievers; weep for those who differ in nowise from
them, those who depart hence without the illumination, without the
seal! They indeed deserve our wailing, they deserve our groans; they
are outside the Palace, with the culprits, with the condemned: for,
'Verily I say unto you, Except a man be born of water and the Spirit,

432

he shall not enter into the kingdom of Heaven' (Jn. 3:5). Mourn for those who have died in wealth and did not from their wealth think of any solace for their soul, who had power to wash away their sins and would not. . . . Let us weep for these; let us assist them according to our power; let us think of some assistance for them, small though it be, yet still let us assist them. How and in what way? By praying and entreating others to make prayers for them, by continually giving to the poor on their behalf. . . . Not in vain did the Apostles order that remembrance should be made of the dead in the dreadful Mysteries. They know that great gain results to them, great benefit; for when the whole people stands with uplifted hands, a priestly assembly, and that awful Sacrifice lies displayed, how shall we not prevail with God by our entreaties for them. And this we do for those who have departed in faith.

HOMILIES ON PHILIPPIANS, 3:4
MG 62, 203
NPNF XIII, 197

ST. AMBROSE
See No. 833.

ST. AUGUSTINE

Whoever says that those children who depart out of this life without partaking of that sacrament shall be made alive in Christ, certainly contradicts the apostolic declaration, and condemns the universal Church, in which it is the practice to lose no time and run in haste to administer baptism to infant children, because it is believed, as an indubitable truth, that otherwise they cannot be made alive in Christ.

847
(1439)

LETTERS, 166:7:21
ML 33, 730
FC XXX, 25

The Christians of Carthage have an excellent name for the sacraments, when they say that baptism is nothing else than 'salvation,' and the sacrament of the body of Christ nothing else than 'life.' Whence, however, was this derived, but from that primitive, as I suppose, and apostolic tradition, by which the Churches of Christ maintain it to be an inherent principle, that without baptism and partaking of the supper of the Lord it is impossible for any man to

848
(1717)

433

attain either to the kingdom of God or to salvation and everlasting life? So much also does Scripture testify.

ON THE MERITS AND REMISSION OF SINS, AND ON THE BAPTISM
OF INFANTS, Bk. 1, Ch. 24

ML 44, 128

See No. 533.   *NPNF* V, 28

849
(1881)   If you wish to be a Catholic, refrain from believing, or saying, or teaching that 'infants which are forestalled by death before they are baptized may yet attain to forgiveness of their original sins.'

ON THE SOUL AND ITS ORIGIN, Bk. 3, Ch. 9

ML 44, 516

See No. 302.   *NPNF* V, 348

ST. LEO THE GREAT
See No. 496.

ST. FULGENTIUS
See No. 134.

186. For adults the baptism of desire can take the place of the baptism of water.

ST. AUGUSTINE

850
(1629)   Nor do I hesitate to put a catholic catechumen burning with divine love before a baptized heretic. . . . For the centurion Cornelius, not yet baptized, is better than Simon baptized. For he was filled with the Holy Spirit before baptism, but the other, after baptism was filled with the evil spirit.

ON BAPTISM, Bk. 4, Ch. 21

ML 43, 172

NPNF IV, 460

187. For adults, and infants as well, martyrdom can take the place of the baptism of water.

TERTULLIAN

851
(309)   We have indeed, likewise, a second font (itself, that is, one with the former) of blood; concerning which the Lord said, 'I have to be

434

baptized with a baptism' (Lk. 12:50), when He had been baptized already. For He had come 'by means of water and blood,' just as John has written; that He might be baptized by the water, glorified by the blood; to make us, in like manner, called by water, chosen by blood. These two baptisms He sent out from the wounds in His pierced side, in order that they who believed in His blood might be bathed with the water; they who had bathed in the water might likewise drink the blood. This is the baptism which both stands in lieu of the fontal bathing when that has not been received, and restores it when lost.

ON BAPTISM, Ch. 16
ML 1, 1217
ANF III, 677

ST. CYPRIAN

Some, as if by human reasoning they were able to make void the truth of the Gospel declaration, object to us the case of catechumens; asking if any one of these, before he is baptized in the Church, should be apprehended and slain on confession of the name, whether he would lose the hope of salvation and the reward of confession, because he had not previously been born again of water? Let men of this kind, who are aiders and favorers of heretics, know therefore, first, that those catechumens hold the sound faith and truth of the Church, and advance from the divine camp to do battle with the devil, with a full and sincere acknowledgment of God the Father, and of Christ, and of the Holy Spirit; then, that they certainly are not deprived of the sacrament of baptism who are baptized with the most glorious and greatest baptism of blood, concerning which the Lord also said, that He had 'another baptism to be baptized with' (Lk. 12:50). But the same Lord declares in the Gospel, that those who are baptized in their own blood, and sanctified by suffering, are perfected, and obtain the grace of the divine promise, when He speaks to the thief believing and confessing in His very passion, and promises that he should be with Himself in paradise.

852
(598)

LETTERS, No. 73:22
ML 3, 1124
ANF V, 385

ST. CYRIL OF JERUSALEM
See No. 845.

ST. GREGORY NAZIANZEN

853
(1010)
I know also a Fourth Baptism (besides that of Moses, John, and Jesus)—that by Martyrdom and blood, which also Christ Himself underwent; —and this one is far more august than all the others, inasmuch as it cannot be defiled by after-stains.

ORATIONS, 39:17
MG 36, 356
NPNF VII, 358

ST. AUGUSTINE

854
(1759)
For whatever unbaptized persons die confessing Christ, this confession is of the same efficacy for the remission of sins as if they were washed in the sacred font of baptism. For He who said, 'Except a man be born of water and of the Spirit, he cannot enter into the kingdom of God' (Jn. 3:5), made also an exception in their favor, in that other sentence where He no less absolutely said, 'Whosoever shall confess me before men, him will I confess also before my Father Who is in heaven' (Mt. 10:32).

THE CITY OF GOD, Bk. 13, Ch. 7
ML 41, 381
NPNF II, 248

ST. FULGENTIUS
See No. 134.

188. *The Church has always recognized that even infants are capable of receiving baptism.*

TERTULLIAN
See No. 839.

ST. AUGUSTINE
See No. 847.

855
(1440)
The blessed Cyprian, indeed, said, in order to correct those who thought that an infant should not be baptized before the eighth day, that it was not the body but the soul which behoved to be saved from perdition—in which statement he was not inventing any new doctrine, but preserving the firmly established faith of the Church; and he,

436

along with some of his colleagues in the episcopal office, held that a child may be properly baptized immediately after its birth.

LETTERS, 166:8
ML 33, 731
FC **XXX**, 27–28

If any man, however, is still perplexed by the question why the children of baptized persons are baptized, let him briefly consider this: . . . The sacrament of baptism is undoubtedly the sacrament of regeneration. Wherefore, as the man who has never lived cannot die, and he who has never died cannot rise again, so he who has never been born cannot be born again. From which the conclusion arises, that no one who has not been born could possibly have been born again in his father.

856
(1725)

ON THE MERITS AND REMISSION OF SINS, AND THE BAPTISM
OF INFANTS, 2:27
ML 44, 177
NPNF V, 62

189. *The effect of baptism is a spiritual regeneration, which consists in the remission of every sin and punishment and the infusion of the first grace.*

LETTER TO BARNABAS
See No. 829.

THE SHEPHERD OF HERMAS
See No. 832.

ST. THEOPHILUS OF ANTIOCH
See No. 788.

ST. IRENAEUS
See No. 536.

TERTULLIAN
See Nos. 830, 800, and 801.

ST. CLEMENT OF ALEXANDRIA
See No. 625.

ST. CYPRIAN
See No. 574.

ST. METHODIUS
See No. 642.

APHRAATES
See No. 487.

ST. CYRIL OF JERUSALEM
See No. 834.

ST. AMBROSE
See No. 805.

ST. AUGUSTINE
See Nos. 580, 526, and 856.

857
(1768)

As, then, there are two regenerations, of which I have already made mention, —the one according to faith, and which takes place in the present life by means of baptism; the other according to the flesh, and which shall be accomplished in its incorruption and immortality by means of the great and final judgment, —so are there also two resurrections, —the one the first and spiritual resurrection, which has place in this life, and preserves us from coming into the second death; the other the second, which does not occur now, but in the end of the world, and which is of the body, not of the soul, and which by the last judgment shall dismiss some into the second death, others into that life which has no death.

THE CITY OF GOD, Bk. 20, Ch. 6
ML 41, 666
NPNF II, 426

858
(1874)

By this laver of regeneration and word of sanctification all the evils of regenerate men of whatever kind are cleansed and healed, —not the sins only which are all now remitted in baptism, but those also which after baptism are committed by human ignorance and frailty; not, indeed, that baptism is to be repeated as often as sin is repeated, but that by its one only ministration it comes to pass that pardon is secured to the faithful of all their sins both before and after their regeneration.

ON MARRIAGE AND CONCUPISCENCE, Bk. 1, Ch. 33
ML 23, 163
NPNF V, 279

CONFIRMATION

190. Confirmation is a true sacrament.

ST. THEOPHILUS OF ANTIOCH

Are you unwilling to be anointed with the oil of God? Wherefore we are called Christians on this account, because we are anointed with the oil of God.

859
(174)

TO AUTOLYCUS, Ch. 1:12
MG 6, 1041
ANF II, 92

TERTULLIAN
See Nos. 800, 827, and 801.

ST. CYPRIAN
See Nos. 808 and 803.

ST. CYRIL OF JERUSALEM

But beware of supposing this to be plain ointment. For as the Bread of the Eucharist, after the invocation of the Holy Spirit is mere bread no longer, but the Body of Christ, so also this holy ointment is no more simple ointment, nor (so to say) common, after invocation, but it is Christ's gift of grace, and, by the advent of the Holy Spirit, is made fit to impart His Divine Nature. Which ointment is symbolically applied to your forehead and your other senses; and while your body is anointed with the visible ointment, your soul is sanctified by the Holy and life-giving Spirit.

860
(842)

CATECHESES, 21:3
MG 33, 1089
NPNF VII, 150

ST. JEROME
See No. 205.

ST. AUGUSTINE
See No. 794.

191. The remote matter is blessed oil (chrism).

TERTULLIAN
See No. 827.

ST. CYRIL OF JERUSALEM
See No. 835.

ST. BASIL
See No. 203.

*192. The proximate matter is the unction of the chrism made on
the forehead in the form of a cross.*

TERTULLIAN
See Nos. 826 and 800.

ST. CYPRIAN
See No. 808.

ST. CYRIL OF JERUSALEM
See Nos. 860 and 808.

ST. BASIL
See No. 203.

ST. AUGUSTINE
See No. 796.

193. The ordinary minister of confirmation is the bishop.

ST. JEROME
See No. 806.

194. The extraordinary minister is any priest.

ST. GREGORY THE GREAT

861
(2294)
It has also come to our ears that some have been offended by our having
forbidden presbyters to touch with chrism those who are to be baptized.

And we indeed acted according to the ancient use of our Church: but, if any are in fact hereby distressed, we allow that, where there is a lack of bishops, presbyters may touch with chrism, even on their foreheads, those who are to be baptized.*

LETTER TO BISHOP JANUARIUS, Bk. 4, No. 26
ML 77, 696
NPNF XII, 153

195. The effect of confirmation is a more abundant effusion of grace and of the gifts of the Holy Spirit.

TERTULLIAN
See No. 801.

ST. CYRIL OF JERUSALEM
See No. 860.

THE EUCHARIST

THE REAL PRESENCE

196. The sacrament of the Eucharist was instituted by Christ in memory of His passion and death.

ST. JUSTIN MARTYR

'And the offering of fine flour, sirs,' I said, 'which was prescribed to be presented on behalf of those purified from leprosy, was a type of the bread of the Eucharist, the celebration of which our Lord Jesus Christ prescribed, in remembrance of the suffering which He endured on behalf of those who are purified in soul from all inquity. . . . Hence God speaks by the mouth of Malachi, one of the twelve [prophets] as I said before, about the sacrifices at that time presented by you: "I have no pleasure in you, says the Lord; and I will not accept your sacrifices at your hands: for, from the rising of the sun unto the going down of

862
(135)

* This is a disputed passage; it may not refer to confirmation.

the same, My name has been glorified among the Gentiles, and in every place incense is offered to My name, and a pure offering: for My name is great among the Gentiles, says the Lord: but you profane it." '

DIALOGUE WITH TRYPHO, Ch. 41
MG 6, 564
ANF I, 215

ST. JOHN CHRYSOSTOM

863
(1192)

'The cup of blessing which we bless, is it not a communion of the Blood of Christ?' (1 Cor. 10:16). Very persuasively spoke he, and with awe. For what he says is this: 'This which is in the cup is that which flowed from His side, and of that do we partake.' But he called it a cup of blessing, because holding it in our hands, we so exalt Him in our hymn, wondering, astonished at His unspeakable gift, blessing Him, among other things, for the pouring it out, but also for the imparting thereof to us all. 'Wherefore if you desire blood,' says He, 'redden not the altar of idols with the slaughter of brute beasts, but My altar with My blood.' Tell me, what can be more tremendous than this? What more tenderly kind?

HOMILIES ON FIRST CORINTHIANS, 24:1
MG 61, 199
NPNF XII, 138

864
(1195)

When you see [the Body of Christ] set before you, say to yourself: 'Because of this Body I am no longer earth and ashes, no longer a prisoner, but free: because of this I hope for heaven, and to receive the good things therein, immortal life, the portion of angels, converse with Christ; this Body, nailed and scourged, was more than death could stand against. . . . This is even that Body, the blood-stained, the pierced, and that out of which gushed the saving fountains, the one of blood, the other of water, for all the world.' . . . This Body has He given to us both to hold and to eat; a thing appropriate to intense love.

HOMILIES ON FIRST CORINTHIANS, 24:4
MG 61, 203
NPNF XII, 143

ST. AMBROSE

865
(1270)

'My Flesh is meat indeed, and My Blood is drink' (Jn. 6:56). You hear Him speak of His Flesh and of His Blood, you perceive the sacred pledges (conveying to us the merits and power) of the Lord's death, and you dishonor His Godhead? Hear His own words: 'A spirit has not flesh and bones' (Lk. 24:39). Now we, as often as we receive the Sacramental Elements, which by the mysterious efficacy of holy prayer are transformed into the Flesh and the Blood, 'do show the Lord's Death' (1 Cor. 11:26).

TO GRATIAN, ON THE CHRISTIAN FAITH, Bk. 4, Ch. 10
ML 16, 641
NPNF X, 278

ST. AUGUSTINE

You ought to know what you have received, what you are going to receive, and what you ought to receive daily. That Bread which you see on the altar, consecrated by the word of God, is the Body of Christ. That chalice, or rather, what the chalice holds, consecrated by the word of God, is the Blood of Christ. Through those accidents the Lord wished to entrust to us His Body and the Blood which He poured out for the remission of sins. If you have received worthily, you are what you have received, for the Apostle says: 'The bread is one; we though many, are one body' (1 Cor. 10:17). Thus he explained the Sacrament of the Lord's table: 'The bread is one; we though many, are one body.' So, by bread you are instructed as to how you ought to cherish unity. Was that bread made of one grain of wheat? Were there not, rather, many grains? However, before they became bread, these grains were separate; they were joined together in water after a certain amount of crushing.

866
(1519)

SERMONS, No. 227
ML 38, 1099
FC XXXVIII, 195–196

'Except you eat the flesh of the Son of man,' Christ says, 'and drink His blood, you have no life in you' (Jn. 6:54). This seems to enjoin a crime or a vice; it is therefore a figure, enjoining that we should have a share in the sufferings of our Lord, and that we should retain a sweet and profitable memory of the fact that His flesh was wounded and crucified for us.

867
(1587)

ON CHRISTIAN DOCTRINE, Bk. 3, Ch. 16
ML 34, 74
NPNF II, 563

868
(1604)

'He that offers the sacrifice of praise glorifies me, and in this way will I show him my salvation' (Ps. 49:23). Before the coming of Christ, the flesh and blood of this sacrifice were foreshadowed in the animals slain; in the passion of Christ the types were fulfilled by the true sacrifice; after the ascension of Christ, this sacrifice is commemorated in the sacrament.

REPLY TO FAUSTUS THE MANICHAEAN, 21:20
ML 42, 385
NPNF IV, 262

869
(1652)

[Paul] was able to preach the Lord Jesus Christ significantly, in one way by his tongue, in another by epistle, in another by the sacrament of His body and blood (since, certainly, we do not call either the tongue of the apostle, or the parchments, or the ink, or the significant sounds which his tongue uttered, or the alphabetical signs written in skins, the body and blood of Christ; but that only which we take of the fruits of the earth and consecrate by mystic prayer, and then receive duly to our spiritual health in memory of the passion of our Lord for us.

ON THE TRINITY, Bk. 3, Ch. 4
ML 42, 873
NPNF III, 59

197. *In the words which John records (6:48 ff.) Christ promised that He would give Himself, flesh and blood, in a real sense, in food and drink.*

ST. CYPRIAN

870
(559)

'I am the bread of life which came down from heaven. If any man eat of my bread he shall live forever. Moreover, the bread that I shall give is my flesh for the life of the world' (Jn. 6:51, 2). Since then He says that, if anyone eats of His bread, he lives forever, as it is manifest that they live who attain to His body and receive the Eucharist by right of communion, so on the other hand we must fear and pray lest anyone, while he is cut off and separated from the body of Christ, remain apart from salvation, as He Himself threatens, saying: 'Unless you eat the flesh of the Son of Man and drink His blood, you shall not have life in you' (Jn. 6:54). And so we petition that our bread, that is Christ, be given us daily, so that we, who abide and live in Christ, may not withdraw from His sanctification and body.

THE LORD'S PRAYER, Ch. 18
ML 4, 531
FC XXXVI, 142–143

ST. HILARY

We speak in an absurd and godless manner about the divinity of Christ's nature in us—unless we have learned it from Him. He Himself declares: 'For my flesh is food indeed, and my blood is drink indeed. He who eats my flesh and drinks my blood abides in me and I in him' (Jn. 6:56, 7). It is no longer permitted us to raise doubts about the true nature of the body and the blood, for, according to the statement of the Lord Himself as well as our faith, this is indeed flesh and blood. And these things that we receive bring it about that we are in Christ and Christ is in us. Is not this the truth? Those who deny that Jesus Christ is the true God are welcome to regard these words as false. He Himself, therefore, is in us through His flesh, and we are in Him, while that which we are with Him is in God.

ON THE TRINITY, Bk. 8, Ch. 14
ML 10, 247
FC XXV, 286

871
(870)

ST. BASIL

It is good and beneficial to communicate every day, and to partake of the holy body and blood of Christ. For He distinctly says, 'He that eats my flesh and drinks my blood has eternal life' (Jn. 6:55). And who doubts that to share frequently in life, is the same thing as to have manifold life. I, indeed, communicate four times a week, on the Lord's day, on Wednesday, on Friday, and on the Sabbath, and on the other days if there is a commemoration of any Saint. It is needless to point out that for anyone in times of persecution to be compelled to take the communion in his own hand without the presence of a priest or minister is not a serious offence, as long custom sanctions this practice from the facts themselves. All the solitaries in the desert, where there is not a priest, take the communion themselves, keeping communion at home.

LETTERS, No. 93
MG 32, 484
NPNF VIII, 179

872
(916)

ST. AMBROSE
See No. 865.

ST. AUGUSTINE

873
(1480)

'Except a man eat my flesh, he shall not have eternal life' (Jn. 6:54). Some received this foolishly [the Capharnaites], they thought of it carnally, and imagined that the Lord would cut off parts from His body, and give unto them; . . . But He instructed them, and said unto them, 'It is the Spirit that quickens, but the flesh profits nothing; the words that I have spoken unto you, they are spirit, and they are life' (ib. 64). Understand spiritually what I have said; you are not to eat this body which you see; nor to drink that blood which they who will crucify Me shall pour forth. I have commended unto you a certain mystery; spiritually understood, it will quicken you. Although it is needful that this be visibly celebrated, yet it must be spiritually understood.

EXPOSITIONS ON THE PSALMS, 98:9
ML 37, 1264

· See No. 867.   *NPNF* VIII, 488

874
(1824)

'My flesh,' He says, 'is for the life of the world' (Jn. 6:52). Believers know the body of Christ, if they neglect not to be the body of Christ. Let them become the body of Christ, if they wish to live by the Spirit of Christ. None lives by the Spirit of Christ but the body of Christ. . . . It is for this that the Apostle Paul, expounding this bread, says: 'One bread,' says he, 'we being many are one body' (1 Cor. 10:17). O mystery of piety! O sign of unity! O bond of charity! He that would live has where to live, has whence to live. Let him draw near, let him believe; let him be embodied, that he may be made to live.

ON THE GOSPEL OF ST. JOHN, Tr. 26:13
ML 35, 1612
NPNF VII, 172

ST. LEO THE GREAT

875
(2214)

For when the Lord says, 'unless you have eaten the flesh of the Son of Man, and drunk His blood, you will not have life in you' (Jn. 6:54), you ought so to be partakers at the Holy Table, as to have no doubt whatever concerning the reality of Christ's Body and Blood. For that is taken in the mouth which is believed in Faith, and it is vain for them to respond Amen who dispute that which is taken.

SERMONS, No. 91:3
ML 54, 452
NPNF XII, 202

198. Christ is really present in the Eucharist under the species of bread and wine.

ST. IGNATIUS OF ANTIOCH
See No. 116.

[The Docetics] abstain from the Eucharist and from prayer, because they do not admit that the Eucharist is the flesh of our Savior Jesus Christ, the flesh which suffered for our sins and which the Father, in His graciousness, raised from the dead. And so denying the gift of God, these men perish in their disputatiousness. It would be better for them to love and so to rise again. (It is well for you to keep away from such persons and not even to speak of them in private or in public. It is better to keep to the prophets and especially to the Gospel in which the passion is presented and the resurrection is an accomplished fact.)

876
(64)

LETTER TO THE SMYRNAEANS, Ch. 6:3–7
MG 5, 713
FC I, 120–121

ST. JUSTIN MARTYR
See No. 24.

ST. IRENAEUS
See No. 433.

TERTULLIAN
See Nos. 827 and 801.

ST. CLEMENT OF ALEXANDRIA

Now, the blood of the Lord is twofold: one is corporeal, redeeming us from corruption; the other is spiritual, and it is with that we are anointed. To drink the blood of Jesus is to participate in His incorruption. Yet, the Spirit is the strength of the Word in the same way that the blood is of the body. Similarly, wine is mixed with water and the Spirit is joined to man; the first, the mixture, provides feasting

877
(410)

that faith may be increased; the other, the Spirit, leads us on to incorruption. The union of both, that is, of the potion and the Word, is called the Eucharist, a gift worthy of praise and surpassingly fair; those who partake of it are sanctified in body and soul, for it is the will of the Father that man, a composite made by God, be united to the Spirit and to the Word mystically.

CHRIST THE EDUCATOR, Bk. 2, Ch. 2
MG 8, 409
FC XXIII, 111

ST. CYRIL OF JERUSALEM

878
(845)
Wherefore with full assurance let us partake as of the Body and Blood of Christ: for in the figure of Bread is given to you His Body, and in the figure of Wine His Blood; that you by partaking of the Body and Blood of Christ, may be made of the same body and the same blood with Him. For thus we come to bear Christ in us, because His Body and Blood are distributed through our members; thus it is that, according to the blessed Peter, we become partakers of the divine nature (2 Pet. 1:4).

CATECHESES, 22:3
MG 33, 1100
NPNF VII, 151

879
(848)
Having learnt these things, and been fully assured that the seeming bread is not bread, though sensible to taste, but the Body of Christ; and that the seeming wine is not wine, though the taste will have it so, but the Blood of Christ; and that of this David sung of old, saying, "And bread strengthens man's heart, to make his face to shine with oil" (Ps. 103:15), strengthen your heart by partaking thereof as spiritual, and make the face of your soul to shine.

CATECHESES, 22:9
MG 33, 1104
NPNF VII, 152

ST. HILARY
See No. 871.

ST. JOHN CHRYSOSTOM
See Nos. 14 and 863.

880
(1194)
'For we, who are many, are one bread, one body' (1 Cor. 10:17). 'For why speak I of communion?' says he, 'we are that self-same body.'

For what is the bread? The Body of Christ. And what do they become who partake of it? The Body of Christ: not many bodies, but one body. For as the bread consisting of many grains is made one, so that the grains nowhere appear; they exist indeed, but their difference is not seen by reason of their conjunction; so are we conjoined both with each other and with Christ: there not being one body for you, and another for your neighbor to be nourished by, but the very same for all.

HOMILIES ON FIRST CORINTHIANS, 24:2
MG 61, 200
See No. 864.   NPNF XII, 140

The Offering is the same, whether a common man, or Paul or Peter offer it. It is the same which Christ gave to His disciples, and which the Priests now minister. This is nowise inferior to that, because it is not men that sanctify even this, but the Same who sanctified the one sanctifies the other also. For as the words which God spake are the same which the Priest now utters, so is the Offering the same, and the Baptism, that which He gave. Thus the whole is of faith. The Spirit immediately fell upon Cornelius, because he had previously fulfilled his part, and contributed his faith (cf. Acts 10:44). And this is His Body, as well as that. And he who thinks the one inferior to the other, knows not that Christ even now is present, even now operates.

881
(1207)

HOMILIES ON SECOND TIMOTHY, 2:4
MG 62, 612
NPNF XIII, 483

ST. AMBROSE

Perhaps you will say, 'I see something else, how is it that you assert that I receive the Body of Christ?' And this is the point which remains for us to prove. And what evidence shall we make use of? Let us prove that this is not what nature made, but what the blessing consecrated, and the power of blessing is greater than that of nature, because by blessing nature itself is changed.

882
(1333)

ON THE MYSTERIES, 9:50
ML 16, 405
NPNF X, 324

In that sacrament [of the Eucharist] is Christ, because it is the Body of Christ, it is therefore not bodily food but spiritual. Whence the

883
(1334)

449

Apostle says of its type: 'Our fathers ate spiritual food and drank spiritual drink' (1 Cor. 10:3, 4), for the Body of God is a spiritual body.

ON THE MYSTERIES, 9:58
ML 16, 408
NPNF X, 325

ST. AUGUSTINE
See Nos. 866 and 869.

ST. LEO THE GREAT
See No. 875.

ST. JOHN OF DAMASCUS
See No. 720.

199. The truth of the real Presence is evident from the words of institution.

ST. JUSTIN MARTYR
See No. 24.

ST. IRENAEUS

884
(232)
Again, giving directions to His disciples to offer to God the first-fruits of His own created things—not as if He stood in need of them, but that they might be themselves neither unfruitful nor ungrateful—He took that created thing, bread, and gave thanks, and said, 'This is My Body' (Mt. 26:26). And the cup likewise, which is part of that creation to which we belong, He confessed to be His blood, and taught the new oblation of the new covenant; which the Church receiving from the apostles, offers to God throughout all the world, to Him who gives us as the means of subsistence the first-fruits of His own gifts in the New Testament, concerning which Malachi, among the twelve prophets, thus spoke beforehand: 'I have no pleasure in you, says the Lord Omnipotent, and I will not accept sacrifice at your hands. For from the rising of the sun, unto the going down [of the same], My name is glorified among the Gentiles, and in every place incense is offered to My name, and a pure sacrifice; for great is My name among the Gentiles, said the Lord Omnipotent' (Mal. 1:10f.); —indicating

in the plainest manner, by these words, that the former people [the Jews] shall indeed cease to make offerings to God, but that in every place sacrifice shall be offered to Him, and that a pure one; and His name is glorified among the Gentiles.

AGAINST HERESIES, Bk. 4, Ch. 17
MG 7, 1023
ANF I, 484

Moreover, how could the Lord, with any justice, if He belonged to another father, have acknowledged the bread to be His body, while He took it from that creation to which we belong, and affirmed the mixed cup to be His blood?

885
(240)

AGAINST HERESIES, Bk. 4, Ch. 33
MG 7, 1073
ANF I, 507

ST. CYRIL OF JERUSALEM

Even of itself the teaching of the blessed Paul (1 Cor. 11:23) is sufficient to give you a full assurance concerning those Divine Mysteries, of which having been deemed worthy, you are become of the same body and blood with Christ. For you have just heard him say distinctly, That Our Lord Jesus Christ in the night in which He was betrayed, took bread, and when He had given thanks He broke it, and gave to His disciples, saying, 'Take, eat, this is My Body'; and having taken the cup and given thanks, He said, 'Take, drink, this is My Blood' (Mt. 26:26ff.). Since then He Himself declared and said of the Bread, This is My Body, who shall dare to doubt any longer? And since He has Himself affirmed and said, This is My Blood, who shall ever hesitate, saying, that it is not His Blood?

886
(843)

CATECHESES, 22:1
MG 33, 1097
NPNF VII, 151

ST. JOHN CHRYSOSTOM
See No. 14.

ST. AUGUSTINE

How was Christ carried in His Own Hands? Because when He commended His Own Body and Blood, He took into His Hands that which

887
(1464)

the faithful know; and in a manner carried Himself, when He said, 'This is My Body.'

EXPOSITIONS ON THE PSALMS, No. 33:1:10
ML 36, 306
NPNF VIII, 73

ST. JOHN OF DAMASCUS
See No. 720.

200. *This Presence of Christ does not depend on the faith and disposition of the receiver.*

ORIGEN
See No. 825.

ST. AUGUSTINE

888
(1820)
'Jesus answered and said unto them, This is the work of God, that you believe on Him whom He has sent' (Jn. 6:29). This is then to eat the meat, not that which perishes, but that which endures unto eternal life. To what purpose do you make ready teeth and stomach? Believe, and you have eaten already.

ON THE GOSPEL OF ST. JOHN, 25:12
ML 35, 1602
NPNF VII, 164

201. *The bread and wine through the words of consecration are converted into the body and blood of Christ.*

ST. CYRIL OF JERUSALEM

889
(840)
For as the Bread and Wine of the Eucharist before the invocation of the Holy and Adorable Trinity were simple bread and wine, while after the invocation the Bread becomes the Body of Christ, and the Wine the Blood of Christ, so in like manner such meats belonging to the pomp of Satan, though in their own nature simple, become profane by the invocation of the evil spirit.

CATECHESES, 19:7
MG 33, 1072
NPNF VII, 145

He once in Cana of Galilee, turned the water into wine, akin to blood, and is it incredible that He should have turned wine into blood? When called to a bodily marriage, He miraculously wrought that wonderful work; and on the children of the bridechamber, shall He not much rather be acknowledged to have bestowed the fruition of His Body and Blood?

890
(844)

CATECHESES, 22:2
MG 33, 1097

See No. 435.

NPNF VII, 151

ST. GREGORY OF NYSSA

Since it has been shown that in no other way was it possible for our body to become immortal, but by participating in incorruption through its fellowship with that immortal Body, it will be necessary to consider how it was possible that that one Body, being for ever portioned to so many myriads of the faithful throughout the whole world, enters, through that portion, whole into each individual, and yet remains whole in itself . . . which Body also by the indwelling of God the Word was transmuted to the dignity of Godhead. Rightly, then, do we believe that now also the bread which is consecrated by the Word of God is changed into the Body of God the Word. For that Body was once, by implication, bread, but has been consecrated by the inhabitation of the Word that tabernacled in the flesh. Therefore, from the same cause as that by which the bread that was transformed in that Body was changed to a Divine potency, a similar result takes place now. For as in that case, too, the grace of the Word used to make holy the Body, the substance of which came of the bread, and in a manner was itself bread, so also in this case the bread, as says the Apostle, 'is sanctified by the Word of God and prayer'; not that it advances by the process of eating to the stage of passing into the body of the Word, but it is at once changed into the body by means of the Word, as the Word itself said, 'This is My Body.' . . . By dispensation of His grace, He disseminates Himself in every believer through that flesh, whose substance comes from bread and wine, blending Himself with the bodies of believers, to secure that, by this union with the immortal, man, too, may be a sharer in incorruption. He gives these gifts by virtue of the benediction through which He trans-elements the natural quality of these visible things to that immortal thing.

891
(1035)

THE GREAT CATECHISM, Ch. 37
MG 45, 93
NPNF V, 504–506

ST. AMBROSE
See Nos. 865 and 882.

ST. JOHN OF DAMASCUS
See No. 720.

202. The matter of the Eucharist is bread and wine.

ST. JUSTIN MARTYR
See No. 24.

ST. CYPRIAN

892
(581)

[To Caecilian] 'You are a priest forever, after the order of Melchisedech' (Ps. 109:4); which order is assuredly this coming from that sacrifice and thence descending; that Melchisedech was a priest of the most high God; that he offered wine and bread; that he blessed Abraham. For who is more a priest of the most high God than our Lord Jesus Christ, who offered a sacrifice to God the Father, and offered that very same thing which Melchisedech had offered, that is, bread and wine, His body and blood?

> LETTERS, No. 63:4
> *ML* 4, 376
> *ANF* V, 359

893
(582)

[To Caecilian] In which portion we find that the cup which the Lord offered was mixed, and that that was wine which He called His blood. Whence it appears that the blood of Christ is not offered 'if there be no wine in the cup, nor the Lord's sacrifice celebrated with a legitimate consecration unless our oblation and sacrifice respond to His passion.

> LETTERS, No. 63:9
> *ML* 4, 380
> *ANF* V, 361

ST. CYRIL OF JERUSALEM
See No. 889.

ST. AUGUSTINE
See No. 866.

203. The minister of the Eucharist to be confected is the priest.

ST. IGNATIUS OF ANTIOCH
See No. 117.

ST. CYPRIAN

For if Jesus Christ, our Lord and God, is Himself the chief priest of God the Father, and has first offered Himself a sacrifice to the Father, and has commanded this to be done in commemoration of Himself, certainly that priest truly discharges the office of Christ, who imitates that which Christ did; and he then offers a true and full sacrifice in the Church to God the Father, when he proceeds to offer it according to what he sees Christ Himself to have offered.

894
(584)

LETTERS, 63:14
ML 4, 385
ANF V, 362

ST. JOHN CHRYSOSTOM
See No. 881.

ST. JEROME

Far be it from me to censure the successors of the apostles, who with holy words consecrate the body of Christ, and who make us Christians. Having the keys of the kingdom of heaven, they judge men to some extent before the day of judgment, and guard the chastity of the bride of Christ.

895
(1345)

See No. 124.

LETTERS (TO HELIODORUS), No. 14
ML 22, 352
NPNF VI, 16

204. For licit and fruitful communion the state of grace is required.

THE DIDACHE

And on the Lord's Day, after you have come together, break bread and offer the Eucharist, having first confessed your offences, so that your

896
(8)

sacrifice may be pure. But let no one who has a quarrel with his neighbor join you until he is reconciled, lest your sacrifice be defiled. For it was said by the Lord: 'In every place and time let there be offered to me a clean sacrifice, because I am the great king'; and also: 'and my name is wonderful among the Gentiles' (Mal. 1:11, 14).

Ch. 14:1
F 1, 32
FC I, 182

TERTULLIAN

897
(368)

A whole day the zeal of faith will direct its pleadings to this quarter: bewailing that a Christian should come from idols into the Church; . . . should apply to the Lord's body those hands which confer bodies on demons. Nor is this sufficient. Grant that it be a small matter, if from other hands they receive what they contaminate; but even those very hands deliver to others what they have contaminated. Idol-artificers are chosen even into the ecclesiastical order. Oh, wickedness! Once did the Jews lay hands on Christ; these mangle His body daily. Oh, hands to be cut off!

ON IDOLATRY, Ch. 7
ML 1, 669
ANF III, 64

ORIGEN
See No. 825.

ST. CYPRIAN

898
(551)

Spurning and despising all these warnings, before their sins have been expiated, before confession of their crime has been made, before their conscience has been purged by the sacrifice and hand of the priest, before the offence of an angry and threatening Lord has been appeased, violence is done to His body and blood, and they sin more against the Lord with their hands and mouth than when they denied the Lord.

THE LAPSED, Ch. 16
ML 4, 479
See No. 802.
FC XXXVI, 71

ST. JOHN CHRYSOSTOM

Consider how indignant you are against the traitor, against them that crucified Him. Look therefore, lest you also yourself become guilty of the body and blood of Christ. They slaughtered the all-holy body, but you receive it in a filthy soul after such great benefits. For neither was it enough for Him to be made man, to be smitten and slaughtered, but He also commingles Himself with us, and not by faith only, but also in very deed makes us His body. What then ought not he to exceed in purity that has the benefit of this sacrifice?

899
(1180)

HOMILIES ON ST. MATTHEW, 82:5
MG 58, 743
NPNF XI, 495

THE HOLY SACRIFICE OF THE MASS

205. The Mass is a true sacrifice.

ST. IRENAEUS
See No. 884.

ST. CYPRIAN
See No. 894.

ST. CYRIL OF JERUSALEM

Then, after the spiritual sacrifice, the bloodless service is completed, over that sacrifice of propitiation we entreat God for the common peace of the Churches; for the welfare of the world; for kings; for soldiers and allies; for the sick; for the afflicted: and, in a word, for all who stand in need of succour we all pray and offer this sacrifice.

900
(851)

CATECHESES, 23:8
MG 33, 1116
NPNF VII, 154

ST. GREGORY NAZIANZEN

901
(1019)

But cease not both to pray and to plead for me when you draw down the Word by your word, when with a bloodless cutting you sever the Body and Blood of the Lord, using your voice for the sword.

LETTERS, 171
MG 37, 280
NPNF VII, 469

ST. JOHN CHRYSOSTOM

902
(1183)

Reverence, now, oh reverence, this Table whereof we all are partakers! Christ, Who was slain for us, the Victim that is placed thereon.

EPISTLE TO THE ROMANS, 8
MG 60, 465

See No. 863.   *NPNF* XI, 394

903
(1193)

And in the old covenant, because they were in an imperfect state, the blood which they used to offer to idols He Himself submitted to receive, that He might separate them from those idols; which very thing again was a proof of His unspeakable affection: but here He transferred the service to that which is far more awesome and glorious, changing the very sacrifice itself, and instead of the slaughter of irrational creatures, commending to offer up Himself.

HOMILIES ON FIRST CORINTHIANS, 24:2
MG 61, 200
NPNF XII, 139

206. The Mass is a representation of the sacrifice of the cross.

ST. CYPRIAN
See No. 893.

ST. AUGUSTINE
See Nos. 868 and 771.

ST. GREGORY THE GREAT

904
(2323)

This Sacrifice alone has the power of saving the soul from eternal death, for it presents to us mystically the death of the only-begotten Son. Though He is now risen from the dead and dies no more, and 'death has no more power over him' (Rom. 6:9), yet, living in Himself immortal and incorruptible, He is again immolated for us in the mystery of the holy Sacrifice. Where His Body is eaten, there His Flesh is distributed among the people for their salvation. His Blood no longer stains the hands of the godless, but flows into the hearts of His faithful followers. See, then, how august the Sacrifice that is offered for us, ever reproducing in itself the passion of the only-begotten Son for the remission of our sins.

DIALOGUES, Bk. 4, 58
ML 77, 425
FC XXXIX, 272–273

207. *Christ is the victim offered in the sacrifice of the Mass.*

ST. CYRIL OF JERUSALEM

And I wish to persuade you by an illustration. For I know that many say, what is a soul profited, which departs from this world whether with sins, or without sins, if it be commemorated in the prayer? For if a king were to banish certain who had given him offence, and then those who belong to them should weave a crown and offer it to him on behalf of those under punishment, would he not grant a remission of their penalties? In the same way we, when we offer to Him our supplications for those who have fallen asleep, though they be sinners, weave no crown, but offer up Christ sacrificed for our sins, propitiating our merciful God for them as well as for ourselves.

905
(853)

CATECHESES, 23:10
MG 33, 1116
NPNF VII, 154–155

ST. JOHN CHRYSOSTOM

For when you see the Lord sacrificed, and laid upon the altar, and the priest standing and praying over the victim, and all the worshippers empurpled with that precious blood, can you then think that you are still among men, and standing upon earth?

906
(1118)

ON THE PRIESTHOOD, Bk. 3, Ch. 4
MG 48, 642

See Nos. 902, 863, and 903.

NPNF IX, 46

PENANCE

208. The Church received from Christ the power of remitting or retaining sins.

TERTULLIAN
See No. 156.

FIRMILIAN
See No. 169.

LACTANTIUS
See No. 131.

ST. JOHN CHRYSOSTOM

907
(1119)

For they who inhabit the earth and make their abode there are entrusted with the administration of things which are in Heaven, and have received an authority which God has not given to angels or archangels. For has it not been said to them, 'Whatsoever you shall bind on earth shall be bound in Heaven, and whatsoever you shall loose on earth shall be loosed in Heaven' (Mt. 18:18)? They who rule on earth have indeed authority to bind, but only the body: whereas this binding lays hold of the soul and penetrates the heavens: and what priests do here below God ratifies above, and the Master confirms the sentence of his servants. For indeed what is it but all manner of heavenly authority which He has given them when He says, 'Whose sins you remit they are remitted, and whose sins you retain they are retained' (Jn. 20:23)? What authority could be greater than this? 'The Father has committed all judgment to the Son' (Jn. 5:22). But I see it all put into the hands of these men by the Son.

ON THE PRIESTHOOD, Bk. 3, Ch. 5
MG 48, 643
NPNF IX, 47

ST. AMBROSE

908
(1287)

See that sins are forgiven through the Holy Spirit. But men make use of their ministry for the forgiveness of sins, they do not exercise the right of any power of their own. For they forgive sins not in their own name but in that of the Father and of the Son and of the Holy Spirit. They ask, the Godhead gives, the service is of man, the gift is of the Power on high.

ON THE HOLY SPIRIT, Bk. 3, Ch. 18
ML 16, 808
See Nos. 820 and 831.   *NPNF* X, 154

ST. JEROME
See No. 895.

ST. AUGUSTINE

Let us not heed those who deny that the Church of God can remit all sins. Failing to recognize in Peter the 'rock', these unhappy souls have accordingly lost possession of the keys; they are unwilling to believe that the keys of the kingdom of heaven have been given to the Church.

909
(1579)

THE CHRISTIAN COMBAT, Ch. 31:33
ML 40, 308
FC IV, 350

209. *This power of remitting or retaining sins extends to all sins committed after baptism.*

ST. IGNATIUS OF ANTIOCH

For, wherever there is division or anger, God has no place. Now God forgives all who repent, so long as their repentance turns to union with God and to communion with the bishop.

910
(59)

LETTER TO THE PHILADELPHIANS, Ch. 8
MG 5, 704
FC I, 116

TERTULLIAN

To all sins, then, committed whether by flesh or spirit, whether by deed or will, the same [God] who has destined penalty by means of judgment, has indeed engaged to grant pardon by means of repentance, saying to the people, 'Repent, and I will save you' (Ezek. 18:21);

911
(312)

461

and again, 'I live, says the Lord, and I will [have] repentance rather than death' (Ezek. 33:11). Repentance, then, is 'life,' since it is preferred to 'death.' That repentance, O sinner, like myself (nay, rather, less than myself, for pre-eminence in sins I acknowledge to be mine), do you so hasten to so embrace, as a shipwrecked man the protection of some plank. This will draw you forth when sunk in the waves of sins, and will bear you forward into the port of the divine clemency.

ON PENANCE, Ch. 4
ML 1, 1233
ANF III, 659

912
(385)

If the sins are deficient in speech, hard by [the door of the church] stands an idolator, hard by stands a murderer; in their midst stands, too, an adulterer. Alike, as the duty of repentance bids, they sit in sackcloth and bristle in ashes; with the self-same weeping they groan; with the self-same prayers they make their circuits; with the self-same knees they supplicate; the self-same mother they invoke. What are you doing, gentlest and most humane Discipline? Either to all these will it be your duty so to be, for 'blessed are the peacemakers'; or else, if not to all, it will be your duty to range yourself on our side. Do you once for all condemn the idolator and the murderer, but take the adulterer out from their midst? —[the adulterer] the successor of the idolater, the predecessor of the murderer, the colleague of each? It is 'an accepting of person': the more pitiable repentances you have left [unpitied] behind!

ON MODESTY, Ch. 5
ML 2, 989
ANF III, 78

913
(386)

But if the clemency of God is applicable to such as are ignorant still, and unbelieving, of course it follows that repentance invites clemency to itself; without prejudice to that species of repentance after believing, which either, for lighter sins, will be able to obtain pardon from the bishop or else, for greater and irremissible ones, from God only.

ON MODESTY, Ch. 18
ML 2, 1017

See No. 156.

ANF III, 94

ST. CYPRIAN

When there has been a withdrawal hence, then there is no opportunity for repentance, no accomplishment of satisfaction. Here life is either lost or kept; here by the worship of God, and by the fruit of faith provision is made for eternal salvation. Let no one either by sins or by years be retarded from coming to the acquiring of salvation. To him who still remains in this world no repentance is too late. The approach to God's forgiveness is open, and for those who seek and understand the truth the access is easy. Although you entreat for your sins at the very end and sunset of temporal life and you implore God who is one and true by the confession and faith of the acknowledgment of Him, pardon is granted to him who confesses, and to him who believes saving forgiveness is conceded out of God's goodness, and there is a crossing into immortality at the very moment of death.

914
(561)

TO DEMETRIAN, Ch. 25
ML 4, 563
FC XXXVI, 190

We certainly think that no one is to be restrained from the fruit of satisfaction, and the hope of peace, since we know, according to the faith of the divine Scriptures, God Himself being their author, and exhorting in them, both that sinners are brought back to repentance, and that pardon and mercy are not denied to penitents.

915
(577)

LETTERS, No. 55:27
ML 3, 793
ANF V, 334-335

But if we find that none ought to be restrained from repenting,* and that peace may be granted by His priests to those who entreat and beseech the Lord's mercy, inasmuch as He is merciful and loving, the groaning of those who mourn is to be admitted, and the fruit of repentance is not to be denied to those who grieve. And because in the place of the departed there is no confession, neither can confession be made there, they who have repented from their whole heart, and have asked for it, ought to be received within the Church, and to be kept in it for the Lord.

916
(578)

LETTERS, No. 55:29
ML 3, 794
ANF V, 335

* Or, "doing penance."

ST. CYRIL OF JERUSALEM

See No. 158.

ST. AMBROSE

917
(1294)

But [the Novatians] say that, with the exception of graver sins, they grant forgiveness to those of less weight. This is not the teaching of your father, Novatian, who thought that no one should be admitted to penance. . . . But God does not make a distinction, Who has promised His mercy to all, and granted to His priests the power of loosing without any exception.

ON REPENTANCE, Bk. 1, Ch. 3
ML 16, 469
NPNF X, 330–331

918
(1298)

Therefore most evidently are we bidden by the teaching of the Lord to confer again the grace of the heavenly sacrament of those guilty even of the greatest sins, if they with open confession bear the penance due to their sin.

ON REPENTANCE, Bk. 2, Ch. 3
ML 16, 501
NPNF X, 347

ST. AUGUSTINE

919
(1501)

Some think that they only sin against the Holy Spirit, who having been washed in the laver of regeneration in the Church, and having received the Holy Spirit, as though unthankful for so great a gift of the Saviour, have plunged themselves afterwards into any deadly sin; as adultery, or murder, or an absolute apostasy, either altogether from the Christian name, or from the Catholic Church. But how this sense of it may be proved, I know not; since the place of repentance is not denied in the Church to any sins whatever.

SERMONS, No. 71
ML 38, 448

See No. 858.

NPNF VI, 320

920
(1919)

But even crimes themselves, however great, may be remitted in the Holy Church; and the mercy of God is never to be despaired of by men who truly repent, each according to the measure of his sin. And in the act of repentance, where a crime has been committed of such a nature as to cut off the sinner from the body of Christ, we are not to take account so much of the measure of time as of the measure of sorrow.

ON FAITH, HOPE, AND LOVE (ENCHIRIDION), Ch. 65
ML 40, 262
NPNF III, 258

210. Of all sins, the greatest were adultery, homicide, and apostasy or heresy.

TERTULLIAN
See No. 912.

ORIGEN

There is the debt of the widow, who is provided for by the Church; the debt of the deacon; that of the priest; and the heaviest of all, that of the bishop exacted from him under penalty of punishment by the Saviour of the whole Church.

921
(473)

ON PRAYER, Ch. 28
MG 11, 524
ACW, 108

And this is their method of procedure, both with those who are sinners, and especially with those who lead dissolute lives . . . [the Christians] lament as dead those who have been vanquished by licentiousness or any other sin, because they are lost and dead to God, and as being risen from the dead (if they manifest a becoming change) they receive them afterwards, at some future time, after a greater interval than in the case of those who were admitted at first, but not placing in any office or post of rank in the church of God those who, after professing the Gospel, lapsed and fell.

922
(526)

AGAINST CELSUS, Bk. 3, Ch. 51
MG 11, 988
ANF IV, 485

ST. CYPRIAN

But if any one of them [virgins consecrated to God] be found to be corrupted, let her abundantly repent, because she who has been guilty

923
(568)

of this crime is an adulteress, not [indeed] against a husband, but against Christ; and therefore, a due time being appointed, let her afterwards, when confession has been made, return to the Church. But if they obstinately persevere, and do not mutually separate themselves, let them know that, with this their immodest obstinacy, they can never be admitted by us into the Church, lest they should begin to set an example to others to go to ruin by their crimes.

LETTERS, No. 4
ML 4, 370
ANF V, 358

ST. BASIL

924
(922)

The woman who has been abandoned by her husband, ought, in my judgment, to remain as she is. The Lord said, 'If any one leave his wife, saving for the cause of fornication, he causes her to commit adultery' (Mt. 5:32); thus, by calling her adulteress, He excludes her from intercourse with another man. For how can the man being guilty, as having caused adultery, and the woman, go without blame, when she is called adulteress by the Lord for having intercourse with another man?

LETTERS, 199
MG 32, 732
NPNF VIII, 240

ST. AUGUSTINE
See No. 919.

211. In the early Church a public penance was imposed for the most serious external crimes.

TERTULLIAN

925
(315)

The narrower, then, the sphere of action of this second and only remaining repentance, the more laborious is its probation; in order that it may not be exhibited in the conscience alone, but may likewise be carried out in some [external] act. This act, which is more usually expressed and commonly spoken of under a Greek name, is ᾽εξομολόγησις, whereby we confess our sins to the Lord, not indeed as if He were ignorant of them, but inasmuch as by confession satisfaction is settled;

466

of confession repentance is born; by repentance God is appeased. And thus exomologesis is a discipline for man's prostration and humiliation, enjoining a demeanor calculated to move mercy. With regard also to the very dress and food, it commands [the penitent] to lie in sackcloth and ashes, to cover his body in mourning, to lay his spirit low in sorrows, to exchange for severe treatment the sins which he has committed; moreover to know no food and drink but such as is plain, —not for the stomach's sake, to wit, but the soul's; for the most part, however, to feed prayers on fastings, to groan, to weep and roar unto the Lord your God; to roll before the feet of the presbyters, and kneel to God's dear ones; to enjoin on all the brethren to be ambassadors to bear his deprecatory supplication [before God]. All this exomologesis [does], that it may enhance repentance; may honor God by its fear of the [incurred] danger; may, by itself pronouncing against the sinner, stand in the stead of God's indignation, and by temporal mortification (I will not say frustrate, but) discharge eternal punishments. Therefore, while it abases the man, it raises him; while it covers him with squalor, it renders him more clean; while it accuses, it excuses; while it condemns, it absolves. The less quarter you give yourself, the more (believe me) will God give you.

ON PENANCE, Ch. 9
ML 1, 1243
ANF III, 664

See No. 912.

ORIGEN
See No. 922.

ST. CYPRIAN
See Nos. 923, 802, and 916.

ST. AUGUSTINE

Vice, however, sometimes makes such inroads among men that, even after they have done penance and have been readmitted to the Sacrament of the altar, they commit the same or more grievous sins, yet God makes His sun to rise even on such men (Mt. 5:45) and gives His gifts of life and health as lavishly as He did before their fall. And although that same opportunity of penance is not again granted them in the Church, God does not forget to exercise His patience toward them. . . . It may therefore be a careful and useful

926
(1435)

enactment that the opportunity of that very humble penance be granted only once in the Church, lest that remedy, by becoming common, be less helpful to sick souls, for it is now more effective by being more respected. Yet, who would dare to say to God: "Why do you pardon this man a second time when he has been caught again in the snare of sin after his first penance?"

LETTERS, No. 153
ML 33, 655
FC XX, 284–285

See No. 580.

212. However, "reconciliation" was made by the imposition of hands, ordinarily by the bishop.

ST. CYPRIAN
See Nos. 923 and 802.

927
(570)

Since, however, I see that there is not yet any opportunity of coming to you, and that the summer has already begun—a season that is disturbed with continual and heavy sickness, —I think that our brethren must be dealt with; —that they who have received certificates from the martyrs, and may be assisted by their privilege with God, if they should be seized with any misfortune and peril of sickness, should, without waiting for my presence, before any presbyter who might be present, or if a presbyter should not be found and death begins to be imminent, before even a deacon, be able to make confession of their sin, that, with the imposition of hands upon them for repentance, they should come to the Lord with the peace which the martyrs have desired, by their letters to us, to be granted to them.

LETTERS, 18:1 (A.D. 250)
ML 4, 259
ANF V, 293

ST. AMBROSE
See No. 805.

ST. AUGUSTINE
See No. 926.

468

213. *Penance is necessary to obtain the remission of sin.*

THE SHEPHERD OF HERMAS

He answered and said: 'Those who repent with their whole heart and cleanse themselves of all the wickedness just described, without ever adding to their former sins, will receive from the Lord a remedy for their former sins. Provided they are not beset by doubt in fulfilling my commandments, they will live to God. But, those who add to their sins and revert to the lusts of this world will bring the judgment of death on themselves.'

928
(90)

SIMILITUDES, 8, 11:3
MG 2, 980
FC I, 316

THE SO-CALLED SECOND LETTER OF ST. CLEMENT OF ROME TO THE CORINTHIANS

While we are still in this world, let us repent with our whole heart of the evil things we have done in the flesh, that we may be saved by the Lord while we have time for repentance. For, after leaving the world, we cannot there confess or repent any more.

929
(103)

8:2
MG 1, 341
FC I, 70

TERTULLIAN
See Nos. 925 and 913.

ST. CYPRIAN

Do full penance, prove the sorrow of a soul that sorrows and laments. Let neither the imprudent error nor the vain stupidity of some move you, who, although they were involved in so grave a crime were struck by such blindness of soul that they neither realized their sins nor lamented them.

930
(554)

THE LAPSED, Ch. 33
ML 4, 491
FC XXXVI, 85

ST. AUGUSTINE
See No. 920.

214. *Some confession not made only to God, but external, is required for the remission of sins.*

THE DIDACHE

931
(3)

You shall confess your offences in church, and shall not come forward to your prayer with a bad conscience. This is the way of life.

Ch. 4:13

F 1, 14

See No. 896.

FC I, 175

LETTER TO BARNABAS

932
(37)

Do not cause quarrels, but bring together and reconcile those who quarrel. Confess your sins. Do not go to prayer with an evil conscience.

Ch. 19:12

MG 2, 780

FC I, 220–221

ST. IRENAEUS

933
(193)

Such are the words and deeds by which, in our own district of the Rhone, they [the gnostic disciples of Marcus] have deluded many women, who have their consciences seared as with a hot iron (1 Tim. 4:2). Some of them, indeed, make a public confession of their sins; but others of them are ashamed to do this, and in a tacit kind of way, despairing of [attaining to] the life of God, have, some of them, apostatized altogether; while others hesitate between the two courses.

AGAINST HERESIES, Bk. 1, Ch. 13

MG 7, 592

ANF I, 336

TERTULLIAN
See No. 925.

934
(316)

Yet [we see] most men either shun this work, as being to public exposure of themselves, or else defer it from day to day. I presume [they do so as being] more mindful of modesty than of salvation; just like men, who, having contracted some malady in the more private parts of the body, avoid the doctors and so perish with their own bashfulness. . . . Grand indeed is the reward of modesty, which the concealment of our fault promises us! If we do hide somewhat from the knowledge of man, shall we equally conceal it from God? Are the judgment of men and the knowledge of God so put upon a par? Is it better to be damned in secret than absolved in public?

ON PENANCE, Ch. 10
ML 1, 1244
ANF III, 664

ST. CYPRIAN
See Nos. 898 and 927.

ST. JOHN CHRYSOSTOM

Let us then also imitate this woman, and in the case of our own sins not be ashamed of men, but fear, as is meet, God who now beholds what is done, and who hereafter punishes those who do not now repent. . . . I exhort you therefore, that although no one see what we do, yet that each of us enter into his own conscience, and set reason for his judge, and bring forward his transgressions, and if he desire them not to be exposed to public view then in that fearful day, let him now heal his wounds, let him apply to them the medicines of repentance.

935
(1164)

HOMILIES ON ST. JOHN, 34:3
MG 59, 196
NPNF IV, 120

ST. AMBROSE
See No. 918.

If you wish to be justified, confess your sin. For a shamefaced confession of sins looses the bands of transgression. You see what God requires of you, that you remember that grace which you have received, and boast not as though you had not received it. You see by how complete a promise of remission He draws you to confession.

936
(1299)

ON REPENTANCE, Bk. 2, Ch. 6
ML 16, 507
NPNF X, 350

471

INDULGENCES

215. Because of the intercession of martyrs some of the canonical penance could be remitted.

ST. CYPRIAN

See Nos. 773, 923, and 927.

216. In the Church there exists a treasury of merits, from which an indulgence for sinners can be applied for punishment due.

ST. AMBROSE

937
(1296)

For he is purged as by certain things done by the whole people, and is washed in the tears of the multitude, and redeemed from sin by the weeping of the multitude, and is purged in the inner man. For Christ granted to His Church that one should be redeemed by means of all, as she herself was found worthy of the coming of the Lord Jesus, in order that through One all might be redeemed.

ON REPENTANCE, Bk. 1, Ch. 15
ML 16, 490
NPNF X, 342

EXTREME UNCTION

217. Extreme unction is a true sacrament, whose effect is to blot out the residue of sin and to increase the forces of the soul and the body.

ST. INNOCENT I

938
(DB 99)

Since your love prompts you to seek advice on this as on other matters, my son Celestine the deacon also mentioned in his letter that Your

Excellency had put up for discussion the text in the epistle of St. James the Apostle: 'If anyone among you is sick, let him call the presbyters, and let them pray over him, anointing him with oil in the name of the Lord. And the prayer of faith will save the sick man, and the Lord will restore him, and if he has sinned, He will forgive him' (Jas. 5:14f.). There is no doubt that this ought to be understood of the faithful who are sick and who can be anointed with the holy oil of chrism which is prepared by a bishop. It is not just priests but all as Christians who may be anointed with this oil when it is necessary for themselves or their families. However, it seems to Us that an idle point is raised when doubt is expressed in the case of a bishop about something that is certainly permitted to priests. For the very reason that it was assigned to priests is that bishops are burdened with other business and are not able to go to all the sick. However, if a bishop is able or thinks someone worthy of a visit from him, then he, whose duty it is to prepare the chrism, can without any hesitation bless and anoint the sick with chrism. But the chrism cannot be poured on those doing penance because this is one of the sacraments. How is it conceivable that one sacrament can be granted to a person to whom the rest of the sacraments are denied?

LETTER TO DECENTIUS
TCT, 322–323

ORDERS

218. Holy Orders is a true sacrament.

ST. BASIL
See No. 804.

ST. AUGUSTINE
See No. 809.

ST. LEO THE GREAT

And finally, now that the mystery of this Divine priesthood has descended to human agency, it runs not by the line of birth, nor is that

939
(2190)

which flesh and blood created, chosen, but without regard to the privilege of paternity and succession by inheritance, those men are received by the Church as its rulers whom the Holy Ghost prepares: so that in the people of God's adoption, the whole body of which is priestly and royal, it is not the prerogative of earthly origin which obtains the unction, but the condescension of Divine grace which creates the bishop.

SERMONS, 3:1

ML 54, 145

NPNF XII, 116

219. *In the Church, the clergy constitute a distinct order from the laity.*

ST. CLEMENT OF ROME
See No. 110.

TERTULLIAN

940
(300)
Even the heretic women, how wanton are they! they who dare to teach, to dispute, to enact exorcisms, to promise cures, perchance also to baptize! Their ordinations are careless, capricious, inconsistent. At one time they place in office novices, at another men tied to the world, at another apostates from us, that they may bind them to themselves by vainglory, since they cannot by truth. Nowhere is promotion readier than in the camp of rebels, where, even to be there, is a merit. Wherefore one man is Bishop today, another tomorrow; today Deacon, who tomorrow will be Reader: today Presbyter, who tomorrow will be Layman; for even to laymen they commit the priestly offices.

THE PRESCRIPTION OF HERETICS, Ch. 41

ML 2, 56

ANF III, 263

See No. 841.

ST. CLEMENT OF ALEXANDRIA
See No. 121.

ST. ATHANASIUS

941
(753)
Theognius, Maris . . . came into our Diocese alleging that they had received orders to investigate certain ecclesiastical affairs, among which

474

they spoke of the breaking of a cup of the Lord, of which information was given them by Ischyras, whom they brought with them, and who says that he is a Presbyter, although he is not, —for he was ordained by the Presbyter Colluthus who pretended to the Episcopate, and was afterwards ordered by a whole Council, by Hosius and the Bishops that were with him, to take the place of a Presbyter, as he was before; and accordingly all that were ordained by Colluthus resumed the same rank which they held before, and so Ischyras himself proved to be a layman.

DEFENSE AGAINST THE ARIANS, ca. 348

MG 25, 385

NPNF IV, 140

ST. BASIL
See No. 804.

ST. JEROME
See No. 895.

220. *Episcopacy, priesthood, and diaconate constitute major orders.*

ST. IGNATIUS OF ANTIOCH
See Nos. 113, 114, and 115.

ST. CLEMENT OF ALEXANDRIA
See Nos. 119 and 120.

ST. JOHN CHRYSOSTOM
See No. 123.

ST. JEROME

The virgin Christ and the virgin Mary have dedicated in themselves the first fruits of virginity for both sexes. The apostles have either been virgins or, though married, have lived celibate lives. Those persons who are chosen to be bishops, priests, and deacons are either virgins or

942
(1350)

widowers; or at least, when once they have received the priesthood, are vowed to perpetual chastity.

LETTERS, 48:21
ML 22, 510
NPNF VI, 79

221. The bishops constitute a superior order to the priests.

ST. CLEMENT OF ROME
See No. 110.

ST. CLEMENT OF ALEXANDRIA
See No. 119.

ST. JOHN CHRYSOSTOM
See No. 123.

ST. JEROME
See Nos. 124 and 806.

222. The deacons are assistants of the bishops and priests in holy functions.

THE DIDACHE
See No. 109.

ST. CLEMENT OF ROME
See No. 103.

ST. IGNATIUS OF ANTIOCH
See No. 167.

ST. JUSTIN MARTYR
See No. 24.

ST. JEROME
See No. 124.

223. *Subdeacons are assistants of the deacons, instituted by the Church at a later time.*

THE CONSTITUTIONS OF THE APOSTLES (ca. 400)

A bishop blesses, he is not blessed; he imposes hands, he ordains, he offers; he receives a blessing from bishops, but never from priests. A bishop deposes every worthy cleric to be deposed, except a bishop; this he cannot do alone. A priest blesses, he is not blessed; he receives blessing from the bishop and co-priest and likewise gives it to co-priest. He imposes hands, he does not ordain; he does not depose, he excommunicates inferiors however if they merit punishment. A deacon does not bless, he does not give a blessing, he receives it however from bishop and priest; he does not baptize nor offer [the Holy Sacrifice]. He can give it to the people, when the bishop or priest has officiated, not as a priest, but as one ministering for priests. None of the other priests can make a deacon, however. A deaconess does not bless, nor do any of those things which priests or deacons do; she only minds the doors and ministers to the priests when they baptize women, for decency sake. A deacon excommunicates a subdeacon, a reader, a cantor, a deaconess, if in the absence of a priest the situation requires it. A subdeacon cannot excommunicate either a cleric or a layman, nor can a reader, a cantor, or a deaconess, for they are the ministers of the deacons.

943
(1236)

8:28:2
MG 1, 1124
ANF VII, 493–494

224. *In the early Church women could be consecrated to God in a special manner as deaconesses or widows; however, they received no order properly so called.*

TERTULLIAN
See No. 940.

ST. CLEMENT OF ALEXANDRIA
See No. 119.

ORIGEN
See No. 921.

225. The matter of orders is the imposition of hands.

ST. CYPRIAN

944
(588)

[To the clergy and people in Spain] For which reason you must diligently observe and keep the practice delivered from divine tradition and apostolic observance, which is also maintained among us, and almost throughout all the provinces; that for the proper celebration of ordinations all the neighboring bishops of the same province should assemble with that people for which a prelate is ordained. And the bishop should be chosen in the presence of the people, who have most fully known the life of each one, and have looked into the doings of each one as respects his habitual conduct. And this also, we see, was done by you in the ordination of our colleague Sabinus; so that, by the suffrage of the whole brotherhood, and by the sentence of the bishops who had assembled in their presence, and who had written letters to you concerning him, the episcopate was conferred upon him, and hands were imposed on him in the place of Basilides.

LETTERS, 67
ML 3, 1027
ANF V, 371

ST. BASIL
See No. 804.

ST. JOHN CHRYSOSTOM
See No. 123.

ST. LEO THE GREAT
See No. 165.

226. The form of orders is the prayer which is conjoined with that imposition.

ST. JOHN CHRYSOSTOM

945
(1214)

See how the writer does not speak superfluously; for he does not say how, but simply that they are ordained through prayer, for this is

478

ordination. The hand of a man is superimposed, God does the whole thing, it is His hand that touches the head of the ordinandus, if it is fitting that in some manner he be ordained.

HOMILIES ON THE ACTS OF THE APOSTLES, 14:3
MG 60, 116
NPNF XI, 90

227. *Already the ancient custom in the Church was that celibacy be imposed on clerics in major orders, or at least that they be prohibited from a second marriage.*

TERTULLIAN
See Nos. 841 and 155.

ST. JEROME
See No. 942.

ST. GREGORY THE GREAT

Three years ago the subdeacons of all the churches in Sicily, in accordance with the custom of the Roman Church, were forbidden all conjugal intercourse with their wives. But it appears to me hard and improper that one who has not been accustomed to such continence, and has not previously promised chastity, should be compelled to separate himself from his wife, and thereby (which God forbid) fall into what is worse. Hence it seems good to me that from the present day all bishops should be told not to presume to make any one a subdeacon who does not promise to live chastely.

946
(2293)

LETTERS, Bk. 1, No. 44
ML 77, 505
NPNF XII, 91

There was a priest who ruled the church entrusted to his care in the fear of the Lord. From the moment of his ordination to the priesthood, he loved his wife as a brother loves his sister, but avoided her as he would an enemy, never allowing her to come near him nor permitting himself an opportunity of going near her. In this way he cut off all possible occasion of familiarity with her.

947
(2319)

DIALOGUES, Bk. 4, Ch. 11
ML 77, 336
FC XXXIX, 203

MATRIMONY

228. The purposes of matrimony are the generation of children, mutual conjugal help, and a remedy for concupiscence.

ST. AUGUSTINE

948
(1642)

Therefore the good of marriage throughout all nations and all men stands in the occasion of begetting, and faith of chastity: but, so far as pertains unto the People of God, also in the sanctity of the Sacrament, by reason of which it is unlawful for one who leaves her husband, even when she has been put away, to be married to another, so long as her husband lives, no not even for the sake of bearing children: and, whereas this is the lone cause, wherefore marriage takes place, not even where that very thing, wherefore it takes place, follows not, is the marriage bond loosed, save by the death of the husband or wife. In like manner as if there take place an ordination of clergy in order to form a congregation of people, although the congregation of people follow not, yet there remains in the ordained persons the Sacrament of Ordination; and if, for any fault, any be removed from his office, he will not be without the Sacrament of the Lord once for all set upon him, albeit continuing unto condemnation.

ON THE GOOD OF MARRIAGE, Ch. 24

ML 40, 394

See No. 809.

NPNF III, 412

949
(1869)

In matrimony, however, let these nuptial blessings be the objects of our love—offspring, fidelity, the sacramental bond. Offspring, not that it be born only, but born again; for it is born to punishment unless it be born again to life. Fidelity, not such as even unbelievers observe one towards the other, in their ardent love of the flesh. . . . The sacramental bond, again, which is lost neither by divorce nor by adultery, should be guarded by husband and wife with concord and chastity.

ON MARRIAGE AND CONCUPISCENCE, Bk. 1, Ch. 11

ML 44, 424

NPNF V, 271

229. *Christian matrimony is a true sacrament.*

ST. IGNATIUS OF ANTIOCH

Tell my sisters to love the Lord and to be satisfied with their husbands
in flesh and spirit. In the same way tell my brothers in the name of
Jesus Christ to love their wives as the Lord does the Church. If anyone
is able to persevere in chastity to the honor of the flesh of the Lord,
let him do so in all humility. If he is boastful about it, he is lost; if he
should marry, the union should be made with the consent of the bishop,
so that the marriage may be according to the Lord and not merely out of
lust. Let all be done to the glory of God.

950
(67)

LETTER TO ST. POLYCARP
MG 5, 724
FC I, 126

TERTULLIAN

If, then, a marriage of this kind (faithful with unfaithful) is approved
by God, why will it not also be a successful marriage, in spite of
difficulties and anxieties and obstacles and defilements, since it already
enjoys the patronage of divine grace, at least in part?

951
(319)

TO HIS WIFE, Bk. 2:7
ML 1, 1299
See No. 80.   *ACW*, 32

Accordingly, among us, secret connections as well—connections,
that is, not first professed in presence of the church—run risk of being
judged akin to adultery and fornication.

952
(384)

ON MODESTY, Ch. 4
ML 2, 987
ANF III, 77

ORIGEN

It is God who has joined together the two in one so that they are no
more two, it is said, 'but one flesh.' And it is God who has joined
together the two in one so that they are no more two, from the time
that the woman is married to the man. And, since God has joined
them together, on this account in the case of those who are joined
together by God, there is a 'gift'; and Paul knowing this, that mar-

953
(505)

riage according to the Word of God was a 'gift,' like as holy celibacy was a gift.

COMMENTARY ON MATTHEW, Bk. 14, Ch. 16
MG 13, 1229

ST. JOHN CHRYSOSTOM

954
(1176)
'What God has joined together, let not man put asunder' (Mt. 19:6). See a teacher's wisdom. I mean, that being asked, Is it lawful? He did not at once say, It is not lawful, lest they should be disturbed and put in disorder, but before the decision by His argument He rendered this manifest, showing that it is itself too the commandment of His Father, and that not in opposition to Moses did He enjoin these things, but in full agreement with him. . . . But now both by the manner of the creation, and by the manner of lawgiving, He showed that one man must dwell with one woman continually, and never break off from her.

HOMILIES ON ST. MATTHEW, 62:1
MG 58, 597
NPNF X, 382

ST. AMBROSE

955
(1249)
[To Vigilius] There is hardly anything more deadly than being married to one who is a stranger to the faith, where the passions of lust and dissension and the evils of sacrilege are inflamed. Since the marriage ceremony ought to be sanctified by the priestly veiling and blessing, how can that be called a marriage ceremony where there is no agreement in faith?

LETTERS, No. 19
ML 16, 984
FC XXVI, 176

956
(1253)
[To Siricius] We do not say that marriage was not sanctified by Christ, since the Word of God says: 'The two shall become one flesh' (Mt. 19:5) and one spirit. But we are born before we are brought to our final goal, and the mystery of God's operation is more excellent than the remedy for human weakness. Quite rightly is a good wife praised, but a pious virgin is more rightly preferred.

LETTERS, No. 42
ML 16, 1124
FC XXVI, 225–226

ST. AUGUSTINE

Therefore, concerning the good of marriage, which the Lord also confirmed in the Gospel, not only in that He forbade to put away a wife, save because of fornication, but also in that He came by invitation to a marriage, there is good ground to inquire for what reason it be a good. And this seems not to me to be merely on account of the begetting of children, but also on account of the natural society itself in a difference of sex. . . . Marriages have this good also, that carnal or youthful incontinence, although it be faulty, is brought unto an honest use in the begetting of children, in order that out of the evil of lust the marriage union may bring to pass some good.

957
(1640)

ON THE GOOD OF MARRIAGE, 3:3
ML 40, 375
NPNF III, 400

And for this cause, therefore, did the Lord, on being invited, come to the marriage, to confirm conjugal chastity, and to show forth the sacrament of marriage. For the bridegroom in that marriage, to whom it was said, 'You have kept the good wine until now' (Jn. 2:10), represented the person of the Lord. For the good wine—namely, the gospel—Christ has kept until now.

958
(1812)

ON THE GOSPEL OF ST. JOHN, 9:2
ML 35, 1459
NPNF VII, 63

See No. 530.

ST. LEO THE GREAT

A wife is different from a concubine, even as a bondwoman from a freewoman. For which reason also the Apostle in order to show the difference of these persons quotes from Genesis, where it is said to Abraham, 'Cast out the bondwoman and her son: for the son of the bondwoman shall not be heir with my son Isaac' (Gen. 21:10). And hence, since the marriage tie was from the beginning so constituted as apart from the joining of the sexes to symbolize the mystic union of Christ and His Church, it is undoubted that that woman has no part in matrimony, in whose case it is shown that the mystery of marriage has not taken place.

959
(2189)

LETTERS, 167:4
ML 54, 1204
NPNF XII, 110

ST. JOHN OF DAMASCUS

960
(2374)

Virginity is the rule of life among the angels, the property of all incorporeal nature. This we say without speaking ill of marriage: God forbid! (for we know that the Lord blessed marriage by His presence, and we know him who said, Marriage is honorable and the bed undefiled), but knowing that virginity is better than marriage, however good.

EXPOSITION OF THE ORTHODOX FAITH, Bk. 4, Ch. 24
MG 94, 1209
NPNF IX, 97

230. *Matrimony effects a bond which is completely indissoluble.*

THE SHEPHERD OF HERMAS

961
(86)

I said to him: 'Sir, allow me to ask you a few questions.' 'Ask them,' he said. 'Sir,' I said, 'if a man has a wife who believes in the Lord and surprises her in adultery, does he commit sin if he lives with her?' 'Before he finds out,' he said, 'he does not. But, if her husband knows the sin, and she does not repent, but persists in her fornication, he becomes guilty of her sin, as long as he lives with her, and an accomplice in her adultery.' 'Sir,' I said, 'what then is he to do, if the wife continues in this passion?' 'Let him divorce her,' he said, 'and remain single. But, if he divorces her and marries another woman, he himself commits adultery.'

PRECEPTS, 4, 1:4
MG 2, 918
FC I, 262

TERTULLIAN

962
(342)

But, observe, if this Christ be yours when he teaches contrary to Moses and the Creator, on the same principle must He be mine if I can show that His teaching is not contrary to them. I maintain, then, that there was a condition in the prohibition which He now made of divorce; the case supposed being, that a man put away his wife for the express purpose of marrying another. His words are: 'Whoever puts away his wife, and marries another, commits adultery; and whoever marries her that is put away from her husband, also commits adultery,'—'put away,' that is, for the reason wherefore a woman ought not to be dismissed, that another wife may be obtained. For he who marries a woman who is unlawfully put away is as much of an adulterer as the man who marries one who is undivorced. Permanent is the marriage which is not rightly dissolved; to marry, therefore, while matrimony is undissolved, is to commit adultery. Since, therefore, His prohibition of divorce was a conditional one, He did not prohibit absolutely; and what He did not absolutely forbid, that He permitted on some occasions, when there is an absence of the cause why He gave His prohibition. In very deed His teaching is not contrary to Moses, whose precept He partially defends, I will not say confirms.

AGAINST MARCION, Bk. 4, Ch. 34
ML 2, 442
ANF III, 404–405

ST. CLEMENT OF ALEXANDRIA

Now that the Scripture counsels marriage, and allows no release from the union, is expressly contained in the law, "You shall not put away your wife, except for the cause or fornication" (Mt. 5:32, 19:9); and it regards as fornication, the marriage of those separated while the other is alive. . . . 'He that takes a woman that has been put away,' it is said, 'commits adultery; and if one puts away his wife, he makes her an adulteress' (Mk. 10:11), that is, compels her to commit adultery. And not only is he who puts her away guilty of this, but he who takes her, by giving to the woman the opportunity of sinning; for did he not take her, she would return to her husband.

CHRIST THE EDUCATOR, Bk. 2, Ch. 23
MG 8, 1096
ANF II, 379

963
(420)

ORIGEN

But now contrary to what was written, some even of the rulers of the church have permitted a woman to marry, even when her husband was living, doing contrary to what was written, where it is said, 'A wife is bound for so long time as her husband lives; shall she be joined to another man she shall be called an adulteress' (Rom. 7:2, 3) not indeed altogether without reason, for it is probable this concession was permitted in comparison with worse things, contrary to what was from the beginning ordained by law, and written.

COMMENTARY ON MATTHEW, 14:23
MG 13, 1245

964
(506)

965
(507)

And even he who withholds himself from his wife makes her often an adulteress when he does not satisfy her desires, even though he does so under the appearance of greater gravity and self-control. And perhaps this man is more culpable who, so far as it rests with him, makes her an adulteress when he does not satisfy her desires than he who, for other reason than fornication, has sent her away—for poisoning or murder or any of the most grievous sins. But as a woman is an adulteress, even though she seem to be married to a man, while the former husband is still living, so also the man who seems to marry her who has been put away, does not so much marry her as commit adultery with her according to the declaration of our Saviour.

COMMENTARY ON MATTHEW, 14:24
MG 13, 1249

LACTANTIUS

966
(642)

Lest anyone think that he can circumscribe the divine precepts, there are added those that take away all calumny and occasion of fraud; he is an adulterer who marries a divorced spouse, and he who dismisses his wife commits adultery (Mt. 5:32) for God is unwilling to dissociate the body.

THE DIVINE INSTITUTES, Bk. 6, Ch. 23
ML 6, 720
ANF VII, 190

ST. BASIL
See No. 924.

ST. GREGORY NAZIANZEN

967
(1002)

For what was the reason why [the Parisees] restrained (see Mt. 19:1ff.) the woman, but indulged the man, and that a woman who practises evil against her husband's bed is an adulteress, and the penalties of the law for this are very severe; but if the husband commits fornication against his wife, he has no account to give? I do not accept this legislation; I do not approve this custom.

ORATIONS, 37:6
MG 36, 289
NPNF VII, 339

ST. JEROME

The apostle has thus cut away every plea and has clearly declared that, if a woman marries again while her husband is living, she is an adulteress. . . . A husband may be an adulterer or a sodomite, he may be stained with every crime and may have been left by his wife because of his sins; yet he is still her husband and, so long as he lives, she may not marry another.

968
(1351)

LETTERS, 55
ML 22, 562
NPNF VI, 110

The laws of Caesar are different, it is true, from the laws of Christ: Papinianus* commands one thing; our own Paul another. Earthly laws give a free rein to the unchastity of men, merely condemning seduction and adultery; lust is allowed to range unrestrained among brothels and slave girls, as if the guilt were constituted by the rank of the person assailed and not by the purpose of the assailant. But with us Christians what is unlawful for women is equally unlawful for men, and as both serve the same God both are bound by the same obligations.

969
(1352)

LETTERS, 77
ML 22, 691
NPNF VI, 158

ST. AUGUSTINE
See No. 809.

ST. GREGORY THE GREAT

For, if they say that marriages should be dissolved for the sake of religion, be it known that, though human law has conceded this, yet divine law has forbidden it. For the Truth in person says, 'What God has joined together let not man put asunder' (Mt. 19:6). He also says, 'It is not lawful for a man to put away his wife except for the cause of fornication' (ib. 9). Who then may contradict this heavenly legislator?

970
(2297)

LETTERS, Bk. 11, 45
ML 77, 1161
NPNF XIII, 65

* A Roman jurist of great renown who held high legal office under Marcus Aurelius and afterwards under Severus, —put to death by Caracalla.

231. The sacrament of matrimony effects an exclusive bond.

ATHENAGORAS

971
(167)

For we bestow our attention, not on the study of words, but on the exhibition and teaching of actions—that a person should either remain as he was born, or be content with one marriage; for a second marriage is only a specious adultery. 'For whosoever puts away his wife,' says He, 'and marries another commits adultery' (Mt. 19:9); not permitting a man to send her away whose virginity he has brought to an end, nor to marry again. For he who deprives himself of his first wife, even though she be dead, is a cloaked adulterer, resisting the hand of God, because in the beginning God made one man and one woman, and dissolving the strictest union of flesh with flesh, formed for the intercourse of the race.

A PLEA FOR THE CHRISTIANS, Ch. 33
MG 6, 965
ANF II, 146–147

ST. THEOPHILUS OF ANTIOCH

972
(186)

For with [Christians] temperance dwells, self-restraint is practiced, monogamy is observed, chastity is guarded, iniquity exterminated, sin extirpated, righteousness exercised, law administered, worship performed, God acknowledged: truth governs, grace guards, peace screens them; the holy word guides, wisdom teaches, life directs, God reigns.

TO AUTOLYCUS, Bk. 3:15
MG 6, 1141
ANF II, 115

MINUCIUS FELIX
See No. 89.

ST. JOHN CHRYSOSTOM
See No. 954.

ST. LEO THE GREAT
See No. 959.

232. The Church has authority to establish impediments to marriage.

ST. BASIL

First of all I have to urge, what is of most importance in such matters [matrimonial], our own custom, which has the force of law, because the rules have been handed down to us by holy men. It is as follows: if any one, overcome by impurity, falls into unlawful intercourse with two sisters, this is not to be looked upon as marriage, nor are they to be admitted at all into the Church until they have separated from one another.

973
(918)

LETTERS, No. 160:2
MG 32, 624
NPNF VIII, 213

ST. GREGORY THE GREAT

A certain earthly law in the Roman republic allows the son and daughter, whether of a brother and sister, or of two brothers, or of two sisters, to marry together. But we have learnt by experience that progeny cannot ensue from such marriages. And the sacred law forbids to uncover the nakedness of kindred. Whence it follows that only the third or fourth generations of believers may be lawfully joined together. For the second, which we have spoken of, ought by all means to abstain from each other. But to have intercourse with a stepmother is a grave offence.

974
(2299)

LETTERS, Bk. 11, No. 64
ML 77, 1189
NPNF XIII, 76

Know then that what I wrote to Augustine, bishop of the nation of the Angli (who was, as you remember, your pupil), about marriages of consanguinity was written specially to him and to the nation of the Angli which had recently come to the faith, lest from alarm at anything too austere they should recede from their good beginning; but it was not written generally to others. Of this the whole Roman city is my witness. Nor did I thus order in those writings with the intention that, after they had been settled in the faith with a firm root, they should not be separated, if found to be below the proper degree of con-

975
(2301)

sanguinity, or should be united, if below the proper line of affinity, that is as far as the seventh generation.

LETTERS, Bk. 14, No. 17
ML 77, 1325
NPNF XIII, 76

233. *Matrimony is licit and good.*

ST. JOHN CHRYSOSTOM

976
(1115)

'Marriage is right,' you say; I also assent to this. For 'marriage,' we read, 'is honorable and the bed undefiled; but fornicators and adulterers God will judge' (Heb. 13:4); but it is no longer possible for you to observe the right conditions of marriage. For if he who has been attached to a heavenly bridegroom deserts him, and joins himself to a wife the act is adultery, even if you call it marriage ten thousand times over; or rather it is worse than adultery in proportion as God is greater than man.

LETTER TO THE FALLEN THEODORE, Bk. 2, Ch. 3
MG 47, 312
NPNF IX, 113

ST. JEROME
See No. 781.

ST. AUGUSTINE
See No. 530.

ST. JOHN OF DAMASCUS
See No. 960.

234. *Celibacy and especially virginity are however preferable to marriage.*

ST. IGNATIUS OF ANTIOCH
See No. 950.

ST. AMBROSE
See No. 956.

ST. JOHN OF DAMASCUS
See No. 960.

XIII.

The Last Things

At death, the soul is separated from the body and man is judged, for it is no longer possible for him either to commit sin or to merit. Those who must expiate the temporary punishment due to sin are detained in purgatory where they can be helped by the prayers of the living. Purgatory has only a temporary existence until the day of judgment. Those who die in mortal sin are cast into hell where they are eternally deprived of God and must eternally suffer the pain of sense—true and corporeal fire. Although both souls and demons will be tortured eternally their punishments will be unequal and less than what they truly deserve.

Various signs will precede the end of the world. All the dead will rise with their same bodies and undergo a general judgment. The just will enjoy the perfect beatitude of heaven which consists in the vision and the love of God. Although there will be various degrees according to merit, the bodies of the blessed will be immortal and glorious, they will no longer be able to sin, and their beatitude will endure for all eternity.

Death as a separation of the soul from the body is graphically described in St. Augustine's *City of God,* but the idea has already been set forth by St. Irenaeus in the second century, by Tertullian in the third, and by St. Gregory of Nyssa in the fourth. As early as St. Clement of Rome we read that after death there is no possibility of meriting or demeriting; St. Cyprian mentions this several times, and later St. Gregory Nazianzen and St. John Chrysostom. It occurs again in St. Gregory the Great. Lactantius, St. John Chrysostom, and

St. Augustine testify that the soul undergoes a particular judgment when it leaves the body and, typically, Tertullian (but also St. Justin Martyr and St. Irenaeus) reminds us that even before the general judgment souls are either blessed or tortured. Lactantius and Origen say so too, and the teaching appears in the *Demonstrations* of Aphraates. Testimony from St. Augustine is not wanting, nor from St. Gregory the Great.

Purgatory exists, where the souls for whom something more must be expiated undergo temporary punishments. Tertullian believes this, as does Lactantius, and St. Augustine refers to it several times. But the souls of the dead detained in purgatory can be helped by the suffrages of the living. The *Epitaph* of Abercius shows this; Tertullian declares it, and then later St. Cyril of Jerusalem, St. John Chrysostom, and St. Augustine in his *On Care to be had for the Dead.* He adds that purgatory will not exist after the day of judgment.

Those who die in mortal sin are cast into hell. St. Ignatius of Antioch makes this clear, and of course, Tertullian, and later St. Gergory Nazianzen and St. John Chrysostom. St. Augustine emphasizes the pain of the damned as an eternal privation of God, leaving to others the emphasis on the pain of sense and the true and corporeal fire of hell. The fire of hell seems to fascinate almost everyone. St. Ignatius of Antioch alludes to it, and in *The Martyrdom of St. Polycarp* it is compared to the temporal fire endured by the martyrs on earth. St. Justin Martyr warns that it is the punishment of immoral actions and Tertullian is almost eloquent on the matter. Athenagoras and Minucius Felix allude to it, as well as St. Hippolytus, St. Cyprian, and Lactantius. All three Cappadocians have something to say about hell, not to overlook St. Augustine and St. Gregory. The pain of the damned torments both souls and demons, and it will last for all eternity. In addition to St. Ignatius of Antioch and St. Polycarp, the *Letter to Diognetus* and the *So-called Second Letter of St. Clement of Rome to the Corinthians* indicate this. St. Justin Martyr holds it with St. Theophilus of Antioch and St. Irenaeus in the second century. Minucius Felix, Tertullian, St. Hippolytus, and St. Clement of Alexandria in the third testify to it, and at least one passage in Origen, whatever his final sentiments may have

been. St. Cyprian and Lactantius complete the ante-Nicene list. Several passages in St. Augustine can be found, usually in *The City of God* or the *Enchiridion,* and the roster is completed with St. Gregory and the Damascene. This is not to say that the punishments of the damned are equal, for the mitigation of punishment occupies the attention of a few writers such as Minucius Felix, St. Hippolytus, St. Cyprian, not to mention the Bishop of Hippo.

Various signs preceding the end of the world are mentioned in the *Didache,* and a somewhat longer account occurs in St. Cyril of Jerusalem. That the dead will rise is affirmed by practically everybody. The earliest references are in the *Didache* and St. Clement of Rome. St. Polycarp, Aristides, and St. Justin Martyr are not far behind, Tatian discusses it in his *Oration* against the Greeks, Athenagoras, St. Theophilus of Antioch, St. Irenaeus, and Minucius Felix, and we are only up to the third century. The list goes on to include the Alexandrians, St. Methodius, St. Hilary, and St. Ambrose. St. Augustine emphasizes that all of the dead will rise, and the general testimony of the Fathers is that they will rise with their same bodies. After this the general judgment will be given.

Origen, however, cannot quite go along with the notion of an eternal hell, and the reasons for this he discusses in his work *On First Principles,* Book 1, Chapter 6, and also in Book 3, Chapter 6. St. Gregory of Nyssa, in *The Great Catechism* (Ch. 26), at least shows some sympathy for "Origenism" and the ultimate restitution of all things. Be that as it may, the overwhelming majority of writers do not agree.

The object of beatitude is God alone. Perfect beatitude in heaven consists in the vision and the love of God. St. Augustine is most eloquent here, although he is preceded by St. Irenaeus and St. Clement of Alexandria, not to mention St. Cyprian. That beatitude is eternal and cannot be lost is the testimony of St. Clement of Rome, St. Theophilus of Antioch, St. Irenaeus, Tertullian, St. Clement of Alexandria, and Origen; and St. Augustine adds that the blessed will no longer be able to sin, and that while eternal life is one, symbolized by the laborers who gained the penny in the parable, nonetheless the many mansions point to the different grades of merit in that one eternal life.

THE LAST THINGS OF MAN

235. Death is a separation of the soul from the body.

TERTULLIAN
    See No. 515.

APHRAATES
    See No. 487.

ST. GREGORY OF NYSSA
    See No. 69.

ST. AUGUSTINE

977
(1772)

The soul is so connected with the body that it succumbs to great pain and withdraws; for the structure of our members and vital parts is so infirm that it cannot bear up against that violence which causes great or extreme agony. But in the life to come this connection of soul and body is of such a kind, that as it is dissolved by no lapse of time, so neither is it burst asunder by any pain. . . . Death will be eternal, since the soul will neither be able to enjoy God and live, nor to die and escape the pains of the body. The first death drives the soul from the body against her will: the second death holds the soul in the body against her will.

THE CITY OF GOD, Bk. 21, Ch. 3
ML 41, 710
NPNF II, 435

236. After death there is no possibility of meriting or demeriting.

ST. CLEMENT OF ROME
    See No. 929.

ST. CYPRIAN

978
(560)

An ever burning Gehenna and a devouring punishment of lively flames will consume the condemned, and there will be no means whereby the torments can at any time have respite and end. Souls with their bodies

494

will be reserved in infinite tortures for suffering. . . . Then there will be the pain of punishment without the fruit of repentance, useless weeping, and ineffectual prayer. Too late do they believe in eternal punishment who were unwilling to believe in eternal life.

TO DEMETRIAN, Ch. 24
ML 4, 561
FC XXXVIII, 189

See Nos. 914 and 916.

ST. GREGORY NAZIANZEN

I know the emptying, the making void, the making waste, the melting of the heart, and knocking of the knees together, such are the punishments of the ungodly. I do not dwell on the judgments to come, to which indulgence in this world delivers us, as it is better to be punished and cleansed now than to be transmitted to the torment to come, when it is the time of chastisement, not of cleansing.

979
(980)

ORATIONS, 16:7
MG 35, 944
NPNF VII, 249

ST. JOHN CHRYSOSTOM

Let us now, I pray you, take courage at His love toward man, and let us show forth an anxious repentance, before the day come on, which permits us not to profit thereby. For as yet all depends on us, but then He that judges has alone control over the sentence. 'Let us therefore come before His face with confession' (Ps. 94:2); let us bewail, let us mourn. For if we should be able to prevail upon the Judge before the appointed day to forgive us our sins, then we need not so much as enter into the court; as on the other hand, if this be not done, He will hear us publicly in the presence of the world, and we shall no longer have any hope of pardon.

980
(1172)

HOMILIES ON MATTHEW, 14:4
MG 57, 222
NPNF X, 90

Wherefore I entreat and beseech, and lay hold of your very knees, that while we have this scant viaticum of life, you would be pricked in your hearts by what has been said, that you would be converted, that you would become better men; that we may not, like that rich man,

981
(1200)

495

lament to no purpose in that world after our departure, and continue thenceforth in incurable wailings. For though you should have father or son or friend or any soever who has confidence towards God, none of these shall ever deliver you, your own works having destroyed you. For such is that tribunal: it judges by our actions alone, and in no other way is it possible there to be saved. . . . For if we be slothful, there will be neither righteous man nor prophet nor apostle nor any one to stand by us.

HOMILIES ON FIRST CORINTHIANS, 42:3
MG 61, 367
NPNF XII, 258

ST. GREGORY THE GREAT

982
(2321)

Each one will be presented to the Judge exactly as he was when he departed this life. Yet, there must be a cleansing fire before judgment, because of some minor faults that may remain to be purged away. Does not Christ, the Truth, say that if anyone blasphemes against the Holy Spirit he shall not be forgiven 'either in this world or in the world to come' (Mt. 12:32)? From this statement we learn that some sins can be forgiven in this world and some in the world to come. For, if forgiveness is refused for a particular sin, we conclude logically that it is granted for others. This must apply, as I said, to slight transgressions.

DIALOGUES, 4:39
ML 77, 396
FC XXXIX, 248

237. *The soul undergoes a particular judgment when it leaves the body.*

ST. JOHN CHRYSOSTOM
See No. 981.

ST. AUGUSTINE

983
(1880)

Now with regard to the point, which with perfect propriety and great soundness of view (Vicentius Victor) believes, that souls after quitting the body are judged, before they come to that final judgment to which they must submit when their bodies are restored to them, and are either tormented or glorified in the very same flesh wherein they once lived here on earth; is it, let me ask you, the case that you were really ignorant of this? Whoever has his mind so obstinately set against the gospel as not to hear these truths, and after hearing to believe them, in the parable of the poor man who was carried away after death to Abraham's bosom, and of the rich man who is set forth as suffering torment in hell (Lk. 16:22 ff.).

ON THE SOUL AND ITS ORIGIN, Bk. 2, Ch. 4
ML 44, 498
NPNF V, 334

238. Even before the general judgment souls are either saved or lost.

ST. JUSTIN MARTYR
See No. 484.

TERTULLIAN

As long as the earth remains, Heaven is not open; in fact, the gates are barred. When the world shall have passed away, the portals of Paradise will be opened. In the meantime, then, will our resting place be in the ether with those lovers of boys of Plato, or in the air with Arius, or around the moon with Endymions of the Stoics? 'Oh, no,' you say, 'but in Paradise whither the Patriarchs and the prophets have traveled as a result of the Lord's Resurrection.' If that is so, how is it that the region of Paradise which was revealed in the spirit of St. John as being 'under the altar' contains no other souls but those of the martyrs? How is it that St. Perpetua, that bravest martyr of Christ, on the day of her death saw only the souls of the martyrs in Paradise, unless it be that the sword which guarded the entrance allowed none to pass save those that had died in Christ and not in Adam? Those who die this new death for God, and violently as Christ did, are welcomed into a special abode. Here, then is the difference between pagan and Christian in death: If you lay down your life for God as the Paraclete recommends, then it will not be of some gentle fever in a soft bed, but in the torture of martyrdom. You must take up your cross and follow Him, according to the precept of Christ. The only key that unlocks the gates of Paradise is your own blood. Look at my Treatise on Paradise where I

984
(351)

showed that all [other] souls are kept in Hell until the Second Coming of the Lord.

ON THE SOUL, Ch. 55
ML 2, 744
ANF III, 231ʳ

ORIGEN
See No. 477.

APHRAATES

985
(688)

But our faith thus teaches, that when men fall asleep, they sleep this slumber without knowing good from evil. And the righteous look not forward to their promises, nor do the wicked look forward to their sentence of punishment, until the Judge come and separate those whose place is at His right hand from those whose place is at His left. And be instructed by that which is written, that when the Judge shall sit, and the books be opened before Him and the good and evil deeds recited, then they that have wrought good works shall receive good rewards from Him Who is good; and they that have done evil deeds shall receive evil penalties from the just Judge.

DEMONSTRATIONS, 8:20
PS 1, 398
NPNF XIII, 381

986
(695)

'And the wicked shall not arise in the judgment, nor sinners in the congregation of the righteous' (Ps. 1:5). And even as the righteous who are perfected in good works shall not come into the judgment to be judged, so if the wicked also whose sins are many, and the measure of whose offences is overflowing, it shall not be required that they should draw nigh unto the judgment, but when they have risen again they shall turn back to Sheol, as David said, 'The wicked shall turn back to Sheol, and all the nations that forget God' (Ps. 9:18).

DEMONSTRATIONS, 22:17
PS 1, 1026
NPNF XIII, 408

ST. AUGUSTINE

987
(1829)

All souls have, when they quit this world, their different receptions. The good have joy; the evil, torments. But when the resurrection takes place, both the joy of the good will be fuller, and the torments of the wicked heavier, when they shall be tormented in the body. . . . For the rest, which is given immediately after death, every one, if worthy of it, receives when he dies. . . . Thus some have now been in that rest for long, some not so long; others for fewer years, and others whose entrance therein is still less than recent.

ON THE GOSPEL OF ST. JOHN, 49:10
ML 35, 1751
NPNF VII, 274

239. Purgatory exists, where the souls—for whom something more must be expiated—undergo temporary punishments.

ST. AUGUSTINE

'Neither chasten me in your hot displeasure' (Ps. 37:2). . . so that you may cleanse me in this life, and make me such, that I may after that stand in no need of the cleansing fire, for those 'who are to be saved, yet so as by fire' (1 Cor. 3:15). And because it is said, 'he shall be saved,' that fire is thought lightly of. For all that, though we should be 'saved by fire,' yet will that fire be more grievous than anything that man can suffer in this life whatsoever.

EXPOSITIONS ON THE PSALMS, 37:3
ML 36, 397
NPNF VIII, 103

988
(1467)

Temporary punishments are suffered by some in this life only, by others after death, by others both now and then; but all of them before that last and strictest judgment. But of those who suffer temporary punishments after death, all are not doomed to those everlasting pains which are to follow that judgment.

THE CITY OF GOD, Bk. 21, Ch. 13
ML 41, 728
NPNF II, 464

989
(1776)

For some of the dead, indeed, the prayer of the Church or of pious individuals is heard; but it is for those who, having been regenerated in Christ, did not spend their life so wickedly that they can be judged unworthy of such compassion, nor so well that they can be considered to have no need of it.

THE CITY OF GOD, Bk. 21, Ch. 24
ML 41, 737
NPNF II, 470

990
(1780)

991
(1920)

And it is not impossible that something of the same kind may take place even after this life. It is a matter that may be inquired into, and either ascertained or left doubtful, whether some believers shall pass through a kind of purgatorial fire, and in proportion as they have loved with more or less devotion the goods that perish, be less or more quickly delivered from it.

ON FAITH, HOPE, AND LOVE (ENCHIRIDION), Ch. 69
ML 40, 265
NPNF III, 260

ST. GREGORY THE GREAT
See No. 982.

240. The souls of the dead detained in purgatory can be helped by the suffrages of the living.

TERTULLIAN

992
(382)

Indeed, she [the woman] prays for his soul [her husband's], and requests refreshment for him meanwhile, and fellowship [with him] in the first resurrection; and she offers [her sacrifice] on the anniversaries of his falling asleep.

ON MONOGAMY, Ch. 10
ML 2, 942
ANF IV, 67

ST. CYRIL OF JERUSALEM
See No. 905.

ST. JOHN CHRYSOSTOM
See No. 846.

ST. AUGUSTINE
See No. 990.

993
(1934)

In the books of the Maccabees we read of sacrifice offered for the dead. Even if it were nowhere at all read in the Old Scriptures, not small is the authority, which in this usage is clear, of the whole Church, namely, that in the prayers of the priest which are offered to the Lord God at His altar, the commendation of the dead has also its place.

ON CARE TO BE HAD FOR THE DEAD, Ch. 1:3

ML 40, 593

NPNF III, 540

241. Those who die in mortal sin are cast into hell.

ST. IGNATIUS OF ANTIOCH

Make no mistake, brethren; the corrupters of families will not inherit the kingdom of God. If, then, those are dead who do these things according to the flesh, how much worse if, with bad doctrine, one should corrupt the faith of God for which Jesus Christ was crucified. Such a man, for becoming contaminated, will depart into unquenchable fire; and will any one who listens to him.

994

(41)

LETTER TO THE EPHESIANS, Ch. 16:1

MG 5, 657

FC I, 93

TERTULLIAN

If you shrink back from exomologesis, consider in your heart hell, which exomologesis will extinguish for you; and imagine first the magnitude of the penalty, that you may not hesitate about the adoption of the remedy. What do we esteem that treasure-house of eternal fire to be, when small vent-holes* of it rouse such blasts of flames that neighboring cities either are already no more, or are in daily expectation of the same fate? The haughtiest mountains start asunder in the birth-throes of their inly-gendered fire; and—which proves to us the perpetuity of the judgment—though they start asunder, though they be devoured, yet come they never to an end. Who will not account these occasional punishments inflicted on the mountains as examples of the judgment which menaces [sinners]? Who will not agree that such sparks are but some few missiles and sportive darts of some inestimably vast centre of fire?

995

(317)

ON PENANCE, Ch. 12

ML 1, 1247

ANF III, 605

* *fumariola*

ST. GREGORY NAZIANZEN
See No. 979.

ST. JOHN CHRYSOSTOM
See No. 846.

242. The pain of the damned is twofold: (a) damnation—the privation of God.

ST. AUGUSTINE
See No. 977.

996
(1932)

It is in vain, then, that some, indeed very many, make moan over the eternal punishment, and perpetual, unintermitted torments of the lost, and say they do not believe it shall be so; . . . But let them suppose, if the thought gives them pleasure, that the pains of the damned are, at certain intervals, in some degree assuaged. For even in this case the wrath of God, that is, their condemnation (for it is this, and not any disturbed feeling in the mind of God that is called His wrath), abides upon them; that is, His wrath, though it still remains, does not shut up His tender mercies; though His tender mercies are exhibited, not in putting an end to their eternal punishment, but in mitigating, or in granting them a respite from their torments.

ON FAITH, HOPE, AND LOVE (ENCHIRIDION), Ch. 112
ML 40, 284
NPNF III, 273

243. The pain of the damned is twofold: (b) the pain of sense —true and corporeal fire.

ST. IGNATIUS OF ANTIOCH
See No. 994.

THE MARTYRDOM OF ST. POLYCARP

997
(78)

Because they kept in mind the grace of Christ, the martyrs despised the tortures of the world, thus purchasing eternal life at the price of a single hour. And the fire of their savage torturers was cool to them; for they kept before their eyes the escape from eternal and unquenchable fire, and with the eyes of their heart they looked up to the good things which are stored up for those who have persevered.

Ch. 2:3
MG 5, 1032
FC I, 152

ST. JUSTIN MARTYR

And more than all other men are we your helpers and allies in promoting peace, seeing that we hold this view, that it is alike impossible for the wicked, the covetous, the conspirator, and for the virtuous, to escape the notice of God, and that each man goes to everlasting punishment or salvation according to the value of his actions. For if all men knew this, no one would choose wickedness even for a little, knowing that he goes to the everlasting punishment of fire; but would by all means restrain himself, and adorn himself with virtue, that he might obtain the good gifts of God, and escape the punishments.

998
(115)

•

THE FIRST APOLOGY, Ch. 12
MG 6, 341
ANF I, 166

ATHENAGORAS
See No. 288.

MINUCIUS FELIX
See No. 90.

TERTULLIAN

Then shall the entire human race be restored to settle the account for the good or the evil it has merited in this world, from then on to be requited for a limitless and unending eternity. And so, no longer will there be death or resurrection again and again, but we will be the same as we now are and not someone else afterwards; being really worshippers of God, we will always be with God, clad in the eternity of our own proper substance which we have put on. But the profane, and those who have not turned wholly to God will be in the punishment of perpetual fire, and they shall have from the very nature of this fire a divine supply, as it were, of incorruptibility.

999
(284)

Even the philosophers knew of the difference between this mysterious fire and ordinary fire. That which serves mankind's use is far different from that which serves the judgment of God, whether it casts thunderbolts from heaven or belches forth from the earth through the mountain peaks. It does not consume what it burns, but, while it destroys, it restores. So it is that volcanoes remain, though they are always on fire, and one who has been struck by lightning is safe, for now no fire can ever reduce him to ashes. This is a proof of the fire of eternity, this is a foreshadowing of the eternal judgment which renews its punishment: mountains burn, but continue to exist. How will the guilty and the enemies of God fare?

APOLOGY, Ch. 48
ML 1, 527
FC 120–121

See No. 995.

ST. HIPPOLYTUS
See No. 667.

ST. CYPRIAN
See No. 978.

ST. CYRIL OF JERUSALEM

1000
(837)

For this body shall be raised, not remaining weak as now; but raised the very same body, though by putting on incorruption it shall be fashioned anew, —as iron blending with fire becomes fire, or rather as He knows how, the Lord who raises us. This body therefore shall be raised, but it shall abide not such as it now is, but an eternal body; no longer needing for its life such nourishment as now, nor stairs for its ascent, for it shall be made spiritual, a marvellous thing, such as we cannot worthily speak of. Then, it is said, shall the righteous shine forth as the sun, and the moon, and as the brightness of the firmament (Mt. 13:43; Dan. 12:3). And God, foreknowing men's unbelief, has given to little worms in the summer to dart beams of light from their body, that from what is seen, that which is looked for might be believed; for He who gives in part is able to give the whole also, and He who made the worm radiant with light, will much more illuminate a righteous man. We shall be raised therefore, all with our bodies eternal, but not all with bodies alike: for if a man is righteous, he will receive a heavenly body, that he may be able worthily to hold converse with Angels; but if a man is a sinner, he shall receive an eternal body, fitted to endure the penalties of sins, that he may burn eternally in fire, nor ever be consumed. And righteously will God assign this portion to either company; for we do nothing without the body. We blaspheme with the mouth, and with the mouth we pray. With the body we commit fornication, and with the body we keep chastity. With the hand we rob, and by the hand we bestow alms; and the rest in like manner. Since then the body has been our minister in all things, it shall also share with us in the future the fruits of the past.

CATECHESES, 18:18
MG 33, 1040
NPNF VII, 139

ST. GREGORY NAZIANZEN

For I know a cleansing fire which Christ came to send upon the earth, and He Himself is anagogically called a Fire. . . . I know also a fire which is not cleansing, but avenging; either that fire of Sodom which He pours down on all sinners, mingled with brimstone and storms, or that which is prepared for the Devil and His Angels or that which proceeds from the face of the Lord, and shall burn up his enemies round about; and one even more fearful still than these, the unquenchable fire which is ranged with the worm that dies not but is eternal for the wicked. For all these belong to the destroying power; though some may prefer even in this place to take a more merciful view of this fire, worthily of Him That chastises.

1001
(1013)

ORATIONS, 40:36
MG 36, 409
NPNF VII, 373

ST. GREGORY OF NYSSA

Indeed, the sinner's life of torment presents no equivalent to anything that pains the sense here. Even if some one of the punishments in that other world be named in terms that are well known here, the distinction is still not small. When you hear the word fire, you have been taught to think of a fire other than the fire we see, owing to something being added to that fire which in this there is not; for that fire is never quenched, whereas experience has discovered many ways of quenching this; and there is a great difference between a fire which can be extinguished, and one that does not admit of extinction.

1002
(1036)

THE GREAT CATECHISM, Ch. 40
MG 45, 104
NPNF V, 508–509

ST. AUGUSTINE

1003
(1774)

For why may we not assert that even immaterial spirits may, in some extraordinary way, yet really be pained by the punishment of material fire, if the spirits of men, which also are certainly immaterial, are both now contained in material members of the body, and in the world to come shall be indissolubly united to their own·bodies? . . . But that hell, which also is called a lake of fire and brimstone, will be material fire, and will torment the bodies of the damned, whether men or devils, —the solid bodies of the one, aerial bodies of the others; or if only men have bodies as well as souls, yet the evil spirits, though without bodies, shall be so connected with the bodily fires as to receive pain without imparting life. One fire certainly shall be the lot of both, for thus the truth has declared.

THE CITY OF GOD, Bk. 21, Ch. 10
ML 41, 724
NPNF II, 462

244. *The punishments of the damned will be eternal.*

ST. IGNATIUS OF ANTIOCH
See No. 994.

ST. POLYCARP
See No. 997.

LETTER TO DIOGNETUS

1004
(100)

You will condemn the deceit and error of the world as soon as you realize that true life is in heaven, and despise the seeming death in this world, and fear the real death which is reserved for those who are to be condemned to eternal fire which shall torment forever those who are committed to it. When you have faith, you will admire those who, for the sake of what is right, bear the temporal fire, and you will think them blessed when you come to know that fire. . . .

Ch. 9:2
MG 2, 1181
FC I, 364

THE SO-CALLED SECOND LETTER OF ST. CLEMENT OF ROME TO THE CORINTHIANS

And understand, brothers, that the lingering of our flesh in this world is short and passing, but the promise of Christ is great and wonderful and is a repose in the kingdom to come and in eternal life. . . . For if we do the will of Christ, we shall find repose; but if not, nothing shall save us from eternal punishment, if we neglect His commandments.

1005
(102)

Ch. 5:5
MG 1, 336
FC I, 68

ST. JUSTIN MARTYR
See No. 998.

And we have learned that those only are deified who have lived near to God in holiness and virtue; and we believe that those who live wickedly and do not repent are punished in everlasting fire.

1006
(121)

THE FIRST APOLOGY, Ch. 21
MG 6, 361

See No. 756.

ANF I, 170

ST. THEOPHILUS OF ANTIOCH

But read the prophetic Scriptures, and they will make your way plainer for escaping the eternal punishments, and obtaining the eternal prizes of God. For He who gave the mouth speech, and formed the ear to hear, and made the eye to see, will examine all things, and will judge righteous judgment, rendering merited awards to each. To those who by patient continuance in well-doing seek immortality, He will give life everlasting, joy, peace, rest, and abundance of good things, which neither has eye seen, nor ear heard, nor has it entered the heart of man to conceive (1 Cor. 2:9). But to the unbelieving and despisers, who obey not the truth, but are obedient to unrighteousness, when they shall have been filled with adulteries and fornications, and filthiness, and covetousness, and unlawful idolatries, there shall be anger and wrath, tribulation and anguish, and at the last everlasting fire shall possess such men (Rom. 2:8,9).

1007
(176)

TO AUTOLYCUS, Ch. 1:14
MG 6, 1045
ANF II, 93

ST. IRENAEUS
See No. 211.

MINUCIUS FELIX
See No. 90.

TERTULLIAN
See Nos. 999, 53, and 995.

ST. HIPPOLYTUS
See No. 667.

ST. CLEMENT OF ALEXANDRIA

1008
(437)

Do not you judge who is worthy or who is unworthy. For it is possible you may be mistaken in your opinion. As in the uncertainty of ignorance it is better to do good to the undeserving for the sake of the deserving, than by guarding against those that are less good to fail to meet in with the good. For though sparing, and aiming at testing, who will receive meritoriously or not, it is possible for you to neglect some that are loved by God; the penalty for which is the punishment of eternal fire.

WHO IS THE RICH MAN THAT SHALL BE SAVED?, Ch. 33
MG 9, 637
ANF II, 600

ORIGEN
See No. 477.

ST. CYPRIAN
See No. 978.

1009
(579)

Oh, what and how great will that day be at its coming, beloved brethren, when the Lord shall begin to count up His people, and to recognise the deservings of each one by the inspection of His divine knowledge, to send the guilty to Gehenna, and to set on fire our persecutors with the perpetual burning of a penal fire, but to pay to us the reward of our faith and devotion! What will be the glory and how great the joy to be admitted to see God, to be honored to receive with Christ, your Lord God, the jot of eternal salvation and light—to greet Abraham, and Isaac, and Jacob, and all the patriarchs, and prophets, and apostles, and martyrs—to rejoice with the righteous and the friends of God in the kingdom of heaven, with the pleasure of immortality given to us—to receive there what neither eye has seen, nor ear heard, neither has entered into the heart of man! For the apostle announces that we shall receive greater things than anything that we here either do or suffer, saying, 'The sufferings of this present time are not worthy to be compared with the glory to come hereafter which shall be revealed in us' (Rom. 8:18). When that revelation shall come, when that glory of God shall shine upon us, we shall be as happy and joyful, honored with the condescension of God, as they will remain guilty and wretched, who, either as deserters from God or rebels against Him, have done the will of the devil, so that it is necessary for them to be tormented with the devil himself in unquenchable fire.

LETTERS (EXHORTATION TO THE PEOPLE OF THIBARIS), 58:10
ML 4, 357
ANF V, 350

ST. GREGORY NAZIANZEN
See No. 1001.

ST. AUGUSTINE
See Nos. 988 and 977.

The crimes which are punished with these most protracted sufferings are perpetrated in a very brief space of time. Nor is there any one who would suppose that the pains of punishment should occupy as short a time as the offense; or that murder, adultery, sacrilege, or any other crime, should be measured, not by the enormity of the injury or wickedness, but by the length of time spent in its perpetration.

1010
(1775)

THE CITY OF GOD, Bk. 21, Ch. 11
ML 41, 726
NPNF II, 462

What a fond fancy is it to suppose that eternal punishment means long continued punishment, while eternal life means life without end, since Christ in the very same passage spoke of both in similar terms in one and the same sentence.' These shall go away into eternal punishment, but the righteous into life eternal!' (Mt. 25:46). If both destinies are 'eternal,' then we must either understand both as long-continued but at last terminating, or both as endless. For they are correlative, —on the one hand, punishment eternal, on the other hand, life eternal. And to say in one and the same sense, life eternal shall be

1011
(1779)

endless, punishment eternal shall come to an end, is the height of absurdity.

THE CITY OF GOD, Bk. 21, Ch. 23

ML 41, 736

NPNF II, 469

1012
(1931)

After the resurrection, however, when the final, universal judgment has been completed, there shall be two kingdoms, each with its own distinct boundaries, the one Christ's, the other the devil's; the one consisting of the good, the other of the bad—both, however, consisting of angels and men. The former shall have no will, the latter no power, to sin, and neither shall have any power to choose death; but the former shall live truly and happily in eternal life, the latter shall drag a miserable existence in eternal death without the power of dying; for the life and the death shall both be without end. But among the former there shall be degrees of happiness, one being more pre-eminently happy than another; and among the latter there shall be degrees of misery, one being more endurably miserable than another.

ON FAITH, HOPE, AND LOVE (ENCHIRIDION), Ch. 111

ML 40, 284

NPNF III, 273

1013
(1932)

It is in vain, then, that some, indeed very many, make moan over the eternal punishment, and perpetual, unintermitted torments of the lost, and say they do not believe it shall be so; . . . But let them suppose, if the thought gives them pleasure, that the pains of the damned are, at certain intervals, in some degree assuaged. For even in this case the wrath of God, that is, their condemnation (for it is this, and not any disturbed feeling in the mind of God that is called His wrath), abides upon them; that is, His wrath, though it still remains, does not shut up His tender mercies; though His tender mercies are exhibited, not in putting an end to their eternal punishment, but in mitigating, or in granting them a respite from, their torments.

ON FAITH, HOPE, AND LOVE (ENCHIRIDION), Ch. 112

ML 40, 284

NPNF III, 273

ST. GREGORY THE GREAT

1014
(2322)

There is one kind of fire in hell, but it does not torment all sinners in the same way, for each one feels its torments according to his degree

510

of guilt. . . . That truth stands solid and unshaken: Just as the joys of heaven will never cease, so, too, there is no end to the torments of the damned.

DIALOGUES, Bk. 4:43

ML 77, 401

FC XXXIX, 254

ST. JOHN OF DAMASCUS

We shall therefore rise again, our souls being once more united with our bodies, now made incorruptible and having put off corruption, and we shall stand beside the awful judgment-seat of Christ; and the devil and his demons and the man that is his, that is the Antichrist and the impious and the sinful, will be given over to everlasting fire: not material fire* like our fire, but such fire as God would know. But those who have done good will shine forth as the sun with the angels into life eternal, with our Lord Jesus Christ, ever seeing Him and being in His sight and deriving unceasing joy from Him, praising Him with the Father and the Holy Spirit throughout the limitless ages of ages. Amen.

1015

(2376)

EXPOSITION OF THE ORTHODOX FAITH, Bk. 4, Ch. 27

MG 94, 1228

NPNF IX, 101

THE LAST THINGS OF THE WORLD

245. Various signs precede the end of the world.

ST. CYRIL OF JERUSALEM

Since the true Christ is to come a second time, the adversary, taking occasion by the expectation of the simple, and especially of them of the circumcision, brings in a certain man who is a magician, and most expert in sorceries and enchantments of beguiling craftiness; who shall seize for himself the power of the Roman empire, and shall falsely style himself Christ; by this name of Christ deceiving the Jews, who

1016

(832)

* See Migne's Preface to St. John of Damascus, *Dial., Contr. Manichaeos.*

are looking for the Anointed, and seducing those of the Gentiles by his magical illusions. . . . At first indeed he will put on a show of mildness (as though he were a learned and discreet person), and of soberness and benevolence: and by the lying signs and wonders of his magical deceit having beguiled the Jews, as though he were the expected Christ, he shall afterwards be characterized by all kinds of crimes of inhumanity and lawlessness, so as to outdo all unrighteous and ungodly men who have gone before him; displaying against all men, but especially against us Christians, a spirit murderous and most cruel, merciless and crafty. And after perpetrating such things for three years and six months only, he shall be destroyed by the glorious second advent from heaven of the only-begotten Son of God, our Lord and Saviour Jesus, the true Christ, who shall slay Antichrist with the breath of His mouth, and shall deliver him over to the fire of hell.

CATECHESES, 15:11
MG 33, 884
NPNF VII, 107–108

ST. AUGUSTINE

1017
(1771) Christ will not come to judge quick and dead unless Antichrist, His adversary, first come to seduce those who are dead in soul; although their seduction is a result of God's secret judgment already passed.

THE CITY OF GOD, Bk. 20, Ch. 19
ML 41, 687
NPNF II, 438

246. The dead shall rise.

ST. CLEMENT OF ROME
See No. 73.

ST. POLYCARP
See No. 210.

ARISTIDES
See No. 87.

ST. JUSTIN MARTYR
See No. 480.

TATIAN

And on this account we believe that there will be a resurrection of   1018
bodies after the consummation of all things; not, as the Stoics affirm,   (155)
according to the return of certain cycles, the same things being produced and destroyed for no useful purpose, but a resurrection once for
all, when our periods of existence are completed, and consequence
solely of the constitution of things under which men alone live, for
the purpose of passing judgment upon them. . . . And, although you
regard us as mere triflers and babblers, it troubles us not, since we
have faith in this doctrine. For just as, not existing before I was born,
I knew not who I was, and only existed in the potentiality ($\dot{v}\pi\hat{\eta}\rho\chi ov$)
of fleshly matter, but being born, after a former state of nothingness, I
have obtained through my birth a certainty of my existence; in the
same way, having been born, and through death existing no longer,
and seen no longer, I shall exist again, just as before I was not, but was
afterwards born. Even though fire destroy all traces of my flesh, the
world receives the vaporized matter; and though dispersed through
rivers and seas, or torn in pieces by wild beasts, I am laid up in the
storehouses of a wealthy Lord. And, although the poor and the godless
know not what is stored up, yet God the Sovereign, when He pleases,
will restore the substance that is visible to Him alone to its pristine
condition.

ORATION AGAINST THE GREEKS, Ch. 6

MG 6, 817

ANF II, 67

See No. 486.

ATHENAGORAS

But that which was created for the very purpose of existing and living   1019
life naturally suited to it, since the cause itself is bound up with its   (169)
nature, and is recognised only in connection with existence itself, can
never admit of any cause which shall utterly annihilate its existence.
But since this cause is seen to lie in perpetual existence, the being so
created must be preserved for ever, doing and experiencing what is
suitable to its nature, each of the two parts of which it consists, contributing what belongs to it.

THE RESURRECTION OF THE DEAD, Ch. 12

MG 6, 997

ANF II, 155

ST. THEOPHILUS OF ANTIOCH
See No. 11.

MINUCIUS FELIX

1020
(272)

It is more difficult to give a beginning to what does not exist than to recall into existence what has once existed. Do you believe that, if something is removed from our feeble eyes, it is also lost to God? The whole body, whether it withers away to dust, or dissolves into moisture, or crumbles away to ashes or passes off in vapor, is removed from our eyes, but it still exists for God, the Preserver of the elements. Nor are we, as you imagine, afraid of any damage resulting from the manner of burial, but we practice the time-honored and more dignified custom of consigning the dead body to the earth. Notice, also, how all nature hints at a future resurrection for our consolation. The sun sets and rises again; the stars sink below the horizon and return; the flowers die and come to life again; the shrubs spend themselves and then put forth buds; seeds must decompose in order to sprout forth new life. Thus, the body in the grave is like the tree in the winter, which conceals its live sap under an apparent dryness. Why do you urge that in the depths of winter it should revive and return to life? We must also wait for the spring of the body. I know perfectly well, of course, that many because of their guilty conscience, hope rather than believe that they are reduced to nothing after death. They prefer to be annihilated rather than to be restored for punishment.

LETTER TO OCTAVIUS, Ch. 34
ML 3, 347
FC X, 393–394

TERTULLIAN
See Nos. 515 and 452.

1021
(364)

The entire cause, then, or rather necessity of the resurrection, will be this, namely, that arrangement of the final judgment which shall be most suitable to God. Now, in effecting this arrangement, you must consider whether the divine censure superintends a judicial examination of the two natures of man—both his soul and his flesh. For that which is a suitable object to be judged, is also a competent one to be raised. Our position is, that the judgment of God must be believed first of all to be plenary, and then absolute, so as to be final, and therefore irrevocable; to be also righteous, not bearing less heavily on any par-

514

ticular part; to be moreover worthy of God, being complete and definite, in keeping with His great patience. Thus it follows that the fulness and perfection of the judgment consists simply in representing the interests of the entire human being. Now, since the entire man consists of the union of the two natures, he must therefore appear in both, as it is right that he should be judged in his entirety; nor, of course, did he pass through life except in his entire state. As therefore he lived, so also must he be judged, because he has to be judged concerning the way in which he lived. For life is the cause of judgment, and it must undergo investigation in as many natures as it possessed when it discharged its vital functions.

ON THE RESURRECTION OF THE FLESH, Ch. 14
ML 2, 813
ANF III, 554–555

ST. CLEMENT OF ALEXANDRIA

For He said again, that the soul never returns a second time to the body in this life; and that which has become angelic does not become unrighteous or evil, so as not to have the opportunity of again sinning by the assumption of flesh; but that in the resurrection the soul returns to the body, and both are joined to one another according to their peculiar nature, adapting themselves, through the composition of each, by a kind of congruity like a building of stones.

ADUMBRATIONS IN 1 PETER 1:3
MG 9, 729
ANF II, 571

1022
(441)

ORIGEN

Let no one, however, suspect that, in speaking as we do, we belong to those who are indeed called Christians, but who set aside the doctrine of the resurrection as it is taught in Scripture. . . . We, therefore, do not maintain that the body which has undergone corruption resumes its original nature, any more than the grain of wheat which has decayed returns to its former condition. But we do maintain, that as above the grain of wheat there arises a stalk, so a certain power is implanted in the body, which is not destroyed, and from which the body is raised up in incorruption (1 Cor. 15:42).

AGAINST CELSUS, Bk. 5, Ch. 22
MG 11, 1216
ANF IV, 552

1023
(528)

515

ST. METHODIUS

1024
(616)
Wherefore observe that these are the very things which the Lord wished to teach to the Sadducees, who did not believe in the resurrection of the flesh. For this was the opinion of the Sadducees. Whence it was that, having contrived the parable about the woman and the seven brethren, that they might cast doubt upon the resurrection of the flesh, 'There came to Him,' it is said, 'the Sadducees also, who say that there is no resurrection' (Mt. 22:23). Christ, then, if there had been no resurrection of the flesh, but the soul only were saved, would have agreed with their opinion as a right and excellent one. But as it was, He answered and said, 'In the resurrection they neither marry, nor are given in marriage, but are as the angels in heaven,' not on account of having no flesh, but of not marrying nor being married, but being henceforth incorruptible.

ON THE RESURRECTION, Ch. 12
MG 18, 281
ANF VI, 367

APHRAATES
See No. 336.

ST. AMBROSE

1025
(1276)
If the earth and heaven are renewed, why should we doubt that man, on account of whom heaven and earth were made, can be renewed? If the transgressor be reserved for punishment, why should not the just be kept for glory? If the worm of sins does not die, how shall the flesh of the just perish? For the resurrection, as the very form of the word shows, is this, that what has fallen should rise again, that which has died should come to life again. And this is the course and ground of justice, that since the action of body and soul is common to both (for what the soul has conceived the body has carried out), each should come into judgment, and each should be either given over to punishment or reserved for glory.

ON THE DEATH OF HIS BROTHER SATYRUS, Bk. 2:87
ML 16, 1340
NPNF X, 188

ST. AUGUSTINE
See No. 857.

Far be it from us to fear that the omnipotence of the Creator cannot, for the resuscitation and reanimation of our bodies, recall all the portions which have been consumed by beasts or fire, or have been dissolved into dust or ashes, or have decomposed into water, or evaporated into the air. Or if it is contended that each will rise with the same stature as that of the body he died in, we shall not obstinately dispute this, provided only there be no deformity, no infirmity, no languor, no corruption.

1026
(1785)

THE CITY OF GOD, Bk. 22, Ch. 20
ML 41, 782
NPNF II, 498

ST. JOHN OF DAMASCUS

We believe also in the resurrection of the dead. For there will be, in truth there will be, a ressurection of the dead, and by resurrection we mean resurrection of bodies. For resurrection is the second state of that which has fallen. For the souls are immortal, and hence how can they rise again? . . . It is, then, this very body, which is corruptible and liable to dissolution, that will rise again incorruptible.

1027
(2375)

EXPOSITION OF THE ORTHODOX FAITH, Bk. 4, Ch. 27
MG 94, 1220
NPNF IX, 99

247. *The dead will rise with their same bodies.*

THE SO-CALLED SECOND LETTER OF ST. CLEMENT OF ROME TO THE CORINTHIANS

And let not any one of you say that this flesh is not judged and does not rise again. Understand: In what state were you saved, in what did you recover your sight, except in this flesh? We must, therefore, guard the flesh as a temple of God. Just as you were called in the flesh, so shall you come in the flesh. If Christ the Lord, who saved us, being spirit at first, became flesh and so called us. so also shall we receive our reward in this flesh.

1028
(104)

Ch. 9:1
MG 1, 341
FC I, 70

ST. JUSTIN MARTYR

1029
(120) Such favor as you grant to these [Pythagoreans, Platonists, *et al.*] grant also to us, who not less but more firmly than they believe in God; since we expect to receive again our own bodies, though they be dead and cast into the earth, for we maintain that with God nothing is impossible. And to any thoughtful person would anything appear more incredible, than, if we were not in the body, and some one were to say that it was possible that from a small drop of human seed bones and sinews and flesh be formed into a shape such as we see? . . . But as at first you would not have believed it possible that such persons could be produced from the small drop, and yet now you see them thus produced, so also judge that it is not impossible that the bodies of men, after they have been dissolved, and like seeds resolved into earth, should in God's appointed time rise again and put on incorruption.

THE FIRST APOLOGY, Ch. 18
MG 6, 356
ANF I, 169

TATIAN
See No. 1018.

TERTULLIAN
See No. 515.

ST. HIPPOLYTUS
See No. 516.

ORIGEN
See No. 477.

1030
(468) Into this condition, then, we are to suppose that all this bodily substance of ours will be brought, when all things shall be re-established in a state of unity, and when God shall be all in all. And this result must be understood as being brought about, not suddenly, but slowly and gradually, seeing that the process of amendment and correction will take place imperceptibly in the individual instances during the lapse of countless and unmeasured ages, some outstripping others, and tending by a swifter course towards perfection, while others again follow close at hand, and some again a long way behind; and thus, through the numerous and uncounted orders of progressive beings who are being

reconciled to God from a state of enmity, the last enemy is finally reached, who is called death, so that he also may be destroyed, and no longer be an enemy. When therefore, all rational souls shall have been restored to a condition of this kind, then the nature of this body of ours will undergo a change into the glory of a spiritual body. For as we see it not to be the case with rational natures, that some of them have lived in a condition of degradation owing to their sins, while others have been called to a state of happiness on account of their merits; but as we see those same souls who had formerly been sinful, assisted, after their conversion and reconciliation to God, to a state of happiness; so also are we to consider, with respect to the nature of the body, that the one which we now make use of in a state of meanness, and corruption, and weakness, is not a different body from that which we shall possess in incorruption, and in power, and in glory; but that the same body, when it has cast away the infirmities in which it is now entangled, shall be transmuted into a condition of glory, being rendered spiritual, so that what was a vessel of dishonor may, when cleansed, become a vessel unto honor, and an abode of blessedness. And in this condition, also, we are to believe, that by the will of the Creator it will abide for ever without any change, as is confirmed by the declaration of the apostle, when he says, 'We have a house, not made mith hands, eternal in the heavens' (2 Cor. 5:1).

ON FIRST PRINCIPLES, Bk. 3, Ch. 6
MG 11, 338
ANF IV, 345

APHRAATES

Therefore, O fool, be instructed by this, that each of the seeds is clothed in its own body. Never do you sow wheat and yet reap barley, and never do you plant a vine and yet it produced figs; but everything grows according to its nature. Thus also the body that was laid in the earth is that which shall rise again. And as to this, that the body is corrupted and wastes away, you ought to be instructed by the parable of the seed, that as the seed, when it is cast into the earth, decays and is corrupted, and from its decay it produces and buds and bears fruit.

1031
(686)

DEMONSTRATIONS, 8:3
PS 1, 363
NPNF XIII, 375

ST. CYRIL OF JERUSALEM
See Nos. 662 and 1000.

ST. AUGUSTINE
See Nos. 1026 and 983.

1032
(1923)
But just as if a statue of some soluble metal were either melted by fire, or broken into dust, or reduced to a shapeless mass, and a sculptor wished to restore it from the same quantity of metal, it would make no difference to the completeness of the work what part of the statue any given particle of the material was put into, as long as the restored statue contained all the material of the original one; so God, the Artificer of marvellous and unspeakable power, shall with marvellous and unspeakable rapidity restore our body, using up the whole material of which it originally consisted. Nor will it affect the completeness of its restoration whether hairs return to hairs, and nails to nails, or whether the part of these that had perished be changed into flesh, and called to take its place in another part of the body, the great Artist taking careful heed that nothing shall be unbecoming or out of place.

ON FAITH, HOPE, AND LOVE (ENCHIRIDION), Ch. 89
ML 40, 273
NPNF III, 265–266

ST. JOHN OF DAMASCUS
See No. 1027.

248. Afterwards, the general judgment will be given.

ST. POLYCARP
See No. 210.

TERTULLIAN
See No. 1021.

ST. HIPPOLYTUS
See No. 667.

ST. CYPRIAN
See No. 1009.

ST. JOHN CHRYSOSTOM
See No. 980.

ST. AUGUSTINE
  See Nos. 857 and 983.

ST. JOHN OF DAMASCUS
  See No. 1015.

BEATITUDE

249. The object of beatitude is God alone.

ST. AUGUSTINE

And man, being a part of your creation, desires to praise You. You
move us to delight in praising You; for You have made us for Yourself, and our hearts are restless till they find rest in You.

CONFESSIONS, Bk. 1, Ch. 1
ML 32, 661
NPNF I, 45

See No. 4.

1033
(1591)

From all this, it will readily occur to any one that the blessedness
which an intelligent being desires as its legitimate object results from a
combination of these two things, namely, that it uninterruptedly enjoy
the unchangeable good which is God; and that it be delivered from all
dubiety, and know certainly that it shall eternally abide in the same
enjoyment.

THE CITY OF GOD, Bk. 11, Ch. 13
ML 41, 328
NPNF II, 212

1034
(1749)

How great shall be that felicity, which shall be tainted with no evil,
which shall lack no good, and which shall afford leisure for the praises
of God, who shall be all in all! . . . What power of movement such
bodies shall possess, I have not the audacity rashly to define, as I
have not the ability to conceive. Nevertheless I will say that in any
case, both in motion and in rest, they shall be, as in their appearance,
seemly; for into that state nothing which is unseemly shall be admitted.
One thing is certain, the body shall forthwith be wherever the spirit

1035
(1788)

wills, and the spirit shall will nothing which is unbecoming either to the spirit or to the body. . . . God Himself, who is the Author of virtue, shall there be its reward; for, as there is nothing greater or better, He has promised Himself. . . . This, too, is the right interpretation of the saying of the apostle, 'That God may be all in all' (1 Cor. 15:28). He shall be the end of our desires who shall be seen without end, loved without cloy, praised without weariness. . . . There we shall rest and see, see and love, love and praise. This is what shall be in the end without end.

THE CITY OF GOD, Bk. 22, Ch. 30
ML 41, 801
NPNF II, 509

250. *Perfect beatitude in heaven consists in the vision and the love of God.*

ST. CLEMENT OF ALEXANDRIA

1036
(432)

For it is said, 'To him that has shall be given' (Mt. 25:29; Lk. 19:26): to faith, knowledge; and to knowledge, love; and to love, the inheritance. And this takes place, whenever one hangs on the Lord by faith, by knowledge, by love, and ascends along with Him to where the God and guard of our faith and love is. Whence at last (on account of the necessity for very great preparation and previous training in order both to hear what is said, and for the composure of life, and for advancing intelligently to a point beyond the righteousness of the law) it is that knowledge is committed to those fit and selected for it. It leads us to the endless and perfect end, teaching us beforehand the future life that we shall lead, according to God, and with gods; after we are freed from all punishment and penalty which we undergo, in consequence of our sins, for salutary discipline. After which redemption the reward and the honors are assigned to those who have become perfect; when they have got done with purification, and ceased from all service, though it be holy service, and among saints. They become pure in heart, and near to the Lord, there waits them restoration to everlasting contemplation; and they are called by the appellation of gods, being destined to sit on thrones with the other gods that have been first put in their places by the Saviour.

STROMATA, Bk. 7, Ch. 10
MG 9, 480
ANF II, 539

ST. CYPRIAN
See No. 1009.

ST. AUGUSTINE
See Nos. 476 and 1035.

ST. JOHN OF DAMASCUS
See No. 1015.

TABLE OF REFERENCE TO ROUËT DE JOURNEL'S

Enchiridion Patristicum

In the table on the following pages, when the number of a selection in *The Teachings of the Church Fathers* is given as corresponding to the number of a selection in Rouët de Journel's *Enchiridion Patristicum,* this means that at least part of the document is here translated in the number given.

Occasionally, one number of the *Enchiridion* is divided among several numbers of *The Teachings of the Church Fathers.*

RJ	TCF	RJ	TCF	RJ	TCF	RJ	TCF
3	931	32	630	66	775	104	1028
4	828	34	829	67	950	109	65
5	22	35	671	68	659	110	243
8	896	36	631	69	673	112	88
9	109	37	932	74	210	113	322
11	97	39	687	75	767	113	470
12	613	40	320	78	997	114	445
13	73	41	994	79	147	115	998
14	439	42	627	80	321	116	71
15	653	44	113	83	469	117	323
16	649	47	51	86	961	120	1029
17	468	48	167	89	340	121	1006
18	670	49	114	90	928	122	59
19	110	50	115	91	341	123	488
20	103	51	52	92	832	124	756
21	111	54	159	94	42	125	60
22	177	56	116	97	87	126	324
23	318	59	910	98	429	127	61
25	112	60	23	100	1004	128	24
27	163	62	107	101	674	129	30
28	319	64	876	102	1005	130	247
29	164	65	117	103	929	131	675

RJ Rouët de Journel's *Enchiridion Patristicum*
TCF *The Teachings of the Church Fathers*

TABLE OF REFERENCE

RJ	TCF	RJ	TCF	RJ	TCF	RJ	TCF
132	484	180	326	235	327	297	153
133	485	181	788	237	151	298	125
135	862	183	514	240	885	299	826
136	676	184	489	241	140	300	940
137	384	185	179	242	199	302	830
138	194	186	972	243	98	303	789
139	31	191	211	246	660	304	800
140	772	192	101	247	592	306	844
141	32	193	933	248	679	307	329
143	33	194	278	251	620	308	126
144	76	195	46	253	498	309	851
146	624	196	457	255	522	310	839
147	480	197	218	256	108	311	661
149	178	198	198	256	328	312	911
150	446	199	448	257	141	314	810
151	462	200	385	264	44	315	925
152	229	202	289	267	441	316	934
153	377	203	180	268	36	317	995
154	440	204	358	269	244	319	951
155	1018	207	463	270	8	320	80
156	430	208	25	271	89	321	267
157	486	209	168	272	1020	323	279
158	656	210	150	273	90	324	449
158	638	211	160	274	77	325	280
159	481	212	43	275	9	326	442
160	677	213	139	277	395	327	450
162	183	214	34	279	78	328	451
163	184	215	26	280	91	329	154
165	325	216	35	281	92	330	777
166	288	218	678	282	79	332	231
167	971	219	639	283	93	333	827
168	456	219	632	284	999	334	16
169	1019	220	536	285	94	335	490
170	482	221	726	286	513	336	680
171	277	222	62	287	220	339	37
172	230	224	502	290	53	341	38
173	11	225	497	291	200	342	962
174	859	226	129	292	142	343	688
176	666	228	219	293	152	345	515
176	1007	231	459	294	172	348	537
178	447	232	884	295	170	350	681
179	185	234	431	296	143	351	984

RJ   Rouët de Journel's *Enchiridion Patristicum*
TCF   *The Teachings of the Church Fathers*

525

RJ	TCF	RJ	TCF	RJ	TCF	RJ	TCF
356	475	419	650	510	102	575	161
357	689	420	963	511	82	577	915
358	778	422	222	512	246	578	916
362	801	424	268	513	17	579	1009
363	452	425	249	514	12	581	892
364	1021	426	690	515	232	582	893
366	841	427	120	516	83	584	894
368	897	428	654	519	47	586	523
369	81	429	290	520	55	587	145
371	201	431	364	522	66	588	944
373	378	431	388	523	74	590	790
376	330	432	1036	524	67	591	842
377	331	436	157	525	95	592	818
380	779	437	1008	526	922	592ᵃ	811
381	155	438	121	527	578	593	812
382	992	439	39	528	1023	594	819
384	952	441	1022	529	617	595	803
385	912	442	371	531	56	596	334
386	913	443	209	533	740	597	836
387	156	444	215	534	223	598	852
388	186	445	212	535	224	600	843
389	298	446	477	546	122	601	840
391	379	447	464	548	574	602	169
392	396	448	471	551	898	604	691
393	386	449	621	552	773	605	722
394	432	451	269	554	930	606	727
395	516	453	721	555	104	607	633
396	667	454	465	556	144	609	389
401	387	459	443	557	130	611	335
402	281	460	708	558	538	612	506
403	248	461	709	559	870	613	642
404	181	462	460	560	978	614	233
405	54	466	491	561	914	615	454
406	682	468	1030	562	13	616	1024
407	625	473	921	564	622	617	683
409	397	478	453	565	774	618	68
410	877	479	333	566	505	619	48
411	245	503	40	567	499	620	49
412	641	504	825	568	923	621	84
413	119	505	953	569	802	622	593
414	332	506	964	570	927	624	234
416	221	507	965	571	105	629	18

RJ Rouët de Journel's *Enchiridion Patristicum*
TCF *The Teachings of the Church Fathers*

RJ	TCF	RJ	TCF	RJ	TCF	RJ	TCF
631	1	764	374	843	886	949	424
632	359	765	375	844	890	952	404
633	780	766	644	845	878	953	349
634	365	767	399	847	808	954	203
635	2	768	342	848	879	973	500
637	131	769	400	850	435	979	190
638	63	771	741	851	900	980	979
639	96	772	757	853	905	981	579
640	99	773	728	857	251	984	227
642	966	774	762	859	362	987	237
644	19	776	343	860	259	988	284
645	22	785	174	861	260	989	285
647	775	786	271	863	746	990	421
654	72	787	401	865	146	991	261
657	213	794	692	866	376	992	763
658	45	795	743	867	420	993	252
659	27	808	558	868	402	994	405
681	336	809	807	870	871	995	702
682	749	810	158	871	437	996	350
683	487	811	845	873	694	997	351
686	1031	812	834	874	730	999	352
688	985	813	391	876	695	1000	837
692	684	816	360	877	392	1001	731
695	986	817	693	878	363	1002	967
703	519	822	283	911	272	1003	539
719	787	823	380	912	403	1005	461
746	235	826	381	914	415	1008	353
747	236	827	729	915	344	1009	366
748	444	828	758	916	872	1010	853
749	507	829	518	917	202	1011	635
750	508	830	744	918	973	1012	532
753	941	831	745	919	804	1013	1001
754	258	832	1016	920	347	1014	297
755	398	834	361	922	924	1015	253
756	270	835	634	923	273	1017	354
757	338	836	622	924	226	1018	715
758	372	837	1000	926	348	1019	901
759	701	838	138	928	696	1027	618
760	390	839	148	943	433	1029	355
761	373	840	889	944	640	1031	69
762	750	841	835	947	831	1032	70
763	517	842	860	948	645	1034	599

RJ   Rouët de Journel's *Enchiridion Patristicum*
TCF   *The Teachings of the Church Fathers*

RJ	TCF	RJ	TCF	RJ	TCF	RJ	TCF
1035	891	1206	846	1329	797	1451	607
1036	1002	1207	561	1330	833	1452	608
1037	425	1207	881	1333	882	1453	668
1107	339	1213	204	1334	883	1455	541
1114	286	1214	945	1345	895	1460	393
1115	976	1217	478	1346	132	1461	614
1117	238	1219	540	1347	195	1464	887
1118	906	1236	943	1348	765	1465	100
1119	907	1249	955	1350	942	1467	988
1158	594	1250	175	1351	968	1468	643
1160	697	1253	956	1352	969	1470	64
1163	651	1254	698	1357	124	1471	75
1164	935	1256	626	1358	205	1473	609
1165	559	1264	407	1359	806	1475	792
1167	712	1266	274	1360	821	1477	665
1168	406	1267	723	1361	781	1478	127
1169	426	1268	769	1383	663	1480	873
1170	50	1269	345	1385	492	1481	262
1171	646	1270	865	1405	292	1489	254
1172	980	1271	382	1417	196	1501	919
1176	954	1271	408	1418	162	1502	669
1177	560	1272	291	1419	176	1506	57
1178	764	1273	647	1421	197	1508	240
1179	14	1275	759	1422	149	1518	685
1180	899	1276	1025	1423	814	1519	866
1182	239	1279	300	1427	307	1535	106
1183	902	1280	816	1428	308	1536	580
1184	524	1281	838	1430	717	1557	20
1185	525	1282	436	1430	785	1559	494
1186	427	1283	412	1431	718	1561	414
1188	595	1284	416	1431	733	1562	128
1189	823	1285	413	1432	791	1563	483
1191	575	1286	182	1433	619	1578	703
1192	863	1287	908	1435	926	1579	909
1193	903	1293	820	1436	600	1580	137
1194	880	1294	917	1437	228	1581	171
1195	864	1295	805	1439	847	1587	687
1198	752	1296	937	1440	855	1590	655
1200	981	1297	831	1441	493	1591	1033
1202	299	1298	918	1446	652	1592	576
1203	656	1299	936	1447	309	1595	760
1205	123	1321	15	1449	664	1597	41

RJ Rouët de Journel's *Enchiridion Patristicum*
TCF *The Teachings of the Church Fathers*

RJ	TCF	RJ	TCF	RJ	TCF	RJ	TCF
1601	793	1723	601	1794	584	1882	302
1603	3	1725	856	1800	658	1883	521
1604	868	1727	520	1801	585	1886	627
1605	511	1730	623	1807	610	1888	586
1608	770	1731	556	1808	713	1890	545
1609	187	1736	562	1809	554	1894	587
1612	192	1737	583	1810	817	1899	206
1614	85	1740	293	1811	747	1902	546
1629	850	1741	282	1812	958	1903	547
1640	957	1742	294	1814	815	1905	505
1642	809	1743	4	1816	394	1908	534
1642	948	1744	795	1817	798	1910	628
1643	786	1745	771	1818	710	1914	548
1644	704	1746	21	1820	888	1916	736
1645	824	1747	466	1823	602	1917	768
1647	794	1748	266	1824	874	1919	920
1649	255	1749	1034	1825	28	1920	991
1650	337	1751	458	1829	987	1921	588
1652	869	1752	287	1830	605	1923	1032
1654	761	1753	476	1832	543	1924	535
1656	409	1757	467	1834	799	1926	596
1657	367	1759	854	1835	544	1928	295
1660	275	1760	509	1836	748	1931	1012
1661	428	1761	512	1837	310	1932	996
1662	417	1762	503	1839	418	1934	993
1664	263	1765	216	1840	419	1936	549
1666	264	1766	188	1841	10	1937	550
1668	356	1767	193	1842	735	1938	551
1669	256	1768	857	1847	796	1939	606
1670	411	1771	1017	1851	611	1940	563
1672	346	1772	977	1856	603	1941	557
1676	265	1774	1003	1858	133	1944	657
1677	410	1775	1010	1869	949	1946	311
1680	734	1776	989	1871	528	1951	303
1681	368	1777	648	1872	529	1952	504
1687	189	1779	1011	1874	858	1953	711
1715	526	1780	990	1876	530	1954	552
1717	848	1782	472	1877	531	1955	474
1718	577	1783	86	1878	533	1956	510
1719	542	1785	1026	1879	495	1958	589
1720	581	1788	1035	1880	983	1961	604
1722	582	1791	527	1881	849	1963	597

RJ   Rouët de Journel's *Enchiridion Patristicum*
TCF   *The Teachings of the Church Fathers*

RJ	TCF	RJ	TCF	RJ	TCF	RJ	TCF
1978	564	2056	739	2190	939	2343	383
1979	565	2057	724	2192	501	2344	422
1981	566	2064	776	2193	637	2345	257
1982	567	2077	58	2194	783	2346	423
1984	568	2081	276	2208	725	2348	370
1985	304	2093	250	2213	753	2349	455
1986	312	2126	438	2214	874	2350	473
1988	305	2137	241	2236	5	2352	434
1989	313	2142	214	2269	134	2354	479
1990	314	2158	191	2274	135	2358	301
1992	590	2168	207	2275	136	2359	296
1993	591	2170	705	2291	29	2361	742
1996	598	2171	706	2293	946	2362	357
1997	315	2172	208	2294	861	2363	751
1998	316	2174	217	2296	766	2364	716
2001	317	2177	782	2297	970	2365	714
2002	306	2179	165	2298	629	2366	732
2005	569	2181	496	2299	974	2367	754
2006	570	2182	686	2300	822	2368	739
2044	612	2183	707	2301	975	2371	720
2045	571	2183	738	2319	947	2372	784
2046	615	2184	699	2321	982	2374	960
2047	616	2186	166	2322	1014	2375	1027
2052	572	2187	173	2323	904	2367	1015
2053	573	2188	700	2338	242	2377	6
2054	719	2189	959	2342	369	2378	7

RJ   Rouët de Journel's *Enchiridion Patristicum*
TCF   *The Teachings of the Church Fathers*

Index to the Church Fathers
(REFERENCES ARE TO MARGINAL NUMBERS)